Southern Governors and Civil Rights

Southern Governors and Civil Rights

Racial Segregation
as a Campaign Issue
in the Second Reconstruction

EARL BLACK

HARVARD UNIVERSITY PRESS
Cambridge, Massachusetts, and London, England   1976

Library of Congress Cataloging in Publication Data

Black, Earl, 1942-
  Southern Governors and civil rights.

  Includes bibliographical references and index.
  1. Southern States—Politics and government—1951-
2. Elections—Southern States. 3. Negroes—Southern
States—Segregation. 4. Negroes—Southern States—
Civil rights. I. Title.
F216.2.B52   323.1'19'6073075   75-25607
ISBN 0-674-82510-1

For my parents
Dorothy O. and Penny E. Black

PREFACE

More than two decades have elapsed since the Supreme Court outlawed racial segregation in public education and, by doing so, initiated a new era in the history of black-white relations. This book examines the ensuing controversy over southern race relations from the perspective of the region's white politicians. It argues that southern office seekers' attitudes on racial segregation changed significantly during the course of the Second Reconstruction. Segregationist stances, which were pervasive at the time of the Court's school desegregation decision, have been increasingly replaced by nonsegregationist orientations. If there is a central implication for public policy to be drawn from this study, it is that substantial change in southern racial traditions, change toward a society less rigidly dedicated to white supremacy, is largely dependent upon the sustained penetration of southern social structures by the national government. "No federal intervention, no racial change" may oversimplify the realities of southern politics, but not by much. Prior to passage of the Civil Rights Act of 1964 and the Voting Rights Act of 1965, southern politicians revealed exceedingly little interest in, or desire for, reform of the Jim Crow system. National action was thus essential to any strategy of racial change in the South, and, at least in terms of the southern campaigners' rhetoric on racial segregation, national intervention was highly successful. National stateways can indeed modify regional folkways.

A number of individuals and institutions have my gratitude for helping me to write this book. In classifying the campaign stances on segregation of southern politicians, I have relied primarily upon accounts of campaign activities in state newspapers. The basic research was conducted in the late fall and early winter of 1966-67 and in the winter of 1970 at the Library of Congress, and the staff of the Library's Newspaper Reference Room has my appreciation for their efficiency in making newspapers available to me. Libraries at Harvard University, the University of Michigan, the University of South Carolina, and the University of South Florida have been utilized, and the Eugene Barker Texas History Center at the University of Texas at Austin allowed me to examine its files on Texas politicians. My second trip to the Library of Congress was made possible by a release time grant from the Research Council of the University of South Florida, while a summer research grant from the University of South Carolina gave me time to attend to the final details of completing the manuscript. Secretaries of State for the southern states generously made primary and general election voting returns available to me; Brian Harrington was an able and industrious student assistant.

Parts of the book have appeared elsewhere, and I wish to thank the authorities of three journals for permission to incorporate material from the following articles: "Southern Governors and Political Change: Campaign Stances on Racial Segregation and Economic Development, 1950-69," *Journal of Politics*, 33 (August 1971), 703-734; "The Militant Segregationist Vote in the Post-*Brown* South: A Comparative Analysis," *Social Science Quarterly*, 54 (June 1973), 66-84; and, coauthored with Merle Black, "The Demographic Basis of Wallace Support in Alabama," *American Politics Quarterly*, 1 (July 1973), 279-304. Permission to quote from V. O. Key, Jr., *Southern Politics in State and Nation* (New York, 1949), was generously given by the holder of the copyright, Alfred A. Knopf, Inc. As I hope is clear in the text, my intellectual debt to the late Professor Key, a man I never met, is enormous.

I am particularly pleased to acknowledge the aid of H. Douglas Price of the Department of Government at Harvard University, who suggested the specific topic of this study and sustained the original enterprise with criticism, encouragement, and wit. For additional constructive advice I am grateful to Milton C. Cummings, Jr.

Special thanks are due my wife, Sena, and my brother, Merle, who have spent more time on this book than they or I care to recall. If they characteristically gave me withering criticism rather than the fulsome praise I would have preferred, I have to admit that their objections were frequently justified.

For errors of fact and interpretation, of commission and omission, I assume responsibility.

CONTENTS

PART ONE   Introduction

1   The Scope of the Study   3
2   The Analytic Framework   10

PART TWO   Historical Perspectives

3   Candidates, Campaigns, and Racial Segregation before
    1954   29
4   The Deep South States and Racial Segregation   48
5   The Peripheral South States and Racial Segregation   87

**PART THREE   Racial Segregation and the
Southern Electoral Process**

6   The Major Candidates   145
7   The Democratic First Primary   162
8   The Democratic Second Primary   199
9   The General Election   244
10 The Governors   281

PART FOUR   Conclusion

11 Explaining Racial Change in Southern Electoral Politics   309

    Appendixes   347   Notes   356   Index   401

TABLES

1. Properties of economic development typology   18

2. Rank ordering of racial segregation and economic development categories   21

3. Hypothetical rank ordering of support by demographic categories for militant segregationist candidates   25

4. Campaign stances on racial segregation and economic development, 1950-53   30

5. The demographic setting of electoral politics in the Deep South   50

6. Campaign racial stance and pattern of support for winning candidates for governor in Alabama   53-54

7. Campaign racial stance and pattern of support for winning candidates for governor in Mississippi   61-62

8. Campaign racial stance and pattern of support for winning candidates for governor in Georgia   67

9. Campaign racial stance and pattern of support for winning candidates for governor in Louisiana   74-75

10. Campaign racial stance and pattern of support for winning candidates for governor in South Carolina   81

11. The demographic setting of electoral politics in the Peripheral South   89

12. Campaign racial stance and pattern of support for winning candidates for governor in Florida   94-95

13. Campaign racial stance and pattern of support for winning candidates for governor in Arkansas   101-102

14. Campaign racial stance and pattern of support for winning candidates for governor in North Carolina   107-108

15. Effect of first primary field size on second primary results in 1960 and 1964 Democratic primaries for governor in North Carolina   110

16. Campaign racial stance and pattern of support for winning candidates for governor in Virginia   114

17. Campaign racial stance and pattern of support for winning candidates for governor in Tennessee   121

18. Campaign racial stance and pattern of support for winning candidates for governor in Texas   126-127

19. The demographic core of militant segregationist voting in the post-*Brown* South   133

20. Deviant case analysis: number of core segregationist urban and low black rural counties and percentage of deviant cases explained   139

21. Campaign racial segregation stances of major candidates for governor in the South, 1954-73   148

22. Campaign economic development stances of major candidates for governor in the South, 1954-73   149

23. Campaign stances on racial segregation and economic development in Democratic first primaries   151

24. Campaign stances on racial segregation and economic development in Democratic first primaries in the Deep South states   153

25. Campaign stances on racial segregation and economic development in Democratic first primaries in the Peripheral South states   155

26. Racial segregation position of first primary leaders in contested Democratic first primaries, 1954-73   164

27. Racial segregation position of first place finishers in contested Democratic first primaries, 1954-73   165

28. Racial segregation position of first place finishers in contested Democratic first primaries, before and after the Voting Rights Act   166

29. Campaign racial stances of first and second place finishers in contested Democratic first primaries, 1954-73   168-169

30. Position on racial segregation of southern politicians who won the Democratic nomination for governor in a contested first primary, 1954-73   197

31. Racial segregation position of first place finishers in contested Democratic first primaries requiring runoffs and in Democratic second primaries, 1954-73   201

32. Racial segregation position of winners in Democratic second primaries, 1954-73   203

33. Racial segregation position of winners in Democratic second primaries, before and after the Voting Rights Act   204

34. Campaign racial stance of winners and losers in Democratic second primaries, 1954-73   209

35. The growth of party competition for southern governorships   247

36. Campaign stances on racial segregation and economic development of participants in selected general elections, 1954-73   253

37. Indexes of dissimilarity for racial segregation and economic development categories in selected general elections, 1954-73   256

38. Campaign racial stances of winners in competitive general elections, 1954-73   259

39. Campaign racial stances of Republican and
Democratic winners in competitive general elections, 1954-73   260

40. Campaign racial stances of winners and losers in
selected general elections, 1954-73   262

41. Campaign racial segregation stances of southern
governors, 1954-73   284

42. Campaign economic development stances of
southern governors, 1954-73   285

43. Campaign stances on racial segregation and
economic development of southern governors   289

44. Indexes of dissimilarity on racial segregation and
economic development dimensions for southern governors   291

45. Campaign stances on racial segregation and
economic development of governors in the Deep South
states, 1954-73   293

46. Campaign stances on racial segregation and
economic development of governors in the Peripheral
South states, 1954-73   295

47. Ranking of southern political units on index of
demographic traditionalism   314

48. Indexes of racial change for Democratic gubernatorial nominees   319

49. The impact of federal intervention on the racial
stances of campaigning southern politicians   323

50. Patterns of black voter mobilization I   327

51. Southern governors' campaign stances on racial
segregation and differences in white and black voter registration rates, 1954-73   329

52. Patterns of black voter mobilization II   330

53. Understanding the new southern politics   332

54. Generational change within the southern political
elite   337

FIGURES

1. The demographic setting of electoral politics in the Deep South   51

2. Alabama political demography and the geographic core of segregationist voting after the *Brown* decision   58

3. Mississippi political demography and the geographic core of segregationist voting after the *Brown* decision   59

4. Georgia political demography and the geographic core of segregationist voting after the *Brown* decision   71

5. Louisiana political demography and the geographic core of segregationist voting after the *Brown* decision   73

6. South Carolina political demography and the geographic core of segregationist voting after the *Brown* decision   79

7. The demographic setting of electoral politics in the Peripheral South   91

8. Florida political demography and the geographic core of segregationist voting after the *Brown* decision   92

9. Arkansas political demography and the geographic core of segregationist voting after the *Brown* decision   99

10. North Carolina political demography and the geographic core of segregationist voting after the *Brown* decision   112

11. Virginia political demography and the geographic core of segregationist voting after the *Brown* decision   119

12. Tennessee political demography and the geographic core of segregationist voting after the *Brown* decision   120

13. The demographic setting of electoral politics in Texas   124

14. The geographic core of segregationist voting in Texas after the *Brown* decision   125

15. Median percentage of segregationist counties for rural, urban, and total counties of the South, Deep South, and Peripheral South   136

16. Campaign stances on racial segregation of major candidates for governor in Democratic first primaries, 1950-73   159

17. Campaign stances on economic development of major candidates for governor in Democratic first primaries, 1950-73   161

18. The Faubus vote in Arkansas before and after the Little Rock crisis   177

19. The evolution of the Wallace first primary vote in Alabama   187

20. Comparison of racial segregation positions of southern politicians   206

21. The evolution of the Wallace second primary vote in Alabama   224

22. Maddox country   233

23. Southern governors' campaign stances on economic development, 1950-73   298

24. Southern governors' campaign stances on racial segregation, 1950-73   300

25. Comparison of major candidates and winners who campaigned as strong segregationists and nonsegregationists in southern elections for governor, 1950-73   303

26. The "opening" of southern electoral politics   311

27. The constraints of demography   315

28. The limitations of party competition   321

29. The timing of racial change in southern electoral politics   340

PART ONE

Introduction

1

The Scope of the Study

In its grand outlines the politics of the South revolves around the position of the Negro. It is at times interpreted as a politics of cotton, as a politics of free trade, as a politics of agrarian poverty, or as a politics of planter and plutocrat. Although such interpretations have a superficial validity, in the last analysis the major peculiarities of southern politics go back to the Negro. Whatever phase of the southern political process one seeks to understand, sooner or later the trail of inquiry leads to the Negro.

Southern sectionalism and the special character of southern political institutions have to be attributed in the main to the Negro. The one-party system, suffrage restrictions departing from democratic norms, low levels of voting and of political interest, and all the consequences of these political arrangements and practices must be traced ultimately to this one factor. All of which amounts to saying that the predominant consideration in the architecture of southern political institutions has been to assure locally a subordination of the Negro population and, externally, to block threatened interferences from the outside with these local arrangements.

The race issue broadly defined thus must be considered as the number one problem on the southern agenda. Lacking a solution for it, all else fails.

Key

"Of books about the South there is no end. Nor will there be so long as the South remains the region with the most distinctive character and tradition."[1] V. O. Key's remark is as true of the 1970s as it was of the 1940s. In this book one central element of the southern political tradition is examined—the commitment of white politicians to a racially segregated social order. Because the division between the dominant white majority and the subordinate black minority has been a "primordial" conflict, one that is rooted in differences of "race, language, religion, and the like as bases for the definition of a

3

terminal community," to analyze racial conflict in the South is to concentrate on the most unyielding and therefore most significant cleavage the region has produced.[2]

The broad objective of this inquiry is to present a systematic and comprehensive description and analysis of the issue of racial segregation in southern electoral politics over the past quarter century. Few periods in southern political history are more deserving of intensive study than the Second Reconstruction, the era which began with the Supreme Court's decision of May 17, 1954, abolishing racial segregation in the public schools.[3] Although it would be an exaggeration to interpret the ruling in *Brown v. Board of Education* as any single determinant of subsequent social and political change in the South, it was a landmark case in two respects.[4] An obvious long-run consequence of *Brown* has been the gradual and still incomplete desegregation of southern public schools.[5] The larger significance of the *Brown* decision, however, is that it effectively restored to the agenda of southern politics an issue of fundamental importance: the status of black southerners in a society dominated by whites.

The Supreme Court's repudiation of racial segregation occurred at a time when the South was beginning to experience considerable change in its social structure and economy. Writing in the late 1940s, Key concluded his unexcelled *Southern Politics* by suggesting that such factors as urbanization, black out-migration, and the spread of commerce and industry would gradually "create conditions favorable to [political] change" in the South.[6] In the years since Key wrote, the southern economy has been steadily moving "from rural-agricultural to urban-industrial."[7] Only a tenth of the region's labor force was employed in agriculture by 1960, a decline of almost 60 percent since 1940. Out-migration reduced the percentage of blacks in the 1960 southern population to 21 percent, and majorities of both blacks (58 percent) and whites (56 percent) resided in urban areas. Socioeconomic changes such as these, together with challenges to the South's caste system of race relations like the *Brown* decision and the civil rights legislation of the mid-1960s, have produced a "slow-moving social revolution of significant proportions."[8]

Through an examination of campaigns for governor from 1950 through 1973, I have sought to document and to assess the views of one set of white politicians in the South concerning a crucial aspect of this "social revolution"—racial segregation.[9] The theoretical and practical importance of a study of elite orientations to racial segregation is readily apparent from Key's research. In *Southern Politics* he argued persuasively that the region had constructed "no system or practice of political organization and *leadership* adequate to cope with its problems."[10] A decade later Key reached the general conclusion that "the critical element for the health of a democratic order consists in the beliefs, standards, and competence of those who constitute the influentials, the opinion-leaders, the political activists in the order."[11] The central question raised here concerns the ways in which white politicians, in an era of rapid socioeconomic and political change, have treated an issue of manifest substantive importance. To over-simplify somewhat, this is an investigation of the extent to which the South has begun to acquire political leadership less representative of traditional segregationist approaches to "the number one problem on the southern agenda."[12]

The focus on white elites is also designed as a contribution to the literature of contemporary southern politics. White politicians possess an important but inadequately developed perspective on political change.[13] A great deal has been written about the political activities of black southerners at both the elite and mass levels,[14] but there has been no systematic, comparative study of white politicians that encompasses the entire region and extends over a fairly lengthy period of time. Since white politicians have monopolized state office holding in the past and seem likely to continue to do so indefinitely, their stances on racial segregation deserve particular scrutiny. The white elite under consideration consists of major candidates for governor in the eleven ex-Confederate states during a twenty-four year period, 1950-73. Governorships were chosen for study because the governor's constitutional role as chief executive has frequently made him a central figure in racial disputes. Data have been gathered on all the 80 governorships decided between 1950 and 1973, involving more than 250 candidacies. The study is thus based on six waves of elections for each of the eleven southern states: one pre-*Brown* campaign (1950-53), three campaigns following the *Brown* decision but pre-ceding decisive federal intervention to modify the racial status quo (1954-65), and two campaigns following national intervention (1966-73).[15] By classifying candidates for governor according to their campaign stances on segregation, the racial positions of a large and important group of southern politicians can be summarized for the entire post-*Brown* period, and trend data can be generated to map out the changing racial attitudes of white candidates over a critical era in southern political history.

Although the book is regional in scope, it should be emphasized that I am not attempting a genuinely comprehensive analysis of the segregation issue in southern politics. For reasons of time and practicality, the focus is limited to a consideration of segregation as a *campaign* issue. No systematic attempt will be made to relate the racial stances of governors during a campaign to their actual performance in office, though that is clearly an important topic, deserving of detailed comparative analysis. It is recognized, of course, that the rhetoric employed by campaigners may bear little relationship to their behavior once they are elected. Nonetheless, since campaigns determine who assumes formal control of the government, an examination of what types of candidates could and could not win popular approval should contribute to an understanding of contemporary southern politics.

It may be useful to introduce at the outset several analytic themes which will recur throughout the book. First, the segregation controversy will be examined from the perspective of the dominant (that is, white) elite in southern politics. It is safe to assume that dominant groups everywhere are reluctant at best to surrender whatever advantages they have gained over subordinate groups. Opposition to change in dominant-subordinate group relations by the dominant elite is particularly likely when the subordinate group lacks resources and when the cleavage between the groups is firmly anchored in history. Most students of the South have stressed the centrality of racial conflict; and it is clear that the enactment of suffrage restrictions and the institutionalization of the Jim Crow system in the late nineteenth and early twentieth centuries formally relegated black southerners to an inferior and marginal status.[16] The simple but nonetheless essential point is that the continued dominance of whites over blacks was characteristically taken for granted, accepted as a "given" of southern politics, by white office seekers at the time of the *Brown* decision. By following the racial stances of white campaigners across the South from 1950 through 1973, I wish to determine the degree to which candidates for governor have significantly altered their traditional commitment to the maintenance of a racially segregated society. The issue of broad theoretical importance is this: under what circumstances or conditions have representatives of the dominant group ceased to advocate racial segregation as a desirable form of social stratification? If the hostility of white politicians to racial change is viewed as thoroughly predictable, the primary explanatory task is to account for observed deviations from the historically segregationist posture of the white elite.

A second theme of this book is the relation between the racial stances of campaigners and their ability to compete successfully at different stages (Democratic first primary, Democratic second primary, and the general election) of the southern electoral process. Students of comparative politics have devoted considerable attention to the consequences of electoral rules of the game,[17] and an objective of this study is to examine the southern process of candidate selection in terms of the region's most important political cleavage. Since general elections in most southern states were of little significance until the mid-1960s in determining the governorship, particular attention will be given to the consequences of the dual primary system. Instituted to determine Democratic nominations for governor in all southern states except Tennessee, the dual primary system requires (or in some cases permits) a second primary in the event that no candidate in the first primary wins a majority of the vote. I am interested in determining the racial stances of winners and losers at each step of the electoral process and in ascertaining whether or not significant changes in the results of elections have accompanied federal intervention to alter the racial status quo.

Although this book is primarily a case study of a white elite, aggregate voting data will be utilized in simple ways to develop linkages between the racial stances of southern candidates and their support bases in the electorate. Given a significant change in the agenda of southern politics—that is, the revival of racial segregation as an explicit campaign issue after 1954—how has support for the preservation of traditional racial norms or support for racial change been related to the demographic structure of southern politics? Without going into detail at this point, a variety of southern studies (see notes to Chapter 2) suggest that considerable variation in demographic support for regional norms would be expected. Election returns have been assembled from the 1,000-odd southern counties for each of the Democratic first primaries ($N = 80$), Democratic second primaries ($N = 36$), and closely contested general elections for governor ($N = 26$) held in the South between 1950 and 1973. These votes will be used to compare the demographic setting of campaigns from one state to another, to acquire an understanding of the demographic and geographic characteristics of the votes for particular candidates, and to identify and analyze those counties within each southern state which consistently supported the most militant segregationists. Through these devices, elite attitudes on segregation will be related to mass voting behavior for the post-*Brown* period.

Examination of the segregation issue invites attention to the role of the national government in the American federal system, and in this study I will attempt to contribute to the growing literature concerning the impact of the national government on southern race relations.[18] Even if it is assumed that national legislation to desegregate public accommodations and public schools (Civil Rights Act of 1964) and to enfranchise blacks (Voting Rights Act of 1965) represented major victories for the civil rights movement in the South, the question still remains as to the consequences of national intervention on the racial stances of southern office seekers. A comparison of campaign rhetoric on racial segregation in the periods before and after enforcement of the Voting Rights Act will provide a rough basis for assessing the achievements and limitations of the national government's attempts to change the South's racial traditions.

A final interest concerns method more than substance. Although generalizations will be presented that summarize the campaign stances of politicians across the South, efforts will be made to make the study as comparative as possible. Southwide findings for specific years will ordinarily be accompanied by subregional generalizations, and results for the subregions will be supplemented whenever feasible by comparisons between the individual southern states. White elite attitudes will thus be quantified and analyzed at three distinct levels (region, subregion, and state) and for three different periods of time (pre-*Brown*, post-*Brown* but pre-federal intervention, and post-federal intervention). My basic objective is to convey a detailed sense of continuity and change in the segregation issue for the entire South and over a crucial era.

The book is divided into four parts. To complete the introductory section, Chapter 2 defines and discusses a number of terms that will be used throughout the study. Although I have not tried to write a history of the segregation issue in recent southern politics, attention to historical developments before and after 1954 is essential if the full import of the Supreme Court's school desegregation decision is to be comprehended. Part Two therefore explores segregation as a campaign issue in the early 1950s (Chapter 3) and provides state-by-state summaries of the segregation issue in gubernatorial campaigns for the first two decades following the *Brown* decision (Chapters 4 and 5). Part Three analyzes the post-*Brown* segregation issue in terms of the process of candidate selection that has prevailed in the South. A persistent theme of Chapters 6-10 is the relationship between the campaign racial stances of candidates for the southern governorship and their ability to survive at consecutive steps of the electoral process. Because of the region's traditional attachment to the Democratic party, the inquiry necessarily begins with the Democratic primaries. Chapter 6 characterizes the racial stances of all those southern politicians who aspired to the Democratic nomination for governor and who were successful enough to win 10 percent or more of the total vote in a Democratic first primary. The results of the Democratic first and second primaries—who defeated whom—are evaluated in Chapters 7 and 8. Chapter 9 assesses segregation as an issue in selected general election campaigns, and Chapter 10 completes the third section by examining the policy views of those politicians who actually won governorships between 1954 and 1973. A final section seeks to explain observed changes over time in the politicians' campaign stances on racial segregation (Chapter 11).

2

The Analytic Framework

A comparative analysis of any phenomenon presupposes an explicit frame of reference, a set of categories to structure the identification of similarities and differences in the objects being compared. In this chapter three typologies will be introduced, two of which attempt to differentiate candidates according to their campaign stances on selected issues. Any classification of elite attitudes which is regional in scope is unlikely to do justice to the subtleties of political life within any given state, yet the effort to devise more abstract categories and to apply them to all states should generate an overview of southern electoral politics which cannot be extrapolated from highly specialized studies of individual states. On the assumption that a southwide comparative analysis of campaign stances (though doubtless lacking in nuance from the perspective of the state specialist) would yield greater theoretical payoffs than an intensive and particularized study of one or two states, the typologies of campaign stances presented below have deliberately sacrificed depth of analysis for breadth of scope. A third classification scheme, one designed to compare the southern states in terms of their demographic composition, suffers from the same defect. By ignoring intrastate geographic sectionalism, which by its nature cannot be systematically compared from one state to another, some of the richness and uniqueness of the setting of electoral politics in individual states is lost. On the other hand, the use of objectively defined demographic criteria permits comparisons to be made across state boundaries. Neither the more intensive study of one or a few states nor the more abstract examination of many states is inherently more meritorious. I have opted for the latter because of a conviction that enough campaigns have accumulated to justify a southwide analysis of electoral politics in the Second Reconstruction.

Classifying Campaign Stances: Preliminary Considerations

In this book I have explored the positions adopted by white politicians toward racial segregation and, secondarily, toward the achievement of economic development. To reduce the topic to manageable size and to facilitate longitudinal and cross-sectional comparisons, these elite orientations will be ascertained through an examination of the politicians' campaign rhetoric. Since all candidates necessarily campaign for the governorship, campaign rhetoric may be utilized as a common and accessible indicator of elite policy views. Racial segregation and economic development were selected for examination because the caste system and the comparative lack of economic development have long been recognized as fundamental regional problems. Because of the difficulty of devising typologies applicable to politicians across eleven states over a 24-year period, the analysis will be confined to two policy issues considered especially useful for an understanding of white elites. Clearly racial segregation and economic development have not been the only important issues in southern campaigns, but they have been significant ones, with implications for the nature of race relations and for the allocation of economic resources. The central question may be expressed as follows: among those white southerners who sought and won governorships, what changes in attitudes toward racial segregation and the achievement of economic development have become apparent since 1950?

Using terms employed by Donald Matthews and James Prothro, regional findings will be controlled for differences between two subregions, the Deep South (Alabama, Georgia, Louisiana, Mississippi, and South Carolina) and the Peripheral South (Arkansas, Florida, North Carolina, Tennessee, Texas, and Virginia).[1] Previous research has established the importance of subregional comparisons. With regard to white political behavior, Matthews and Prothro used survey data to show that Deep South whites were more committed to "strict segregation" and less aware of the true racial attitudes of blacks than were Peripheral South whites.[2] Bernard Cosman, analyzing the 1964 presidential election, found Peripheral South whites less willing to vote on the basis of racial prejudice than whites in the Deep South.[3]

Distinctive subregional patterns, it will be demonstrated, exist for white politicians as well as for whites generally.

Since any conclusions rest upon the accuracy of the original classifications, the procedures used to code individual politicians need to be elaborated. Data on the campaign stances of gubernatorial candidates have been gathered primarily from state newspapers.[4] Because southern newspapers vary widely in terms of the frequency, comprehensiveness, and biases of their campaign coverage, the more elaborate techniques of content analysis were not considered appropriate. No attempt has been made to produce generalizations on the order of "Candidate *A* advocated defiance of the *Brown* decision in twice as many speeches as Candidate *B*." I am essentially concerned with the substance of a politician's references to racial segregation and economic development. To determine these policy orientations, two newspapers were selected for each state and all articles pertaining to a given gubernatorial election, including reports of stump speeches, television addresses, profiles of candidates, and the like, were read. For Arkansas, Louisiana, and Mississippi, where coverage seemed adequate or where a second newspaper was unobtainable, a single source was used. Campaign reportage was followed on a day-by-day basis for each stage (Democratic first primary, Democratic second primary, and, when closely contested, the general election) of the southern electoral process. Coverage typically began some six weeks before the first primary. Depending upon whether a second primary was necessary to determine the Democratic nominee and whether a Republican actively sought the office, each campaign was followed for a period of six to fourteen weeks. Notes (ranging from lengthy quotations to brief comments) were taken on the policy stances of each politician. Using these notes and applying criteria to be specified shortly, candidates for governor were then classified according to their campaign stances on racial segregation and the achievement of economic development. Classifications of individual candidates are listed in Appendix A.

Southern Candidates and Racial Segregation

With respect to southern electoral politics, the Supreme Court's 1954 school desegregation decision ultimately accomplished what the white primary and Fair Employment Practices Committee controversies of the 1940s failed to achieve: the revival of an extraordinarily divisive issue—the "place" of the Negro—that most white southerners had considered settled beyond challenge. There might be differences of style, tone, and emphasis, but white politicians in the years before *Brown v. Board of Education* were united by "a common resolve indomitably maintained—that it shall be and remain a white man's country."[5] It seems worthwhile, therefore, to examine systematically the white politician's historic commitment to racial segregation during the years in which the legal basis for the caste system was destroyed.[6] If southern racial traditions *have* been appreciably altered since 1954, significant changes should be discernible in the rhetoric of candidates for the governorship.

In terms of racial segregation, campaigners will be categorized as strong or militant segregationists, moderate segregationists, or non-segregationists. Since the purpose of the analysis is to gauge change (or continuity) in southern racial norms, the typology has been designed to identify the point at which candidates for a major state office, as a practical matter, cease to campaign as racial segregationists. Failure to advocate and defend the caste system will be regarded as a significant break with tradition, whether or not such politicians openly align themselves with efforts to end racial segregation. No nominal classification of this sort, relying on newspaper accounts of campaign rhetoric, can aspire to complete objectivity, but this typology at least affords one means of comparing the campaign racial stances of white politicians over a period of time and between subregions and (where feasible) states. The results appear to be, to borrow one of Key's phrases, "within shouting distance of the realities."

Campaigners who satisfied at least one (most met more) of the following criteria have been considered strong or militant segregationists:

1. The candidate expresses unambiguous, emphatic, and more or less unqualified opposition to racial desegregation and support for racial segregation. No countervailing values (for example, the duty to comply with federal court orders) that would dilute this commitment to the maintenance of a caste system are recognized.
2. The candidate makes his defense of racial segregation (or opposition to desegregation, HEW guidelines, and so on) a leading campaign theme. The segregation issue is discussed incessantly and can be traced in most campaign speeches.
3. The candidate appeals to racial prejudice (for example, designating an opponent as the NAACP candidate) to discredit his opposition.

Though found in far greater proportion in the Deep South than in the Peripheral South, militant segregationists were elected governor of every southern state at some point after the *Brown* decision. Representative strong segregationists include J. Lindsay Almond of Virginia, Ross Barnett of Mississippi, and George Wallace of Alabama. Statements taken from Almond's 1957 general election campaign against Theodore Dalton illustrate the militants' opposition to racial change. A champion of massive resistance to school desegregation, Almond dismissed the *Brown* decision as a ruling which merely expressed the "sociological predilections and wild hallucinations of nine men contrary to the language of the Constitution." His moderate segregationist opponent might favor a pupil placement plan even though it "opens the doors for mass integration" and "embraces, accepts, promotes and legalizes race-mixing," but Almond promised to "defend our way of life" and to "fight relentlessly to prevent amalgamation of races in Virginia." Voters could expect Almond to devise a "defense in depth" against attempts to desegregate the state's public schools.[7]

Other southern politicians shared the militants' antipathy for racial desegregation without treating segregation as an issue of commanding importance. Candidates who described themselves as racial segregationists in their campaigns but who did not meet the criteria established for strong segregationists have been designated moderate segregationists. Moderate is employed merely for want of a better label. Since the word was often used by militant segregationists in the 1950s and early 1960s to describe a white who was deemed insufficiently committed to the caste system and since the term has been used in more recent times to characterize a politician who accepts some racial change but does not crusade for racial equality, it should be noted that neither connotation is implied. Here all moderates are by definition segregationists. The following statements describe most moderates:

1. The candidate favors racial segregation and opposes desegregation, but these preferences are usually qualified by other values and commitments. While promising to do his best to preserve segregation or limit desegregation, he often expresses his intention to respect decisions of the federal judiciary.

2. The candidate does not make the defense of racial segregation a leading campaign theme. Racial segregation is supported primarily as a matter of regional tradition, a commitment routinely expected of serious office seekers. References to segregation tend to

be brief and perfunctory; campaign speeches typically focus on nonracial issues.

3. The candidate avoids appealing to racial prejudice to discredit his opposition. On the contrary, more militant opponents may be attacked for race baiting.

Victorious moderate segregationists include LeRoy Collins of Florida, Carl Sanders of Georgia, Terry Sanford of North Carolina, and Earl Long of Louisiana. Collins's 1956 reelection campaign against Sumter Lowry, a militant opponent of desegregation, exemplifies the approach of the moderate segregationist. Although Collins attacked Lowry for "inciting hate" between the races and refused to offer "leadership that is founded in hatred," the governor's own preference for racial segregation was clearly expressed. There would be no desegregation of Florida's schools, he said, "if there is any lawful way to prevent it." As Collins told the electorate, "I will maintain segregation."[8]

Southern office seekers traditionally supported the region's Jim Crow system. Depending upon the situation, racial segregation might or might not become an explicit issue in pre-*Brown* campaigns, but it could safely be assumed that all serious politicians regarded themselves as racial segregationists. Candidates who doubted the justice of the social order did not ordinarily share their reservations with the electorate. In view of the tenacity of southern racial norms, the emergence of nonsegregationists is a development of considerable significance. This category is purposively inclusive. Nonsegregationists range from a minority of governors who adopted fairly explicit pro-civil rights stances to politicians who simply chose, for varying reasons, not to identify themselves publicly as racial segregationists. Many of these candidates, then, were essentially indifferent to the merits of segregation versus desegregation in their campaigns and sought generally to be as noncommittal as possible concerning the caste system. These politicians usually fall into one of the following categories:

1. Whatever his private beliefs, the candidate does not campaign openly as a segregationist. For all practical purposes, he seeks to avoid explicit stands on racial issues; he champions neither segregation nor desegregation.

2. The candidate does not describe himself as a segregationist or as an integrationist, but he expresses qualified support for some black demands. Statements concerning race tend to be indirect and

highly abstract (for example, the candidate favors "equality of opportunity"). Black support is welcomed.

3. The candidate explicitly and unambiguously favors various Negro rights. Racial segregation may be explicitly repudiated; black support is welcomed.

A curiosity until the early 1970s in the Deep South, nonsegregationists have become increasingly numerous in the Peripheral South. Examples include Buford Ellington of Tennessee (in 1966), John Connally of Texas, Winthrop Rockefeller of Arkansas, and Linwood Holton of Virginia. While Ellington's remarks in his 1966 campaign are not representative of nonsegregationists, they do demonstrate a change of attitude. The committed segregationist of the 1958 gubernatorial campaign told Tennesseans eight years later that the time had come to "bury the word and practice of segregation."[9]

Southern Candidates and the Achievement of Economic Development

Politicians throughout the South have encouraged the development of economic systems grounded less on agriculture and more on commerce and industry. "Southern governors have become the *de facto* executive directors of the state chambers of commerce," Dunbar has written, "and spend their time competing with each other as supplicants for new plants."[10] But if the goal of economic development has been universally shared, there has been less agreement concerning what southern state governments should do to expedite economic growth. (We take for granted that southern politicians routinely support various state-authorized subsidies for new industry and invariably claim to be better qualified than their opponents to attract new payrolls into their states.) Differing conceptions of the state government's role in the encouragement of economic development are particularly significant because of the long-standing deficiencies of public education in the South. A recent analysis of the southern labor force emphasizes the relation between economic development and quality education and concludes:

The shortages of skilled workers, of technicians, of scientists, of managerial ability among small businessmen, and of risk-taking entrepreneurs are serious stumbling blocks to further industrialization and technological development of the South. Education and training that sufficed for the southern agricultural labor force are not adequate to meet the demands of today's manpower market and certainly will not be adequate in the years to come in the industries of the South and elsewhere in the nation.[11]

In view of comparatively low standards of living and inadequate educational systems, what roles have white politicians envisioned that state governments should play in promoting economic development? What strategies to achieve economic development have been advanced, implicitly or explicitly, by southern campaigners? On the basis of the candidate's stances toward public education and class politics, four responses will be differentiated: marginalist, adaptive, redistributive, and progressive.[12]

The primary indicator of attitudes concerning the achievement of economic development is the candidate's position on the question of substantially increased expenditures for public education. Greater investment in public education is viewed as conceptually related to the economic development of a state in two ways. Improved educational opportunities permit individuals to acquire the skills necessary to compete for more attractive jobs; and the aggregate improvement in the quality of a state's labor force is an inducement to outside industry to locate in the state. Candidates who did not advocate significantly higher appropriations for public education are considered more traditional in their approach to the achievement of economic development than politicians who supported the investment of much larger sums in public education. Hence the politician's attitude on educational expenditures is theoretically related to the realization of economic development as means to an end. Examination of these elite views has the advantage of dividing southern politicians—who are in general agreement concerning the desirability of economic development—into two categories: those who are prepared to finance it through the improvement of public education and those who are not.

Class politics—the extent to which a politician does or does not campaign as a neo-Populist, championing the interests of economic have-nots—has been used as the second indicator of elite attitudes toward the achievement of economic development. Although class politics is less clearly related to the goal of economic development than is public education, here too a means-end relationship can be specified. Depending upon their attitudes toward class politics, candidates may obscure class cleavages, avoid redistributive taxing and spending policies, and encourage economic development through close cooperation between government and the business community, or they may emphasize class economic issues and attempt to achieve economic development through the adoption of redistributive taxing and spending policies intended to improve the quality (among other services) of public education. Because the relationship between the politician and the business community will vary greatly depending upon whether (conflict) or not (conciliation) a candidate proposes redistributive economic policies and because it will be important for subsequent analysis to distinguish neo-Populists from other southern politicians, class politics has been incorporated as a secondary aspect of the classification scheme. The properties of this achievement of economic development typology are summarized in Table 1.

Many politicians in the South have favored an approach to public education and the achievement of economic development that has minimized both the financial responsibilities of the state and class politics. Marginalists have been defined as follows:

1. The candidate does not advocate substantially increased state spending for public education. Although marginal improvements in the educational system may be supported, the candidate's campaign rhetoric reflects overriding concern with the present costs of state government. Economy in government is commonly stressed; budget cutting may be advised.

2. The candidate's speeches do not reflect a view of politics as (more or less) a struggle between haves and have-nots. Redistributive taxing and spending programs are not emphasized.

Marginalist campaigners did not propose that social welfare programs such as old age pensions be significantly expanded, nor did they align themselves conspicuously with have-not groups. A. S. Harrison of Virginia, Allan Shivers of Texas, and Jimmie Davis of Louisiana

Table 1. Properties of achievement of economic development typology

		Candidate Favors Substantially Increased Spending for Public Education	
		No	Yes
Candidate Views Politics as Conflict between Haves and Have-nots and Champions Cause of Have-nots	No	Marginalist	Adaptive
	Yes	Redistributive	Progressive

exemplify the marginalist. Harrison, the Byrd Organization's candidate in 1961, attacked his opponent's "ultra-liberal approach to state finances" and promised to preserve Virginia's "sound, economical, constructive, progressive, honest government." The root issue for Harrison was whether the state would "abandon the sound political philosophies we have followed for 50 years." If the national business community thought Virginia was becoming a "free-wheeling, free-dealing, socialist, spending state, we might as well fold up our tents and steal away as far as getting new industry is concerned."[13]

Other candidates have followed marginalists in deemphasizing class politics but have nonetheless taken the position that long-range economic growth requires far greater financial support for public education by the states themselves. By proposing the expansion or creation of trade schools, community colleges, state university systems, and the like, adaptives have attempted to enhance job opportunities for individuals and to make their states more competitive in attracting industry. Politicians who met the following criteria have been considered adaptives:

1. The candidate favors substantially increased state support for public education and commonly describes the improvement of education as having a high priority in his administration. Increased expenditures for education may be explicitly defended as an investment in future economic development.
2. The candidate's speeches do not reflect a view of politics as (more or less) a struggle between haves and have-nots. Redistributive taxing and spending programs are not emphasized.

Like the marginalists, adaptives have typically been indifferent, if not hostile, to increased spending for social welfare programs. Representative adaptives include John Connally of Texas (in 1964 and 1966), Terry Sanford of North Carolina, and Carl Sanders of Georgia. Campaigning for reelection in 1964, for example, Connally described his fundamental goal as an improvement of the state's educational system so that more Texans might "share in the economic fruits of the technological space age."[14]

A small number of office seekers may be described as redistributives. The rhetoric of these politicians has been grounded in a more or less articulate conception of politics as a conflict between haves and have-nots. Redistributives have urged the reallocation of state resources in directions calculated to benefit have-not groups, and this neo-Populist orientation differentiates them from marginalists and adaptives. However, redistributives resemble marginalists in that they have not envisioned a significantly larger role for public education in the effort to achieve economic development. Redistributives may be characterized as follows:

1. The candidate does not advocate substantially increased state spending for public education. Marginal improvements (for example, salary increases for teachers, hot lunch programs for schoolchildren) may be vigorously supported.
2. The candidate's rhetoric reflects a view of politics as (more or less) a struggle between haves and have-nots (for example, "special interests" versus "the people"). The candidate emphasizes his willingness to expand such social welfare programs as old age pensions.

Few campaigners of this type successfully competed for the governorship in the post-*Brown* years. Orval Faubus of Arkansas was the only redistributive to win in the 1960s, and Faubus defies easy classification. While he originally ran as a redistributive in the Sid McMath tradition, he later established close ties with leading segments of the Arkansas business community. Since his campaign rhetoric, which emphasized the concrete economic benefits provided by his administrations, remained basically consistent over the years, he has been designated a redistributive.[15] James Folsom of Alabama and Earl Long of Louisiana are additional examples of this category.

Over a period of time southern neo-Populists have become more aware of the advantages of increased investment in public education, so that it is possible to identify a small but influential group of progressives. It should be stressed that I am using the term progressive in a narrow and specialized sense; the progressive is a campaigner who combines the neo-Populism of the redistributive with the adaptive's interest in the improvement of public education. The following statements describe progressives:

1. The candidate favors substantially increased state support for public education and commonly describes the improvement of education as having a high priority in his administration. Increased expenditures for education may be explicitly defended as an investment in future economic development.
2. The candidate's rhetoric reflects a view of politics as (more or less) a struggle between haves and have-nots (for example, "special interests" versus "the people"). The candidate emphasizes his willingness to expand such social welfare programs as old age pensions.

Lester Maddox of Georgia, George Wallace of Alabama, and Reubin Askew of Florida illustrate the progressive. Though his economic proposals received far less attention than his bizarre views on race, Maddox wanted to double educational expenditures in Georgia and denounced his Republican opponent as a rich man who "would be a lot better off if he knew about people as well as dollars." While he led Georgia, Maddox claimed, there would be "no more of the rich getting richer and the poor poorer."[16]

Much greater attention will be given to the candidates' stances on racial segregation than to their positions on the achievement of economic development, but at various points the relationship between the two policy dimensions will be examined. In contrast to classifications of politicians which subsume in a single phrase a multitude of policy orientations,[17] the approach of this study is to define campaign stances for each of two dimensions having theoretical and practical importance for comprehending elite policy views and then to investigate as an empirical question the relationship between the selected policy areas. Stated in general terms, I wish to establish the degree to which traditional (or less traditional) stances on racial segregation have been associated with traditional (or less traditional) positions on the achievement of economic development. Table 2 provides a rank ordering of categories from the "most traditional" combination of campaign stances (the militant segregationist-marginalist) to the two "least traditional" combinations (the nonsegregationist-progressive,

Table 2. Rank ordering of racial segregation and achievement of economic development categories from most traditional to least traditional orientations[a]

Campaign Stance on Achievement of Economic Development	Campaign Stance on Racial Segregation		
	Strong Segregationist	Moderate Segregationist	Nonsegregationist
Marginalist	I	V	IX
Redistributive	II	VI	X
Adaptive	III	VII	XI
Progressive	IV	VIII	XII

[a]Racial segregation categories are ranked in decreasing traditionalism from left to right; achievement of economic development types are ranked in decreasing traditionalism from top to bottom. See the text for an explanation of ranking procedures.

followed closely by the nonsegregationist-adaptive). In the table racial segregation categories are ranked in decreasing traditionalism from left to right, while economic development types are ranked in decreasing traditionalism from top to bottom. The cell rankings assume that racial segregation (my primary interest) is the more important policy dimension. Thus any strong segregationist, whatever his views may be on the achievement of economic development, is treated as more traditional than any moderate segregationist, and so forth. Since educational expenditure has a stronger conceptual relationship than does class politics to the achievement of economic development, candidates who have opposed significantly greater appropriations for public education (marginalists and redistributives) are considered more traditional than politicians who have advocated larger expenditures (adaptives and progressives). Within the constraints imposed by this initial ordering of the economic development categories, office seekers who have championed the economic have-nots (progressives and redistributives) are interpreted as less traditional than those who have not emphasized class politics (adaptives and marginalists). Of the twelve possible combinations of racial segregation and economic development types, several are of considerably more theoretical interest than others. Cross-tabulation of the policy dimensions permits an assessment of the relative prominence of Cell I candidates (the most traditional combination) as compared to Cell XII and XI campaigners (the two most innovative combinations) and reveals how frequently traditional positions on one dimension have been accompanied by innovative stances on the second dimension (for example, Cells III, IV, and IX). Examination of the joint distribution of segregation and economic development categories should clarify the policy orientations of southern politicians in the post-*Brown* era as a whole and help determine whether or not significant changes have occurred since 1954.

The Segregation Issue and Southern Political Demography

As was suggested in Chapter 1, a central goal of this work is to relate the segregation issue to the demographic structure of southern politics.[18] One of the more widely accepted generalizations concerning the political demography of the South has been Key's hypothesis that "the hard core of the [white] political South—and the backbone of [white] southern unity [on the race issue]—is made up of those counties and sections of the southern states in which Negroes constitute a substantial proportion of the population."[19] More specifically, the locus of white southern traditionalism on race has been the rural county with a large black population. "It is not the Negro in general," Key observed, "that provides the base for white Democratic unity in national affairs; it is fundamentally the rural Negro in areas of high concentration of colored population."[20] As Key elaborated:

> It is the whites of the black belts who have the deepest and most immediate concern about the maintenance of white supremacy. Those whites who live in counties with populations 40, 50, 60, and even 80 percent Negro share a common attitude toward the Negro. Moreover, it is generally in these counties that large-scale plantation or multiple-unit agriculture prevails. Here are located most of the large agricultural operators who supervise the work of many tenants, sharecroppers, and laborers, most of whom are colored. As large operators they lean generally in a conservative direction in their political views.[21]

Advocacy of Secession, opposition to Populism, enthusiasm for the "legal" disfranchisement of blacks, and support for the Democratic party nationally in 1928 (despite the nomination of an anti-Prohibition Catholic) and for the Dixiecrats in 1948 (after the Democratic national convention adopted a civil rights plank) were all most pronounced among the whites of the southern black belts.[22]

Key's "black belt hypothesis"[23] thus suggests that opposition to racial change in the South would be strongest in rural counties with substantial black populations. Rural areas with small black populations would be relatively less concerned with the perpetuation of the racial status quo; and the region's cities, while far from liberal on civil rights, would be even less preoccupied with the race issue.[24] Stated in terms of comparisons between the southern states, resistance to the *Brown* decision could be expected to vary according to the importance—as a fraction of the state vote—of the rural areas with large black populations.

Although Key's research dealt primarily with electoral politics, the utility of his black belt hypothesis is that it is stated in sufficiently general terms to be potentially applicable to any aspect of race and politics in the South. A review of the literature concerning voting behavior, black voter registration, and school desegregation indicates that numerous social scientists have followed Key in viewing the size of the black population and urban-rural differences as significant variables in accounting for the region's politics. Particular studies may have qualified the argument from time to time, but in general the relevance of the demographic variables Key emphasized has been reinforced by subsequent work.[25]

Key's findings suggest the utility of grouping each state's counties (including Virginia's independent cities as counties) into classifications which range from the demographic setting hypothetically least supportive of the racial status quo to that setting most opposed to change in southern racial traditions.[26] Basic divisions have been established between urban and rural areas and between rural areas with large and small black populations. Two categories have been devised to differentiate the more populous from the less populous urban centers. The phrase large metropolitan refers to counties which were part of a Standard Metropolitan Statistical Area with a 1960 population exceeding 250,000. The use of 250,000 as a cut-off point between urban categories is admittedly arbitrary. However, it has the advantage of being a figure that is fairly high yet still isolates at least one large metropolitan center in nine of the eleven southern states. Counties included in the remaining southern SMSAs plus counties with a central city of 25-50,000 population in 1960 have been classified as medium urban. While Key had contrasted broadly between rural counties with low and high black populations, Matthews and Prothro demonstrated empirically that there existed "a critical point, at about 30 per cent Negro, where white hostility to Negro political participation becomes severe."[27] I have incorporated this finding by grouping rural counties into low black (those with 1960 black populations of less than 30 percent) and high black (those with 1960 black populations of 30 percent or more) categories. High black rural counties have been subdivided into medium black (30-49 percent black) and black belt (over 50 percent black) classifications. (It will be recognized that the term black belt is used here in a more restrictive and technical sense than in the phrase black belt hypothesis.) None of the southern SMSA counties contained 1960 black populations in excess of 50 percent; the few counties with black population majorities and a central city of 25-50,000 in 1960 (for example, Dallas County, Alabama) have been treated as black belt rather than medium urban. With this qualification, the categories are mutually exclusive.

The demographic categories outlined above will be employed in three different ways: to compare the southern states with respect to the demographic setting in which electoral politics takes place; to acquire an understanding of the demography of the vote for particular gubernatorial candidates, especially militant segregationists; and to analyze those counties within each state which furnished core electoral support after 1954 for selected militant segregationists. Each of these objectives necessitates a brief explanation.

Comparative analysis of the states' demographic settings for electoral politics should help explain why resistance to racial deseg-regation varied from state to state. Southern states in which there were few large cities and in which a substantial proportion of the state vote was contributed by whites residing in rural areas with large black populations (Mississippi is the classic example) could be expected, on the basis of their demographic characteristics alone, to give more con-spicuous support to militant segregationists than states (such as Texas and Tennessee) in which the high black rural vote was trivial and in which a sizable fraction of the electorate lived in urban areas.

In examining individual candidates, the demography of the vote for militant segregationists is of particular interest. Table 3 rank-orders the electorates of the demographic categories in terms of their hypoth-esized level of support for militant segregationists. The percentage of the vote obtained by a given militant segregationist would be expected to increase along a demographic continuum beginning with the large metropolitan areas and ending with the black belt counties.[28] This specific rank ordering, however, would apply only to elections in which the black vote was effectively disfranchised. How would this typology be affected by the mobilization of blacks? Counties with majority black electorates (that is, the black belt counties, assuming blacks were fully mobilized) would obviously be expected to oppose militant segregationists. It is plausible that these counties would now provide the lowest percentage of electoral support for such candi-

Table 3. Hypothetical rank ordering of support by demographic categories for militant segregationist candidates in southern elections before and after black mobilization (after Key)

Demographic Category	Pre-Black Mobilization	Post-Black Mobilization
Large Metropolitan	5	4
Medium Urban	4	3
Low Black Rural	3	2
High Black Rural		
Medium Black Rural	2	1
Black Belt Rural	1	5

dates. Yet in the remaining demographic categories, whites would continue to constitute the majority of the electorate, and there seems to be no compelling reason to expect dramatic reversals in levels of relative support. The theoretical importance of the typology lies in its potential for ordering levels of support by demographic categories for the most racially conservative candidates in southern elections in which race is the dominant issue, both before and after the mobilization of black voters.[29]

Much of the research since Key that has employed black-white population and urban-rural criteria has been concentrated on particular states, a few states, or the region as a whole; there have been few systematic attempts to compare all eleven states in terms of the black belt hypothesis.[30] By using the state as the principal unit of analysis and focusing on the demography of the militant segregationist vote in the post-*Brown* years, Key's argument may be tested on an explicitly comparative basis. The significance of the attempt extends beyond the question of the applicability of Key's general theory of southern racial politics to elections in eleven different states. Although black political participation and the achievement of racial desegregation in many areas of southern life have made unadulterated militant segregationists less the wave of the future than "the last living examples of a different—and soon to be extinct—breed," during much of the Second Reconstruction the segregation issue assumed great salience in political campaigns.[31] Given the importance of the issue, an analysis of those counties within each state which consistently supported the most militant defenders of the racial status quo should provide insight into the structure of southern electoral cleavages in the post-1954 era. Appendix B explains how "core segregationist" counties have been identified and lists the candidates and elections used to measure the segregationist vote.

The classification schemes presented above, insensitive though they may be to subtleties of elite policy orientations or to the significance of demographic factors other than the size of the black population and urban-rural composition, at least provide a vocabulary for comparative analysis. Having defined the central concepts of the study, I will begin this exploration of the segregation issue by examining campaign stances in the period that immediately preceded the Supreme Court's attack on the southern caste system.

PART TWO
Historical Perspectives

3

Candidates, Campaigns, and Racial Segregation before 1954

In the years preceding the *Brown* decision, when racial segregation could be understood by white politicians as an intrinsic, seemingly immutable characteristic of southern life, references to race in political campaigns were sporadic and commonly pertained to occurrences outside the South. Campaign oratory concerning segregation in the 1940s usually related to the wartime Fair Employment Practices Committee (FEPC) established by executive order of President Franklin D. Roosevelt in 1941, to the Supreme Court's 1944 decision abolishing the white primary, or to President Harry S Truman's civil rights proposals of 1948 and the adoption of a civil rights plank by the 1948 Democratic national convention, the acts which precipitated the Dixiecrat revolt.[1] Except for scattered instances to be considered shortly, these issues had largely dissipated in state elections by 1950, and from then until 1954 campaigning southern politicians gave relatively little attention to racial matters.

The Candidates

For the overwhelming majority of candidates for governor in the early 1950s, racial segregation was, at most, a secondary concern. None of the major candidates from 1950 to 1953 could be classified as a nonsegregationist, but only a small minority ran as militant segregationists. Most campaigners may be described as moderate segregationists. These politicians would readily affirm their satisfaction with southern racial norms when the situation required them to do so; otherwise they ignored the racial question or minimized its importance by asserting that the Negro's position in society was a settled issue.

The predominance of moderate segregationists in pre-*Brown* campaigns is clearly shown in Table 4, which compares the racial segregation and economic development positions of major candidates for governor with those of the eventual Democratic nominees. During this period the traditional consensus among white office seekers on the principle of racial segregation was maintained. Of those campaigners who received at least 10 percent of the vote in a Democratic first primary, 95 percent were moderate segregationists and the rest were militant segregationists. No serious candidate challenged the prevailing segregationist ethos, for a public commitment to the caste system was generally regarded as a necessary but not sufficient step toward electoral success. White politicians who favored the gradual elimination of racial segregation, if they existed, kept their preferences to themselves.

Table 4.   Campaign stances on racial segregation and achievement of economic development of major candidates and Democratic nominees for governor in the South, 1950-53 (percent)

Campaign Stance	Major Candidates[a]		Democratic Nominees[b]	
Strong Segregationist	5		14	
SS-Marginalist		3		7
SS-Redistributive		3		7
SS-Adaptive		0		0
SS-Progressive		0		0
Moderate Segregationist	95		86	
MS-Marginalist		63		71
MS-Redistributive		29		7
MS-Adaptive		3		7
MS-Progressive		0		0
Nonsegregationist	0		0	
NS-Marginalist		0		0
NS-Redistributive		0		0
NS-Adaptive		0		0
NS-Progressive		0		0
Totals	100		100	
Number of Cases	(38)		(14)	

[a]Includes all candidates who received at least 10 percent of the vote in a Democratic first primary for governor. Percentages in this and subsequent tables have been rounded to the nearest whole number. As a result, columns may not always sum to 100.

[b]All Democratic nominees during this period won the general election.

Moderate segregationists won twelve (86 percent) of the fourteen governorships decided in the South from 1950-53. In two instances strong segregationists were elected, so that segregationists of one variety or another governed every southern state. The comparative absence of strident race baiting in the pre-*Brown* years was rooted less in the moderate attitudes of individual candidates than in the lack of a concrete threat to the maintenance of racial segregation. Once the Supreme Court ordered the desegregation of public schools, many ostensible moderate segregationists became militants overnight.

Conventional views on the achievement of economic development accompanied the politicians' status quo racial policies. Two thirds of the gubernatorial candidates campaigned as marginalists, and these politicians, who believed the state could best encourage economic growth by carefully limiting its own expenditures and by authorizing tax concessions to recruit new industry, won approximately four fifths of the pre-*Brown* governorships. Redistributives, who comprised one third of the candidates but only 14 percent of the nominees, were more concerned with the reallocation of existing resources than with economic development per se.

With respect to the joint distribution of racial segregation and economic development types, by far the most significant bloc (63 percent of the major candidates and 71 percent of the Democratic nominees) consisted of moderate segregationists who were marginalists. Seven out of ten winners of this variety achieved their nominations without facing a second primary. None of the first primary victors—Gordon Persons of Alabama, William Umstead of North Carolina, Gordon Browning and Frank Clement of Tennessee, and, in two consecutive elections, Allan Shivers of Texas—allocated much time to racial issues in their campaigns.

Economy in government was a favorite theme of Shivers, for example, when he sought reelection in 1950. The Texas governor considered himself "basically a conservative man, but one progressive enough to want Texas to have good schools, good highways and farm-to-market roads and a good welfare program." A newspaper advertisement for Shivers a few days before the election ignored the Negro but reiterated the need for conservative leadership. "We must," the ad read, "preserve a sound government and a sound economy—must find a way to stop the trend toward bigger and bigger state spending, without depriving our people of essential services."[2]

Another incumbent, Gordon Browning of Tennessee, likewise avoided race in his 1950 campaign. Browning stressed his administrative accomplishments. No other American governor had "met an expanding program, balanced the budget, and appreciably reduced taxes at the same time," he claimed. "I am the only man who has reduced taxes at all."[3] Two years later Browning was defeated by another moderate segregationist-marginalist. Frank Clement's efforts in 1952 consisted primarily of "singing hymns, saying prayers, counting the sins of the Browning administration and calling for Godliness and honesty in Tennessee."[4] Clement proposed a sweeping legislative investigation of the "corruption in state government which has flourished under the Administration of Governor Browning." What Tennessee needed most was "honesty, decency and morality" in government. "There'll be no millionaires made in the Clement Administration," he promised. Browning, in return, described Clement as the "cheapest, most garrulous, and the most loud-mouthed character assassin this state has ever seen."[5] Throughout a bitter, name calling campaign, neither candidate engaged in race baiting.

Three moderate segregationist-marginalists were nominated as a result of second primaries; and none of these candidates—Robert Kennon of Louisiana (see below), Francis Cherry of Arkansas, and Dan McCarty of Florida—exploited the segregation issue. Cherry, a proponent of economy, efficiency, and "a return to decency in government," did attack Governor Sidney McMath in 1952 as "Harry Truman's boy," a charge that some voters might have interpreted as a hint that McMath was insufficiently committed to segregation. Actually, Cherry's position on the Negro involved a balancing of interests not uncommon in the pre-*Brown* era. It would be improper for him to "make a special appeal to any minority," but he could promise that "all people are to be treated equally."[6] Equality of treatment, of course, would be extended on a racially segregated basis. Dan McCarty's 1952 platform did not mention race; rather, he emphasized the need to "promote economic growth, expand school and highway construction," and enforce Florida's gambling, liquor, and racing laws. McCarty would use "good business judgment" to improve the efficiency of state government.[7] For the moderate segregationist-marginalist, then, racial segregation was not treated as a significant issue. To the extent that substantive issues were discussed, these campaigners were principally interested in restraining state spending.

Moderate segregationists with redistributive economic views formed a second sizable bloc of potential governors. Like the moderate segregationist-marginalists, such politicians as Philip Hamm of Alabama, Carlos Spaht of Louisiana, and Ralph Yarborough of Texas (discussed later) typically subordinated race to economics. Although they campaigned in seven states and totaled 29 percent of the major candidates, moderate segregationist-redistributives were usually defeated. Sidney McMath of Arkansas, seeking a traditional second term in 1950, was the sole moderate segregationist and redistributive elected governor, and McMath himself was defeated in 1952. In the 1952 campaign he defended his "program of progress" and regularly assailed the "ruthless special interests" which sought his defeat. Little was said about civil rights.[8]

Elections for governor before 1954, then, were essentially contested by moderate segregationists who were either marginalists or redistributives. Since these combinations include more than 90 percent of the major candidates, many conceivable variations of racial segregation and economic development types appeared occasionally or not at all. The single moderate segregationist with an adaptive orientation was James F. Byrnes of South Carolina. Following a lengthy career which included service in all three branches of the national government, Byrnes returned home and easily won the governorship in 1950. Supreme Court decisions against racial segregation in higher education were "disturbing," but Byrnes was more worried about the size of the national government. "Now is the time," he told the electorate, "to halt the federal government from encroaching on the states and embarking on further socialistic experiments . . . Big government is bad government." Yet Byrnes did not use states' rights rhetoric as a shield for state inaction. Byrnes was acutely dissatisfied with the quality of education in his state and thought South Carolina needed nothing less than an "educational revival." Promising to provide the necessary leadership, he suggested that "nothing is so wrong with our educational system that money wouldn't help it."[9]

Whatever their economic predilections, moderate segregationists from 1950 through 1953, in contrast to their performance after the *Brown* decision, rarely discussed the racial issue. Negro support might even be solicited, generally on a private basis, but bargaining would be in terms of patronage or promises of fair play within the context of a racially segregated society.

Candidates who waged unadulterated segregationist campaigns in the early 1950s were atypical, and the peripheral role of the militants is further indicated by the fact that several of the most vociferous strong segregationists failed to win even 10 percent of the vote. Both Bruce Henderson, a state senator from the Black Belt, and Eugene "Bull" Connor, Birmingham Police Commissioner, finished far out of the competition (fourth and sixth, respectively) in the 1950 Alabama first primary. Henderson stated his political philosophy succinctly: "I am for States Rights! PERIOD!" Whites in Alabama were imperiled, he warned, by the "indiscriminate registration and mass voting" of blacks.[10] Connor, who was to attain international notoriety in 1963 for his repression of civil rights demonstrators in Birmingham, shared Henderson's anxiety over black voting and thus opposed any repeal of the state's poll tax. Alabama already contained 50,000 Negro voters, he estimated, and if the poll tax were eliminated, "there'll be 500,000." Connor considered himself the only candidate with "guts enough to make states' rights the No. 1 plank in his platform."[11] Mary Cain, perhaps the most undiluted reactionary to seek a southern governorship in the early 1950s, placed fifth in the 1951 Mississippi primary. Editor of the *Summit Sun*, Cain thought white southerners had already done too much for the Negro, preferred to close white schools rather than desegregate them, and asserted that "the boys in Washington want us to become a mongrel race." Mississippi civilization was endangered by "smart alecks in Washington who think they can improve on God's plan of different races by making us abolish segregation and absorb the negro into the white." Nor was Cain's conservatism confined to race. Social Security was denounced as the "most socialistic of all New Deal socialism," and the candidate was unsympathetic to the political demands of the indigent elderly. "These dear old people," she believed, "are mostly dear old moochers."[12]

On the whole, campaigning politicians in the pre-*Brown* era had little cause to exacerbate what appeared to be a settled debate on the status of the Negro. Despite the formal destruction of the white primary, blacks were far from cohesively organized as voters. In 1952 there were one million registered black voters in the South, but this represented only 20 percent of the potential black electorate.[13] With black voting strength still minimal, as long as no serious, sustained extraregional challenge was mounted against the caste system and as long as segregated institutions were not confronted by an indigenous civil rights movement, most white politicians could afford to ignore or deemphasize the issue of racial segregation. Moderate segregationists generally referred to the Negro only as a matter of political protection against militant opponents or as a means of demonstrating to white voters their adherence to southern racial norms.

The Campaigns

If attention is limited to the two candidates who received the most first primary votes in each election, pre-*Brown* campaigns may be divided into two groups: elections in which militant segregationists were involved and elections in which both politicians ran as moderate segregationists. The typical election for governor (11 out of 14 contests) matched moderate segregationists against each other. Since there were no nonsegregationists and since moderate segregationists tended to avoid the issue, racial segregation was a significant, much discussed issue only in those campaigns (approximately one fifth of the total) in which militants had widespread appeal. The three elections which matched militant segregationists against more moderate opponents will be described in some detail.

In the 1950 Georgia primary, Governor Herman Talmadge appealed to racial prejudice frequently in his campaign against a veteran anti-Talmadge opponent, M. E. Thompson of Valdosta. Although Herman was as accomplished a race baiter as his late father, his redistributive tendencies differentiated him from Ole Gene. Talmadge favored an increase in old age benefits, wanted all the federal aid he could get, and argued that "the Talmadge administration has made more material and permanent achievements for the benefit of the people of Georgia than any other administration in history." Real and imagined attacks on Georgia institutions, however, rather than economic progress, received the governor's fullest attention. Talmadge stressed racial themes repeatedly, pointing out his own unambiguous commitment to segregation while portraying Thompson as an ally of integrationists. "I am opposed to the FEPC proposition and the opposition is for it," he announced. "I am for the county unit system and the opposition is against it. Those are the chief and only issues in this race." Black political participation, hardly excessive at the time, would be reduced by a new voter registration law. Talmadge told an enthusiastic audience—shouts of "You tell 'em, Hummon" were recorded—that "the people I'm going to disenfranchise are those FEPC people." "As long as Talmadge is your governor," he explained on another occasion, "not a single white voter is going to be denied the ballot. It's that FEPC crowd I'm after."[14]

Thompson, a moderate segregationist and marginalist, spent much of his time denying Talmadge's accusations. It was untrue that he associated with "that FEPC crowd" or failed to appreciate the county unit system, an extraordinary electoral arrangement that left Georgia's urban voters without influence in statewide elections. Nor was segregation an issue. "If radicals like Henry Wallace in the East and demagogues like the present governor in the South would quit stirring up the race matter," Thompson argued, "it would be no problem in the South." Talmadge's references to the FEPC question were attempts to disguise "his own miserable record of extravagance, waste, indecision and broken promises." Thompson contended, without apparent success, that Talmadge had betrayed his white followers by attending a Negro gathering. "It must have been embarrassing," he commented, "for the worthy Negro citizens . . . to have their orderly meeting interrupted by the governor's bodyguard preventing a photographer from getting a picture of him, as he shuffled about, shaking hands and nibbling food and begging for votes."[15]

When the Supreme Court issued several decisions favorable to graduate and professional school desegregation, Talmadge announced that the rulings would have no effect in Georgia. "As long as I am Governor," he promised, "Negroes will not be admitted to white schools." Two days later he let black Georgians know exactly where they stood with him. "I am not ashamed of being a white man," he informed a rally. "I am glad I was elected by the white people. I did not solicit votes from Negroes in 1948, and I am not soliciting their votes now." Thompson could not be trusted on the segregation issue. "If you want to hire a night watchman you wouldn't hire someone convicted of arson," Talmadge reasoned. "If you want someone to protect Georgia's segregation laws, I wouldn't recommend a fellow that vetoed a white primary bill." While Talmadge governed Georgia, "they will not break down the Jim Crow laws in this state."[16]

Thompson responded to Talmadge's bid for a white bloc vote by affirming his support for school segregation. Some equalization of resources was required to save the dual system, he believed, but the Governor was merely "yelling, 'Nigger, nigger,' hoping to holler loud enough to make you forget his broken promises about state employees and taxes." Talmadge's "hollering about the racial issue and the FEPC," he complained, "is nothing but drawing a red herring across his own failure as Governor."[17]

In the final week of the campaign Talmadge enlisted motherhood in the fight for continued white supremacy. "The good women of Georgia," he predicted, "will never stand for the mixing of the races in our schools . . . The parents of Georgia, particularly the mothers, are rallying to our standard." Toward the end Thompson sought to convince the electorate that Talmadge had failed to resist with vigor the desegregation of the armed forces. Unmistakably the hard-lining segregationist in the primary, Talmadge won a narrow plurality (49 percent of the vote to 48 percent for Thompson) but swamped Thompson in county units, 305 to 115.[18] While Thompson polled twice as many votes as Talmadge in Atlanta, Talmadge had overwhelming strength in the countryside. Eighty-six percent of the state's 121 most rural counties (those alloted two units each under the county unit system, as opposed to the six units given to the most populous counties) gave the governor a plurality or better; and Talmadge's greatest vote (55 percent) was supplied by rural counties with black populations of 30 percent or more. Thompson was strongest among urban voters in northern Georgia and several rural counties in extreme southern Georgia surrounding his hometown.

The 1950 Arkansas primary matched Governor Sidney McMath, a moderate segregationist and redistributive who was seeking a second two-year term, against former Governor Ben Laney, a militant segregationist and marginalist who had been prominent in the Dixiecrat movement. Although there were definite racial overtones to the election, economic policy was the more debated issue. McMath, a lawyer from Hot Springs, campaigned largely on his redistributive economic programs and worked to deemphasize racial questions. Laney, a wealthy planter-banker from Quachita County in the delta, combined outspoken resistance to FEPC legislation with a hold-the-line approach to government spending.

In his opening speech Laney called for economy in government as well as the repeal of a state income tax enacted the previous year. McMath's spending policies were disparagingly contrasted with Laney's own frugal approach to public finance, and civil rights matters were mentioned briefly. The candidate assailed FEPC yet promised fair treatment for all races.[19] McMath began his campaign by attacking Laney's proposed "business-like" administration. The central issue was whether the governor's office would be "operated in the interest of a privileged few, or in the interest of all people." FEPC, socialized medicine, and the centralization of political power in Washington were matters which both candidates opposed. "We both have talked about states' rights, but I have done something about states' rights," McMath asserted, citing his decision to retain necessary Washington ties by remaining a loyal Democrat and his efforts to construct more roads, increase teacher pay, raise old age pensions, and induce more industry to settle in Arkansas. Beyond his hostility to FEPC McMath said nothing about race. Atlhough Laney ran a strong states' rights campaign, McMath could also use the vocabulary of states' rights effectively and did not hesitate to trace his southern roots. "I am a Democrat," he would say, "yes, a states' rights Democrat—because I am fighting for the rights of states and individual citizens."[20]

Unlike Talmadge, Laney appealed for black as well as white support. To whites he emphasized his refusal to make special concessions to Negroes and his renunciation of the national Democratic Party. He did not mind being called a Dixiecrat because he was "proud of Dixie." Negro support was solicited, in a fashion, by the argument that blacks would be foolish to believe the special (though unspecified) promises McMath was rumored to be making. McMath was "playing the colored citizens of the state for the biggest suckers of all time." Laney favored more aid for Negro education but denounced politicians who promise everything to Negroes:[21]

> I absolutely refuse to follow the example of my opponent, who, when in Washington or some Northern city, pictures himself as a young dragon slayer, who, with one bold stroke, broke the back of all Southern tradition, and crammed the so-called civil rights ideas down your throat and mine, and then came home mealy-mouthed, telling you that he sees this thing just like you and I have seen it all the time.

McMath's redistributive economic policies were as objectionable to Laney as the governor's weak stand against civil rights. "The people should be warned that a continuation of this extravagance means deficit spending, increased debt or higher taxes," Laney said. "The present governor is pledging an expansion of his so-called liberal program which cannot be accomplished without an enormous increase in expenditures." A Laney advertisement urged voters to deliver "a smashing victory for Arkansas and our southern Democratic way of life and a crushing defeat for the Tax-O-Crats and their deficit spending and dangerous socialistic philosophies!"[22]

McMath, who was confident of reelection, continued to express his disapproval of FEPC and refused to be drawn into an elaborate presentation of his racial views. Instead, he emphasized the class implications of Laney's election. The little man in Arkansas could anticipate no benefits from a politician whose gospel was that "only the rich shall rule and the favored shall have privilege." Arkansas did not need a governor who was "bound up, body and soul, with the Dixiecrat movement in the South." Compared to the crude racism of

Talmadge, Laney's appeal to white prejudice against blacks was relatively subtle. It consisted essentially of telling whites that McMath supported FEPC and had made Negroes undisclosed promises. Against these tactics, McMath emphatically denied that he liked FEPC and stressed his progressive economic program. Arkansas voters, inclined by tradition to give incumbents a second term, preferred McMath over Laney by close to a two-to-one margin.[23] McMath received majorities in all but eight counties and ran especially well in the mountain and border regions, while Laney was comparatively strong in several counties of the delta, the most traditional section of the state.[24]

The 1951 Mississippi primaries provide the final instances of pre-*Brown* campaigns in which the issue of racial segregation received prominent treatment. It should be added that race was far less a dominant, pervasive issue in 1951, particularly in the first primary, than it became after the school desegregation decision. There was no disagreement between the candidates concerning the state's racial traditions, but none of the major candidates in the first primary ran as militant segregationists.[25] The strongest campaigners were former Governor Hugh White, founder of the state's "Balance Agriculture with Industry" program and an economic marginalist, and Paul B. Johnson, Jr., son of another Mississippi governor and (in 1951) a redistributive. Other major candidates included Lieutenant Governor Sam Lumpkin of Tupelo and Jackson lawyer Ross Barnett. Lumpkin feared desegregation would result in "mongrelization." As the "real States' Rights candidate," he would "lead the fight against Harry S Truman and any or all of the so-called civil rights planks" the Democrats might debate at their 1952 national convention. Barnett, in his first race for governor, urged Democrats to return to "Jeffersonian principles," advocated "an all-out fight against communism," and promised to maintain racial segregation. If he had his way, there would "never be an FEPC law, nor any other violation of States' Rights."[26]

In the first primary White ran on his previous record as governor, stressing industrial development through the BAWI program, underlining his dedication to the concept of States' Rights, and announcing his opposition to "FEPC, Civil Rights and any program contrary to our Southern beliefs." "General industrial expansion," he believed, "is the answer to our economic problem." Johnson, a Hattiesburg attorney, supported a severance tax on oil and higher old age pensions but disassociated himself from the national Democratic Party. Allegations that he admired President Truman were "pusillanimous lies." The candidate favored segregated schools and more money for Negro education.[27]

None of the candidates was remarkably successful in the first primary. White led the field with only 23 percent of the vote, dividing the delta vote with Lumpkin and demonstrating strength in several southwestern counties around his native Pike County and his home in Marion County. Johnson, who placed second with 21 percent, made his best showing in the hill counties of the eastern half of the state.

Appeals to racial prejudice, especially on the part of White, who ran as a militant segregationist, increased significantly in the second primary. Both White and Johnson frequently questioned each other's integrity as a States' Righter. Johnson asserted that White had betrayed the States' Rights cause by not working in 1936 to preserve the two thirds rule on presidential nominations in Democratic conventions, a provision which had given the South a veto over the Democratic nominee. According to Johnson, White was "the man who put Truman in Trumanism by that very lack of action." White, in turn, pressed his charge that Johnson's loyalty to Mississippi could not be taken for granted. "States' rights versus Trumanism" was the real issue in the second primary. "You people know how I stand on our cherished southern traditions," White said. "I don't believe you want to compromise these ideals with a crowd which already has shown its Trumanite colors." These remarks elicited an angry and florid response. "I thought that my opponent was a high-class, Christian gentleman," Johnson protested, "but the mud-slinging, vicious, cruel and untrue attack that he has made upon me is enough to make the blush of shame mantle the cheeks of every clear-thinking, red-blooded Mississippian." A few wealthy individuals, he maintained on another occasion, had "hoisted the States' Rights flag over their big estates and attempted to take possession of a movement that belongs to the people." "The real issue," Johnson asserted, "is not States' Rights at all. It is selfish interests versus the people." White was merely a "profiteer," and the runoff offered voters a choice between "youth and progress versus hate and fear uttered by a 70-year-old man with 70-year-old ideas."[28]

As the campaign proceeded White became more specific about Johnson's deficiencies as a segregationist. "It was the little black gang," he contended, "that defeated Sam Lumpkin and put Paul Johnson in the second primary." The election of Johnson would threaten the future of racial segregation:[29]

There are 20,000 Negroes voting in Mississippi. In a few years there may be 50,000. Are you going to take chances on the Negro vote dominating elections in Mississippi?

The issue in this campaign is not Hugh White but the customs and traditions of Mississippi and whether we will be returned to the National Democratic party under President Truman and the Civil Rights crowd. The time to decide is now.

If the Negro vote continues to play such an important part, it won't be long before the Negroes will be sitting next to you in public places, churches, and attending school with your children.

A vote for Johnson is a vote for the Truman crowd and Civil Rights. Are you going to sell your birthright?

"If you turn Mississippi over to the Truman crowd, you have lost all hope for white supremacy," White told the electorate. "This is the most serious matter that has faced you since reconstruction." By contrast, Johnson argued that race was not an issue, since both candidates were committed to racial segregation. Endorsement of his "program of progress and clean government" would inform future candidates "that they cannot win on a platform that pits race against race, creed against creed, religion against religion and class against class." White's assertion to the contrary, Johnson would not turn the state over to the blacks. "For twenty years," he said, "my opponent has known nothing to run on but prejudice, hate, fear and the Negro question." Johnson's position on the use of the racial issue in 1951 was temperate by Mississippi standards:[30]

If I had to base my candidacy on race vs. race, class against class, religion against religion, I would . . . get my old shotgun, stand it on its butt, stick my toe to the trigger, and blow my brains out. I don't want to win by making the Negro the whipping boy when he isn't even an issue in the race.

Despite White's insistence that Johnson was weak on segregation, their differences were matters of style and emphasis rather than substance; Johnson pledged that "no negroes will go to school with white children" while he was governor.[31] With the vote dividing roughly along a delta versus hills cleavage, White won the election with 51 percent of the vote. Strong support from the black belt counties (59 percent) enabled White to overcome losses (46 percent) in rural counties with low black populations. Johnson's majorities came from the hill counties, while White swept the delta and southwestern Mississippi.

In the remaining eleven primaries the two leading candidates were both moderate segregationists. The segregation issue in these elections was either latent or of tangential interest. Moderate segregationists who were marginalists won seven of the eight nominations which were decided by first primaries. Three of these victories came against other marginalists (North Carolina, 1952; Tennessee, 1952; and Virginia, 1953); four were at the expense of redistributives (Alabama, 1950; Tennessee, 1950; and Texas, 1950 and 1952). While there is no need to summarize all the first primaries in which segregation was not a central issue, two of these campaigns deserve mention.

Race might be considered a quasi-issue in the 1950 Alabama primary. Among the more prominent candidates it was agreed that one could be a more effective advocate of States' Rights by remaining within the Democratic Party than by bolting it, and there was considerable clamor from extremist minor candidates (see above) about the dangers of black voting. Yet to the degree that issues, rather than personalities, were discussed, the leading politicians were more interested in taxing and spending policies. Gordon Persons, President of the Alabama Public Service Commission and a marginalist, campaigned against increased state spending. The Montgomery attorney, who had first sought the governorship in 1946, made few explicit commitments. His platform had no "wild promises and, in fact, it contains probably fewer promises than any other." Persons' fiscal conservatism differed significantly from the redistributive stance of State Commissioner of Revenue Philip Hamm. A former schoolteacher from Geneva County and the protégé of Governor James Folsom, Hamm (accompanied by Folsom) defended the neo-Populist programs of the Folsom administration and promised more of the same. Special interest "hogs" had been "soaked," 3,000 miles of black-top road had been constructed, teacher salaries had been raised, and the number of Alabamians receiving old age benefits had doubled. Folsom had achieved all this without higher taxes, Hamm explained, "Just like Big Jim told you it would be done—by weaning the pigs and hogs." Hamm himself had used his office to make "the big hogs pay their fair share." Persons received a plurality in every demographic area and won the first primary with 34 percent of the vote. Hamm obtained only 14 percent despite the fact that Folsom actively supported him, and when campaign funds proved difficult to raise, Hamm decided not to participate in a runoff election. Persons was therefore declared the Democratic nominee.[32]

"Political controversy in Texas since 1944," Key wrote, "has been pitched on the broad level of progressive versus conservative government."[33] The 1952 Texas gubernatorial primary, though not a close election, is the best example of a pre-*Brown* campaign fought out basically in terms of economic ideology, with virtually no attention given to racial segregation. Governor Allan Shivers, leader of the Texas conservatives, was a marginalist and States' Righter. (It should be emphasized that the most controversial States' Rights issue in Texas at this time was not race, but whether the state or the national government controlled rights to Tideland oil deposits.) Shivers, a native of East Texas, viewed his campaign against Ralph Yarborough, a redistributive and a lawyer from Austin, as a struggle for the control of Texas between the national Democratic Party and men committed to "middle-of-the-road, conservative policies." According to Shivers, Yarborough had been encouraged to run by certain Washington Democrats who disliked Shivers because of the governor's efforts to "get the government out of the hands of the liberals and parlor pinks." Would the voters, Shivers asked, line up

with the Democratic Party of Texas, with the advocates of Jeffersonian principles, sound government and the sacred, constitutionally guaranteed rights of individuals and states—or will it be with the proponents of federalism, creeping socialism, paternalism, tax-spend-and-electism, paramount rightsism and all the other isms so eloquently expounded by the left-wing logicians and tumbleweed thinkers of our day and time?[34]

While the governor may not have been in full command of his rhetoric, his statement did express the ideological orientation of the Texas conservative Democrats.

Yarborough, who was making his first race for the Texas governorship and who was not well known in 1952, waged what the *Dallas Morning News* described as a "frank overalls-versus-silk stocking campaign." He demanded more farm-to-market roads, higher old age pensions, and soil and water conservation programs; and he attacked Shivers personally in strong terms. The Shivers administration, he claimed, functioned "without a heart, without a soul, and without a conscience." Texans were said to be increasingly "fed up with a silver-spoon, aristocratic, dictatorial governor who has no sympathy for the people of the state."[35]

Shivers cut short his campaign to attend the Democratic national convention, and, while in Chicago, he accused a Texas liberal of attempting to deliver the state's convention votes "to the New York politicians, the CIO-PAC, the ADA, the NAACP and the synthetic

Southerner [Estes Kefauver] who now has publicly identified himself with forces openly hostile to Texas." This reference to the National Association for the Advancement of Colored People exhausted the racial issue in 1952. With landslide majorities in every demographic category, Shivers easily (62 percent of the total) won renomination.[36]

Three elections in which the two leading candidates were moderate segregationists required runoffs to settle the nominations. Without exception racial segregation did not emerge as a significant issue in either the first or second primaries. In two instances (Arkansas, 1952; and Louisiana, 1951-52) redistributives won the first primary but were defeated by marginalists in the runoff. A marginalist maintained a first primary lead over a redistributive in the 1952 Florida second primary.

Interest in the segregation issue was minimal, for example, in the Louisiana elections. Candidates for governor, as was the custom, were associated with Long and anti-Long factions.[37] Alternatives to Longism included Judge Robert Kennon of Minden and Congressman Hale Boggs of New Orleans, both marginalist and "good government" types, and Alexandria's James McLemore, a marginalist who was the leading States' Righter. Judge Carlos Spaht of Baton Rouge, a redistributive, was Governor Earl Long's candidate. As Uncle Earl assured the electorate, Spaht wanted "our good, liberal government" to continue. "The Sam Jones-*Times-Picayune*-Shreveport *Times*-big corporation combination don't care what you do just so they beat Judge Spaht," Long declared. "They'll take Boggs, Kennon or McLemore but when they do you can be sure of one thing—the people will lose."[38]

No candidate emphasized segregation in the first primary, which Spaht (23 percent) led narrowly over Kennon (22 percent), nor did race become a runoff issue. Kennon continued to advocate "good government," while Spaht denounced his opponent as a "political prisoner of the multi-millionaire oil interests, the professional politicians, the mayor of the city of New Orleans and the other vested interests of the state." The only explicit reference to race occurred when Kennon complained that the Long forces were spreading rumors that he was prejudiced. "I am friendly toward Catholics, toward Protestants, to all races, and toward all creeds," he said. "Everywhere in Louisiana people know that."[39] In a reaction against Earl Long's rule but not necessarily against his redistributive economic programs,[40] Kennon won the second primary with 61 percent of the vote.

Since general elections for governor in the South were rarely meaningful events in the early 1950s, no effort has been made to examine racial segregation as a factor in each of them. Only the 1953 Virginia general election was closely contested, and much of its significance derives from its probable effect upon later Virginia politics. Republican Theodore Dalton, a state senator from Radford, surprised the entrenched Byrd Organization by polling 45 percent of the vote in that election. Race was not an issue. Earlier in 1953 the Republican State Convention, fearing judicial disapproval of school segregation, had asked Governor John S. Battle to establish a commission to study inequalities in school facilities and to consider what the state might do in the event desegregation might be required. Governor Battle thought the suggestion was premature and neither party discussed racial segregation in the general election campaign.[41]

Dalton, a moderate segregationist who championed a $100 million bond program for highways, repeal of the poll tax, and a teacher pay raise, ridiculed the tendency of his Byrd Organization opponent, Thomas Stanley, to evade all issues. "If there's anything unknown in Virginia," Dalton remarked, "it's where my opponent stands on the issues." Stanley, a farmer and manufacturer from Henry County with considerable experience in state politics, remained quiet, confident that Virginians wanted no basic political changes. Portraying Dalton as a reckless, spendthrift politician, Stanley argued that the Republicans would destroy "the sound principles upon which we have built this Commonwealth."[42] Dalton's impressive showing, especially in the large metropolitan areas where he drew 48 percent of the vote, indicated that substantial numbers of Virginians were questioning the Byrd Organization's policies, and it has been suggested that a desire to bolster the organization's public support was a significant factor in the willingness of the Byrd Organization to advocate "massive resistance" to the *Brown* decision.[43]

Racial Segregation: The Submerged Issue

As I have attempted to demonstrate, racial segregation was of relatively little import as an *overt* campaign issue in the early 1950s. In the lull between the Dixiecrat revolt of 1948 and the *Brown* decision of 1954, few prominent southern politicians campaigned as hard-lining, gallus-snapping white supremacists of the old school; and none, for obvious political reasons, questioned the status quo on segregation. With no effective external or internal challenges to the caste system, most candidates for governor could afford to avoid or minimize the segregation question. The militant segregationist was thus an exceptional figure rather than the regional norm. Despite the apparently submerged character of the issue, a tacit commitment to racial segregation was a minimum qualification for access to the largely white southern electorate. In the modal case the segregation issue might be virtually absent or present only in the sense that candidates would praise what they invariably perceived as their state's harmonious and mutually satisfactory tradition of relations between the races. In a small number of campaigns there were substantial differences of emphasis and style with respect to civil rights, but all within the context of complete acceptance of racial segregation as a form of social stratification. Key's assessment as of the late 1940s applies with equal validity to the campaigns of the early 1950s:

> It would be incorrect to say that the problem of race relations is a constant preoccupation of politicians or a matter of continuous debate. Campaign after campaign is waged in which the question of race is not raised; in campaign after campaign candidates most unrestrained in Negro baiting find themselves defeated when the votes are counted. The situation is, rather, that the struggles of politics take place within an institutional framework fixed by considerations of race relations, a framework on the order of a mold which gives shape and form to that which it contains. It is chiefly when the equilibrium in race relations is threatened that the issue of the Negro comes to the fore in political discussion.[44]

The little that white southern politicians did say about blacks—their intentions, their attitudes, their aspirations—was essentially patronizing, self-serving, or false. Apologists for the white majority have often contended that the *Brown* decision undermined race relations in the region and that southerners were slowly "working out the problem" on their own. An examination of the tone and content of campaign rhetoric in the early 1950s indicates the mythical nature of this belief. The relative absence of stem-winding racist oratory in southern campaigns did not signify that a segregated social order was being gradually transformed from within or that southern office seekers were becoming less strenuously opposed to racial desegregation than their predecessors. A few white politicians did propose that steps be taken to improve the quality of black education, but certainly no major candidate for governor argued against the principle of racially segregated schools. The belated interest in Negro education was mainly an effort to put a measure of equality into the "separate but equal" doctrine. If it is fair to conclude that the Negro "was and is the neglected man in Mississippi, though not the forgotten man," for the South generally in the pre-*Brown* period, blacks were typically both neglected and very largely forgotten in campaigns for governor.[45]

4

The Deep South States
and Racial Segregation

Since the extent to which white politicians have resisted racial change has varied from state to state, some knowledge of the politics of individual states is essential to an understanding of the segregation controversy. Racial segregation as an issue in southern campaigns could be examined by devoting a chapter to each of the eleven southern states. That approach has been rejected, however, in favor of an attempt to develop regional and subregional generalizations concerning the racial stances of gubernatorial candidates and to investigate the segregation issue at successive stages of the southern electoral process. Because it will not be feasible in later chapters to trace events in any single state chronologically, at this point I wish to summarize the states' responses to the threat of school desegregation in the years after the *Brown* decision. Case studies of specific campaigns which will be offered in subsequent chapters may then be related to the recent political history of a state. In this chapter developments within the five states of the Deep South will be assessed. The history of the segregation issue in campaigns will be narrated; data concerning the racial stance and the demography of the vote for each successful candidate will be presented in tabular form; and paired maps will be used to indicate the demographic setting of electoral politics and to identify areas of greatest resistance to racial change within each state. By beginning with the Deep South states where the status of blacks has been a persistent source of political conflict, and moving toward the Peripheral South states (Chapter 5) which have been relatively least preoccupied with racial divisions, a sense of the range of southern reactions to the *Brown* decision should be conveyed.

The Demographic Setting of Electoral Politics

Consideration of the demographic setting of electoral politics provides a starting point for differentiating the states of the Deep South. As was argued in Chapter 2, Key's findings in *Southern Politics* suggest the utility, for purposes of comparative analysis, of dividing the electorates of the various states into demographic components based on the size of the black population and urban-rural differences. A series of categories—large metropolitan, medium urban, low black rural, high black rural (with the latter classification subdivided into medium black and black belt categories)—has been devised; and each county within a state has been assigned to an appropriate classification. Expressed in unqualified terms, the greater the weight (as a percentage of the total state vote) of the most traditional category, the high black rural counties, the greater the probability that militant segregationists would dominate a state's electoral process once the *Brown* decision placed the issue of racial segregation explicitly on the agenda of southern politics. Conversely, moderate segregationists or nonsegregationists might be expected to be comparatively successful in those states in which the least traditional component, the large metropolitan counties, contributed a substantial proportion of the total state vote.

The highly traditional political demography of the Deep South states is indicated by Table 5, which displays the mean proportion of the total vote in Democratic first primaries for governor (1950-73) contributed by each demographic category. As the means of the Deep South states show, the high black rural counties cast approximately one third of the total vote in gubernatorial primaries, far more than the low black rural, large metropolitan, or medium urban classifications. The high black vote was greater than one quarter of the total in every state except Alabama (22 percent); and it exceeded the large metropolitan contribution in Mississippi, South Carolina, and Georgia. Mississippi, with over half its vote furnished by high black counties and with no large metropolitan areas, was clearly the most demographically traditional of the Deep South states. During this period the Deep South vote was more rural than urban. Louisiana was the single state in which the two urban categories combined produced over 50 percent of the state vote. Although the significance of the high black component in the Deep South electorates is readily apparent, it should be noted that the black belt counties (restricting the term black belt to rural counties with black population majorities) were less

Table 5. The demographic setting of electoral politics in the Deep South: mean percentage distribution of the vote in Democratic first primaries for governor, 1950-73, by states and subregion

Demographic Category	Deep South States					
	Ala	Ga	La	Miss	SC	DS[a]
Large Metropolitan	23	24	33	0	28	22
Medium Urban	25	18	20	26	17	21
Low Black Rural	30	28	20	23	16	24
High Black Rural	22	30	26	51	39	34
Medium Black Rural	15	21	22	28	24	22
Black Belt	7	9	4	23	15	12
Totals	100	100	100	100	100	100

[a]Deep South means were computed from means of the five states in the subregion.

important numerically than the medium black counties, the rural counties with black populations of 30 to 49 percent. Only in Mississippi (23 percent) and South Carolina (15 percent) did the black belts comprise as much as 10 percent of the total vote.

The use of means derived from elections which span more than two decades might well underestimate the potential significance of demographic changes (for example, increased urbanization) commonly associated with a lessened concern for the maintenance of traditional racial norms. When the first primary votes are plotted over time for each state (see Figure 1), a general impression emerges of relative stability in the proportion of the vote contributed by various demographic categories. Throughout the era under consideration the high black counties were consistently the largest component of the vote in Mississippi, South Carolina, and Georgia. Moderate increases in the large metropolitan sector are evident in Alabama and Georgia (where the county unit system was ruled unconstitutional in 1962). Even by the early 1970s the rural character of the Democratic electorates in the Deep South had not appreciably diminished. More than 70 percent of the total Mississippi vote was cast by rural counties, and the Georgia electorate was still more rural than urban. There was a rough balance between urban and rural categories in Alabama, while in Louisiana the urban categories contributed a majority of the vote but were

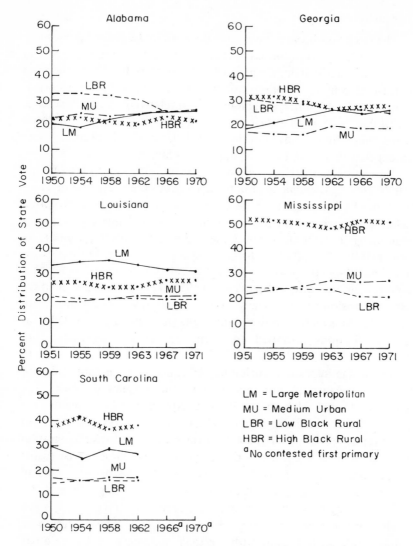

Figure 1. The demographic setting of electoral politics in the Deep South: distribution of total state vote in Democratic first primaries for governor, 1950-71 (percent)

virtually stable over the entire period. South Carolina did not have contested Democratic primaries in 1966 or 1970. Campaigns for governor in the Deep South were thus waged in highly traditional demographic settings.

Alabama

The Deep South states have generally exhibited a greater preoccupation with the segregation issue than states in the Peripheral South. Alabama and Mississippi, without much question, have been the most consistent centers of opposition to racial change, while Georgia, Louisiana, and South Carolina have been relatively less conservative. There has been no shortage of strong segregationists in the latter states, but militants have not dominated electoral politics to the same extent that they have in Mississippi and Alabama.

The campaign racial stances and the patterns of support for winning candidates in Alabama gubernatorial elections are presented in Table 6.[1] From 1958 through 1970 the Alabama electorate without exception selected as governor the most militant of the available segregationist candidates. Former Governor James "Big Jim" Folsom, a moderate segregationist (comparable to Louisiana's Earl Long) famed for his uninhibited campaign style and redistributive economics, achieved a first primary majority (51 percent) in 1954. The primary preceded the *Brown* decision by a few days, and segregation was not a significant issue. In the general election campaign, the outcome of which was certain, Folsom promised to keep the schools segregated but advocated "adequate" schooling for both races. White opposition to racial change intensified during his term, and Folsom found himself attacked because of his comparatively mild views on race. The governor toured Alabama in 1956 to explain his stand against the Citizens Council and his ridicule of a nullification resolution passed by the state legislature. His solution for preventing racial integration was to convince black leaders privately that it would be unwise to file school desegregation suits. "Don't you think that's better," Folsom would ask, "than getting out on the stump and yelling 'nigger?' "[2]

The tragedy of Alabama politics has been that "nigger" (or some euphemism) has been precisely what a majority of white voters have wanted to hear. Beginning with the 1958 campaigns of John Patterson, a young attorney general who was originally given little chance to win, successful candidates for governor in Alabama have supplied a proven demand for race baiting. Patterson's highly publicized attacks on the NAACP during his term as attorney general were instrumental to his victory. The most extreme segregationist in the 1958 primaries, Patterson urged his opponents to take a more definite stand "where the NAACP is concerned" and expressed surprise that "we haven't heard more from them on the subject." It was the attorney general's boast that he had "run the NAACP out of the state." George

Table 6. Campaign racial stance and pattern of support for winning candidates for governor at successive stages of the electoral process in Alabama, 1950-70

Year	Winning Candidate	Campaign Racial Stance of		Winner's Share of Vote within Demographic Categories						
		Winner	Closest Opponent	Large Metro	Medium Urban	Low Black Rural	High Black Rural	Medium Black	Black Belt	State
Democratic First Primary										
1950	Gordon Persons	MS	MS	40 P[a]	35 P	27 P	38 P	40 P	35 P	34 P[b]
1954	James Folsom	MS	MS	36 L	48 P	63	50	54	41 P	51
1958	John Patterson	SS	SS	26 P	29 P	32 P	41 P	43 P	35 L	32 P
1962	George Wallace	SS	MS	24 L	31 L	34 L	43 P	40 P	49 P	33 P
1966	Lurleen Wallace	SS	NS	47 P	53	60	56	62	47 P	54
1970	Albert Brewer	NS	SS	47 P	42 P	36 L	43 L	39 L	50	42 P
Mean percentage distribution of state vote				23	25	30	22	15	7	100
Democratic Second Primary										
1958	John Patterson	SS	SS	57	52	56	58	60	51	56

(continued)

Table 6. (cont.)

Year	Winning Candidate	Campaign Racial Stance of		Winner's Share of Vote within Demographic Categories						
		Winner	Closest Opponent	Large Metro	Medium Urban	Low Black Rural	High Black Rural	Medium Black	Black Belt	State
1962	George Wallace	SS	MS	46	50	61	68	67	72	56
1970	George Wallace	SS	NS	47	51	58	51	58	41	52
	Mean percentage distribution of state vote			25	25	29	21	14	7	100

Symbols: SS = Strong Segregationist; MS = Moderate Segregationist; NS = Nonsegregationist; P = Plurality for candidate; L = Loss for candidate

[a] Percentages for candidates in this and similar tables for other states have been rounded to the nearest whole number. Decimals have been used, however, in those few cases in which the reader would otherwise be unable to determine whether or not a candidate had received a majority of the vote within a given demographic category.

[b] The first primary winner became the Democratic nominee when his closest opponent declined to contest the second primary.

Wallace, Patterson's main opponent, also ran as a militant segregationist. "I was fighting against civil rights 10 years ago," Wallace
claimed, "before many knew what civil rights were."[3] However,
Wallace was less outspoken on segregation in 1958 than in 1962 and
his statements were relatively less inflammatory than those of Patterson. Patterson led the first primary field and defeated Wallace handily
in the second primary with 55 percent of the vote.

The victory of Patterson signaled a qualitative change in the posture
of successful Alabama candidates on racial segregation. The threat of
school desegregation (however token) as a consequence of the *Brown*
decision created circumstances under which segregation became transformed from a more or less latent campaign issue, with candidates
routinely agreeing on the virtues of the caste system, into a question of
such salience that the most militant segregationist candidate possessed
the best chance to win the governorship. Alabama political lore
reports that Wallace, in defeat, drew the proper inference for future
electoral success: "No one is ever going to out-nigger me again."[4]

Four years later Wallace's rhetoric was sufficiently defiant to make
him the leading segregationist among major candidates for governor.
It was apparent during the 1962 campaign that token desegregation in
a few school districts might soon be ordered by federal courts, and
Wallace categorically announced that he would not "obey any order
of any federal court that orders integration of any schools."[5] Wallace
won the first primary with 33 percent of the vote and easily defeated
(56 percent) a moderate segregationist, State Senator Ryan deGraffenried, in the second primary. In both these elections, Wallace's vote
ascended steadily along a demographic continuum from the state's
large metropolitan areas to the black belt counties. Wallace delivered
an inaugural address, one of the most belligerent ever given in the
modern South, in which he promised to preserve "segregation now
. . . segregation tomorrow . . . segregation forever."[6] During his first
term as governor Wallace praised the methods used by Police Commissioner Eugene "Bull" Connor in breaking up nonviolent civil
rights demonstrations in Birmingham, attempted unsuccessfully to
halt the desegregation of the University of Alabama, and in general
created a new standard of gubernatorial intransigence with respect to
racial change.

By virtue of his performance in office Wallace was securely established by 1966 as the most militant segregationist in Alabama politics.
When the state senate defeated his proposal to amend the state constitution to permit a governor to succeed himself, Wallace circumvented

the constitution's intent and spirit by persuading his (late first) wife Lurleen to run instead. Hence the 1966 Democratic primary amounted to a referendum on Wallace's term as governor. As an incumbent Wallace's strategy was to ignore his opposition (except for Attorney General Richmond Flowers, who was frequently assailed as a tool of Alabama's multifarious enemies) and concentrate on his administration's record of economic benefits and undying hostility to federal intervention concerning race relations. Racial segregation, the main issue of Wallace's 1962 campaigns, was not explicitly defended, and references to blacks were generally limited to the claim that they had benefited prodigiously from Wallace's economic and educational programs. Strident segregationist oratory disappeared, to be replaced by a set of euphemisms which indicated that the Wallaces would firmly resist further racial changes. "We will continue," Wallace would say, "to stand up for Alabama."[7] Lurleen Wallace's first primary majority (54 percent), achieved despite the growth of a black electorate estimated at 246,000, was an impressive confirmation of Wallace's popularity among white Alabamians, and two years later Wallace mounted a third party campaign for the Presidency.[8]

When he again sought the Alabama governorship in 1970, Wallace emphasized the economic achievements of past Wallace administrations and proposed a series of neo-Populist programs (for example, free transportation for commuting college students, the reduction of utility rates) calculated to have working class appeal. He continued to refrain from explicitly segregationist rhetoric but did not avoid race-oriented appeals. Wallace believed his election would "serve notice to President Nixon that he cannot be President again unless he fulfills his promises to return control of the schools to the states." As the election neared Wallace began to warn of an impending "black militant bloc vote" against himself.[9] In the 1970 first primary Wallace received only 41 percent of the vote, far from the landslide majority of his wife in 1966, and actually trailed Governor Albert Brewer, a former Wallace protégé who had succeeded to the governorship when Mrs. Wallace died in office, by 12,000 votes. In the second primary Wallace defined the issues much more directly in racial terms. Throughout the campaign he contended that Brewer had won the first primary because of the "black bloc vote." Alabamians were informed that Brewer had obtained 99 percent of the vote in certain all-black wards in Birmingham, and Wallace newspaper advertisements denounced the "spotted alliance" between Brewer and the blacks. The fundamental question for Wallace was which race would dominate the state. "If the bloc vote controls the runoff," Wallace told his audiences, "it's going to control politics for the next 50 years in Alabama. I know you won't let that happen."[10] Wallace's second primary victory over Brewer, though less than overwhelming (52 percent), demonstrated that blatant appeals for a white bloc vote, when orchestrated by Wallace, were still feasible in Alabama. Wallace carried every demographic category except for the black belt (41 percent) and the large metropolitan counties (47 percent) and ran particularly well in rural counties with white population majorities (the medium black and low black classifications). Thus despite the creation of a substantial black electorate, the basic characteristic of the traditional political order in Alabama—white supremacy—remained unaltered through the early 1970s. In contrast to the other Deep South states, which opted for nonsegregationist gubernatorial candidates in the 1970-72 elections, Alabama electoral politics continued to be rooted in the racial conflicts of previous decades.

To supplement this overview of the segregation issue in campaigns and provide insight into the structure of electoral conflict, a pair of maps has been constructed which contrast the broad demographic setting of electoral politics with the demographic characteristics of those counties which consistently supported militant segregationists after 1954. The map labeled "political demography" in Figure 2 simply portrays the geography of the demographic categories—large metropolitan, medium urban, low black, and high black—introduced previously, while the map named "segregationist voting" identifies the Alabama core segregationist counties in terms of their demographic classification. (The methods used to determine core segregationist counties are discussed in Appendix B.)

The relationship between the demographic setting of Alabama politics and segregationist voting is strikingly apparent in Figure 2. By and large, consistent segregationist voting has been most pronounced in the high black rural counties. A north-south sectional division between low black and high black rural counties is roughly paralleled by the absence of segregationist counties in northern Alabama and by their presence in southwestern Alabama.[11] (A "friends and neighbors" vote for Wallace over Patterson in the 1958 primaries prevents several of the southeastern Alabama counties from ranking as core segregationist.) Neither of the two large metropolitan SMSAs (Birmingham and Mobile) qualified as core segregationist, and a compara-

Figure 2.   Alabama political demography and the geographic core of segregationist voting after the *Brown* decision: comparison of the demographic setting of Alabama's electoral politics with counties consistently in the upper half of the vote for selected militant segregationist candidates for governor, 1954-73

Political Demography   Segregationist Voting

Large Metropolitan: blank   Large Metropolitan and Medium
Medium Urban: dotted   Urban: dotted
Low Black Rural: striped   Low Black Rural: striped
High Black Rural: shaded   High Black Rural: shaded

tively rural county attached to the Montgomery SMSA (Elmore) was the single medium urban county which consistently supported strong segregationists.

Mississippi

The political demography of Mississippi is by far the most traditional of the southern states.[12] Approximately two thirds of the state's 82 counties were classified as high black rural, and there were no large metropolitan SMSAs. All but three counties in the western half of the state were high black, and the eastern half was divided primarily between high black rural and low black rural counties (see Figure 3). In this bastion of white resistance to racial change, the counties which consistently ranked in the upper half of the vote for selected militant segregationists were located essentially in the southern half of the state, with a particular concentration in south-western Mississippi. The north-south cleavage in the core segrega-tionist vote is more difficult to interpret than are the results for most southern states. Although most of the segregationist counties in Mississippi possessed high black concentrations, none of the northern delta counties, the counties with the heaviest black populations, qualified as segregationist. In large measure this finding reflects the fact that several of the most extreme segregationist candidates after 1954 (for example, Ross Barnett, Paul Johnson, Jr., and Jimmy Swan) did not reside in the delta and were more often identified as hill than as delta politicians. Since a militant stance on segregation was the norm in Mississippi campaigns, especially in the period 1955-63, delta counties could give relatively less consistent support to the most irreconcilable segregationist without rejecting in any way a strong stand against racial change.

Figure 3.   Mississippi political demography and the geographic core of segre-gationist voting after the *Brown* decision: comparison of the demographic setting of Mississippi's electoral politics with counties consistently in the upper half of the vote for selected militant segregationist candidates for governor, 1954-73

Political Demography   Segregationist Voting

Large Metropolitan: none   Medium Urban: dotted
Medium Urban: dotted   Low Black Rural: striped
Low Black Rural: striped   High Black Rural: shaded
High Black Rural: shaded

White Mississippians had long been extraordinarily disturbed by the prospect of challenges to white supremacy,[13] and as Table 7 shows, strong segregationists won every Democratic nomination except the final one in the years 1955-71. All the major candidates in 1955 campaigned as militant segregationists. Paul Johnson, Jr., who led the first primary field but lost to Attorney General J. P. Coleman in the runoff election, promised that "Negroes and whites will not go to school together in Mississippi" while he was governor. Blacks were advised to ignore representatives of civil rights organizations: "When these birds from the NAACP come around to collect a dollar or five dollars from you and say they're going to do something for you, don't believe them. You should see them in the night clubs in Washington spending your money on whiskey and women." Coleman believed that his relatively calm and legalistic approach was more likely to preserve total school segregation than combative denunciations of the national government. "A threatening governor screaming for federal bayonets or a totally inexperienced man in the same position will only lose that which we are determined to keep in our great state," he said. As examples of his legal expertise Coleman cited his success in securing the execution of a black man convicted of raping a white woman and his efforts to foil an "absolutely worthless" petition for school desegregation in Vicksburg. "I am strong enough, skilled enough, and morally courageous enough," he emphasized, "to do some riding at night [he had driven all night to reach Vicksburg] whenever and wherever necessary to protect our people from the haunting specter of racial integration."[14] In the second primary both candidates stressed their support for segregation and accused their opponent of weakness on the issue. According to Johnson, "Coleman and [Governor Hugh] White are aligned with the soft-thinkers who tell us that integration is inevitable and that it is the Christian thing to do." Coleman contrasted his "record of performance" on segregation to Johnson's inexperience and suggested that Johnson had attempted to win the black vote.[15] Despite his opposition to desegregation, Coleman was considered a disappointment by the more militant Mississippi segregationists. His shortcomings included describing an interposition resolution as "legal poppycock," failing to support Orval Faubus in 1957, and a willingness to discuss candidly the improbability of using the "police power" to forestall desegregation. Compared to that of his successor, Coleman's career was "relatively free of demagoguery."[16]

Table 7. Campaign racial stance and pattern of support for winning candidates for governor at successive stages of the electoral process in Mississippi, 1951-71

		Campaign Racial Stance of		Winner's Share of Vote within Demographic Categories						
Year	Winning Candidate	Winner	Closest Opponent	Large Metro	Medium Urban	Low Black Rural	High Black Rural	Medium Black	Black Belt	State
Democratic First Primary										
1951	Hugh White	MS	MS	-	23 L	19 L	26 P	25 P	27 P	23 P
1955	Paul Johnson	SS	SS	-	33 P	32 P	24 L	28 L	19 L	28 P
1959	Ross Barnett	SS	SS	-	32 L	32 L	38 P	42 P	33 L	35 P
1963	Paul Johnson	SS	SS	-	37 P	39 P	39 P	43 P	34 P	39 P
1967	William Winter	MS	SS	-	34 P	32 P	32 P	28 L	36 P	33 P
1971	Charles Sullivan	NS	NS	-	39 P	35 P	38 P	35 P	43 P	38 P
	Mean percentage distribution of state vote				26	23	51	28	23	100
Democratic Second Primary										
1951	Hugh White	SS	MS	-	50	46	54	50	59	51
1955	J. P. Coleman	SS	SS	-	46	56	60	58	63	56
1959	Ross Barnett	SS	SS	-	49	54	57	58	56	54
1963	Paul Johnson	SS	SS	-	55	58	58	61	54	57
1967	John Bell Williams	SS	MS	-	55	57	53	57	49.7	55

(continued)

Table 7.   (cont.)

Year	Winning Candidate	Campaign Racial Stance of		Winner's Share of Vote within Demographic Categories						
		Winner	Closest Opponent	Large Metro	Medium Urban	Low Black Rural	High Black Rural	Medium Black	Black Belt	State
1971	William Waller	NS	NS	-	56	56	53	57	47	54
	Mean percentage distribution of state vote			-	26	23	51	28	23	100
	General Election									
1963	Paul Johnson (D)	SS	SS	-	55	65	65	67	62	62
	Percentage distribution of state vote			-	29	21	50	29	21	100

Symbols: SS = Strong Segregationist; MS = Moderate Segregationist; NS = Nonsegregationist; P = Plurality for candidate; L = Loss for candidate

Thus it was not surprising that whites turned to a more defiant seg-regationist in 1959. Jackson attorney Ross Barnett, the most grotesque candidate in the field, had a deserved reputation as the favorite of the white Citizens' Council. Under no circumstances would Barnett "yield one inch on segregation" or tolerate subversive influences in the Magnolia State: "I don't want the NAACP vote, and when I am governor I am going to investigate the NAACP from A to Z and try to get them outlawed from this state."[17] There is no need to retrace Barnett's performance as governor. The University of Mississippi was desegregated in 1962, despite his efforts to prevent it. Barnett's failure to preserve total school segregation, however, did not prevent him from reporting to the legislature, in what he described as a "stewardship summary" of his achievements, that Mississippi was still "the greatest states' rights state in the American union." The 1964 Civil Rights Bill, he told the legislators, was a "vicious, un-American and completely unconstitutional" proposal that would "put all Americans in slavery under a dictatorship—the like of which no nation in this world has ever seen."[18]

The Mississippi electorate, less than a tenth of whom were black, was in an angry mood in 1963, still resentful of the desegregation of Ole Miss, and Lieutenant Governor Paul Johnson, Jr., who had been photographed refusing to admit James Meredith to the University of Mississippi, had no difficulty establishing himself as a candidate in the die-hard Barnett tradition. Johnson presented himself as the politician feared most by John and Robert Kennedy. Their antipathy to him was based, he claimed, on his refusal to "bow to their philosophy of big government, and because they know my love, my loyalty and my life is dedicated to Mississippi and the segregated ways of good people." In one respect Johnson had a better grasp of political realities than his principal opponent, former Governor Coleman. Johnson did not promise that no additional integration would occur while he was governor, only that he would resist racial change. Coleman argued that he could somehow prevent more desegregation.[19] Johnson's blatant appeals to white prejudice, his assertion that segregation was compatible with industrial development, and his attack on Coleman as "the Kennedy candidate" enabled him to compile solid majorities in each demographic category.

After his hard-lining segregationist campaign, Johnson's inaugural address was surprisingly conciliatory, an indication, probably, that he was reluctant to jeopardize opportunities for economic growth by engaging in unnecessary conflicts with the national government. Mississippians were reminded that they were "part of this world, whether we like it or not." The new governor elaborated on his role:

> Hate, or prejudice, or ignorance will not lead Mississippi while I sit in the governor's chair. I will oppose . . . any man, any faction, any party, or any authority which I feel is morally wrong or constitutionally in error . . . and I will stand accountable for my action; but, if I must fight, it will not be a rear-guard defense of yesterday . . . it will be for our share of tomorrow.[20]

Johnson's performance as governor was somewhat better than his campaign rhetoric on civil rights would have suggested. When three civil rights workers were murdered in Neshoba County during the 1964 Freedom Summer, Johnson refrained from "demagogic outbursts, while treading the uneasy path between the demands of the Citizens' Council . . . and the imperatives of the situation." The State Sovereignty Commission, which helped finance the Citizens' Council, declined in influence during his administration, and the governor, fearing the impact of prolonged racial strife on the state's economy, joined leading businessmen, including the Jackson Chamber of Commerce, in requesting compliance with the 1964 Civil Rights Act and with the token desegregation of several Jackson public schools in September 1964. Congressional approval of the Civil Rights Act made it clear even to the more obtuse Mississippi businessmen and politicians that the nation wanted at least a change of tone from the Deep South, and Johnson alluded to this feeling when he declared that "the day for a lot of bull-shooting is over."[21] Yet there were distinct limitations to his conception of "prejudice." If he did not demagogue in the style of Ross Barnett, Johnson was not above the casual and callous slur. Questioned about reports that many blacks in the delta were suffering from severe malnutrition or slowly starving, the governor dismissed the problem. "All the Negroes I've seen lately," he said, "are so fat they shine."[22]

Though specific references to blacks were comparatively rare in the 1967 Democratic primary, only one of the four leading candidates, State Treasurer William Winter, could in any sense be considered a "moderate" on race, and Winter's moderation was implicit, since he sought to discuss nonracial issues and referred to himself as a segregationist and as a conservative. Two lesser candidates should be mentioned. Former Governor Ross Barnett, in contrast to his previous campaigns, did not emphasize segregation in every speech. Barnett did deliver his "racial integrity" address occasionally, but he was overshadowed and outpolled as a segregationist by a Hattiesburg broadcaster and country music singer, Jimmy Swan. Swan promised to create racially segregated and free private schools for all of Mississippi's white school children. Precisely how this private educational system would operate might be unclear, but "thinking" Mississippians would recognize the importance of supporting Swan's efforts to "save our children from the degeneracy of mass integration."[23] Congressman John Bell Williams, who trailed Winter in the first primary but won the second primary easily (55 percent), campaigned against riots in the cities, HEW school desegregation guidelines, and the Johnson administration in Washington. Winter was denounced as a "dedicated, demonstrated liberal," and the congressman defined the leading campaign issue as "whether Mississippi will go down the road of Socialism with the Great Society or stand firm on the bed-rock of conservatism and constitutional government with John Bell Williams."[24] Williams' victory gave Mississippi yet another strong segregationist governor. An estimated 139,000 blacks were registered to vote by 1966, a bloc that amounted to nearly 23 percent of the state total. Although blacks were a larger proportion of the electorate in Mississippi than in any other southern state, the intensity of white opposition to racial change limited the impact of black mobilization in the 1967 elections.[25]

Between 1967 and 1971 the percentage of blacks in the total electorate rose to an estimated 28 percent, and perhaps more important, some degree of school desegregation was achieved throughout Mississippi. Probably because of these developments, the 1971 Mississippi elections did not resemble the explicitly segregationist campaigns of the past. As one experienced observer commented, the campaign was characterized "by the greatest wave of racial moderation to sweep through state politics this century." For the first time in the modern history of the state, the two leading candidates for governor could be described as nonsegregationists. Neither Lieutenant Governor Charles Sullivan, who led the first primary vote, nor Jackson lawyer William Waller, the victor in the second primary, utilized the rhetoric of segregation. Sullivan thought Mississippi needed a governor who would "lead us progressively through the decade of the '70's and not carry us back to the decade of the '60's," and Waller considered economics rather than race to be the state's central problem. The two nonsegregationists divided two thirds of the first primary vote, while

Jimmy Swan, running another militant segregationist campaign, received only 17 percent. In contrast to many second primary campaigns after 1954, neither Sullivan nor Waller used the segregation issue against the other in the runoff.[26] Waller, waging an anti-Establishment campaign, won with 54 percent of the vote and then defeated Charles Evers in the general election by a margin of nearly four-to-one. Two decades after the *Brown* decision, a measure of racial change had come even to "The Closed Society."

Georgia

The racial stances of successful candidates for the Georgia governorship (see Table 8) have been slightly more varied than those of winners in Alabama and Mississippi.[27] Because even token desegregation of Georgia schools was not accomplished until 1961, candidates in the 1954 and 1958 primaries argued incessantly over the question of who was best qualified to preserve completely segregated schools. Marvin Griffin, a rural politician associated with the Talmadge faction, emphasized his determination to prevent desegregation in his successful 1954 campaign. Blacks should work to improve themselves, but they should proceed "in the Georgia way," without benefit of NAACP advice. "If we lose the election this summer," Griffin warned, "we lose all forms of segregation—in schools, churches, and cafes." Only he was qualified to protect Georgians from "outside NAACP agitators and the Ohio-owned carpetbag Atlanta press." Griffin's concern with desegregation was premature but politically effective; when his election was assured, he announced that the voters had chosen a man "who believes in and can be depended on to preserve our great social and political tradition and the Georgia way of life."[28]

Supported by Senators Richard Russell and Herman Talmadge, Ernest Vandiver emerged as the overwhelming favorite in the 1958 Georgia primary. Though not as vocal a segregationist as his sole opponent, an obscure state representative and former executive director of the Georgia States' Rights Council named William T. Bodenhamer, Vandiver was not soft on the segregation issue, as his rival's campaign literature claimed.[29] Vandiver took the position that "there is not enough money in the federal treasury nor enough federal troops to force us to mix the races in the classrooms of the schools and colleges of Georgia while I am your governor." Toward the end of the campaign he again expressed himself unequivocally against any com-

Table 8. Campaign racial stance and pattern of support for winning candidates for governor at successive stages of the electoral process in Georgia, 1950-70

Year	Winning Candidate	Campaign Racial Stance of		Winner's Share of Vote within Demographic Categories						
		Winner	Closest Opponent	Large Metro	Medium Urban	Low Black Rural	High Black Rural	Medium Black	Black Belt	State
Democratic First Primary										
1950	Herman Talmadge	SS	MS	36 L	51	51	55	54	57	49 P[a]
1954	Marvin Griffin	SS	MS	28 P	38 P	39 P	39 P	37 P	43 P	36 P[a]
1958	Ernest Vandiver	SS	SS	86	81	80	77	77	77	81
1962	Carl Sanders	MS	SS	72	62	53	47 L	49 L	43 L	58
1966	Ellis Arnall	NS	SS	36 P	35 P	24 L	26 L	25 L	28 L	29 P
1970	Jimmy Carter	NS	NS	41 L	46 P	56	52	54	47 P	49 P
Mean percentage distribution of state vote				24	18	28	30	21	9	100
Democratic Second Primary										
1966	Lester Maddox	SS	NS	43	47	64	62	64	59	54
1970	Jimmy Carter	NS	NS	49	56	68	65	66	62	59
Mean percentage distribution of state vote				28	20	25	27	19	9	100
General Election										
1966	Lester Maddox (D)	SS	MS	34	33	62	55	58	50	46 L[b]
1970	Jimmy Carter (D)	NS	NS	42	60	68	75	74	78	59
Mean percentage distribution of state vote				31	21	24	24	17	8	100

Symbols: SS = Strong Segregationist; MS = Moderate Segregationist; NS = Nonsegregationist; P = Plurality for candidate; L = Loss for candidate

[a]These candidates received pluralities of the popular vote but majorities of the county unit vote.

[b]Although the Republican candidate received a plurality of the general election vote, in the absence of a majority vote the 1966 governorship was determined by the Georgia legislature. The legislature selected the Democratic candidate.

pliance with the *Brown* decision. "Georgians," he declared on state-wide television, "entertain no thought of surrender" on segregation. The candidate made a "solemn pledge" that "when Ernest Vandiver is your governor, neither my three children nor any child of yours, will ever attend a racially mixed school or college in this state." The following day he suggested that public schools would be abandoned in Georgia before whites submitted to "judicially enforced integration, at bayonet point, or otherwise." Attempts to desegregate the schools would be countered by extensive grassroots opposition:[30]

> You and I say to the United States Supreme Court that we will resist this tyranny at every crossroads, at every filling station, in every hamlet, in every militia district, in every town, in every city and in every county throughout the length and breadth of the State of Georgia until sanity is restored in the land.

Vandiver's subsequent reconsideration of this pledge, when token desegregation of the University of Georgia and the Atlanta public schools occurred in 1961, spared Georgia from a crisis similar to Little Rock. Once the question of *complete* school segregation had been resolved, Carl Sanders was able to frame the segregation issue along new lines. Sanders, a state senator from Augusta, was the first moderate segregationist to win the Georgia governorship. Running against former Governor Griffin, Sanders stood for law and order and opposed those "agitators" who would, in his view, destroy the peace in Georgia. "Race-baiters and hate-mongers, from Marvin Griffin and Roy Harris to Martin Luther King, Jr., and Ralph Abernathy," he promised, "won't be allowed to disrupt the lives of entire communities and sow discord and disunity." Despite a personal preference for racial segregation, he would never "put a padlock on a school house" or undertake activities that would embarrass the state nationally.[31] Georgia's national image was not a serious concern for Griffin, who recommended the selective application of the blackjack sapling as a means of discouraging sit-in demonstrations and urged an expanded turnout among rural and small town whites to "offset the two nigger boxes in Atlanta." His return to the governorship was necessary, Griffin explained, to prevent the NAACP from controlling electoral politics in Georgia.[32] Inordinate corruption in Griffin's previous administration, combined with Sanders' personality and emphasis on economic development, contributed to Griffin's defeat. Sanders did not carry the high black rural counties, but he received a majority (53 percent) in the low black rural counties and had overwhelming support in the medium urban (62 percent) and large metropolitan (72 percent) classifications. Although the election of Sanders represented a victory for progressive forces in Georgia, it should not be forgotten that Sanders had campaigned explicitly as a segregationist.[33]

Relatively few white Georgians sent their children to desegregated schools or shared public accommodations with blacks when Sanders assumed office. Four years later, resentment of the Johnson administration's civil rights legislation, including school desegregation guidelines established by HEW, and black riots in Atlanta helped elect an amateur politician whose "entire public career had been built upon violent racial harangues and defiance of the Federal Government."[34] Dismissed by most observers as a fringe candidate and best known for his frantic efforts to forestall the desegregation of his Atlanta restaurant, Lester Maddox ran a grassroots campaign for the Georgia governorship in 1966 that appealed straightforwardly to the racial prejudices of whites. At various points he promised to autograph ax handles in the governor's office, suggested that Martin Luther King, Jr., be "jailed or deported," deplored President Johnson's "racist, 'We Shall Overcome' attitude," and characterized school desegregation guidelines as "communistic." Maddox considered himself the only authentic "segregationist candidate."[35] Wide appeal to rural Georgians, blue-collar urbanites, and small businessmen, together with support from Republicans voting in the Democratic runoff, made Maddox a surprise Democratic nominee over former Governor Ellis Arnall, an aging New Dealer who ran openly as a national Democrat.

Maddox combined explicit racism with progressive economic rhetoric in his general election campaign against Republican Congressman Howard Callaway. Although he would consistently advocate and practice segregation, Maddox believed his opponent was so confused that he could not say whether or not he was a segregationist. Contrasting Callaway's inherited wealth with his own "poor boy" background, Maddox told crowds that "we've got a few [followers] with dirt under their fingernails—thank God—but none with dirt in their hearts."[36] Majorities in urban Georgia enabled Callaway to win the popular vote, but the Republican candidate, because of a write-in campaign for Arnall, did not receive a majority. State law left the selection of the governor to the legislature under such circumstances, and since that body was overwhelmingly Democratic, Maddox rather than Callaway was elected governor.

The new governor delivered what was, for him, an astoundingly mild inaugural address. There would be no "undue change in the direction or policy of . . . state government." Schools would not be shut, and Maddox perceived "no necessity for any conflict to arise between federal-state authority." Advocates of "extremism or violence" would not be welcome in Georgia.[37] For all of the apparent moderation of his inaugural speech, however, the hard truth of Maddox's election was that "old-fashioned Democratic white suprem- acists"[38] could win in Georgia twelve years after the *Brown* decision and despite the registration of some 290,000 black voters.[39]

In the 1970 Democratic primaries, for the first time in Georgia his- tory, there were no militant segregationists among the major candidates for governor. With blacks constituting around one fifth of the electorate and with Maddox constitutionally unable to succeed himself, the two major candidates both ran as nonsegregationists. Former Governor Sanders, who was generally expected to win a second term, campaigned as a dynamic, experienced leader and no longer described himself, as he had in 1962, as a segregationist. Jimmy Carter, a state senator from southern Georgia, ran a vigorous neo- Populist campaign which was designed to attract the Maddox and Wallace vote without the use of segregationist rhetoric. Carter referred to himself as a "redneck" and suggested that "you can appeal to these people on something other than race." The essence of Carter's campaign was a strong personal attack on Sanders as an aloof, Establishment candidate who had little comprehension of the needs of the average citizen and who had enriched himself through public office.[40] Carter defeated Sanders decisively in the first primary (49 to 38 percent) and won a landslide victory in the runoff election (59 to 41 percent). In his inaugural address Carter challenged Georgians to accept a new standard of racial justice:

> I say to you quite frankly that the time for racial discrimination is over. Our people have already made this major and difficult deci- sion, but we cannot underestimate the challenge of hundreds of minor decisions yet to be made. Our inherent human charity and our religious beliefs will be taxed to the limit. No poor, rural, weak, or black person should ever have to bear the additional burden of being deprived of an education, a job or simple justice. We Georgians are fully capable of making our own judgments and managing our own affairs. We who are strong or in positions of leadership must realize that the responsibility for making correct decisions in the future is ours. As Governor, I will never shirk this responsibility.[41]

Carter's explicit repudiation of racial discrimination, one of the few such statements made by southern politicians, was a far cry from the standard rhetoric of Georgia politics. His subsequent performance, however, failed to match the promise of his inaugural.[42]

The defeat in 1970 of Sanders, the only urban-oriented governor elected in Georgia since the *Brown* decision, underscores the persistence of urban-rural conflict in Georgia. The demographic structure of the second primary votes for Maddox and Carter (see Table 8) is very similar. Both candidates failed to carry the large metropolitan counties (the Atlanta SMSA) but received at least three fifths of the vote in each of the rural categories. It will be recalled from Figure 1 that the Georgia electorate continues to be more rural than urban. While a measure of urban support is needed to win statewide office in Georgia, the careers of Maddox and Carter suggest that rural strength remains the key to success.

With the Atlanta SMSA the only large metropolitan area and with high black rural counties comprising over half of the state's 159 counties, the demographic setting of Georgia politics (see Figure 4)

Figure 4. Georgia political demography and the geographic core of segregationist voting after the *Brown* decision: comparison of the demographic setting of Georgia's electoral politics with counties consistently in the upper half of the vote for selected militant segregationist candidates for governor, 1954-73

Political Demography   Segregationist Voting

Large Metropolitan: blank
Medium Urban: dotted
Low Black Rural: striped
High Black Rural: shaded

Large Metropolitan and Medium
    Urban: dotted
Low Black Rural: striped
High Black Rural: shaded

has been highly conducive to segregationist campaigning.[43] There are clusters of low black rural counties in northern and southeastern Georgia, but the most distinctive feature of Georgia's demography is the wide band of high black counties which covers most of the southern half of the state. The great majority of the state's core segregationist counties were high black counties located south of the fall line, principally in southwestern Georgia. No major urban center ranked consistently in the upper half of the militant segregationist vote.

Louisiana

Stem-winding racist oratory has been less prevalent in Louisiana gubernatorial campaigns during the twentieth century than in most Deep South states. White Louisianians have not been less dedicated to white supremacy than their Deep South neighbors, but the development of bifactional competition—Longs versus anti-Longs—along economic lines reduced the salience of the racial issue.[44] With the revival of the segregation controversy in the late 1950s, electoral support for militant segregationists assumed a distinctive geographical pattern. A simplified version of Louisiana's demographic setting is presented in Figure 5.[45] There are numerous high black rural parishes in North Louisiana, especially along the Mississippi and Red rivers, and in South Louisiana along the Mississippi. Low black rural parishes are prominent in southwestern and southeastern Louisiana, and two large metropolitan centers, New Orleans and Shreveport, are situated at opposite corners of the state. The segregationist voting map for Louisiana reveals an extremely sharp sectional cleavage between North and South Louisiana. Over three quarters of the North Louisiana parishes (including the Shreveport SMSA), as contrasted to a pair of South Louisiana parishes, were consistently in the upper half of the militant segregationist vote. Segregationist voting was pronounced in the Red River valley, the uplands of North Louisiana, and the northern delta of the Mississippi River. High black parishes account for approximately two thirds of the core segregationist parishes, but it is the high black areas of North Louisiana, not South Louisiana, which qualified as segregationist. These variations in the segregationist vote are a reflection of fundamental "religio-cultural" differences within the state. Compared to the Anglo-Saxon and Protestant culture of North Louisiana, the French-Catholic culture of South Louisiana has been relatively less supportive of the more extreme segregationist candidates for governor.[46]

Figure 5. Louisiana political demography and the geographic core of segregationist voting after the *Brown* decision: comparison of the demographic setting of Louisiana's electoral politics with counties consistently in the upper half of the vote for selected militant segregationist candidates for governor, 1954-73

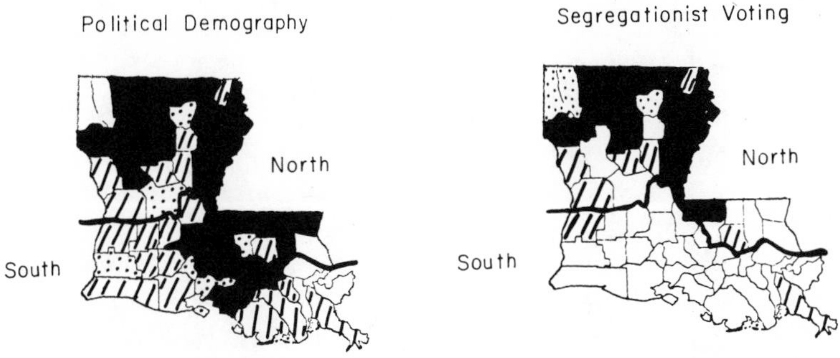

Political Demography

Segregationist Voting

Large Metropolitan: blank
Medium Urban: dotted
Low Black Rural: striped
High Black Rural: shaded

Large Metropolitan and Medium
  Urban: dotted
Low Black Rural: striped
High Black Rural: shaded

Source for sectional divisions: Perry H. Howard, *Political Tendencies in Louisiana,* rev. and exp. ed. (Baton Rouge: Louisiana State University Press, 1971), p. 2. The Florida parishes have been grouped with the North Louisiana parishes to bring out more clearly the geography of the French-Catholic and Anglo-Saxon/Protestant political cultures.

Among the Louisiana governors themselves, there has been considerable change over time with respect to their positions on the segregation issue (see Table 9). So long as school desegregation did not appear eminent, former Governor Earl Long, a paternalistic moderate segregationist who supported the national Democratic Party and did not preach defiance of the Supreme Court, could win a majority (51 percent) in the 1956 first primary on the strength of his flamboyant personality and redistributive economic programs. The major themes of his campaign were the economic advantages of a Long administration (for example, "absolutely free" hot school lunches and increased old age pensions) and the incompetence and insensitivity to public needs that he discerned in his opponents. Long defended racial segregation but saw no need to emphasize racial problems. "I will do every reasonable thing to preserve segregation," he said. "I am one million per cent for segregation. I am the best friend the colored and the white man has ever had. Putting one man against another is not the Christian thing to do. If I have to do that, then I don't want to be

Table 9. Campaign racial stance and pattern of support for winning candidates for governor at successive stages of the electoral process in Louisiana, 1951-72

		Campaign Racial Stance of		Winner's Share of Vote within Demographic Categories						
Year	Winning Candidate	Winner	Closest Opponent	Large Metro	Medium Urban	Low Black Rural	High Black Rural	Medium Black	Black Belt	State
Democratic First Primary										
1951-52	Carlos Spaht	MS	MS	22 L	19 L	25 P	26 P	25 P	27 P	23 P
1955-56	Earl Long	MS	MS	42 P	47 P	60	61	62	58	51
1959-60	deLesseps Morrison	MS	MS	42 P	33 P	30 P	24 L	25 P	19 L	33 P
1963-64	deLesseps Morrison	MS	MS	45 P	30 P	28 P	24 P	24 P	22 L	33 P
1967	John McKeithen	NS	SS	86	79	78	77	77	79	81
1971-72	Edwin Edwards	NS	NS	23 P	24 P	31 P	18 P	20 P	13 L	24 P
	Mean percentage distribution of state vote			33	20	20	26	22	4	100
Democratic Second Primary										
1951-52	Robert Kennon	MS	MS	67	63	58	57	56	60	61
1959-60	Jimmie Davis	SS	MS	48	54	54	62	62	66	54
1963-64	John McKeithen	SS	MS	43	51	57	62	62	64	52

1971-72 Edwin Edwards	NS	NS	45	50	59	49.5	49.7	49	50
Mean percentage distribution of state vote			33	21	20	26	22	4	100
General Election									
1963-64 John McKeithen (D)	MS	MS	51	56	73	67	68	64	61
1971-72 Edwin Edwards (D)	NS	NS	52	54	68	59	59	62	57
Mean percentage distribution of state vote			33	23	19	25	21	4	100

Symbols: SS = Strong Segregationist; MS = Moderate Segregationist; NS = Nonsegregationist; P = Plurality for candidate; L = Loss for candidate.

governor." Long's version of "progressive, humanitarian government" brought him a triumph in which a distant third was the best a
strong segregationist could do. It was a victory, according to the
winner, "for the people in all walks of life and the fine colored
people."[47] Long's somewhat frantic efforts to prevent the state legislature from disfranchising many black voters, widely interpreted in
the national press as yet another illustration of southern buffoonery,
typified the governor's commitment to fair play (within the
framework of a caste system, to be sure), and his failure gave hard-
lining segregationists considerable influence in Louisiana politics after
he left office.[48]

The segregation issue became more explicit in the 1959-60
campaigns. In the first primary former Governor Jimmie Davis ran on
a harmony plank. "I want to be a friend of all the people," Davis
maintained, "and I am not prejudiced against any political faction or
group." After he qualified for the second primary, however, Davis
formed an alliance with William Rainach, the Citizens' Council candidate who had finished third, and used the "bloc vote" charge against
New Orleans Mayor deLesseps Morrison, a moderate segregationist.
Announcing that he intended to "honor our Southern traditions,"
Davis informed his campaign workers that "I don't want one vote
from the NAACP."[49] Aided by this blatant racist appeal, Davis won
majorities in every demographic category except the large metropolitan classification. As governor he called repeated special sessions of
the legislature in an unsuccessful attempt to prevent token school
desegregation in New Orleans.

The 1963 Democratic primaries followed the pattern established in
1959. Morrison again led the first primary balloting but could not
overcome the runoff accusation, this time issued by Public Service
Commissioner John McKeithen, that he was the Negro candidate.
McKeithen, whose political roots were with the Long faction, did not
stress segregation in the first primary. Instead, he campaigned as a
man whom neither Washington nor special interests in Louisiana
could control. Anti-Kennedy talk disappeared after the Kennedy
assassination, and McKeithen, arguing now that the key issue was the
"sorry" record of the Davis administration, promised to give Louisiana a "new image."[50] When he placed second to Morrison, Mc-
Keithen abruptly changed his strategy to take advantage of Morrison's
vulnerability as an urban Catholic who seemed weak on segregation.
Ninety-eight percent of the black voters, he told a press conference,

had supported his opponent, a state of affairs that "shocked and alarmed" McKeithen. He opened his runoff campaign by charging on statewide television that Morrison had conspired with Roy Wilkins of the NAACP to receive massive black support. This Negro bloc vote was likened to "a shot-gun [aimed] at the heads of the citizens of this state." McKeithen argued that Morrison would use the black vote to "force what will be nearly 800,000 registered white voters into submitting to the excessive and unreasonable demands of out-of-state Negro leaders and organizations." If Morrison won, "you will see the darnedest registration of Negroes in the history of the United States," McKeithen predicted. "God pity Louisiana when that happens." Despite Morrison's assurances that he supported racial segregation, McKeithen won the election.[51]

Yet McKeithen's performance in office proved different from what might have been expected. The governor placed law and order above racial traditions and intervened occasionally as a peacemaker in racial disorders.[52] During his first term the issue of racial segregation became less salient at the state level, and McKeithen, whose popularity was reflected in his ability to secure acceptance of a constitutional amendment allowing the governor to succeed himself, found his renomination in 1967 virtually unchallenged. In an exceptionally quiet governor's race McKeithen campaigned only indirectly and sporadically. John Rarick, a rightwing congressman, provided token opposition, and McKeithen won a landslide victory (81 percent) in the first primary. Over 240,000 blacks were registered to vote by 1966, a gain of some 80,000 since 1964.[53] After the election McKeithen told a group of civic leaders, "We believe in equal opportunity for all. We want Negroes in state government and jobs, the state police. Thank goodness for this old Southern state—it has finally turned the clock and got into the 20th Century." When his opponents tried to raise the racial issue against him, "We beat 'em to death." "It was a great day," he believed, "for the South and America."[54]

McKeithen's second term, with one important exception, was comparatively uneventful. In the spring of 1970 he achieved brief national attention as the result of a campaign to arouse opposition to school desegregation policies of HEW and the federal judiciary. Through full-page advertisements in newspapers like the New York *Times* and the Washington *Post,* McKeithen contended that Louisiana "recognized long ago that segregation was dead forever, that integration is the law of the land." What angered the governor were federal requirements for "the *complete, numerical* balancing of the races," particularly desegregation plans which entailed the busing of students. McKeithen's intense opposition to busing was shared, of course, by most white politicians in the South. In a calmer mood late in his second administration, however, he praised the citizens of Louisiana for having adjusted to school desegregation "with a minimum of tension." "Today we have Negroes in positions of high responsibility in the state," McKeithen told the legislature. "We are being given the advantage of their knowledge and leadership in helping Louisiana forward. We are all working together in a degree of harmony that means much for the future well-being of our state."[55]

By the 1971-72 elections the number of registered black voters had increased to 340,000, some 21 percent of the electorate, and the segregation issue was generally avoided by candidates for governor. Former Governor Jimmie Davis, the only major candidate who could even be considered a moderate segregationist, placed fourth with a humiliating 12 percent of the vote, and all the other leading politicians—Congressman Edwin Edwards, State Senator J. Bennett Johnston, and former Congressman Gillis Long—were nonsegregationists who actively solicited the support of blacks. Edwards, a French-Catholic from South Louisiana, led the first primary field, and Johnston, an Anglo-Saxon and Protestant from North Louisiana, finished second. In contrast to the 1960 and 1963 second primaries, where candidates from North Louisiana attacked the South Louisiana candidate as soft on segregation, Johnston and Edwards continued to avoid segregationist postures and emphasized instead their desire to reform Louisiana politics. The electorate divided along sectional lines, and Edwards, with 50.2 percent of the vote, became the first French-Catholic in the twentieth century to win the Democratic nomination for governor. Neither Edwards nor his Republican challenger considered race an issue in the general election, which Edwards won without strain. In his inaugural address Edwards indicated unmistakably that the old-fashioned politics of race, at least in state elections, no longer prevailed in Louisiana. "To the poor, the elderly, the unemployed, the thousands of black Louisianians who have not yet enjoyed the full bounty of the American dream," the governor said, "we extend not a palm with alms, but the hand of friendship. We understand your plight. We shall lighten your burdens and open wide the doors of opportunity."[56]

South Carolina
South Carolina elections occur in one of the most traditional demo-

graphic settings in the South (see Figure 6). In this small state rural counties with high black populations are spread across the Coastal Plains (roughly the eastern half of the state), while the rural counties of the Piedmont (the western half) are divided between high black and low black counties. Three large metropolitan SMSAs (Greenville, Columbia, and Charleston), however, give the state an increasingly urban orientation.[57] Segregationist voting has been most persistent in the high black counties of the Coastal Plains. All but two of the core segregationist counties were located east and south of the fall line, and a substantial majority of them had high black populations. Compared to the other Deep South states, segregationist voting has been moderately strong in South Carolina's urban areas. Charleston, Lexington (part of the Columbia SMSA), and Aiken (part of the Augusta, Georgia, SMSA) were consistently in the upper half of the vote for selected militant segregationists.

South Carolina's reputation as a hotbed of defiant segregationists has been based in the post-*Brown* years largely on the activities of national spokesmen like Senator Strom Thurmond. By the standards of the Deep South, the governors of South Carolina have been rather

Figure 6. South Carolina political demography and the geographic core of segregationist voting after the *Brown* decision: comparison of the demographic setting of South Carolina's electoral politics with counties consistently in the upper half of the vote for selected militant segregationist candidates for governor, 1954-73

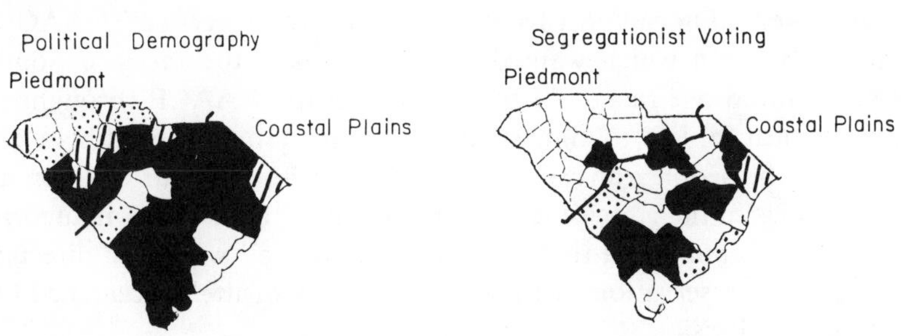

Political Demography

Piedmont

Coastal Plains

Segregationist Voting

Piedmont

Coastal Plains

Large Metropolitan: blank
Medium Urban: dotted
Low Black Rural: striped
High Black Rural: shaded

Large Metropolitan and Medium
   Urban: dotted
Low Black Rural: striped
High Black Rural: shaded

Source for sectional divisions: Chester W. Bain, "South Carolina: Partisan Prelude," in William C. Havard, ed., *The Changing Politics of the South* (Baton Rouge: Louisiana State University Press, 1972), p. 591.

sedate segregationists. Militant resistance to any degree of school desegregation was commonly expressed by candidates in the 1950s, but no governor in the next decade engaged in confrontationist politics with the national government over the enforcement of the *Brown* decision. More significantly, as black voters assumed a more active and sometimes decisive role in state elections, governors have begun to change the tone and substance of public policy toward blacks. Prior to 1966 governorships were decided solely within the Democratic primaries; on the whole, no set of elections in the South has been less dramatic.[58]

Table 10 shows that successful candidates in South Carolina, with the exception of the 1970 general election, all favored racial segregation. George Bell Timmerman, Jr., the winner in 1954, waged a strong segregationist campaign in which he frequently denounced the "agitators of the NAACP." Some two weeks before the original *Brown* decision Timmerman promised to employ "every means available to me to preserve segregation in schools, regardless of any decision whatsoever by the Supreme Court." Following the school desegregation ruling he recommended the establishment of an integrated school system to supplement the dual system in existence. His assumption was that whites would universally choose to remain segregated, but his opponent, Lester Bates, argued that the proposal "will not preserve segregation and would bankrupt the state." Timmerman accused Bates, who also campaigned as a militant segregationist, of "lying in the same political bed with the NAACP," and he indicated clearly that he desired no support from the "viciously subversive" NAACP, an organization which wanted to "amalgamate the races in South Carolina into one race." "I intend to fight the NAACP throughout my political career," Timmerman said. Timmerman viewed his election as "the people's answer to those who wish to use our children as guinea pigs in their sociological experiments," and, in his inaugural address, he announced that his "greatest efforts" would be directed toward the preservation of the southern "way of life" threatened by the *Brown* decision.[59]

The two leading candidates in the 1958 primaries were again militant segregationists. Lieutenant Governor Ernest Hollings, the eventual nominee, considered himself well-qualified to handle "the important task of protecting and defending the Southern way of life," and Donald Russell, a former president of the University of South Carolina, agreed that the new governor must be a spokesman "for South Carolina, our traditions and our way of life." In the runoff campaign

Table 10. Campaign racial stance and pattern of support for winning candidates for governor at successive stages of the electoral process in South Carolina, 1950-70

Year	Winning Candidate	Campaign Racial Stance of		Winner's Share of Vote within Demographic Categories						
		Winner	Closest Opponent	Large Metro	Medium Urban	Low Black Rural	High Black Rural	Medium Black	Black Belt	State
Democratic First Primary										
1950	James Byrnes	MS	MS	69	73	74	72	70	76	72
1954	George Bell Timmerman	SS	SS	59	54	61	66	69	65	61
1958	Ernest Hollings	SS	SS	46 P	31 L	37 L	47 P	46 P	49 P	42 P
1962	Donald Russell	MS	MS	64	65	57	59	56	62	61
1966	No contested primary									
1970	No contested primary									
	Mean percentage distribution of state vote			28	17	16	39	24	15	100
Democratic Second Primary										
1958	Ernest Hollings	SS		57	53	54	60	61	59	57
	Percentage distribution of state vote			30	18	15	37	23	14	100
General Election										
1966	Robert McNair (D)	MS	SS	56	60	67	56	56	57	58
1970	John West (D)	NS	SS	50	53	55	52	51	53	52
	Mean percentage distribution of state vote			34	16	12	38	21	16	100

Symbols: SS = Strong Segregationist; MS = Moderate Segregationist; NS = Nonsegregationist; P = Plurality for candidate; L = Loss for candidate

Hollings emphasized his own segregationist beliefs but questioned Russell's sincerity as a segregationist. His opponent had offered "a lot of fancy talk" but had failed to take a definite stand on segregation. Hollings suggested that his own uncompromising opposition to racial change accounted for his poor showing, compared to his first primary rivals, in selected black precincts in Columbia. A newspaper advertisement placed by a friend of Hollings quoted Russell as saying in 1953 that blacks would probably be admitted to the University of South Carolina in two or three years and raised the question, "Have we another socialistic 'do-gooder' in our midst?" Placed on the defensive by these attacks, Russell argued that Hollings had distorted his position. He had "stated on every stump in South Carolina" that he supported and would enforce the state's segregation laws "without compromise." "I repeat what I have said throughout South Carolina —there will be no mixing of the races in South Carolina while I am governor." Far from advocating the desegregation of the University of South Carolina, Russell could report with self-satisfaction that he had "promptly terminated" a professor who had publicly advocated racial integration. As a result, "I was villified by integrationists all over the United States; I received insulting letters and I was subjected to abusive telephone calls." Russell also claimed that entrance examinations had been administered at the state university so as to preserve segregation; under his leadership the University of South Carolina had "pioneered in protecting our southern way of life and in taking a necessary precautionary step." Hollings won the second primary decisively, receiving majorities in every demographic category, and assumed office with a promise to "resist the dictation of a power-happy federal government."[60]

As a result of the Supreme Court's caution in implementing school desegregation and the multiplicity of extra-legal sanctions available to discourage blacks from exercising their constitutional rights, Timmerman and Hollings could afford to denounce attempts to reform the Jim Crow traditions of South Carolina. In 1962, as scattered desegregation suits neared final decision, Donald Russell's campaign pledge that he possessed the "vision and judgment" to defend school segregation had a hollow ring. Though he was "firmly and irrevocably committed to the segregated way of life," Russell's principal concern was the improvement of educational and occupational opportunities. "A job . . . that's the problem, that's the real campaign issue," he argued. "I want to go out," he remarked on another occasion, "and find new industry and new jobs for the people of this state."[61]

This combination of an adaptive economic orientation and a relatively calm approach to token school desegregation contributed to Russell's landslide (61 percent) victory in the first primary. The Ole Miss desegregation crisis occurred after his nomination, and Russell, who was a man of responsibility compared to Ross Barnett, was not prepared to lead South Carolina through the turmoil that Mississippi had experienced. With Clemson University under federal court order to desegregate shortly, the new governor delivered an inaugural address devoid of segregationist rantings and excoriations of the national government. Russell spoke of "varied difficulties" to be faced in public education but indicated that the state would "meet with courage whatever the future holds for us, and . . . work out our problems peaceably, according to our standards of justice and decency."[62] The moderation of Russell's speech contrasted sharply with George Wallace's defiant call (in the same month) for "segregation forever" in Alabama. In seeking to bring about nonviolent school desegregation, Russell was following the lead of his predecessor. Late in his term Hollings had privately asked the news media to help prepare the state for token desegregation.[63] With protection provided by the state police, school desegregation soon began without violence.

Russell's measured, undramatic approach to racial change was continued by Lieutenant Governor Robert McNair, who became governor when Russell resigned to assume the Senate seat vacated by the death of Olin Johnston. Unopposed in the 1966 Democratic primary, Governor McNair campaigned in the general election on a platform of "peace, progress and prosperity." His Republican opponent, Joseph Rogers, Jr., a Goldwater conservative, described the central issue as "which candidate can best stand up to the federal government." A militant segregationist, Rogers believed that "what we need to deal with the [desegregation] guideline enforcers and others seeking to impose unreasonable demands on our people is a determined leader who will make Washington see him first." McNair, though a segregationist, affirmed that South Carolina would "comply with the [guidelines] law, and live within the law, as distateful as it may be." McNair thought his election, with majorities in every demographic classification and 56 percent of the total vote, proved that "the people of South Carolina will not be swayed by the emotional, smearsheet type of campaign."[64] Black registration was estimated at 190,000 (approximately half of the potential black electorate) in 1966, an increase of 100,000 since 1962, and black votes gave McNair a comfortable margin of victory.[65]

McNair's inaugural contained no race baiting or denunciations of the national government. South Carolinians were urged to forget the ancient, divisive issues and "grasp the new opportunities of this exciting age."[66] Neither "infringement of human rights [nor] flagrant disregard for law and order" would be permitted to tarnish the state's reputation. It was time, McNair contended, for an end to racial animosity and conflict:

> Today's South Carolina has no time for obsession with either "black power" or "white backlash." The time was never better to work for an improved climate of understanding—for opinion leaders and editorial writers to encourage action rather than promote reaction.
>
> With the opportunities that are now before us, this is not the time—and South Carolina is not the place—for those who are preoccupied with extremism or petty frustration.
>
> It is a time and a place for resolving problems rather than contributing to divisive frictions—for breaking down artificial barriers to progress . . . This is the time, and South Carolina is the place, for building communities where only the clearly indolent will bear the bitter burden of poverty and ignorance.

Although his progressive image was grievously damaged in 1968 by his mishandling of civil rights demonstrations in Orangeburg, compared to most southern governors McNair's performance in office concerning race relations was generally constructive. The best example of his leadership came in January 1970 when federal courts ordered the complete desegregation of schools in two counties. Despite considerable white pressure, McNair urged South Carolinians not to defy the courts. As he argued on statewide television, "We've run out of courts, and we've run out of time, and we must adjust to new circumstances."[67]

By 1970 blacks accounted for 25 percent of the electorate in South Carolina, and the general election again offered a clear choice between the racial stances of the two major party candidates. Lieutenant Governor John West, who was unopposed in the Democratic primary, campaigned as a nonsegregationist, actively seeking the support of blacks, while Republican Congressman Albert Watson ran as a militant segregationist in the Strom Thurmond tradition. Watson emphasized the need for "discipline" in the state's desegregated schools and used television commercials which asked, "Are we going to be ruled by the bloc? Look what it did in Watts . . . in the nation's capitol." In contrast to Watson's emotional appeal to the racial prejudices of whites, West took the position that "I will not by word or deed or action do anything to inflame or polarize class against class, rich against poor, color against color." He counseled continued support for public education "despite anything the Supreme Court or HEW might do" and suggested that his election would demonstrate to the nation that "we are not a land of magnolias, segregation and discrimination."[68] West won the general election, but the narrow margin of his victory (52 percent) demonstrated compellingly the growth of party competition for the governorship in South Carolina. The decline of the Democratic vote between 1966 and 1970 may be seen in Table 10. The Democratic Party lost support in every demographic classification in 1970, with the greatest decrease occurring in the low black rural counties. In the 1970 election the Democrats continued to win majorities in every demographic category, but in no case did they receive more than 55 percent of the vote.

In an inaugural address that was liberal even by national standards, West told his state that "the time has arrived when South Carolina for all time must break loose and break free of the vicious cycle of ignorance, illiteracy and poverty which has retarded us throughout our history." The elimination of "hunger and malnutrition and their attendant suffering," the development of "adequate housing for all our people," improved medical care, and expanded educational opportunities were major goals of West's "Progress for People" program. His position on race relations was equally ambitious. "We can, and we shall, in the next four years eliminate from our government any vestige of discrimination because of race, creed, sex, religion or any other barrier to fairness for all citizens," he promised. "We pledge to minority groups no special status other than full-fledged responsibility in a government that is totally color-blind."[69]

By the early 1970s South Carolina had passed the stage where only segregationist candidates could successfully aspire to the governorship. "The people of South Carolina have made their decision about the racial question," West said in August 1971. "There is a working majority determined to solve this problem amicably and justly, not to let every single political question become a racial one."[70] The Republican gubernatorial campaigns of 1966 and 1970 indicate, to be sure, that racism has not been eliminated in state elections, but segregationist rhetoric is no longer as essential to political victory as it once was.

This overview of the segregation controversy in the states of the Deep South illustrates both the tenacity of segregationist perspectives among white candidates for the governorship and the fact that significant changes have nonetheless occurred which make Deep South politicians less monolithically committed to the caste system. In none of these states could it be said with confidence that the politics of racial segregation was dead, but the growth of substantial black electorates (generally in the range of 20 to 25 percent of the registered voters) and the reality of widespread school desegregation provide the basis for a politics relatively less focused on strident opposition to racial change. It is significant that four of the five Deep South states—Georgia, South Carolina, Mississippi, and Louisiana—elected governors in the early 1970s who campaigned as nonsegregationists. In the subregion of the South that once said "never," George Wallace's 1970 election in Alabama provided the only victory for strong segregationists, and even Wallace won by a fairly narrow margin.

5

The Peripheral South States and Racial Segregation

Compared to the states of the Deep South, electoral politics in the Peripheral South states has been less structured around the maintenance of racial segregation. Smaller percentages of major candidates in the Peripheral South campaigned as strong segregationists after 1954; Peripheral South governors were less willing, on the whole, to engage in confrontations with the national government over school desegregation; and in states like Texas and Tennessee the duration of the segregation issue in gubernatorial campaigns was relatively brief. Moreover, of the southern politicians classified in this study as militant segregationists, the more extreme and uncompromising advocates of racial segregation were usually found in the Deep South. Differences between the Deep South and the Peripheral South in the broad demographic setting of their electoral politics provide a partial explanation of the higher degree of segregationist militancy among the Deep South politicians.

The Demographic Setting of Electoral Politics

In several respects the political demography of most Peripheral South states is considerably less traditional than that of the Deep South. Table 11, which compares the six Peripheral South states, the two subregions, and the region in terms of the mean percentage distribution of the vote between demographic categories in contested Democratic first primaries for governor (1950-73), furnishes the relevant data. Large metropolitan SMSAs and low black rural counties contributed a greater share of the total vote in the Peripheral South than in the Deep South, but the most significant subregional difference concerns the size of the high black rural electorates. The high black category accounted for one third of the vote and outweighed the other demographic categories in the Deep South; in the Peripheral South, however, it was by far the smallest component (13 percent) of the vote. Expressed as a ratio, the proportion of the vote contributed by the high black counties was 2.6 times greater in the Deep South than in the Peripheral South. In Tennessee, Texas, and Florida, the percentage of the vote located in the high black counties ranged from 4 to 6 percent; only North Carolina (25 percent) and Arkansas (21 percent) had high black electorates comparable to those which existed in the Deep South states. Since rural counties with heavy concentrations of blacks have historically constituted the most receptive constituency for militant segregationists, the small size of the high black category in several Peripheral South states has presumably given politicians there somewhat less incentive to wage strong segregationist campaigns. In terms of their demographic structure, Texas, Tennessee, Florida, and (to a lesser degree) Virginia were the least traditional of the southern states. All four states were characterized by substantial large metropolitan electorates (rising from 37 percent of the state vote in Texas to 49 percent in Florida) and by relatively insignificant (Virginia excepted) high black rural electorates. North Carolina and Arkansas resembled the Deep South states demographically, though in both cases the low black rural counties produced a much larger proportion of the total vote than the high black rural counties.

As Figure 7 demonstrates, the relative importance of the various demographic categories in the first primary vote remained essentially stable from 1950 through 1973 in Florida, North Carolina, and Arkansas but changed significantly in Tennessee, Texas, and Virginia. It will be recalled (see Figure 1 in the last chapter) that only marginal changes were observed in the demographic composition of the Deep South electorates during the same period. While Florida was the most urban of the Peripheral South electorates, the data show little growth in the relative size of the large metropolitan category. (The increasing competitiveness of the Republican Party probably accounts for the slight decline in the large metropolitan vote in 1970. A closely contested Republican primary in that year attracted many urban voters away from the Democratic primary.) In Tennessee, Texas, and Virginia, however, the large metropolitan proportion of the total vote rose by more than ten percentage points since 1950, so that by the late 1960s more than two fifths of the total vote in these states was con-

Table 11. The demographic setting of electoral politics in the Peripheral South: mean percentage distribution of the vote in Democratic first primaries for governor, 1950-73, by states, subregions, and region

Demographic Category	Peripheral South States								
	Ark	Fla	NC	Tenn	Tex	Va	PS[a]	DS	S
Large Metropolitan	0	49	6	40	37	39	29	22	25
Medium Urban	28	23	33	5	20	20	22	21	21
Low Black Rural	51	21	36	51	38	24	37	24	31
High Black Rural	21	6	25	4	4	17	13	34	22
Medium Black Rural	16	5	19	3	4	11	10	22	15
Black Belt	5	1	6	1	0.4	6	3	12	7
Totals	100	100	100	100	100	100	100	100	100

[a] Subregional and regional means are based on means of the individual states included within each classification.

centrated in the large metropolitan SMSAs. It is also clear from the charts that the growth of the big city electorate in Tennessee, Texas, and Virginia occurred largely at the expense of the low black counties. By the end of the period substantial urban majorities—60 to 70 percent of the total vote—existed in Florida, Virginia, and Texas; the Tennessee electorate was evenly divided between urban and rural voters; and North Carolina and Arkansas were the only Peripheral South states with large rural majorities. The greater urbanism of the Peripheral South, combined with the decline of the low black vote and the absence of sizable high black electorates, produced a demographic setting for electoral politics in most Peripheral South states that was comparatively less tradition-oriented than that of the Deep South states.

Florida

If Alabama and Mississippi stand as the most irreconcilable opponents of racial change after 1954, Texas, Tennessee, and Virginia may be considered the least conservative of the southern states on the segregation issue. By the end of the 1960s these Peripheral South states appeared to have reached a plateau where serious candidates routinely sought black votes, avoided crude techniques of race baiting, and *might* identify themselves as pro-civil rights. Beyond this point, attempts to rank-order the remaining Peripheral South states in terms of the presence or absence of the segregation issue in campaigns for governor involve considerable guesswork. Consequently, Arkansas, North Carolina, and Florida will be grouped and assumed to express basic similarities vis-à-vis the segregation issue. Although explicit segregationist appeals were declining by the late 1960s in these states, segregation remained a campaign issue for a longer period of time in Arkansas, North Carolina, and Florida than in Texas, Tennessee, and Virginia.

Florida campaigns for governor have contained more segregationist rhetoric than the political demography of the state might suggest. Despite an insignificant high black component and the highest degree of urbanization in the South, factors which might facilitate the emergence of a politics less centered around southern racial traditions, the preservation of racial segregation was a campaign theme of most successful candidates for governor after 1954. Demographically, the state may be divided into North Florida, which is predominantly rural and contains ten of Florida's eleven high black counties, and South

Figure 7. The demographic setting of electoral politics in the Peripheral South: distribution of total state vote in Democratic first primaries for governor, 1950-73 (percent)

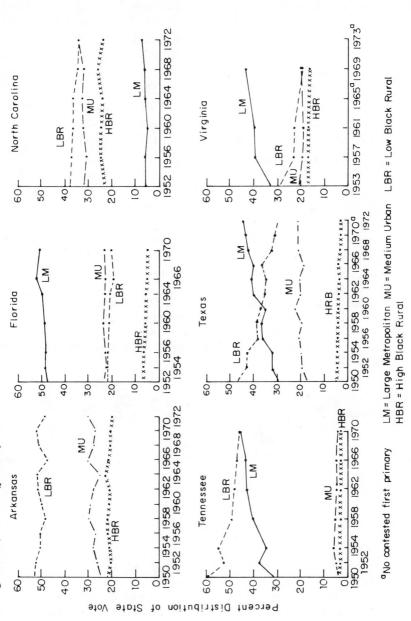

LM = Large Metropolitan MU = Medium Urban LBR = Low Black Rural
HBR = High Black Rural

[a]No contested first primary

Florida, which is overwhelmingly urban. With the exception of Jacksonville, all the large metropolitan SMSAs—Miami, Ft. Lauderdale-Hollywood, Tampa-St. Petersburg, and Orlando—are located in the southern half of the state.[1] Cultural and political extensions of the Deep South, the rural counties of North Florida consistently ranked in the upper half of the vote for selected militant segregationist candidates for governor (see Figure 8). The highly sectional character of strong segregationist voting, a finding developed in previous studies of Florida,[2] is clearly visible in post-*Brown* elections for governor. Two thirds of the 36 counties of North Florida were core segregationist counties, compared to one of the 31 South Florida counties. While any analysis of the demography of these core segregationist counties will be postponed until later in this chapter, it should be noted that in Florida, unlike the Deep South states, there were more segregationist low black than high black counties.

Although Floridians have not always chosen the most extreme segregationist as governor, all but one of the chief executives elected in the period 1954-70 campaigned in some measure as a segregationist

Figure 8.   Florida political demography and the geographic core of segregationist voting after the *Brown* decision: comparison of the demographic setting of Florida's electoral politics with counties consistently in the upper half of the vote for selected militant segregationist candidates for governor, 1954-73

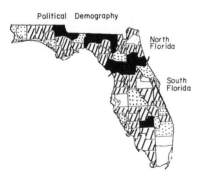

Large Metropolitan: blank
Medium Urban: dotted
Low Black Rural: striped
High Black Rural: shaded

Large Metropolitan and Medium
   Urban: dotted
Low Black Rural: striped
High Black Rural: shaded

Source for sectional divisions: H.D. Price, *The Negro and Southern Politics* (New York: New York University Press, 1957), p. 49.

(see Table 12). LeRoy Collins, who won a two-year term in 1954 after the death of Governor Dan McCarty and a full four-year term in 1956, achieved a national reputation as one of the South's leading racial moderates despite his consistent opposition to school desegregation. Segregation was of little significance as an overt issue in the 1954 Florida elections. In both the first primary and the runoff, Collins denounced Governor Charley Johns for having voted against a bill to unmask the Ku Klux Klan in 1951. Admitting that his pro-Klan vote had been an error, Johns complained that Collins was distributing leaflets among blacks that discredited him. The *Brown* decision, announced while the second primary campaign was in progress, did not elicit much segregationist oratory. Johns was noncommital about the ruling; Collins merely cautioned against "hysteria and political demagoguery" and said he favored segregated schools. In practical terms, the racial issue was limited to Johns' assertion that Collins was falsely claiming that Johns wanted to deny blacks the right to vote. Collins won with a substantial majority.[3]

Two years later, with his chief rival, Sumter Lowry, running exclusively as a militant segregationist, Collins became a more vocal advocate of the racial status quo. "We are just as determined as any other southern state to maintain segregation," the governor argued, "but we will do so by lawful and peaceful means." Collins denounced Lowry as a "one-track candidate" given to "buffoonery and demagoguery." Committed to segregation though he was, Collins refused to have Florida "torn asunder by rioting and disorder and violence and the sort of thing that [Lowry] is seeking to invite."[4] Landslide support from the large metropolitan SMSAs (61 percent) enabled Collins to win the first primary with a majority. Collins' moderation on the segregation issue was expressed more by his efforts to create abstract respect for the *Brown* decision as the law of the land than by any willingness to encourage actual school desegregation. No state university in Florida was desegregated before 1958, and token school desegregation began only in 1959.[5] Yet in the spring of 1960 Collins' qualified support of Negro sit-in demonstrations at Tallahassee lunch counters was unique among southern governors. It was "morally wrong," the governor publicly stated, for businessmen to refuse to serve blacks in one area of their stores while otherwise welcoming their patronage.[6]

No major candidate for governor in 1960 agreed with Collins' assessment of the ethical responsibilities of entrepreneurs, and the election of Farris Bryant, a militant segregationist, over Doyle Carl-

Table 12. Campaign racial stance and pattern of support for winning candidates for governor at successive stages of the electoral process in Florida, 1950-70

Year	Winning Candidate	Campaign Racial Stance of		Winner's Share of Vote within Demographic Categories[a]				
		Winner	Closest Opponent	Large Metro	Medium Urban	Low Black Rural	High Black Rural	State
Democratic First Primary								
1952	Dan McCarty	MS	MS	47 P	53	49 P	51	49 P
1954	Charley Johns	MS	MS	32 L	38 P	48 P	52	38 P
1956	LeRoy Collins	MS	SS	61	52	38 P	25 L	52
1960	Farris Bryant	SS	MS	18 L	20 L	25 P	36 P	21 P
1964	Haydon Burns	SS	NS	31 P	20 L	28 P	29 P	28 P
1966	Haydon Burns	NS	NS	35 L	31 L	41 P	39 L	35 P
1970	Earl Faircloth	NS	NS	28 L	27 L	36 P	33 P	30 P
Mean percentage distribution of state vote				49	23	21	6	100
Democratic Second Primary								
1952	Dan McCarty	MS	MS	51	57	55	56	53
1954	LeRoy Collins	MS	MS	61	55	45	41	55
1960	Farris Bryant	SS	MS	47	60	65	76	55
1964	Haydon Burns	SS	NS	48	65	72	75	58

1966	Robert King High	NS	SS	60	54	43	40	54
1970	Reubin Askew	NS	NS	53	69	56	55	58
	Mean percentage distribution of state vote			51	23	20	6	100
General Election								
1966	Claude Kirk (R)	MS	NS	52	58	61	56	55
1970	Reubin Askew (D)	NS	MS	57	58	55	59	57
	Mean percentage distribution of state vote			56	22	18	4	100

Symbols: SS = Strong Segregationist; MS = Moderate Segregationist; NS = Nonsegregationist; P = Plurality for candidate; L = Loss for candidate

[a]Because the high black rural component accounted for less than 10 percent of the state vote, no breakdown of the medium black and black belt vote will be given.

ton, a moderate segregationist, was widely interpreted as a reaction against Collins. Bryant's stand on racial segregation was less crude in 1960 than it had been in his first campaign for governor. "In the homes of Negroes we find different intellectual levels and moral and sanitary standards," he said in 1956. "I feel it would not be good for the two groups with such different standards to be thrown into direct contact." In 1960 Bryant attacked the *Brown* decision, rejected Collins' position on the morality of sit-in demonstrations, and pledged to "exercise every constitutional power . . . to maintain segregation, and to do so peacefully." Although he would not close the schools to avoid desegregation, he was convinced that "the ingenuity of the Legislature has not been tapped to devise new ways to avoid it." Having established a narrow lead over Carlton in the first primary, Bryant dismissed Carlton's charges in the runoff that he was a "race baiter" and a "school closer" and accused his opponent of "pussyfooting" on the segregation question. The election offered Floridians a clear choice between Carlton's "moderate integrationist approach" and his own unalterable commitment to racial segregation. "He stands for moderate integration," Bryant said. "I am a firm believer in firm segregation. If I am governor, we will maintain seg-regation by every honorable and constitutional means." According to Bryant, the "Negro bloc vote" was instrumental to Carlton's second-place finish in the first primary. "He has the Negro people to thank for his success to date," Bryant maintained. "The only reason he is in the second primary is because of their vote."[7] Segregationist appeals of this variety helped to discredit Carlton, particularly with voters in the rural and medium urban counties, and Bryant won the election with 55 percent of the vote.

The two leading candidates in 1964 were sharply at odds on the segregation issue. Jacksonville Mayor Haydon Burns, who won the first and second primaries without difficulty, campaigned as a militant segregationist. Burns considered the Civil Rights Bill of 1964, then pending before Congress, a "monstrous" proposal. Robert King High, the mayor of Miami, ran as a nonsegregationist and was one of the few southern politicians who endorsed the Civil Rights Bill. In his view the legislation was "designed to divert from the streets into the courthouse the thrust of 22 million Negroes who are seeking the same rights we all enjoy." Strong support from blacks in general and from Dade County in particular enabled High to qualify for the second primary, but as the liberal mayor of the state's largest city, he had no real chance to overcome Burns' 80,000 vote lead. Throughout the runoff campaign Burns attacked High as the "NAACP candidate." "The challenge on next Tuesday will be complacency vs. the NAACP bloc voting," Burns warned; but there was no cause for alarm. Burns received 58 percent of the vote and carried all but three of Florida's counties.[8]

By 1966, with the passage of major civil rights legislation and with some 286,000 blacks (61 percent of the black voting age population) registered to vote, candidates who had previously denounced public accommodations legislation were now soliciting the Negro vote.[9] High doubted that Governor Burns and Scott Kelly, both militant segregationists in 1964, sincerely advocated civil rights. His opponents, High told a gathering of black teachers, "changed their politics as the fashions change—you might call it turncoatism. Even the segregationists can't depend on them." High and Kelly repeatedly questioned Burns' integrity; and when Burns led High by only 30,000 votes in the first primary, he returned to the old standbys of his 1964 campaign—accusations of "ultra-liberalism" and bloc Negro support for High. Burns expressed disgust at the spectacle of blacks who, having been bribed, stroll "to the polls with a lever number in their hand and vote as instructed." Burns' reliance on the bloc vote charge was less successful than High's argument that "Haydon Burns has mismanaged the public business and dishonored the public trust."[10] Heavy support from urban Florida enabled High to win the second primary, but he took a severely disunited Democratic Party into the general election campaign against Republican Claude Kirk. Though Kirk did not identify himself as a segregationist, denounce the NAACP, or discuss the perils of the "bloc vote," he condemned High as "ultra-liberal" and viewed open housing legislation, then being considered in Congress, as unconstitutional. "As far as I am concerned," he would say, "every man's home is his castle."[11] While relatively little time and attention was given to the open housing issue, Kirk's stand did help him become Florida's first Republican governor in modern history. No demographic category favored the Democratic candidate.

In 1970, for the first time in the post-*Brown* era, all the major candidates in the Democratic first and second primaries campaigned as nonsegregationists. The number of registered black voters was estimated at 315,000 and major candidates actively sought black support.[12] In the second primary campaign between Attorney General Earl Faircloth and State Senator Reubin Askew, the leading issue was Askew's proposal for a corporate income tax. Faircloth described

Askew as the "taxing candidate" and dismissed his "harem-scarem" tax plan, while Askew argued that consumers, particularly poor and middle-class citizens, were required to assume too much of the tax burden in Florida. "It's time the little guy had a tax break," Askew said, "that the corporations pay their fair share." In contrast to the three previous Democratic second primaries, neither candidate accused the other of being the NAACP candidate. Askew won handily (58 percent of the vote) and carried his "fair share" tax plan into the general election campaign against Governor Kirk. (Beginning in 1966, Florida governors have been allowed by the state constitution to seek a second term.) Kirk's gift for self-promotion and his erratic performance in office had made him a controversial figure among Republicans as well as Democrats. His most conspicuous action in the field of school desegregation was his brief defiance of a federal court order requiring school busing in Manatee County in the spring of 1970. In his campaign against Askew, as in 1966, Kirk avoided explicitly segregationist oratory while drawing attention to his opposition to "forced busing" and "forced housing." Kirk attacked Askew's ideas on taxation as "a cruel liberal hoax" and promised that "there will be no corporation tax as long as Kirk is governor." With the Democrats united behind a new candidate with a novel proposal—a "fair share program for tax relief through tax reform"—Askew won 57 percent of the vote and obtained majorities in 57 of 67 counties.[13]

Askew's performance on the segregation issue was far more liberal than that of most southern governors. In the fall of 1971, with the emotions of many whites aroused over court-ordered school busing in several counties, Askew appealed for calm and defended busing as an unavoidable means to "put an end to segregation in our society." The following spring he campaigned unsuccessfully against a proposed constitutional amendment to prohibit "forced busing." Florida's governors in the post-*Brown* years thus ranged from explicit defenders of racial segregation to a North Florida politician who urged the electorate to be "more concerned with a problem of justice than a problem of transportation."[14] Only in 1970 was the Florida gubernatorial campaign devoid of manifest (though not of subtle) segregationist appeals at all stages.

Arkansas

A tendency to reject the more extreme segregationists, which has occurred in more southern states than might be expected, has prevailed from time to time in Arkansas, even during the twelve-year career of Governor Orval Faubus (1955-67). Since the early 1960s no politician running as a militant segregationist has won the Arkansas governorship. The maps in Figure 9 compare the political demography of Arkansas with the counties which consistently ranked in the upper half of the vote for a variety of strong segregationist candidates. In Arkansas the high black rural counties are concentrated in the delta of eastern and southern Arkansas; low black rural counties are numerous in the border and mountain sections of northwestern Arkansas; and there were (as of the 1960 census) no large metropolitan SMSAs. Over four fifths of the core segregationist counties were located in the delta, the section with the largest concentration of blacks.[15] Two fifths of the delta counties, compared to less than a tenth of the mountain and border counties, consistently favored militant segregationists. Demographically, segregationist counties were equally divided between the high black and low black categories.

During much of the post-*Brown* era (see Table 13), gubernatorial

Figure 9.   Arkansas political demography and the geographic core of segregationist voting after the *Brown* decision: comparison of the demographic setting of Arkansas's electoral politics with counties consistently in the upper half of the vote for selected militant segregationist candidates for governor, 1954-73

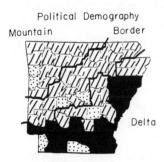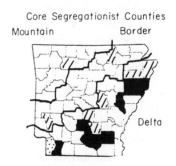

Large Metropolitan: none
Medium Urban: dotted
Low Black Rural: striped
High Black Rural: shaded

Large Metropolitan and Medium
  Urban: dotted
Low Black Rural: striped
High Black Rural: shaded

Source for sectional divisions: Thomas F. Pettigrew and Ernest Q. Campbell, "Faubus and Segregation: An Analysis of Arkansas Voting," *Public Opinion Quarterly,* 24 (Fall 1960), 438-439.

elections in Arkansas were dominated by Orval Faubus. Faubus' efforts in 1957 to resist token school desegregation in Little Rock gave him an unchallengeable position in Arkansas politics and, somewhat misleadingly, an international reputation as an intransigent and virulent segregationist, an image that obscured his decreasing reliance on the racial issue in later campaigns. Faubus was never a rabid, hard-lining racist in the tradition of the Deep South. He could manipulate the language of defiance as well as any politician, though his reliance upon "forced integration" as his main campaign issue was limited to two races, 1958 and 1960. In subsequent campaigns he occasionally flashed the old rhetoric, but only enough to warrant classification as a moderate segregationist. Nor was Faubus considered a militant segregationist in his pre-Little Rock days.[16] In the 1954 Democratic primaries, which marked Faubus' entry into gubernatorial campaigns, civil rights was largely a latent issue. Aside from some early statements (soon dropped) by Faubus that desegregation was a crucial issue, there were few references to Negroes. Faubus promised blacks state jobs and access to the governor's office but did not foresee immediate school desegregation. Incumbent Governor Francis Cherry, a "good-government" type, had nothing to say concerning race. Cherry led the first primary, but Faubus' redistributive economic program helped him capture the runoff. No candidate employed militant segregationist arguments in the second primary.[17] When Faubus ran for a second term in 1956 he argued that segregation was a minor issue because every candidate favored it, and he denounced his extremist opponent, James D. Johnson, as a professional "purveyor of hate." Johnson, organizer of the White Citizens' Council, was described as a "willing mouthpiece" for a "handful of vicious men . . . for whom the stirring up of strife and racial hatreds and tension is a cheerful past-time." Faubus promised the voters he would do his best "to maintain segregation in a calm, orderly, thoughtful and completely legal manner."[18]

Faubus' reputation as a militant segregationist campaigner rests upon his oratory in the 1958 and 1960 primaries. Seeking a third two-year term in 1958, he vigorously defended his resistance to desegregation in Little Rock the previous year. His numerous enemies inside and outside Arkansas, he would tell crowds, were conniving at his political destruction. Since "it's Courage That Counts," however, the governor would continue to defend what he considered to be the principle of local self-government. "I stand now, and always," he said, "in opposition to integration by force, and at bayonet point."

Table 13. Campaign racial stance and pattern of support for winning candidates for governor at successive stages of the electoral process in Arkansas, 1950-72

| Year | Winning Candidate | Campaign Racial Stance of | | Winner's Share of Vote within Demographic Categories | | | | | | |
		Winner	Closest Opponent	Large Metro	Medium Urban	Low Black Rural	High Black Rural	Medium Black	Black Belt	State
Democratic First Primary										
1950	Sidney McMath	MS	SS	-	64	66	59	61	49.6 L	64
1952	Sidney McMath	MS	MS	-	25 L	32 P	34 P	35 P	30 L	31 P
1954	Francis Cherry	MS	MS	-	58	40 P	53	48 P	69	45 P
1956	Orval Faubus	MS	SS	-	50	65	52	51	55	58
1958	Orval Faubus	SS	MS	-	59	72	76	75	79	69
1960	Orval Faubus	SS	MS	-	51	61	64	64	63	59
1962	Orval Faubus	MS	NS	-	43 P	54	56	54	63	52
1964	Orval Faubus	MS	MS	-	60	65	73	70	79	66
1966	James Johnson	SS	NS	-	21 P	22 L	38 P	39 P	35 P	25 P
1968	Marion Crank	NS	MS	-	20 L	28 P	27 L	26 L	28 P	26 P
1970	Orval Faubus	MS	NS	-	32 P	38 P	39 P	36 P	47 P	36 P
1972	Dale Bumpers	NS	NS	-	68	65	68	70	63	67
	Mean percentage distribution of state vote			0	28	51	21	16	5	100
Democratic Second Primary										
1952	Francis Cherry	MS	MS	-	68	62	60	59	63	63

(continued)

Table 13. (cont.)

Year	Winning Candidate	Campaign Racial Stance of		Winner's Share of Vote within Demographic Categories						
		Winner	Closest Opponent	Large Metro	Medium Urban	Low Black Rural	High Black Rural	Medium Black	Black Belt	State
1954	Orval Faubus	MS	MS	-	41	58	46	50	33	51
1966	James Johnson	SS	NS	-	48	53	55	56	50	52
1968	Marion Crank	NS	MS	-	62	66	59	58	61	63
1970	Dale Bumpers	NS	MS	-	64	58	53	55	49	59
	Mean percentage distribution of state vote			0	28	51	21	16	5	100
	General Election									
1964	Orval Faubus (D)	MS	NS	-	51	58	64	64	65	57
1966	Winthrop Rockefeller (R)	NS	SS	-	62	51	50.2	48	55	54
1968	Winthrop Rockefeller (R)	NS	NS	-	58	50.3	49	46	54	52
1970	Dale Bumpers (D)	NS	NS	-	56	67	57	62	47 P	62
	Mean percentage distribution of state vote			0	31	49	20	14	6	100

Symbols: SS = Strong Segregationist; MS = Moderate Segregationist; NS = Nonsegregationist; P = Plurality for candidate; L = Loss for candidate

According to Faubus, there was "only one way to get along with the NAACP and the Daisy Bates [Little Rock NAACP leader] crowd . . . , and that is surrender." Far from surrendering, Faubus announced that he would again order the National Guard into action if circumstances warranted it. When Faubus won an overwhelming victory (69 percent of the vote) against weak opponents, politicians throughout the region sensed the political rewards of confronting a national administration over school desegregation. The voters, Faubus commented as the election results became clear, "have expressed their approval of my efforts to retain the rights of a sovereign state, as set out in the federal constitution; the voting today was a condemnation by the people of illegal federal intervention in the affairs of the state and of the horrific use of federal bayonets on the streets of an American city and in the halls of a public school."[19] In 1960, running again against minor opposition, Faubus reviewed his administration's accomplishments in industrial development, welfare increases, and state services generally. If the voters of Arkansas did not reelect him, they would "surrender the state to a puppet governor," one controlled by "hard-core integrationists." Talking principally about his programs and states' rights, Faubus won another easy majority (59 percent) in the first primary.[20] As in 1958 Faubus received his greatest support from rural counties, especially those with high black populations.

The turbulent, frenzied atmosphere of the post-Little Rock elections had largely dissipated by 1962. Faubus campaigned as the middle-of-the-road candidate, the shrewd and experienced alternative to both "extreme integrationists" and "extreme segregationists." "The big change [from the previous campaigns] is that Mr. Faubus has voluntarily given up the race issue as his main vote-getting device," the *Arkansas Gazette* concluded. "By 1960 he seemed to have lost his enthusiasm for it but this year he has played it down so much that the segregationist vote—once a power to be reckoned with and now an unknown quantity—could split in all directions."[21] Yet Faubus was sufficiently identified with resistance to desegregation that he could probably count on the votes of many segregationists whether or not he constantly drummed up anti-desegregation sentiment. Faced with stronger opponents than in 1958 or 1960, Faubus nonetheless was renominated in the first primary.

Race was even less an issue in Faubus' 1964 campaign, though it should be emphasized that Faubus' views on the merits of desegregation had not altered and that he was still capable of denouncing proponents of racial change. One week before the first primary ended he expressed his opposition to the 1964 Civil Rights Act and assailed "disorderly and violent demonstrators." Faubus "refused to join those forces which seek to impose upon the people of Arkansas a state policy of immorality, atheism, and forced integration." Nor was segregation much of an issue in the 1964 general election, the only significant test for Faubus that year. Faubus and Winthrop Rockefeller, the Republican who was making his first state campaign, said little about civil rights and both, in effect, solicited black votes. The only important exception to Faubus' indifference to race came when the governor, outraged by reports that black demonstrators had tried to block traffic in some areas, personally threatened to drive a truck over anyone who tried that tactic in Arkansas. Faubus later said he regretted this outburst.[22] In his final term the governor began to "redeem himself with Negroes." A few state jobs were opened up, some blacks were appointed to state boards, and Faubus "patched up his old differences" with NAACP leaders in Little Rock.[23] Faubus' career, in short, was not that of the typical true-believing southern segregationist. A remarkably adept politician, his Machiavellian ability to perceive shifts in public opinion and gauge the relative strength of competing groups enabled him to retire undefeated in January 1967.

With Faubus in retirement, the Democratic nomination in 1966 went to James D. "Justice Jim" Johnson, a rural orator and extreme segregationist. Although he usually avoided specific references to blacks, Johnson assured his audiences that his opinions had not changed since his militantly segregationist campaign of 1956 against Faubus: "I suffered the abuse of the press, the pinks, and the pseudo-liberals [in 1956], who called me a racist, a demagogue, and even inferred that I was the personification of Satan, because I dared to tell the people that integration would not stop with the schools."[24] Since it constituted a new test of the salience of racist appeals, the general election campaign between Johnson and Rockefeller created unusual interest. Rockefeller's victory, with 54 percent of the vote, indicated that a majority of Arkansas voters in 1966 preferred a nonsegregationist Republican who promised to create jobs through economic development to a local version of George Wallace. Rockefeller was narrowly reelected in 1968, this time over a Faubus-supported Democrat who did not wage a segregationist campaign. A coalition of traditional Republican voters in the mountain region, urbanites, and blacks (whom the Rockefeller forces actively organized) provided the basis for Rockefeller's victories.[25]

The 1970 elections supplied further evidence of the decline of segregationist rhetoric in Arkansas gubernatorial campaigns. Three of the four major candidates ran as nonsegregationists, and Orval Faubus, ending his retirement after four years, appealed to segregationist sentiment in indirect ways, much as he had done in 1962 and 1964. Faubus frequently expressed concern about "the disorder in the schools" and complained that his rivals were "strangely quiet" on the issue of school busing. By 1970 much of Faubus' appeal had dissipated. In contrast to his first primary majorities of the past (excepting 1954), Faubus received only 36 percent of the vote and was forced into a runoff campaign against a small-town lawyer without previous experience in state politics, Dale Bumpers. While Faubus attacked Bumpers as a "flaming liberal" and soft on busing, Bumpers emphasized his commitment to "change the political climate of Arkansas." "I want to be a governor you don't have to apologize for," he said in reference to Faubus. "I want to create an image for Arkansas that you'll be proud of."[26] The result was a decisive upset victory for Bumpers, who obtained 59 percent of the second primary vote. In the general election, with the Democratic nominee neither a militant segregationist nor identified with the Faubus "Old Guard," Bumpers united the Arkansas Democrats and won 62 percent of the state vote against Rockefeller. Both Bumpers and Rockefeller conducted nonsegregationist campaigns.

Bumpers' inaugural address did not specifically refer to racial issues, but he did promise a government of "open doors." "The future we envision," he observed, "must be shaped and shared by all Arkansans: old and young, black and white, rich and poor."[27] "I hope segregation as a political issue is dead forever," Bumpers said in 1971. "I believe that essentially it is."[28] Again campaigning as a nonsegregationist, Bumpers was reelected without difficulty in 1972. The success of politicians like Rockefeller and Bumpers suggests that the era of die-hard segregationist militancy has passed in Arkansas gubernatorial politics. By 1970 an estimated 72 percent of the black voting age population was registered, and these 138,000 voters constituted 17 percent of the total electorate.[29] Moreover, survey research indicates that Arkansas voters at the end of the 1960s were less supportive of militant segregationists. "The blatant segregationist may still have his way in his own backyard," one study concludes, "but the state-wide candidate who builds his campaign with racial overtones is now appealing to a distinct minority. Arkansas simply will not give a majority to an extremist on the issues of race."[30] With the aging of the Faubus faction, the development of a substantial black electorate, and the moderation of voter attitudes on segregation, it is improbable that militant segregationists will again capture the governorship in Arkansas.

North Carolina

As in Texas and Tennessee (see below), the governors of North Carolina have generally conceived their responsibilities concerning school desegregation in limited, noninterventionist terms. Their principal functions have been to keep the peace and to encourage local solutions to racial problems. Since the late 1950s they have been willing to accept token school desegregation and to promote this comparatively flexible position as the "North Carolina way."[31] Table 14 summarizes the racial stances and support bases of successful candidates for governor from 1952 through 1972.

Industrialist Luther H. Hodges, a political amateur who was elected lieutenant governor in 1952 and assumed the governorship when William Umstead died in office, was easily elected in 1956 on the strength of his ability to recruit new plants and his promise "not to mix the races in our schools." When three school districts were desegregated in 1957 under federal court orders, Hodges repeated his opposition to "mixing the races" but warned that he would not allow "any lawlessness or violence in connection with this problem." At a time when Faubus was deploying National Guardsmen to halt school integration, Hodges refused to intervene in a similar manner. Negro leaders were urged to persuade their people that attendance at segregated schools indicated racial pride. Any "substantial" school desegregation would, according to Hodges, endanger the public school system in North Carolina.[32] While Hodges' analysis of how racial conflict might best be eased reflected no profound understanding of the deficiencies of segregated schools, his acceptance of token desegregation established a tradition of "moderation" which became, in time, a point of pride among many white politicians. The "North Carolina way" prevented the kind of crude federal-state confrontation that seemed to lead to the mobilization of federal troops and to a crisis of confidence among outside entrepreneurs. It had the additional effect of keeping school desegregation at a seemly rate, one

Table 14. Campaign racial stance and pattern of support for winning candidates for governor at successive stages of the electoral process in North Carolina, 1952-72

Year	Winning Candidate	Campaign Racial Stance of		Winner's Share of Vote within Demographic Categories						
		Winner	Closest Opponent	Large Metro	Medium Urban	Low Black Rural	High Black Rural	Medium Black	Black Belt	State
Democratic First Primary										
1952	William Umstead	MS	MS	57	52	52	52	52	50	52
1956	Luther Hodges	MS	-a	80	86	86	86	85	91	86
1960	Terry Sanford	MS	SS	40 P	39 P	46 P	38 P	38 P	37 L	41 P
1964	Richardson Preyer	NS	MS	44 P	40 P	35 L	33 L	32 L	33 L	37 P
1968	Robert Scott	MS	MS	49 P	43 P	56	44 P	45 P	42 P	48 P
1972	Hargrove Bowles	NS	NS	48 P	47 P	45 P	43 P	41 P	49 P	46 P
	Mean percentage distribution of state vote			6	33	36	25	19	6	100
Democratic Second Primary										
1960	Terry Sanford	MS	SS	63	58	59	48	48	47	56
1964	Dan Moore	SS	NS	57	59	64	65	65	65	62
1972	Hargrove Bowles	NS	NS	54	59	53	49.6	49	53	54
	Mean percentage distribution of state vote			6	34	36	24	19	5	100
General Election										
1960	Terry Sanford (D)	MS	MS	53	52	49	75	73	84	54

(continued)

Table 14. (cont.)

		Campaign Racial Stance of		Winner's Share of Vote within Demographic Categories						
Year	Winning Candidate	Winner	Closest Opponent	Large Metro	Medium Urban	Low Black Rural	High Black Rural	Medium Black	Black Belt	State
1964	Dan Moore (D)	MS	MS	52	54	53	73	71	81	57
1968	Robert Scott (D)	NS	SS	56	53	48	61	60	65	53
1972	James Holshouser (R)	NS	NS	55	51	55	39	41	31	51
	Mean percentage distribution of state vote			8	32	44	17	14	4	100

Symbols: SS = Strong Segregationist; MS = Moderate Segregationist; NS = Nonsegregationist; P = Plurality for candidate; L = Loss for candidate

[a]No other candidate received as much as 10 percent of the vote.

approximating a crawl. An estimated 0.003 percent of North Carolina's black students attended classes with whites in 1957-58, and it was 1964-65 before as many as 1 percent of the blacks were in desegregated schools.[33]

Terry Sanford demonstrated in 1960 that a moderate segregationist, equipped with a winning personality, an efficient organization, and a well-publicized plan to improve education, could use his state's record of token desegregation to advantage against a militant segregationist, I. Beverly Lake. Sanford combined talk of a "New Day for North Carolina" with opposition to "domination or direction by the NAACP." Neither candidate favored racial change. Sanford was explicitly opposed to school desegregation, and Lake was pledged to "use all my powers and influence to terminate whatever integration occurs, whether by voluntary action of the school board or by compulsion beyond its capacity to resist."[34] The disparity between Lake's racist speeches and Sanford's calm support of the "North Carolina way" obscured the continuity between the racial policies of Sanford and Hodges. Lake could be dismissed as an extremist, while Sanford could affirm his support for the status quo and denounce race baiting. "We don't need the climate of hate that Dr. Lake is talking about," Sanford argued. "We don't need the climate of fear—of hysteria that Dr. Lake proposes."[35] Heavy support from urban areas and from low black rural counties gave Sanford a comfortable majority (56 percent) in the second primary.

After the campaigns were over, Sanford proved in spirit and in deed to be more attentive to blacks than had been customary in North Carolina. A conciliatory attitude toward black Carolinians was manifest in his inaugural address:

> We are not going to forget, as we move into the challenging and demanding years ahead, that no group of our citizens can be denied the right to participate in the opportunities of first-class citizenship. Let us extend North Carolina's well known spirit of moderation and good will, of mutual respect and understanding, in order that our energies and our resources, our abilities and our skills, may be directed toward building a better and more fruitful life for all the people of our state.[36]

Third party movements have influenced American politics from time to time without winning national elections, and in some southern states, strong segregationists have occasionally determined governorships while losing. Although Lake was defeated in the 1960 runoff, his support four years later was instrumental to the victory of Dan Moore over Richardson Preyer, the candidate of the Sanford faction. Preyer avoided segregationist rhetoric and advocated the continuation of "the North Carolina way in civil rights." Moore described himself as a man of the center on civil rights, an alternative to "extremists of either the right or the left." Lake continued to take an unqualified stand against racial change. In the first primary Lake was eliminated and Preyer established a narrow lead (37 to 34 percent of the vote) over Moore. Moore denounced Preyer as the recipient of the "bloc Negro vote," secured the support of Lake, and won a landslide victory (62 percent) in the second primary.[37]

Although Preyer was a weaker candidate than Sanford, Table 15 suggests that a situational variable—the size of the field in the first primary—contributed strategically to Sanford's success. Two middle-of-the-road candidates canceled each other out in the 1960 first primary, leaving Sanford matched against an extremely conservative opponent. Under these circumstances the more liberal candidate received nearly half of the middle-of-the-road vote. Preyer, facing a conservative rather than the extremist Lake, gained only one additional vote in the second primary for every seventeen which went to Moore. Had Sanford's opponent been an acceptable, mainstream politician, he might well have been defeated.

The segregation issue and the conflict between conservative, liberal, and extremely conservative factions of the Democratic Party were less distinct in the 1968 Democratic primary. However, Lieutenant Governor Robert Scott and Raleigh attorney J. Melville Broughton, Jr., both sons of former governors, repeatedly emphasized their commitment to law and order, an issue with definite racial connotations in 1968. Scott, who was supported by many white liberals but who tried to minimize factional conflict, said bluntly, "We are not going to

Table 15. Effect of first primary field size on second primary results in 1960 and 1964 Democratic primaries for governor in North Carolina (figures in thousands of votes)

Type of Primary	1960			1964		
	Sanford	Lake	Two Others	Preyer	Moore	Lake
First Primary	269	182	202	281	258	217
Second Primary	352	276		294	480	
Net Gain	83	94		13	222	

tolerate law breakers." Long associated with the conservative Democrats, Broughton pledged to "use every resource to put down riots and apprehend the criminals and hoodlums who start and participate in them." Scott won 48 percent of the first primary vote and became the Democratic nominee when Broughton decided not to request a runoff election. In his general election campaign Scott avoided racial controversy. "I don't have a special program for Negroes or Indians or white people," he would say. "But I've got a darn good program for all people, because we are one people." Republican Congressman James Gardner, by contrast, stressed his ineradicable opposition to HEW school desegregation guidelines and appealed for support from followers of George Wallace. "I've never heard [Wallace] say anything I disagree with," Gardner revealed. "Lots of people down here in the East are going to be voting for George Wallace and Jim Gardner." Scott won by 70,000 votes (53 percent), and Gardner explained his defeat in terms of "the Negro vote." "We thought it would not exceed 100,000," he said, "but it came close to exceeding 200,000." Other estimates ranged up to 250,000, with turnout particularly heavy in North Carolina's cities.[38] Few blacks were enthusiastic about Scott's candidacy, but Gardner's defeat suggested that black voters had sufficient leverage to deny—at least occasionally—state office to militant segregationists.

All the major candidates in the 1972 Democratic primaries campaigned as nonsegregationists. The most popular candidates, State Senator Hargrove Bowles and Lieutenant Governor Pat Taylor, expressed opposition to busing, but they did not frame the issue in segregationist terms or make it a central theme of their campaigns. Despite early predictions that Taylor would win, Bowles conducted an extensive media campaign around the issue of "no new taxes" and came within one percentage point of a first primary majority. In contrast to the 1960 and 1964 runoffs, neither candidate utilized racist appeals in the second primary. When Reginald Hawkins, a black dentist who had finished third, announced his support of Taylor, there was no accusation of "bloc vote" or "NAACP candidate" from Bowles. Bowles won the nomination with 54 percent of the vote. In the general election both Bowles and State Senator James Holshouser, the Republican nominee, ran nonsegregationist campaigns. Holshouser, having defeated Gardner in the Republican primary, reversed Gardner's 1968 strategy and made a deliberate effort to win black support. Blacks were urged to divide their votes between the two major parties and were promised a "full partnership in state government.''[39] Substantial support from the large metropolitan and low black rural counties (55 percent in each) offset the traditionally weak Republican vote in the high black rural counties (39 percent) and enabled Holshouser to win the governorship with a narrow majority (51 percent). The decline of segregationist rhetoric evident in the 1972 campaigns reflects in part the fact that an estimated 300,000 blacks were registered to vote by 1970.[40] While black Carolinians were still considerably undermobilized—only 55 percent of the potential black electorate was registered, the lowest figure in the South—the size of the black vote was sufficiently large to discourage unambiguous segregationist campaigns.

As would be expected, electoral support for militant segregationists has been most evident (see Figure 10) in the eastern half of the state.[41] In North Carolina the size of the black population is greatest in the East, declines in the Piedmont (particularly the western half), and is

Figure 10.   North Carolina political demography and the geographic core of segregationist voting after the *Brown* decision: comparison of the demographic setting of North Carolina's electoral politics with counties consistently in the upper half of the vote for selected militant segregationist candidates for governor, 1954-73

Political Demography

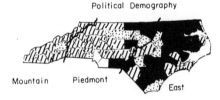

Large Metropolitan: blank
Medium Urban: dotted
Low Black Rural: striped
High Black Rural: shaded

Core Segregationist Counties

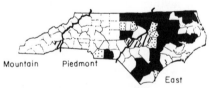

Large Metropolitan and Medium
    Urban: dotted
Low Black Rural: striped
High Black Rural: shaded

Source for sectional divisions: Preston W. Edsall and J. Oliver Williams, "North Carolina: Bipartisan Paradox," in William C. Havard, ed., *The Changing Politics of the South* (Baton Rouge: Louisiana State University Press, 1972), p. 400. To simplify presentation their Piedmont Crescent category has been omitted.

minimal in the mountain region. Charlotte (as of the 1960 census) is the only large metropolitan SMSA, but there are numerous smaller urban centers in the Piedmont and in the East. The maps disclose unusually strong regional differences in the degree of support given militant segregationists, differences that are clearly related to the size of the black population. While there was only one segregationist mountain county, 29 percent of the Piedmont counties (all in the eastern half of that section), and 61 percent of the counties in the East were consistently in the upper half of the segregationist vote. Core segregationist voting in North Carolina was less overwhelmingly a rural phenomenon than in most southern states; however, the segregationist urban counties were located in the more traditional regions of the state, tended to have large black populations, and were invariably contiguous to segregationist high black rural counties.

Virginia

Once conspicuous in the Peripheral South for its advocacy of "massive resistance" to the *Brown* decision, by the late 1960s Virginia ranked with Texas and Tennessee in its relative lack of support for the principle of racial segregation (see Table 16). Apart from Faubus's activities at Little Rock, which were essentially improvised rather than part of a coordinated, regional effort to resist school desegregation, Virginia's governors, guided by the late Senator Harry F. Byrd, Sr., led their counterparts in the Peripheral South in opposing integration. For half a decade after 1954, the delusion persisted within the Byrd Organization that a completely segregated school system could be maintained, and that, if worst came to worst, public schools were less important to Virginians than racial segregation.

Although massive resistance collapsed in 1959, its impact on public education in Virginia was considerable. Other Peripheral South states might reluctantly accept token desegregation, but Virginia Democrats rejected pupil placement laws in 1956 because they would have allowed *some* integration. Governor Thomas Stanley, addressing a special session of the legislature, put the case for complete segregation in graphic terms:

> Do we want to permit the destruction of our schools by permitting "a little integration" and witness its subsequent sure and insidious spread throughout the Commonwealth?
> My answer is a positive "no."

Table 16. Campaign racial stance and pattern of support for winning candidates for governor at successive stages of the electoral process in Virginia, 1953-73

Year	Winning Candidate	Campaign Racial Stance of Winner	Campaign Racial Stance of Closest Opponent	Winner's Share of Vote within Demographic Categories						
				Large Metro	Medium Urban	Low Black Rural	High Black Rural	Medium Black	Black Belt	State
Democratic First Primary										
1953	Thomas Stanley	MS	MS	55	67	74	73	72	76	66
1957	J. Lindsay Almond	SS	MS	70	82	89	86	88	80	80
1961	Albertis S. Harrison	SS	MS	52	60	53	71	74	67	57
1965	No contested primary									
1969	William Battle	NS	NS	34 L	39 P	51	36 P	40 P	31 L	39 P
1973	No contested primary									
	Mean percentage distribution of state vote			39	20	24	17	11	6	100
Democratic Second Primary										
1969	William Battle	NS	NS	46	51	65	53	58	45	52
	Percentage distribution of 1969 state vote			44	19	22	16	9	7	100
General Election										
1953	Thomas Stanley (D)	MS	MS	51	54	53	71	69	76	55
1957	J. Lindsay Almond (D)	SS	MS	61	67	57	78	79	76	63
1965	Mills Godwin (D)	NS	NS	47	46	51	49	49	48	48
1969	Linwood Holton (R)	NS	NS	55	53	53	45	46	43	53
1973	Mills Godwin (R)	MS	NS	50.01	52	51	51	55	45	51
	Mean percentage distribution of state vote			37	18	32	13	8	5	100

Symbols: SS = Strong Segregationist; MS = Moderate Segregationist; NS = Nonsegregationist; P = Plurality for candidate; L = Loss for candidate

On the other hand, shall we take all appropriate measures . . . to resist this illegal encroachment upon our sovereign power?

My answer is a definite "yes," and I believe it is to be the answer of the vast majority of the white people of Virginia, as well as the answer of a large, if unknown, number of Negro citizens.[42]

The legislators responded by approving bills to cut off state funds to desegregated schools and to close any public schools which admitted students on an integrated basis.[43]

Popular approval of the legislature's fight against integration was evident in the results of the 1957 general election. J. Lindsay Almond, the Byrd candidate, vigorously defended massive resistance and promised to keep the schools both open and segregated, while Theodore Dalton, an Eisenhower Republican, argued that the only realistic alternatives to token desegregation were closed schools or heavily integrated ones. Almond, clearly benefiting from the fact that Army troops, dispatched by a Republican President, were enforcing school desegregation in Little Rock at the time of the election, won with 63 percent of the vote.[44]

Opposition to desegregation became more intense when Almond assumed office. The new governor perceived Virginia as a land beset by wily integrationists. "Against these massive attacks," he counseled in his inaugural address, "we must marshall a massive resistance."[45] In September 1958 nine public schools were closed, an act which compelled many Virginians to rethink the wisdom of massive resistance. By the time the state Supreme Court declared the massive resistance legislation unconstitutional in January 1959, increasing numbers of Virginians were apparently persuaded that complete segregation was less important than they had originally believed. Token desegregation seemed preferable to closed schools.[46] Almond's initial response to the judicial repudiation of massive resistance was an intemperate reiteration of his determination to preserve school segregation, but a later speech to a special session of the legislature on the school crisis was radically different in tone. The governor admitted in effect that the police power could not be used to evade federal court orders, and far from suggesting a continuation of massive resistance, he asked the legislators to remain calm and avoid precipitate action.[47] Token school desegregation began in Virginia the following month.

Subsequent Virginia campaigns substantiate the conclusion that, with the failure of the massive resistance movement in 1959, "a certain corner had been turned."[48] Racial segregation has been gradually deemphasized in campaigns for governor. Albertis S.

Harrison, Jr., the successful candidate of the Byrd Organization in 1961, still promised to employ "every legal, honorable and constitutional means to maintain segregated conditions," defended the practice of providing tuition grants to students unwilling to attend desegregated public schools, and attacked his first primary opponent as a tool of the NAACP and the AFL-CIO. What differentiated Harrison's race from the 1957 election was the absence of massive resistance rhetoric. "We want," Harrison proclaimed, "a public school system second to none."[49] Admittedly, this was progress of a meager sort. The segregation issue now turned on techniques to circumscribe school desegregation rather than on the wisdom of preventing integration by abolishing the public schools.

By the 1965 general election it was apparent that controversy over the principle of segregation was declining in Virginia electoral politics.[50] The Byrd Organization, having decided apparently that its future lay not with the more extreme segregationists in Southside Virginia, sought support from liberal Democrats, organized labor, and blacks, as well as from moderate conservatives. Since the Republicans, under the progressive leadership of Linwood Holton, also solicited black votes openly, this election had added significance as one of the first examples of interparty competition for black support to be found in southern gubernatorial contests. While neither Holton nor Lieutenant Governor Mills Godwin, the Democratic candidate, advocated segregation, their appeal for Negro votes was not expressed as support for integration per se. Godwin was no longer the outspoken opponent of racial change that he had been in 1961, but, unlike Holton, he did not promise to appoint blacks to state boards. Usually he was silent on racial matters. When he appeared before a Negro teachers' organization, for example, he said nothing specifically about race.[51] Though he refused to make special promises to Negro groups, Holton frequently described Godwin as an architect of massive resistance and accused his opponent of still seeking support from racially conservative Southsiders.[52] Godwin drew pluralities in every demographic category and won the election with 48 percent of the state vote. His 1966 inaugural, characteristically couched in generalities, contained no hostile references to civil rights. Virginia was proud to be a southern state, Godwin said, but it must be remembered that "the South is also [part] of the nation."[53]

In the 1969 general election, after a Democratic primary in which all three major candidates had waged nonsegregationist campaigns, Holton defeated William Battle to become Virginia's first Republican governor in the twentieth century. Some 255,000 blacks were registered to vote in 1968,[54] and both candidates pledged to end racial discrimination in state government. Battle promised "equality of employment under my administration," and Holton, who was endorsed by the state's largest Negro voter organization, committed himself to a "color-blind administration."[55] There were no significant differences between the candidates on race relations; both were highly conciliatory. Majority support from urban areas and from the low black rural counties gave Holton his victory. Holton's inaugural speech, the first of a new decade in the South, contained an unprecedented commitment to racial change. The Republican governor hoped Virginia would become "a model in race relations." "Let our goal in Virginia be an aristocracy of ability," Holton urged, "regardless of race, color or creed."[56] Once in office Holton's actions corresponded to the idealism of his inaugural. When federal courts in 1970 ordered the busing of Richmond schoolchildren, Holton advocated compliance and personally escorted his children to predominantly black public schools. The governor issued an executive order declaring, "I will not tolerate nor will any state official tolerate racial or ethnic prejudice in the hiring or promotion of employees in the state government," and by the end of his term black employment in state government rose to an estimated 18 percent of all state workers. Although his identification with racial change ran counter to the Nixon administration's "southern strategy" and was unpopular with many Virginia Republicans, Holton considered his efforts to improve race relations as his most significant achievement.[57]

Holton's successor, former Governor Mills Godwin, did not continue the practice of nonsegregationist campaigning which Godwin himself had initiated in 1965. Running as a moderate segregationist Republican, Godwin won a close victory (50.7 to 49.3 percent) over Lieutenant Governor Henry Howell, a Democrat who was listed on the ballot as an Independent and who was by far the most racially and economically liberal politician in recent Virginia history. Godwin did not use explicitly segregationist language and expressed pride in the little black support he received, but his constant attacks on Howell as an advocate of school busing defined his racial posture as that of a moderate segregationist. In 1973 Godwin did not need the votes of blacks (most of whom were already committed to Howell) as badly as he had in his 1965 campaign. There was no Conservative party candidate in 1973 to appeal to segregationist whites, and the conservative faction of the Virginia Republican party, augmented by defections from the Byrd Organization, did not object to antibusing rhetoric. Howell denied that he favored busing and based his campaign around such economic issues as repeal of the state's sales tax on food. After the election was over, Godwin used press conferences and his first official speeches to convey a more positive attitude toward blacks and other minorities than had been apparent in his campaign. An intention to represent "all the people" was expressed, every citizen was promised "the equal rights set forth in Virginia's constitution," and the new governor reasserted the policy of equal employment practices in state government. If Godwin's victory constituted a reversion toward segregationist politics, Holton was convinced that the trend away from racial discrimination "can't be reversed."[58]

Despite the growth of large metropolitan centers such as the Washington suburbs, Richmond, and Norfolk, the demographic setting of electoral politics in Virginia has been more traditional than that of Florida, Tennessee, or Texas.[59] Low black counties predominate in northern and southwestern Virginia, but there is a large concentration of high black counties in southeastern Virginia. A close association has prevailed (see Figure 11) between the size of the black population and segregationist voting, with the high black rural counties of the southeast (particularly Southside Virginia) providing the most consistent support for militant segregationists. In addition to the segregationist high black counties, a number of medium urban areas (all in the southeastern region) and a cluster of low black counties in northern Virginia (basically "friends and neighbors" of the late Senator Byrd, Sr.) also qualified as core segregationist counties.

Tennessee

Tennessee ranks with Texas as the two southern states least supportive of strong segregationist campaigns. If the segregation issue failed to elicit the sustained attention of Tennessee politicians that it did in most states of the South, part of the explanation lies in the demography of Tennessee's electoral politics. Aside from the presence of four large metropolitan areas (Memphis, Nashville, Knoxville, and Chattanooga), Tennessee possessed no geographic concentration of blacks large enough to encourage a politics of race in the tradition of the Deep South. In 1960 there were only five rural counties in the state (see Figure 12) with black populations exceeding 30 percent. Much of the black population resided in the large metropolitan areas and hence

Figure 11. Virginia political demography and the geographic core of segregationist voting after the *Brown* decision: comparison of the demographic setting of Virginia's electoral politics with counties consistently in the upper half of the vote for selected militant segregationist candidates for governor, 1954-73

Political Demography

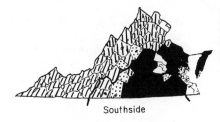

Large Metropolitan: blank
Medium Urban: dotted
Low Black Rural: striped
High Black Rural: shaded

Southside

Core Segregationist Counties

Large Metropolitan and Medium
    Urban: dotted
Low Black Rural: striped
High Black Rural: shaded

Southside

Source for Southside boundary: Ralph Eisenberg, "Virginia: The Emergence of Two-Party Poltics," in William C. Havard, ed., *The Changing Politics of the South* (Baton Rouge: Louisiana State University Press, 1972), p. 60.

was better situated to mobilize in defense of its interests. To the extent that they may be identified with confidence,[60] core segregationist counties have been largely confined to West Tennessee, the region which contained the highest proportions of blacks.

Tennessee chief executives in the post-*Brown* years were disinclined to intervene directly in local situations to prevent school desegregation, and racial segregation dominated electoral politics only once, in the 1958 campaign when memories of the Little Rock crisis were fresh. Since the early 1960s, as Table 17 shows, successful candidates for governor have campaigned as nonsegregationists. Gubernatorial politics during this period turned less on the segregation issue than on personalities, factional conflict, and, to a limited degree, ideological differences. A single faction, led in turn by Frank Clement and

Figure 12.   Tennessee political demography and the geographic core of segregationist voting after the *Brown* decision: comparison of the demographic setting of Tennessee's electoral politics with counties consistently in the upper half of the vote for selected militant segregationist candidates for governor, 1954-73

Political Demography

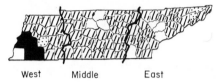

West   Middle   East

Large Metropolitan: blank
Medium Urban: dotted
Low Black Rural: striped
High Black Rural: shaded

Core Segregationist Counties

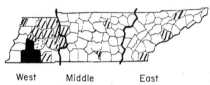

West   Middle   East

Large Metropolitan and Medium
    Urban: dotted
Low Black Rural: striped
High Black Rural: shaded

Source for sectional divisions: Lee S. Greene and Jack E. Holmes, "Tennessee: A Politics of Peaceful Change," in William C. Havard, ed., *The Changing Politics of the South* (Baton Rouge: Louisiana State University Press, 1972), p. 168.

Buford Ellington, controlled the Tennessee governorship from 1952 through 1970, when the Republicans won.[61] Clement, though a segregationist, had national ambitions in the early 1950s which he was unwilling to jeopardize by crusading against racial change. He was less hostile to the *Brown* decision than other southern governors.[62] Segregation bills passed by the Tennessee legislature in 1955 were vetoed, and when Clement eventually signed similar legislation in 1957, including a pupil placement law, he was aware that the state would ultimately be required to comply with the school desegregation ruling.[63]

Beyond his realistic appraisal of the inevitability of token desegregation, Clement called out the National Guard in 1956 to break up a white mob that had gathered to prevent school desegregation in Clinton, Tennessee. The troops were there to maintain law and order, he said, not to prevent integration or to preserve segregation. While the courts remained open, there was no "right to take mob action in

Table 17. Campaign racial stance and pattern of support for winning candidates for governor at successive stages of the electoral process in Tennessee, 1950-70a

| | | Campaign Racial Stance of | | Winner's Share of Vote within Demographic Categoriesb | | | | |
		Winner	Closest Opponent	Large Metro	Medium Urban	Low Black Rural	High Black Rural	State
Year	Winning Candidate							
Democratic First Primary								
1950	Gordon Browning	MS	MS	58	64	53	65	56
1952	Frank Clement	MS	MS	47 P	46 P	47 P	49.5 P	47 P
1954	Frank Clement	MS	SS	70	72	66	70	68
1958	Buford Ellington	SS	SS	24 L	28 L	37 P	32 L	31 P
1962	Frank Clement	NS	NS	38 P	53	45 P	54	43 P
1966	Buford Ellington	NS	NS	54	56	52	55	54
1970	John Jay Hooker	NS	NS	42 P	44 P	47 P	45 P	44 P
	Mean percentage distribution of state vote			40	5	51	4	100
General Election								
1970	Winfield Dunn (R)	NS	NS	54	61	48	46	52
	Percentage distribution of 1970 state vote			49	7	42	3	100

Symbols: SS = Strong Segregationist; MS = Moderate Segregationist; NS = Nonsegregationist; P = Plurality for candidate; L = Loss for candidate

aTennessee does not provide for a second primary; candidates may win the Democratic nomination with a plurality of the vote.

bSince the high black rural component of the total state vote was less than 10 percent, no breakdown of the vote into medium black and black belt categories has been provided.

the streets.'' Clement's behavior contrasted sharply with the approach of Faubus the following year; and this difference was underlined when Clement, days after Faubus had commanded the Arkansas National Guard to keep the peace by preventing black students from attending Central High School in Little Rock, refused to follow the Faubus strategy in Tennessee. His office, he explained, had neither constitutional nor statutory authority to interfere with school desegregation; a governor could intervene at the local level only when "law and order has completely broken down."[64] In effect, the reluctance of Tennessee governors to participate in local racial controversies allowed those school districts which had exhausted their legal means of forestalling desegregation to comply with federal court orders.

The Little Rock crisis stimulated opposition to racial change. (Parenthetically, although Faubus's stand at Little Rock encouraged segregationists throughout the South, its impact on electoral politics was probably greater in Peripheral South states like Tennessee and, to a lesser degree, Texas than in the Deep South, where there was no *immediate* threat of even token desegregation.) Anti-black sentiment reached a peak in the 1958 Democratic primary won by Ellington, who campaigned as an "old-fashioned segregationist." Ellington assured the electorate that he had been strongly opposed to school desegregation for years: "So I'm not a Johnny-come-lately so far as mixing of the races is concerned." His closest rival, Judge Andrew Taylor, was more militant than Ellington and claimed to be "unconditionally and irrevocably opposed to integration of the white and Negro races in our schools."[65]

In succeeding elections racial segregation was not a salient campaign issue. Neither Clement nor his opponents in the 1962 primary found it advisable to campaign as segregationists; instead, all the major candidates "openly courted Tennessee's potent and growing Negro vote."[66] By 1966 Ellington and his opponent, John Jay Hooker, Jr., were soliciting and dividing a black vote estimated at 225,000 (roughly 70 percent of the black voting age population).[67] Hooker called for a "rededication to the ideal that all men are created free and equal." His racial liberalism, however, lacked the dramatic quality of Ellington's public confession that he had been on the wrong side of the segregation controversy in 1958 and that the time had come to eliminate racial segregation. Ellington appointed the first black to a Cabinet-level office in Tennessee and, in his inaugural, promised to seek a "new and better tomorrow for all our citizens."[68] In the 1970 Democratic primary the two leading candidates, Hooker and Stanly

Snodgrass, both conducted nonsegregationist campaigns, while Robert Taylor, who finished third, ran a mildly segregationist race in which he periodically attacked Hooker and Snodgrass for seeking the "bloc vote." Hooker secured the Democratic nomination, but his liabilities as a businessman—the failure of his venture into the fried chicken industry was emphasized daily by the Nashville *Banner*—became an issue and prevented him from unifying the Democratic party. The nomination of Winfield Dunn, chairman of the Republican party in Memphis, gave the Republicans a candidate with a firm political base in the state's largest city, and Dunn's subsequent victory, with 52 percent of the vote, made him Tennessee's first Republican governor since 1920. Both Hooker and Dunn ran nonsegregationist campaigns, though Hooker's ties to black political organizations were much stronger. After the election Dunn expressed a desire to interest more blacks in the Republican party and said that he expected "black people to play a significant role in my administration."[69] Beginning in the early 1960s, then, Tennessee politicians with ambitions for the governorship have tended to avoid segregationist rhetoric and have generally demonstrated considerable respect for the black vote. Approximately 240,000 blacks were registered voters by 1970, a total which represented three quarters of the potential black electorate. Only Texas had a higher rate of black mobilization among the southern states.[70]

Texas

As in Tennessee, the demography of electoral politics in Texas has not facilitated a politics focused around opposition to racial change. There are small clusters of high black rural counties in East Texas, but most of the rural counties of West and South Texas contain small percentages of blacks (see Figure 13). Moreover, Texas has more large metropolitan SMSAs—Houston, Dallas, San Antonio, Fort Worth, El Paso, Beaumont-Port Arthur, and Corpus Christi—than the other southern states, and it is in the urban areas that a majority of black Texans live.[71] In contrast to the sectional cleavages in core segregationist voting discernible elsewhere in the South, Figure 14 does not reveal any impressive grouping of segregationist counties in East Texas, the region with the largest black population. There is a small concentration of segregationist high black counties around Houston, but segregationist counties are equally divided between East and West Texas. The absence of consistent segregationist voting in East Texas suggests that segregation may not have been a highly salient issue in the Texas elections, at least by comparison with other southern states. All the segregationist votes were taken from elections which occurred in the 1950s. Four of the five elections came before the Little Rock crisis increased the visibility of the segregation issue. In each of the pre-Little Rock elections a principal opponent of the militant segregationist was Ralph Yarborough, a native East Texan who emphasized neo-Populist economics and who ran as a moderate segregationist. White resistance to black voter registration, moreover, was less strong in East Texas than in many Deep South states. Under these circumstances the anticipated consistent segregationist vote did not materialize in the most traditional portion of the state. The lack of a clear association between black concentrations and segregationist voting emphasizes the distinctiveness of Texas politics, a difference which Key discussed as a politics of economics as opposed to the standard southern politics of race.[72]

The relative indifference of Texas politicians to the segregation

Figure 13.   The demographic setting of electoral politics in Texas

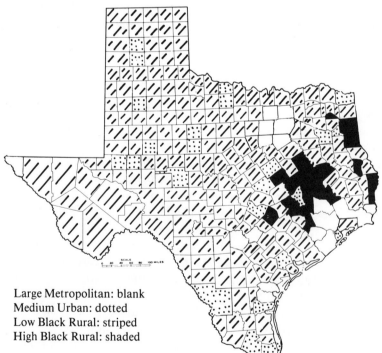

Large Metropolitan: blank
Medium Urban: dotted
Low Black Rural: striped
High Black Rural: shaded

Figure 14. The geographic core of segregationist voting in Texas after the *Brown* decision: counties consistently in the upper half of the vote for selected militant segregationist candidates for governor, 1954-72

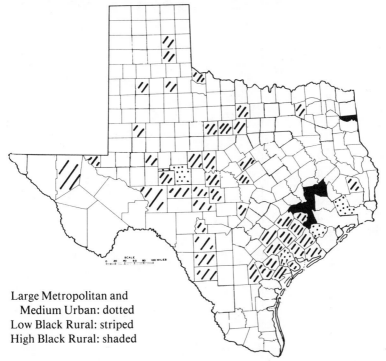

Large Metropolitan and
   Medium Urban: dotted
Low Black Rural: striped
High Black Rural: shaded

issue disappeared in the mid-1950s but was clearly evident in the 1960s and early 1970s (see Table 18). Though Texas has been led by segregationists, no tradition of gubernatorial intervention in local desegregation problems developed. In addition, because some state universities had desegregated prior to the *Brown* decision, Texas politicians could not argue that they were uniquely qualified to preserve a tradition of complete segregation in public education. Texas led the South in the number of school districts voluntarily complying with the *Brown* decision,[73] and Governor Allan Shivers, despite a 1954 campaign pledge that schools would remain segregated, did not interfere with the handful of school districts which desegregated. In 1956, however, Shivers did act on two occasions to prevent court-ordered school desegregation. Texas Rangers were ordered to Texarkana Junior College and to Mansfield, a small town near Fort Worth. In the latter and more important instance, Shivers claimed that the Rangers were dispatched to "protect against violence." The governor had asked the school board to transfer out of the district any students whose

Table 18. Campaign racial stance and pattern of support for winning candidates for governor at successive stages of the electoral process in Texas, 1950-72

Year	Winning Candidate	Campaign Racial Stance of		Winner's Share of Vote within Demographic Categories[a]				
		Winner	Closest Opponent	Large Metro	Medium Urban	Low Black Rural	High Black Rural	State
Democratic First Primary								
1950	Allan Shivers	MS	MS	73	80	77	77	76
1952	Allan Shivers	MS	MS	61	63	61	64	62
1954	Allan Shivers	SS	MS	51	51	48 L	46 L	49.5 P
1956	Price Daniel	MS	MS	45 P	42 P	35 P	31 L	40 P
1958	Price Daniel	MS	NS	61	60	61	62	61
1960	Price Daniel	NS	MS	62	59	58	60	60
1962	John Connally	NS	NS	32 P	29 P	29 P	23 L	30 P
1964	John Connally	NS	NS	68	68	72	67	69
1966	John Connally	NS	NS	71	75	77	78	74
1968	Don Yarborough	NS	NS	29 P	24 P	18 L	23 L	24 P
1970	No contested primary							
1972	Dolph Briscoe	NS	NS	38 P	45 P	52	48 P	44 P
Mean percentage distribution of state vote				37	20	38	4	100
Democratic Second Primary								
1954	Allan Shivers	SS	MS	54	56	52	49	53
1956	Price Daniel	SS	MS	53	50.1	48	48	50.1

1962	John Connally	NS	NS	52	51	51	43	51
1968	Preston Smith	NS	NS	51	56	61	55	55
1972	Dolph Briscoe	NS	NS	48	56	67	62	55
	Mean percentage distribution of state vote			42	21	33	4	100
General Election								
1962	John Connally (D)	NS	MS	51	54	59	62	54
1968	Preston Smith (D)	NS	NS	52	57	67	72	57
1970	Preston Smith (D)	NS	NS	48	55	64	66	54
1972	Dolph Briscoe (D)	NS	MS	43 L	47 P	59	62	48 P
	Mean percentage distribution of state vote			52	21	25	3	100

Symbols: SS = Strong Segregationist; MS = Moderate Segregationist; NS = Nonsegregationist; P = Plurality for candidate; L = Loss for candidate

aBecause the high black rural component was less than 10 percent of the total state vote, no breakdown of the medium black and black belt vote has been provided.

presence "would reasonably be calculated to incite violence." Thus Shivers ignored a white mob that had gathered at Mansfield and, in effect, circumvented a federal court order requiring desegregation. Any possible federal-state confrontation was avoided when the NAACP withdrew its suit. Shivers went on to argue that his behavior had not constituted defiance of the federal judiciary but had only been designed to "prevent trouble." This line of reasoning, later used by Faubus in Little Rock, permitted state officials to preserve law and order by removing the black students, who were exercising their constitutional rights, instead of dispersing the white crowd.[74] Texas governors after Shivers limited their intervention into local desegregation affairs to verbal expressions of support.

Texas gubernatorial elections in the post-*Brown* era have been (at the most) influenced rather than dominated by the segregation issue, and no campaign after the late 1950s centered unambiguously on racial segregation. In the aftermath of the school desegregation decision candidates were expected to defend the caste system, and a moderate segregationist such as Ralph Yarborough could expect to be attacked as the favorite of the NAACP by militant segregationists like Shivers (1954) and Price Daniel (1956).[75] While the Democratic nominees were strong advocates of states' rights, campaigners who ran single-mindedly on the segregation issue and who championed direct intervention by the governor into local desegregation controversies did not receive widespread support. Former Governor W. Lee "Pappy" O'Daniel, the most extreme segregationist among major candidates for governor, placed third in 1956 and 1958. O'Daniel explained to the electorate how the *Brown* decision was conceived. "Both pure blood races were created by God," he said. "We work in perfect harmony. But those nine old men called in the members of the Communist Party for consultation, trying to figure out a way to destroy us. They called in the Communist Party. The Communist Party spread their plan down, and they copied their plan exactly." When O'Daniel became governor school districts that had voluntarily desegregated "had better jump back the other way."[76]

The 1957 Little Rock crisis heightened resistance to school desegregation. Under the leadership of Governor Price Daniel, the Texas legislature enacted a medley of segregation laws, including one measure, never enforced, that would have eliminated state funds to school districts that integrated without obtaining popular approval through a referendum.[77] Daniel's position on school desegregation, as articulated in his 1958 reelection campaign, was to support by legal means the racial policies of local school boards without advocating or practicing state control of local boards. Daniel opposed "forced integration" and thought the time had come "for all who believe in the Constitution, in States' Rights and local self-government to bind ourselves together in a crusade against further federal encroachment." However, the governor would not turn his campaign into such a crusade. "My position [against desegregation] is clear," he announced, "and I do not intend to demagogue on an issue in which common sense is the only answer."[78] In 1960 the major issue in the governor's race was not segregation but the desirability of a general sales tax. Specific references to civil rights were rare, though candidates continued to use the vocabulary of states' rights and Jack Cox, Daniel's opponent, promised to use the Texas Rangers to cope with "lawless" sit-in demonstrations.[79]

A host of new faces in state politics and Daniel's gradual movement toward the center of the Texas political spectrum culminated two years later in the first campaign for governor in which major candidates were able to solicit black support in a comparatively open manner. Pejorative references to opponents as the "NAACP candidate" have been absent from Texas campaigns since 1962. "Racism is dead in statewide Texas politics," the liberal *Texas Observer* commented after the Democratic primaries. "The urban Negro vote has become a significant swing factor here, as happened years ago in the great cities of the North. The Negro bloc was courted to an unprecedented extent in this election." Nor did either candidate resort to race baiting in the 1962 general election, the most bitterly contested general election held in Texas during the 1960s. Both Democrat John Connally and Republican Jack Cox, the *Observer* reported, issued "liberal, although general, statements" on civil rights at a state labor convention. Connally "used his aptitude for platitudes to cover up the plainly integrationist meaning of his stance," while Cox relied upon "his fundamentalist conservative politics to justify a generalized belief in racial liberalism." Neither candidate "dared defy the growing strength of the Negro and Latin-American citizenry."[80] Connally won with 54 percent of the vote.

Far from being an outspoken advocate of racial change, Connally nonetheless pursued a new approach to the segregation issue. His 1963 television report on President John F. Kennedy's proposed Civil Rights Bill commands attention as a reminder that southern governors have not been united in their orientation toward desegregation. The governor protected himself politically by opposing, as an infringement of property rights, any statutory ban on racial segregation in public accommodations. Unlike most of his contemporaries, Connally announced that he supported voluntary desegregation. According to Connally, Texas had made substantial progress in voluntarily ending racial segregation in public schools, restaurants, hotels, and theaters. The governor continued:

> Across the length and breadth of this state desegregation proceeds apace in parks, playgrounds, swimming pools, libraries, and churches. In every corner of Texas the horizons of equality extend to more and more citizens of our state.
> I'm proud of Texas and of Texans for this kind of progress, progress which is continuing day by day.[81]

Promising to enforce public accommodations legislation should Congress pass it, Connally urged whites to grant blacks equal protection of the laws, voting rights, the use of public facilities, and increased educational and economic opportunities. Above all, he counseled a local approach to the problem. The issue of Negro rights provided a chance to prove "our dedication to the sacred principles of local self-government," Connally said. "If we truly believe in the doctrine of states' rights, we never shall have a better opportunity to demonstrate it to the glory of Texas." It may be argued that Connally exaggerated both the amount of voluntary desegregation and the likelihood of localities to deal constructively with civil rights, yet compared to the adamantly segregationist postures of many southern governors at this time, Connally's willingness to interpret desegregation as "progress" was an act of statesmanship.

With his political mentor, Lyndon B. Johnson, in the White House following the assassination of President Kennedy, Connally became the dominant figure in state politics and easily won reelection both times he sought it (in 1964 and 1966). In his 1964 campaign, the only one in which he faced relatively serious opposition, Connally called for "maximum opportunity for every Texan without regard to race, creed, color or background," and his only comment on the then pending Civil Rights Bill was a statement that national laws would be enforced.[82] Although law and order was a favorite theme of Texas politicians in 1968, none of the leading candidates for governor campaigned as segregationists. Don Yarborough, the Houston liberal who led the first primary field, envisioned "a new day . . . that will bring total and complete equality." Yarborough was defeated in the second primary by Lieutenant Governor Preston Smith, a Lubbock business-man who described himself as a "progressive conservative." Pledging a firm stand against riots, Smith suggested that better "vocational programs . . . would go furtherest in solving problems of poverty and lawlessness."[83] The new governor's sympathy for (among other groups) "racial minorities" was indicated in his inaugural address. Though he had no "cheap or easy" answers to complex social problems, Smith claimed to be "AWARE of injustice and WILLING to confront it with the weapons at my disposal."[84] Smith was renominated without Democratic opposition in 1970.

The Democratic primaries of 1972, like those of the past ten years, were devoid of explicitly segregationist rhetoric. All the major candidates except State Representative Francis Farenthold expressed opposition to "forced busing," but three conservatives (Smith, Lieutenant Governor and Connally protégé Ben Barnes, and rancher-banker Dolph Briscoe) and one liberal (Farenthold) routinely sought black support and promised greater opportunities for blacks in state government. A stock fraud scandal in which Governor Smith had profited handsomely made Smith's candidacy hopeless from the outset, and, though he was not directly implicated, undermined support for Barnes as well. Briscoe established a sizable lead over Farenthold in the first primary (44 to 28 percent) and won the second primary without difficulty (55 to 45 percent). In the runoff campaign he criticized Farenthold for supporting "forced busing" but told blacks that he wished to "build a better life for all Texans." "He will assert," a Briscoe advertisement said, "strong and positive leadership aimed at reconciling all segments of our society." In the general election Briscoe defeated a considerably more conservative Republican, State Senator Henry Grover. Grover made no attempt to win the support of minority groups, announcing instead, "I'm going after the conservative vote." He portrayed Briscoe as a liberal who favored busing and George McGovern.[85] Grover's strategy did not result in a higher percentage of Republican votes over the 1970 general election, but the 1972 general election was closer than the preceding election (see Table 18 for the Democratic votes) because 6 percent of the vote went to La Raza Unida, a Mexican-American third party with strength in South Texas. Heavy support from rural Texas counties resulted in a plurality (48 percent) for Briscoe.

By giving blacks a minor voice in their administrations, Connally and Smith probably improved the long-term ability of conservative

Democrats to control the Texas governorship and made it more difficult for liberal Democrats to recruit massive, automatic black support. A tremendous increase in black voter registration lies behind the
decline of explicit campaign race baiting in Texas. The number of
black voters rose from 227,000 in 1960 to 550,000 in 1970. With 85
percent of the black voting age population registered in 1970, Texas
had by far the highest rate of black mobilization in the South.[86] There
may well be sporadic controversy in campaigns over urban rioting, the
use of busing to achieve a racial balance in public education, and the
like, but serious candidates for the governorship are unlikely, given
the size of the black electorate, to challenge the principle of school
desegregation or similar questions.

The Demography of the Militant Segregationist Vote

Finally, before summarizing this overview of the segregation issue
in the different states, attention needs to be directed to the demographic characteristics of the counties within each state which consistently ranked in the upper half of the militant segregationist vote in the
post-*Brown* years. In this chapter and the preceding chapter maps
have been utilized to indicate the geography of the core segregationist
counties, but thus far there has been no systematic and explicitly comparative analysis of their demography. According to Key's black belt
hypothesis (see Chapter 2), militant segregationist voting would be
expected to increase along a demographic continuum from large
metropolitan counties (the least traditional areas) to rural counties
with high black populations (the most traditional areas). Before research began it was anticipated that no exact relationship between
segregationist voting and the black belt hypothesis would be found.
As Key suggested, "The role of the black belts in giving cohesion to
the South appears with most clarity in national politics."[87] Reliance
on state elections raises the possibility that factors peculiar to individual states—for example, "friends and neighbors" voting patterns in
many Democratic first primaries and the mobilization of black voters
in some rural counties with large black populations following the abolition of the white primary in 1944—might operate to obscure black
belt versus nonblack belt electoral conflict.

Yet the demographic structure of the core segregationist vote, which
is summarized in Table 19, tends to reconfirm the black belt hypothesis. Each figure shows the percentage of counties within a given demographic category which ranked in the upper half of the vote for se-

Table 19. The demographic core of militant segregationist voting in the post-*Brown* South: percentage of counties within each demographic category consistently in upper half of vote for selected militant segregationist candidates for governor

Demographic Category	Deep South States						Peripheral South States							
	Ala	Ga	La	Miss	SC	DS[a]	Ark	Fla	NC	Tenn	Tex	Va	PS[a]	S[a]
Large Metropolitan	0	0	33	-[b]	33	17	-[b]	0	50	0	11	29	11	11
Medium Urban	9	9	17	13	25	13	14	20	46	33	8	44	27	17
Low Black Rural	16	25	42	30	14	25	17	46	8	22	23	26	22	23
High Black Rural	61	43	58	28	45	45	43	55	73	60	26	71	57	55
Medium Black Rural	63	44	52	42	36	44	44	56	69	33	19	70	50	44
Black Belt	58	41	70	14	53	53	40	50	88	100	67	73	70	58
State	33	33	47	27	37	33	24	39	38	22	21	42	31	33

[a]DS = Deep South median; PS = Peripheral South median; S = South median
[b]Mississippi and Arkansas contained no large metropolitan counties as of 1960.

lected militant segregationists at least 75 percent of the time. The central tendency of the data, using medians based on the eleven southern states, does reflect the anticipated relationship between segregationist voting and demography: 11 percent of the large metropolitan counties and 17 percent of the medium urban counties, compared to 23 percent of the low black counties and 55 percent of the high black counties, qualified as segregationist. Medians for the Deep South and Peripheral South states, however, show minor discrepancies, and there is considerable variation from one state to another.

The relation between urbanism and segregationist voting may be briefly stated. Large metropolitan counties contributed little consistent support for militant segregationists. Only five of nine states contained any large metropolitan counties which ranked as segregationist, and much of this apparent support was an artifact of the category's definition, which treats all SMSA components as separate and equivalent units.[88] None of the truly populous southern counties were consistently (that is, 75 percent of the time) in the upper half of the segregationist vote. Two borderline large metropolitan centers in the Deep South—Shreveport, Louisiana (both Caddo and Bossier Parishes) and Charleston, South Carolina—qualified,[89] but the segregationist large metropolitan counties of the Peripheral South did not include the central city for which the SMSA was named. Medium urban counties tended to produce larger percentages of segregationist counties (five of nine cases) than the large metropolitan counties; and consistent support for the militants was more characteristic of low black than of medium urban counties in a majority (seven) of the states. North Carolina and Virginia, the major exceptions, were states in which the segregationist vote in the smaller urban areas was rooted in distinct sectional cleavages (see the appropriate maps). In each southern state the two urban classifications provided significantly less core support for militant segregationists than did the high black counties.

Inspection of the rural categories reveals the expected difference between low black and high black counties for ten of the eleven states. The median percentage of high black counties consistently supporting militants is more than double the corresponding figure for low black counties. Although the high black-low black differences are manifest, comparison of the medium black and black belt categories discloses no standard relationship between segregationist voting and size of black concentrations. In six states a higher percentage of black belt counties favored militants, while in four cases the core segregationist vote was more pronounced in the medium black counties.[90] Of all the southern states, the Mississippi figures are the most deviant. Only 14 percent of Mississippi's black belt counties ranked as segregationist, compared to the southern black belt median of 58 percent. The Mississippi findings are probably best explained in terms of the particular candidates selected to represent the militant segregationist vote. As was suggested in the last chapter, a strong segregationist position was the norm for Mississippi politicians during much of the post-*Brown* era. The more extreme segregationists, especially in the first primaries, tended to be less attractive to the delta counties than other militant segregationists.

In general, the data in Table 19 isolate significant demographic variations in the core segregationist vote. Substantial differences exist in most southern states between the high black and urban categories and between the high black and low black categories, all of which is consistent with Key's black belt hypothesis. Given the use of state rather than national elections and the probability that black mobilization before the 1965 Voting Rights Act in some high black counties would reduce the number of segregationist high black counties, these results demonstrate fairly persuasively the durability of Key's argument.

To probe the segregationist vote further, the demographic categories were regrouped into rural and urban divisions and the percentage of segregationist rural and urban counties was calculated, state by state, for varying levels of black population. When median percentages of segregationist counties are graphed for the South, the Deep South, and the Peripheral South (see Figure 15), the thrust of the black belt hypothesis is again confirmed. As would be expected for the South's rural counties, the median proportion of segregationist counties is positively related to the size of the black population. The association between segregationist voting and percent black is virtually linear for rural counties in the Peripheral South, while for the southern states generally and for the Deep South the median percentage of segregationist counties increases steadily until the black population reaches 30-39 percent and remains at a high level thereafter.

The graphs in Figure 15 help explain the segregationist tendencies of many low black counties. Much of the core segregationist voting in low black counties was contributed by rural counties with black populations in the 20-29 percent range. The median percentage of segregationist counties for rural counties with black populations of 20-29 percent (40) was four times the percentage for rural counties with 0-9 percent black concentrations (10). Figure 15 also lends

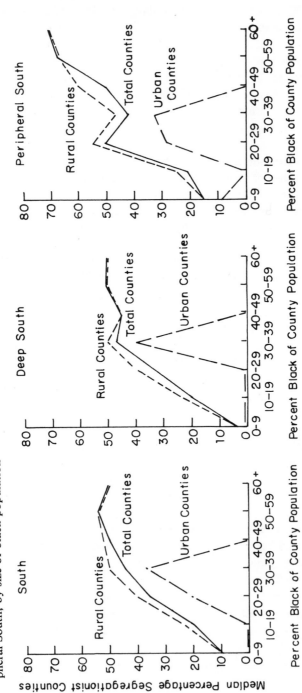

Figure 15. Median percentage of segregationist counties for rural, urban, and total counties of the South, Deep South, and Peripheral South, by size of black population

support to Key's observation that southern "cities seem to be less dominated in their political behavior than rural areas by consideration of the race question."[91] A comparison of medians for rural and urban counties with equivalent black populations shows that, without exception, a higher proportion of rural counties ranked in the upper half of the segregationist vote. Relatively strong urban support for militant segregationists did exist, however, in counties with 30-39 percent black populations. Compared to their counterparts in the rural South, the data suggest that blacks in urban areas have typically been in a better position to mobilize their numbers[92] and that urban whites have been relatively less taken with militant candidates. In the South after 1954 as well as in the pre-*Brown* South that Key analyzed, support for the more outspoken advocates of racial segregation centered demographically in rural counties with large black populations.

While the data tend to confirm the expectation that segregationist voting would be far less characteristic of large metropolitan, medium urban, and low black counties than of high black counties, a number of segregationist urban and low black counties was found. Most of these deviations may be "explained" by one or more of the following variables: 1960 black populations of 20-29 percent for low black rural counties and 20 percent or more for urban counties; spatial contiguity to a high black rural county which scored as segregationist; and black concentrations in 1900 of at least 30 percent.

All these variables are related to the black belt hypothesis. The first variable represents an adjustment of the original division of rural counties into low black (0-29 percent) and high black (over 30 percent) categories. Low black counties with sizable black concentrations (20-29 percent) gave substantially more support to militants than rural counties with black populations of less than 20 percent (see Figure 15). By lowering the cutting point for "high black" status to 20 percent, many deviant counties may still be accounted for in terms of their relatively large black populations. Segregationist urban counties are similarly considered to be explained when their 1960 black populations exceed 20 percent. Since urban counties were not classified according to their black population, black concentrations in excess of 29 percent—and hence even more compatible with the black belt hypothesis—are possible for the large metropolitan and medium urban categories. The sectional clusterings of core segregationist counties, which were apparent in the maps for every southern state except Texas, suggest a second possible explanation of the deviant counties. Many segregationist urban and low black rural counties are spatially contiguous to high black rural counties which consistently supported militant segregationists. Inferentially, these counties share a common regional political culture with the surrounding high black counties which predisposes them to favor militant defenders of the racial status quo. The phenomenon of contiguity is best illustrated by North Carolina, a state in which nearly half its medium urban counties ranked as segregationist. All the segregationist medium urban counties were located in the eastern half of the state and were adjacent to segregationist high black counties. A third suggested explanation concerns the historical size of the black population. In a study of black voter registration in Florida, Douglas Price extended Key's argument by emphasizing the analytic importance of historical black concentrations. Several Florida counties with small 1950 black populations and low rates of black registration had once (1900) possessed large black populations. The migration of blacks by itself did little to change the bias against black political participation of the whites who remained.[93] Several deviant cases did have 1900 black populations of 30 percent or more, but this variable was usually combined with one or both of the other variables. Deviant counties that met at least one of the criteria outlined above have been considered "explained."

As Table 20 shows, the great majority of the segregationist urban and low black rural counties may be accounted for in terms of the suggested variables. All but two of the segregationist urban counties in the South possessed at least one of the specified attributes. Moreover, in contrast to the low black rural counties, the urban counties tended to satisfy all three criteria. The fundamental explanation of segregationist voting in urban areas is that these counties were located in highly traditional sections of their states and contained large percentages of blacks in 1900 as well as in 1960.

Less overwhelming but still impressive results were obtained for the more common low black rural deviations. The three variables collectively account for 75 percent or more of the segregationist low black counties in eight of the eleven states and are particularly useful in explaining the numerous deviant counties (see the appropriate maps) situated in North Florida (89 percent of 18 counties) and eastern and southern Arkansas (75 percent of eight counties). Low black deviations in three Peripheral South states, however, are less satisfactorily explained. Slightly better than half (56 percent of 16 cases) of Virginia's low black deviations are accounted for, with most

Table 20. Deviant case analysis: number of core segregationist urban and low black rural counties and percentage of deviant cases explained, by state[a]

Deviant Counties	Deep South States						Peripheral South States							
	Ala	Ga	La	Miss	SC	DS[b]	Ark	Fla	NC	Tenn	Tex	Va	PS[b]	S[b]
Urban Counties[c]														
Total Deviant Cases	1	1	3	1	3	1	1	2	7	1	4	11	3	2
Percent Explained	100	100	100	100	100	100	100	100	100	100	50	100	100	100
Low Black Counties														
Total Deviant Cases	4	15	8	6	1	6	8	18	4	17	45	16	17	8
Percent Explained	75	80	75	83	100	80	75	89	75	24	16	56	66	75
All Deviant Counties														
Total Deviant Cases	5	16	11	7	4	7	9	20	11	18	49	27	19	11
Percent Explained	80	81	82	86	100	82	78	90	91	28	18	74	76	81

[a]Counties which met one or more of the following criteria have been considered explained: 1960 black population of 20 percent or more; 1900 black population of 30 percent or more; and contiguity to a high black rural county which ranked as core segregationist.
[b]DS = Deep South median; PS = Peripheral South median; S = South median
[c]Includes both large metropolitan and medium urban counties.

of the unexplained low black counties clustered at the northern tip of the state around the home county of the late Senator Harry F. Byrd, Sr.[94] Largely unexplained are the segregationist low black counties in Texas (16 percent of 45 counties) and Tennessee (24 percent of 17 counties). None of the low black counties in the least traditional regions of these states (West Texas and East and Middle Tennessee) and less than half of the low black counties in the most traditional sections (East Texas and West Tennessee) met any of the suggested criteria. Texas' deviant status with respect to the black belt hypothesis has been discussed previously in the chapter; the large percentage of unexplained low black counties in Tennessee is partially the result of the small number of militant segregationist votes (see footnote 60). Generally, the Tennessee findings are more consistent with the black belt hypothesis than those of Texas, for most of the segregationist counties are located in West Tennessee, the expected region.

When the segregationist urban and low black counties are combined, the suggested variables account for a substantial proportion (the median for eleven states is 81 percent) of the total deviant cases. Deviant segregationist voting in Texas and Tennessee remains unexplained, but in nine of the southern states at least three quarters of the total deviant cases meet the specified criteria.

This analysis of segregationist voting has attempted to show that a parsimonious theory of the politics of race, Key's black belt hypothesis, is still highly relevant to an understanding of southern politics. Even if attention is restricted to the size of the black population and urban-rural differences, much can be learned concerning the structure of electoral cleavages.[95] Comparative analysis of the core militant segregationist vote within and between the eleven southern states demonstrated that consistent support for selected militant segregationists in the post-*Brown* era typically increased along a demographic continuum from large metropolitan centers to rural counties with high black populations. Most of the segregationist urban and low black rural counties—the deviant cases—were accounted for by variables related to the black belt hypothesis. These findings, it should be emphasized, were achieved under circumstances (particularly the use of state elections) which constitute a fairly rigorous test of the explanatory power of Key's argument.

Conclusion

The overview of the segregation issue in southern electoral politics that has been presented in the last two chapters suggests a division of the ex-Confederate states into four groups.[96] At one point or another after the *Brown* decision, all the southern states experienced gubernatorial campaigns in which racial segregation was a central (and frequently decisive) issue, but by the late 1960s and early 1970s, many white politicians were reluctant to campaign openly as segregationists. For the post-*Brown* era as a whole, the states of the Deep South were considerably more resistant to racial change than the Peripheral South states. Within the Peripheral South, segregationist oratory has been least prevalent in Texas, Tennessee, and Virginia. The "bloc vote" charge arose frequently in the 1960s in North Carolina, Arkansas, and Florida, yet these states have been less obsessed with segregation than the five Deep South states. Verbal commitments to racial segregation, though not necessarily the crude sort of defiance associated with a Ross Barnett or a George Wallace, were common during the 1960s in South Carolina, Louisiana, and Georgia; and Mississippi and Alabama furnished the most die-hard opposition to desegregation. Campaigns for governor, then, have reflected no single, universally followed "southern" position on racial segregation. While the southern political culture has by no means facilitated equalitarian rhetoric, it has permitted more diversity on race than has been generally perceived. And as blacks have participated more actively in politics, hard-lining segregationist campaigners have become a comparatively rare phenomenon.

In a superficial sense, the disappearance or decline of the segregation issue in the late 1960s and early 1970s in most southern states resembles the virtual absence of an overt racial issue in the early 1950s, before the *Brown* ruling. There is an essential difference. The absence of segregationist rhetoric in the pre-*Brown* era was predicated upon the assumption that racial segregation was a settled question, while the latter decline in campaign racism reflected the reentry of blacks into the southern political system and the political reality that the segregation controversy, in principle and sometimes in actuality, had been revived, fought out, and decided against the historical preferences of most white southerners.

PART THREE

Racial Segregation
and the Southern Electoral Process

6

The Major Candidates

Fundamental changes occurred in the campaign racial stances of gubernatorial candidates during the two decades that followed the school desegregation decision. Moderate segregationists, after having controlled southern governorships in the early 1950s, found their influence sharply diminished after 1954 by the rise of militant segregationists who capitalized on the Supreme Court's challenge to southern racial traditions. Nonetheless, as gradual enforcement of the *Brown* decision and passage of the Civil Rights Act of 1964 and the Voting Rights Act of 1965 brought about a Second Reconstruction, conditions were established which led to the decline of the strong segregationist and to the emergence of a new type of southern politician, the nonsegregationist campaigner. This broadening of choice in southern campaigns with respect to the segregation issue represents one of the most significant long-term consequences of the *Brown* decision. By the mid-1960s in several Peripheral South states, and by the early 1970s in most southern states, it could no longer be safely assumed that leading candidates for governor were explicit advocates of racial segregation.

The purpose of this chapter is to summarize the shifting attitudes of white politicians concerning racial segregation and (secondarily) the achievement of economic development. If candidates in the pre-*Brown* years universally preferred racial segregation and tended to be economic marginalists, to what extent have white elites altered their positions on these policy questions since 1954? To what degree have the political systems of individual states been receptive to a more diversified range of opinions concerning segregation and the achievement of economic development? An assessment of the views of major candidates—defined here as those politicians who received at least 10 percent of the vote in a Democratic first primary for governor—during the years 1954-73 should provide preliminary answers to these questions. Since segregationist and marginalist perspectives have not lacked representation in electoral politics, the "openness" or "breadth" of southern political systems may be estimated by determining where, when, and with what frequency alternative positions have been advanced. Whether or not innovative views on segregation and economic development have been presented successfully will be considered in later chapters.

The Post-*Brown* Era: An Overview

Let us first consider the post-*Brown* era as a whole. Tables 21 and 22 summarize the racial segregation and economic development stances of the approximately 200 major candidates in Democratic first primaries for governor from 1954 through 1973. (Individuals who ran more than once are counted anew for each campaign.) During these two decades one third of the prospective southern governors were militant segregationists, 31 percent were moderate segregationists, and 36 percent were nonsegregationists. Compared to the pre-*Brown* years, when there were no nonsegregationist candidates, it is evident that at some point after 1954 white politicians ceased to present a united defense of racial segregation. The change that has taken place in elite orientations on segregation has not been uniformly distributed throughout the region. Deep South politicians, as would be expected, have been far more resistant to racial change than candidates in the Peripheral South. Until the early 1970s (see below) any shift from traditional segregationist stances was largely confined to the Peripheral South. More than twice as many major candidates in the Deep South (51 percent) as in the Peripheral South (23 percent) were militant segregationists, while 47 percent of the Peripheral South campaigners and 19 percent of the Deep South candidates ran as nonsegregationists. Including moderate segregationists, over four fifths (82 percent) of the Deep South candidates from 1954 through 1973 were segregationists, compared to 54 percent of the major candidates in the Peripheral South. Change has been equally apparent regarding the candidates' views on the achievement of economic development. Although nearly half (46 percent) of the major candidates could be classified as marginalists, 29 percent were adaptives and another tenth campaigned as progressives. In contrast to the segregation dimension, the emergence of new perspectives on economic development has not been more pronounced in one sub-region than the other.

If significant changes have been observed within each policy area since the *Brown* decision, the obvious question arises as to whether these shifts in elite orientations have been complementary. To put it differently, have traditional (segregationist) and innovative (nonsegregationist) positions on race coincided respectively with traditional (marginalist or redistributive) and innovative (adaptive or progressive) stances on the achievement of economic development? The cross-tabulations presented in Tables 21 and 22 reveal several important associations between the segregation and economic development dimensions. For the South generally, strong segregationists were appreciably more likely to be marginalists than adaptives, and a moderate segregationist stance was associated with a traditional position on economic development. Nonsegregationists, by contrast, have characteristically been adaptives or progressives rather than marginalists or redistributives. Some 71 percent of the militant segregationists in the South campaigned as marginalists, while 56 percent of the nonsegregationists were adaptives. Marginalists and (less impressively) redistributives were considerably more likely to be segregationists than nonsegregationists; adaptives and progressives tended to be nonsegregationists. Fifty-one percent of the region's marginalists were strong segregationists, and 70 percent of the adaptives conducted nonsegregationist campaigns. Though the relationship is far from perfect, campaigners who were traditional or innovative on one policy dimension tended to be similarly traditional or innovative on the second dimension.

Basic subregional variations are apparent concerning the economic development stances associated with particular orientations on racial segregation. Segregationists and nonsegregationists in the Peripheral South, for example, have differed markedly on their economic development positions. Nonsegregationists have typically held innovative stances on economic development, while both moderate segregationists and militant segregationists have characteristically advanced tradtional views. The Deep South pattern is less straight-forward, but the principal difference is between strong segregationists and both moderate segregationists and nonsegregationists. Disregarding the redistributive and progressive categories because of the small number of cases, the data show that militants in the Deep South have generally run as marginalists and that moderates and nonsegregation-

Table 21. Campaign racial segregation stances of major candidates for governor in the South, 1954-73, by economic development position and subregion (percent)

Campaign Stance on Racial Segregation	Campaign Stance on Achievement of Economic Development														
	Deep South					Peripheral South					South				
	M	R	A	P	T	M	R	A	P	T	M	R	A	P	T
Strong Segregationist	75	38	14	56	51	35	38	0	0	23	51	38	5	25	33
Moderate Segregationist	25	63	41	0	31	43	43	15	0	31	36	48	25	0	31
Nonsegregationist	0	0	45	44	19	22	19	85	100	47	13	14	70	75	36
Totals	100	100	100	100	100	100	100	100	100	100	100	100	100	100	100
Number of Cases	(36)	(8)	(22)	(9)	(75)	(54)	(21)	(34)	(11)	(120)	(90)	(29)	(56)	(20)	(195)

Symbols: M = Marginalist; R = Redistributive; A = Adaptive; P = Progressive; T = Totals
Tau beta values: Deep South = .51; Peripheral South = .47; South = .47

Table 22. Campaign economic development stances of major candidates for governor in the South, 1954-73, by racial segregation position and subregion (percent)

Campaign Stance on Achievement of Economic De- velopment	Campaign Stance on Racial Segregation											
	Deep South				Peripheral South				South			
	SS	MS	NS	T	SS	MS	NS	T	SS	MS	NS	T
Marginalist	71	39	0	48	70	62	21	45	71	53	17	46
Redistributive	8	22	0	11	30	24	7	18	17	23	6	15
Adaptive	8	39	71	29	0	14	52	28	5	23	56	29
Progressive	13	0	29	12	0	0	20	9	8	0	21	10
Totals	100	100	100	100	100	100	100	100	100	100	100	100
Number of Cases	(38)	(23)	(14)	(75)	(27)	(37)	(56)	(120)	(65)	(60)	(70)	(195)

Symbols: SS = Strong Segregationist; MS = Moderate Segregationist; NS = Nonsegregationist; T = Totals
Tau beta values: Deep South = .51; Peripheral South = .47; South = .47

ists have tended to hold adaptive economic positions. Consideration of the economic development categories indicates more similarity than dissimilarity between the subregions. In both the Deep South and the Peripheral South, traditional stances on economic development have been related to segregationist orientations, while candidates with innovative views on economic development have tended to be non-segregationists.

The changing nature of white elite orientations may be demonstrated through a comparison of the percentage distribution of racial segregation and economic development categories for the years before (1954-65) and after (1966-73) enactment of the Voting Rights Act. If the post-*Brown* era was initially characterized by a revival of the segregation issue, federal intervention to achieve desegregation in schools and public accommodations and to protect the right to vote led to a decline in the use of segregationist rhetoric in southern campaigns. The analytic distinction between the campaign stances of southern politicians before and after the Voting Rights Act applies with particular force to the states of the Deep South, where federal voting registrars were sent to enroll eligible blacks. However, the distinction should not be taken literally for the Peripheral South (only Virginia and some North Carolina counties were directly affected);[1] it is intended to symbolize broadly the intervention of the national government in the mid-1960s to alter the Jim Crow system.

Prior to the Voting Rights Act, candidates for governor in the South assumed highly traditional positions on economic development as well as racial segregation. Table 23 discloses that 36 percent of the southern candidates (49 percent in the Deep South and 26 percent in the Peripheral South) were militant segregationists and marginalists, a combination uncompromisingly hostile toward racial change, unpersuaded that the state should invest substantially greater sums in public education, and generally entranced with the past. An additional 22 percent (16 percent in the Deep South and 26 percent in the Peripheral South) were moderate segregationists and marginalists, the modal type of the pre-*Brown* years. Thus nearly three fifths of the major candidates throughout the region (65 percent in the Deep South and 52 percent in the Peripheral South) from 1954 through 1965 campaigned along essentially traditional lines on both policy dimensions.

The contrast between pre- and post-Voting Rights Act campaign stances is striking. In the years following decisive federal intervention to protect the right to vote and to end racial segregation in public

Table 23. Campaign stances on racial segregation and achievement of economic development of major candidates for governor in Democratic first primaries, before and after the Voting Rights Act of 1965 and 1954-73, by region and subregion (percent)

Campaign Stance	Pre-Voting Rights Act 1954-65			Post-Voting Rights Act 1966-73			Post-*Brown* 1954-73		
	DS	PS	Reg	DS	PS	Reg	DS	PS	Reg
Strong Segregationist	59	36	45	35	2	14	51	23	33
SS-Marginalist	49	26	36	12	0	4	36	16	24
SS-Redistributive	2	10	7	8	2	4	4	7	6
SS-Adaptive	4	0	2	4	0	1	4	0	2
SS-Progressive	4	0	2	12	0	4	7	0	3
Moderate Segregationist	41	42	41	12	15	14	31	31	31
MS-Marginalist	16	26	22	4	8	7	12	19	16
MS-Redistributive	10	11	11	0	2	1	7	8	7
MS-Adaptive	14	4	8	8	4	5	12	4	7
MS-Progressive	0	0	0	0	0	0	0	0	0
Nonsegregationist	0	22	13	54	83	73	19	47	36
NS-Marginalist	0	7	4	0	15	9	0	10	6
NS-Redistributive	0	4	2	0	2	1	0	3	2
NS-Adaptive	0	8	5	38	48	45	13	24	20
NS-Progressive	0	3	2	15	19	18	5	9	8
Totals	100	100	100	100	100	100	100	100	100
Number of Cases	(49)	(72)	(121)	(26)	(48)	(74)	(75)	(120)	(195)

Symbols: DS = Deep South; PS = Peripheral South; Reg = Region

facilities, there has been a steep decline in the proportion of southern politicians assuming traditional positions on both racial segregation and economic development. The modal southern campaigner from 1966 through 1973 was one of the least traditional types, the nonsegregationist and adaptive. Some 45 percent of the region's candidates were of this combination, and it was the most common type in both the Peripheral South (48 percent) and the Deep South (38 percent). Moreover, when the nonsegregationist and progressive candidate is considered, clear majorities in the South (63 percent), the Peripheral South (67 percent), and the Deep South (53 percent) were associated with innovative stances on segregation and economic development. As the controversy over the principle of school desegregation diminished and as the South's need for a better educated labor force became more apparent, far more candidates for governor adopted innovative orientations than had been the case in the past.

While the regional and subregional findings provide an overview of elite views since 1954, they need to be supplemented by an examination of differences and similarities between the gubernatorial candidates of individual states. Comparative analysis of the Deep South states (see Table 24) clearly isolates Mississippi as the state whose elites were least receptive to racial change. The data illustrate, at least with respect to white candidates for governor, the accuracy of Silver's description of Mississippi as a "closed society."[2] "Especially in times of stress," Silver observed, "the [racial] orthodoxy becomes more rigid, more removed from reality, and more extreme conformity to it is demanded."[3] A state in which all the major candidates for governor from 1954 through 1965, and more than four fifths of them from 1954 through 1973, campaigned as militant segregationists has surely been "closed" to substantive racial change during most of the period under consideration. No other Deep South state approached Mississippi in terms of the degree to which strong segregationists dominated gubernatorial campaigns, although more than half of the major candidates were militant segregationists in South Carolina and Georgia. The low figure (26 percent) for strong segregationists in Louisiana is partly an artifact of campaign strategy in that state. Several Louisiana candidates muted their segregationist rhetoric in the first primary, only to emerge as militant segregationists once they qualified for the second primary. The percentage of nonsegregationists ranged from 11 percent in South Carolina to 27 percent in Georgia for the two decades after the *Brown* decision.

Prior to enforcement of the Voting Rights Act all of the Deep South

Table 24. Campaign stances on racial segregation and achievement of economic development of major candidates for governor in Democratic first primaries in the Deep South states, before and after Voting Rights Act of 1965 and 1954-73 (percent)

Campaign Stance	Pre-Voting Rights Act 1954-65					Post-Voting Rights Act 1966-73					Post-*Brown* 1954-73				
	Ala	Ga	La	Miss	SC	Ala	Ga	La	Miss	SC	Ala	Ga	La	Miss	SC
Strong Segregationist	40	67	31	100	71	40	33	17	57	0	40	53	26	82	56
SS-Marginalist	20	67	31	90	43	0	17	17	14	0	13	47	26	59	33
SS-Redistributive	0	0	0	0	14	0	0	0	29	0	0	0	0	12	11
SS-Adaptive	0	0	0	10	14	0	0	0	14	0	0	0	0	12	11
SS-Progressive	20	0	0	0	0	40	17	0	0	0	27	7	0	0	0
Moderate Segregationist	60	33	69	0	29	0	0	17	14	50	40	20	53	6	33
MS-Marginalist	20	22	23	0	14	0	0	17	0	0	13	13	21	0	11
MS-Redistributive	20	0	23	0	0	0	0	0	0	0	13	0	16	0	0
MS-Adaptive	20	11	23	0	14	0	0	0	14	0	13	7	16	6	22
MS-Progressive	0	0	0	0	0	0	0	0	0	50	0	0	0	0	0
Nonsegregationist	0	0	0	0	0	60	67	67	29	50	20	27	21	12	11
NS-Marginalist	0	0	0	0	0	0	0	0	0	0	0	0	0	0	0
NS-Redistributive	0	0	0	0	0	0	0	0	0	0	0	0	0	0	0
NS-Adaptive	0	0	0	0	0	40	33	67	14	50	13	13	21	6	11
NS-Progressive	0	0	0	0	0	20	33	0	14	0	7	13	0	6	0
Totals	100	100	100	100	100	100	100	100	100	100	100	100	100	100	100
Number of Cases	(10)	(9)	(13)	(10)	(7)	(5)	(6)	(6)	(7)	(2)	(15)	(15)	(19)	(17)	(9)

states could be regarded as fundamentally "closed" on the question of segregation. There were no nonsegregationist major candidates in the Deep South before 1965, but this situation changed significantly following the mobilization of black voters. During the period 1966-73, for the first time in the twentieth century, there were more nonsegregationists than militant segregationists among major candidates for governor in Georgia, Louisiana, Alabama, and South Carolina. However, a majority of the Mississippi candidates were still strong segregationists, and, in contrast to the other Deep South states, the proportion of militants in the first primary field did not decline after 1965 in Alabama.

Mississippi politicians, in addition to their racial conservatism, seldom voiced innovative views on economic development. In that relatively unstructured and (apart from race) issueless political system, three fifths of the major candidates have been marginalists, a showing matched only by Georgia. Unlike the other Deep South states, a substantial majority of the gubernatorial candidates in Mississippi (59 percent) and a near majority in Georgia (47 percent) have been strong segregationists and marginalists, the most traditional type. It should be added that this combination was much more characteristic of the pre-Voting Rights Act campaigns than of primaries after 1965. A disproportionately high percentage of adaptives sought the governorship in South Carolina (44 percent) and Louisiana (37 percent). Adaptives constituted well less than 30 percent of the total field in Mississippi, Alabama, and Georgia.

A final comparison concerns Alabama. What differentiates Alabama from the remaining Deep South states is less militancy on the segregation issue than a persistent neo-Populist strain, personified by "Big Jim" Folsom (a redistributive) in the 1950s and by George Wallace (a progressive) in the 1960s. Indeed, Wallace's career represents the *reductio ad absurdum* of the "wholesome contempt for authority and [the] spirit of rebellion" that Key discerned in Alabama politics.[4] Nearly half (47 percent) of the major candidates in Alabama competed as redistributives or progressives, a proportion far greater than that of any other Deep South state.

Table 25 compares the distribution of racial segregation and economic development types within the states of the Peripheral South. The most significant finding for the 1954-73 period concerns the atrophy of segregationist rhetoric in three states: Texas, Tennessee, and Virginia. In contrast to the other southern states, 70 percent of the Texas politicians, 54 percent of the Tennessee candidates, and 50

Table 25. Campaign stances on racial segregation and achievement of economic development of major candidates for governor in Democratic first primaries in the Peripheral South states, before and after Voting Rights Act of 1965 and 1954-73 (percent)

Campaign Stance	Pre-Voting Rights Act 1954-65						Post-Voting Rights Act 1966-73						Post-*Brown* 1954-73					
	Ark	Fla	NC	Tenn	Tex	Va	Ark	Fla	NC	Tenn	Tex	Va	Ark	Fla	NC	Tenn	Tex	Va
Strong Segregationist	33	59	25	38	19	40	6	0	0	0	0	0	20	42	15	23	11	25
SS-Marginalist	11	53	25	38	6	40	6	0	0	0	0	0	6	38	15	23	4	25
SS-Redistributive	22	6	0	0	13	0	6	0	0	0	0	0	14	4	0	0	7	0
SS-Adaptive	0	0	0	0	0	0	0	0	0	0	0	0	0	0	0	0	0	0
SS-Progressive	0	0	0	0	0	0	0	0	0	0	0	0	0	0	0	0	0	0
Moderate Segregationist	56	35	63	25	31	40	24	0	40	20	0	0	40	25	54	23	19	25
MS-Marginalist	28	24	50	25	19	20	18	0	0	20	0	0	23	17	31	23	11	13
MS-Redistributive	28	6	0	0	13	0	6	0	0	0	0	0	17	4	0	0	7	0
MS-Adaptive	0	6	13	0	0	20	0	0	40	0	0	0	0	4	23	0	0	13
MS-Progressive	0	0	0	0	0	0	0	0	0	0	0	0	0	0	0	0	0	0
Nonsegregationist	11	6	13	38	50	20	71	100	60	80	100	100	40	33	31	54	70	50
NS-Marginalist	6	0	0	0	0	0	18	29	0	0	18	0	11	8	0	0	22	0
NS-Redistributive	6	6	0	0	25	0	6	0	0	0	0	0	6	4	0	0	4	0
NS-Adaptive	0	0	13	38	6	20	41	43	40	60	55	67	20	13	23	46	26	38
NS-Progressive	0	0	0	0	13	0	6	29	20	20	27	33	3	8	8	8	19	13
Totals	100	100	100	100	100	100	100	100	100	100	100	100	100	100	100	100	100	100
Number of Cases	(18)	(17)	(8)	(8)	(16)	(5)	(17)	(7)	(5)	(5)	(11)	(3)	(35)	(24)	(13)	(13)	(27)	(8)

percent of the Virginia campaigners waged nonsegregationist races. Although there is no adequate comparative study of the matter, the organization of the metropolitan black vote in these states was probably instrumental to the decline of segregationist campaigning.[5] Since there were twice as many nonsegregationists and moderate segregationists as strong segregationists in Arkansas and since the modal candidate (54 percent) in North Carolina was a moderate segregationist, comparative analysis isolates Florida (at least through the mid-1960s) as the most racially traditional state in the Peripheral South. Despite a demographic setting (numerous large cities and an insignificant high black rural component) that was much less "traditional" than that of most southern states, the amorphousness of Democratic factions in Florida tended to make "balance-of-power politics [by blacks] impracticable, there being no fixed centers of power to be balanced."[6] Forty-two percent of Florida's major candidates, compared to 23 percent for the entire Peripheral South, were militant segregationists.

In contrast to the Deep South states, where major candidates before 1965 were invariably segregationists, nonsegregationist campaigners appeared in some degree in all six Peripheral South states before the mid-1960s. Texas (50 percent) and Tennessee (38 percent) were the only southern states in which nonsegregationists accounted for a substantial proportion of the first primary field prior to federal intervention, but in the post-1965 elections nonsegregationists comprised large majorities of the major candidates for governor in each of the Peripheral South states. During the years 1966-73, the single militant segregationist to campaign in a Democratic primary was Arkansas' James Johnson in 1966.[7] The dramatic rise of the nonsegregationist candidate should not be taken to imply that many politicians in the Peripheral South emphasized the desirability of racial change. However, it seems evident that the growth of black electorates and the achievement of desegregation in schools, public accommodations, and related areas, have created a new status quo in which the advocacy of racial segregation in campaigns has acquired a quixotic quality.

Although the percentage of adaptives has increased significantly in all the Peripheral South states since the mid-1960s, for the post-*Brown* era generally the shift toward innovative orientations has been less apparent concerning economic development than racial segregation. During the period 1954-73, adaptives appeared most frequently (50 percent) in Virginia, where after 1961 neither candidates of the Byrd Organization nor their opponents supported unadulterated "pay-as-you-go" fiscal policies.[8] There were equal percentages (46 percent) of adaptives and marginalists in Tennessee and North Carolina, and in Arkansas and Texas there were considerably more marginalists than adaptives. The distribution of economic development stances again reveals the persistence of traditional perspectives in Florida. Sixty-three percent of the Florida Democratic candidates, well above the Peripheral South figure of 45 percent, were marginalists. For the most part, these politicians corresponded to William Havard and Loren Beth's description of " 'Chamber of Commerce' types—smooth, outwardly sophisticated, skilled in the modern political techniques of radio and television, and making a virtue of a conservative moderation on the Eisenhower model."[9] Finally, Table 25 documents the weakness of neo-Populist orientations (whether redistributive or progressive) in the Peripheral South, especially in North Carolina, Tennessee, and Virginia. Although 27 percent of the subregion's total candidates were neo-Populists of some variety, most of these politicians campaigned in Arkansas and Texas. In Arkansas the substantial percentage of redistributives is primarily a reflection of Orval Faubus's long domination of state politics, and Faubus's neo-Populism was more rhetorical than genuine. Aggressive, though invariably unsuccessful, campaigns for the Texas governorship were conducted by both redistributives (Ralph Yarborough in the 1950s) and by progressives (Don Yarborough in the 1960s and Francis Farenthold in 1972).

Regional and Subregional Trends, 1950-73

On the assumption that the *Brown* decision inaugurated a new era in southern politics, one in which segregation reemerged as an explicit campaign issue, I have attempted to characterize the racial segregation and economic development positions of gubernatorial candidates before and after enactment of the Voting Rights Act as well as for the entire post-*Brown* period. It has been apparent from the discussion thus far that the campaign stances of southern office seekers on the two policy dimensions have shifted considerably since the early 1950s, yet the nature and extent of these changes in white elite perspectives have not been adequately presented. Longitudinal analysis provides an answer to a question posed at the outset of this book: in an era of unprecedented socioeconomic and political change, what changes in attitudes toward racial segregation and the achievement of economic development have occurred since 1950 among white southern politicians who aspired to the governorship?

A historic change in southern electoral politics—the decline of the segregationist candidate and the rise of the nonsegregationist—is evident in the trend lines charted in Figure 16.[10] Moderate segregationists, the dominant type in pre-*Brown* primaries, diminished at a fairly steady rate after 1954. Candidates who advocated a militant defense of the racial status quo reached the height of their influence in the years after the Little Rock crisis (1958-61), but as desegregation became a reality and as black voting increased, the proportion of militant segregationists among major candidates for governor also declined. In the early 1970s, militant and moderate segregationists together furnished less than one fifth of the total field, a striking indication of change among white politicians. Beginning in the late 1950s, a steadily increasing percentage of southern candidates have conducted nonsegregationist campaigns. Although there were no nonsegregationists before 1958, by the late 1960s two thirds of the major candidates were nonsegregationists, and this figure rose to slightly better than 80 percent in the early 1970s.

The southwide pattern, however, conceals fundamental differences between the subregions. In the Deep South, the center of racial conservatism, there was little significant change in the racial stances of campaigning politicians before the early 1970s. Strong segregationist candidates consistently dominated electoral politics from 1954 through the late 1960s, and no major candidate in the Deep South failed to run as a segregationist through 1965. Passage of the Voting Rights Act brought blacks into the Deep South electorates in large numbers and provided a constituency for occasional nonsegregationist candidacies in the late 1960s. With the continued growth of black voter registration and with school desegregation increasingly a fait accompli, in the early 1970s strong segregationist appeals declined drastically and nonsegregationist campaigns became the norm. Compared to the persistence of the segregation issue in the Deep South, significantly different trends are discernible in the Peripheral South. Commencing in the early 1960s, there has been a steady rise in nonsegregationists and a sharp decline in segregationists (both militants and moderates). Strong segregationists, who never constituted a majority of the total field in the Peripheral South, have been exceedingly rare since 1965. By the early 1960s, nearly a decade before the Deep South, the great majority of office seekers in the Peripheral South no longer conformed to the traditional model of the segregationist white candidate.

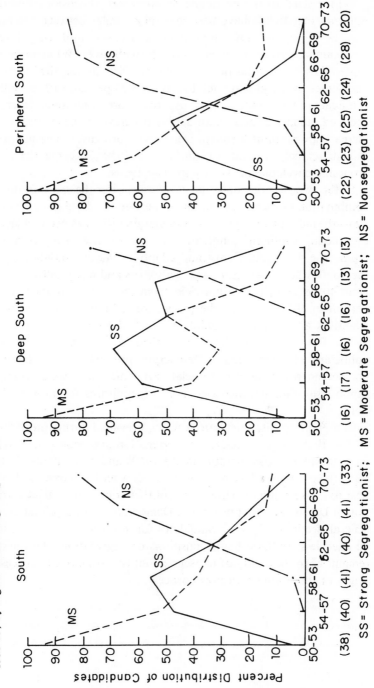

Figure 16. Campaign stances on racial segregation of major candidates for governor in Democratic first primaries in the South, 1950-73, by region and subregion (percent)

SS = Strong Segregationist;   MS = Moderate Segregationist;   NS = Nonsegregationist

With regard to the economic development dimension, Figure 17 indicates that trends have been generally similar between the region and the subregions. Over time fewer and fewer southern politicians have campaigned as marginalists or redistributives. While more than three fifths of the total field were marginalists during the 1950s, the percentage of marginalists fell to less than 20 percent of the southern candidates in the early 1970s. As the more traditional categories declined, adaptives and (secondarily) progressives have assumed an increasingly prominent role in Democratic primaries. The adaptives, though scarcely in evidence during the 1950s, became the modal economic development type by the late 1960s.

In the two decades since the *Brown* decision the most traditional combination of racial segregation and economic development categories—the militant segregationist and marginalist—has been replaced as the modal southern candidate by one of the least traditional types—the nonsegregationist and adaptive. Major candidates across the South who ran as strong segregationists and marginalists declined from 40 percent of the total field from 1954 through 1961 to zero percent in 1970-73, while the proportion of nonsegregationists and adaptives among major candidates reached 60 percent in the early 1970s. By the end of the period, then, a majority of the white politicians who competed in Democratic primaries for governor did not defend the principle of racial segregation and were willing to support substantially increased state expenditures for public education.

Compared to elite orientations which prevailed during the 1950s, it is clear that elite perspectives on segregation and economic development broadened considerably in the 1960s and early 1970s. Putting aside the economic development dimension until Chapter 9, I move next to a discussion of patterns of conflict concerning racial segregation in Democratic first primaries, Democratic second primaries, and general elections. If major candidates for governor have increasingly adopted less tradition-bound positions on segregation, the question remains as to the ability of nonsegregationists to survive at successive stages of the southern electoral process.

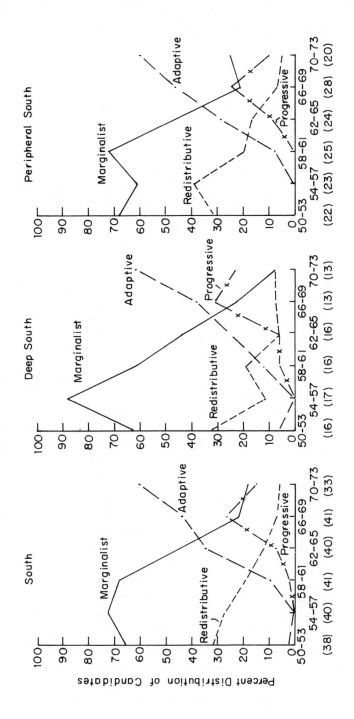

Figure 17. Campaign stances on achievement of economic development of major candidates for governor in Democratic first primaries, 1950-73, by region and subregion (percent)

7

The Democratic First Primary

Although Republican candidates have begun to give Democratic nominees serious competition for the governorship in many southern states, during much of the post-*Brown* era the selection of governors was still determined by Democratic primaries rather than by general elections. Even if it is no longer universally true that "the Democratic primary in the South is in reality the election,"[1] Democratic primaries have generally remained significant arenas for public choice. The nature of the southern primary system is well known and requires only a brief description. All the southern states choose Democratic nominees through primary elections. Ten states provide in various ways for a second (runoff) primary when no contestant receives a majority of the first primary vote. In Tennessee a plurality of the primary vote is ordinarily sufficient for nomination; a runoff would be held only if there were a tie in the first primary. The use of a second primary distinguishes the southern states from the nonsouthern states, where nominations are characteristically won with pluralities of the primary vote.[2] Another feature of southern gubernatorial campaigns worth stating at the outset is the comparative absence of primaries involving incumbent governors. Arkansas and Texas (the only states with a two-year term), Florida (as of 1966), Louisiana (as of 1967), and Alabama (as of 1970) permit incumbents to seek reelection, but otherwise governors are elected for four-year periods and may not run for a second consecutive term. Any advantages or disadvantages that might be associated with an incumbent's performance in office are consequently removed from the great majority of southern contests for governor.

In this chapter we are concerned with patterns of conflict between strong segregationists, moderate segregationists, and nonsegregationists. What have been the campaign racial positions of winners and losers in Democratic first primaries? What changes are discernible over time in the ability of candidates with different racial stances to survive first primary competition? The basic question of theoretical and practical importance may be posed as follows: given the historical opposition of white elites and white electorates to racial change, under what circumstances have candidates relatively less committed to racial segregation won elections in the South? The victory of militant segregationists in the years following the *Brown* decision would be no surprise in view of ingrained southern racial traditions and low rates of black political participation; what need particularly to be analyzed are the conditions under which moderate segregationists have defeated strong segregationists and nonsegregationists have won against segregationists.

The Competitiveness of Moderate Segregationists and Nonsegregationists

In contrast to the situation in the second primary (see Chapter 8), moderate segregationists and nonsegregationists in the post-*Brown* period managed to hold their own in the first primary against more hard-lining segregationists. Nonsegregationists led the field in 22 (36 percent) of the 61 contested Democratic first primaries from 1954 through 1973, compared to 20 (33 percent) first place finishes for moderate segregationists and 19 (31 percent) for militant segregationists.[3] Table 26 demonstrates that strong segregationists did not overwhelm their opponents in the first primary. Of the 21 first primaries in which moderate segregationists and militants competed against each other, moderates won a slight majority. Nonsegregationists placed first in four of the five contests in which they ran against strong segregationists and in five of the eight elections in which they faced moderate segregationists. Yet the impressive showing of the nonsegregationists should not be exaggerated. Nearly two thirds of the first primary leaders campaigned as segregationists, and a majority of the nonsegregationist victories were obtained in primaries where *all* of the major candidates were nonsegregationists. The data in Table 26 also suggest the extent to which racial segregation became an explicit campaign issue after 1954. In the sense that voters were offered a choice between alternative positions (such as strong segregationist

Table 26. Racial segregation position of first primary leaders in contested Democratic first primaries for governor in the South, 1954-73, by racial segregation stance of major opponents

First Primary Leaders	Major Opponents					
	SS	MS	NS	Both[a]	Total	Percent
Strong Segregationist	6	10	1	2	19	31
Moderate Segregationist	11	4	3	2	20	33
Nonsegregationist	4	5	12	1	22	36
Total	21	19	16	5	61	100

[a]First primaries in which all three racial segregation classifications were represented.

versus moderate segregationist), segregation was a significant issue in well over three fifths of the first primaries. Including those primaries in which all major candidates were militant segregationists, segregation was a live issue in approximately three quarters of the post-*Brown* elections.

Table 27 supplies an overview of the relative success of the three segregation categories when consideration is restricted to the racial positions of politicians who placed first and second in contested Democratic first primaries. Although the range of disagreement over the segregation issue is narrowed somewhat by this procedure, the advantage of considering only the two most successful candidates in a given primary is that it reduces the scope of conflict to more manageable proportions. The expected subregional differences concerning racial segregation are apparent. Forty-two percent of the first primary leaders in the Peripheral South, compared to 26 percent in the Deep South, campaigned as nonsegregationists. The modal first primary leader in the Deep South was a militant segregationist (43 percent), but militants placed first in only 24 percent of the Peripheral South primaries. Most of the first primaries in which the two leading candidates were both strong segregationists occurred in the Deep South, while primaries in which nonsegregationists finished first and second were mainly limited to the Peripheral South. Despite the greater overall success of the Deep South militants, however, moderate segregationists broke even against militant segregationists in the Deep South as well as in the Peripheral South, and nonsegregationists were more competitive in the first primary against strong segregationists in the Deep South than in the Peripheral South.

Table 27. Racial segregation position of first place finishers in contested Democratic first primaries for governor in the Deep South, Peripheral South, and South, 1954-73, by racial segregation stance of second place finishers

	Second Place Finishers														
	Deep South					Peripheral South					South				
First Place Finishers	SS	MS	NS	T	%	SS	MS	NS	T	%	SS	MS	NS	T	%
Strong Segregationist	7	2	1	10	43	1	6	2	9	24	8	8	3	19	31
Moderate Segregationist	2	5	0	7	30	5	5	3	13	34	7	10	3	20	33
Nonsegregationist	3	0	3	6	26	0	3	13	16	42	3	3	16	22	36
Total	12	7	4	23	100	6	14	18	38	100	18	21	22	61	100

Significant changes over time in the racial stances of first primary leaders are manifest in Table 28. When the segregation positions of first and second place finishers are compared across the South for primaries held before and after the Voting Rights Act, the impact of federal intervention on the expression of segregationist views in campaigns is clearly suggested. The proportion of strong segregationists who led Democratic first primaries declined from 44 percent in the pre-Voting Rights Act years to 9 percent after 1965; moderate segregationists experienced a similar decrease (from 44 percent to 14 percent); and the percentage of nonsegregationists among first primary leaders rose from 13 to 77 percent. An even more powerful indicator of the decline of the traditional segregationist southern politician is the fact that both leading candidates campaigned as nonsegregationists in three fifths of the first primaries from 1966 through 1973. The competitiveness of moderate segregationists vis-à-vis militants in the first primary campaigns should again be emphasized. Most of the primaries that matched moderate segregationists against militants occurred *before* federal intervention, and moderate segregationists led strong segregationists in six of 14 cases. Nonsegregationists split their matches with moderate segregationists before and after 1965 but were able to lead militant segregationists only in the post-Voting Rights Act period.

Table 28. Racial segregation position of first place finishers in contested Democratic first primaries for governor in the South, before and after the Voting Rights Act, by racial segregation stance of second place finishers

| First Place Finishers | Second Place Finishers | | | | | | | | | |
| | 1954-65 | | | | | 1966-73 | | | | |
	SS	MS	NS	T	%	SS	MS	NS	T	%
Strong Segregationist	8	8	1	17	44	0	0	2	2	9
Moderate Segregationist	6	9	2	17	44	1	1	1	3	14
Nonsegregationist	0	2	3	5	13	3	1	13	17	77
Total	14	19	6	39	100	4	2	16	22	100

It is time to inquire in a detailed manner into the patterns of conflict on the segregation issue that have characterized post-1954 campaigns for governor in the South. Limiting our attention to the racial positions of first and second place finishers in Democratic first primaries, six types of campaign may be differentiated: militant segregationists only, militant segregationist versus moderate segregationist, militant segregationist versus nonsegregationist, moderate segregationists only, moderate segregationist versus nonsegregationist, and nonsegregationists only. These types of campaign establish a continuum that begins with the most traditional contest and ends with the least traditional match. No attempt will be made to recapitulate all 61 first primary contests. However, in order to illustrate general tendencies and to communicate some of the emotional tone and flavor of post-*Brown* electoral politics to readers who lack first-hand knowledge of the period, case studies of selected primaries will be presented. Particular emphasis will be given to elections which matched strong segregationists against moderate segregationists or nonsegregationists, since these contests have offered the clearest differences between candidates on the segregation issue.

Militant Segregationists

In 13 percent of the first primaries from 1954-73, the two most popular candidates were each militant segregationists. These primaries, which were common in the late 1950s, involved Deep South states in seven out of eight cases. As Cell I of Table 29 indicates, Mississippi witnessed more campaigns of this variety (three) than any other southern state. When the two leading candidates have been strong segregationists, campaign strategy has generally involved nothing more elaborate than an attempt by each politician to "out-seg" the other. Occasionally, however, candidates have emphasized their own racial militancy while arguing indirectly or directly that their opponent's views were so extreme as to invite outside attention and perhaps intervention.

The 1959 Mississippi campaign may serve as an illustration of the strong segregationist versus strong segregationist primary. The three major candidates in the 1959 Mississippi first primary—Jackson lawyer Ross Barnett, Lieutenant Governor Carroll Gartin of Laurel, and District Attorney Charles Sullivan of Clarksdale—were all strong segregationists. Although Barnett had the closest ties to the Citizens' Council, each of the candidates passed the Citizens' Council's test on

Table 29. Campaign racial stances of first and second place finishers in contested Democratic first primaries for governor in the South, 1954-73, by subregion (N = 61)

First Place Finishers	Second Place Finishers					
	Strong Segregationist		Moderate Segregationist		Nonsegregationist	
	DS	PS	DS	PS	DS	PS
Strong Segregationist	SC 54ᵃ SC 58 Miss 55 Miss 59 Miss 63 Ala 58 Ga 58	Tenn 58 I	Ga 54 Ala 62 II	Tex 54 Va 57 Va 61 Ark 58 Ark 60 Fla 60	Ala 66 III	Fla 64 Ark 66
Moderate Segregationist	Ga 62 Miss 67	Tenn 54 Ark 56 Fla 56 NC 56 NC 60 IV	Ala 54 La 55-56 La 59-60 La 63-64 SC 62	Fla 54 Ark 54 Ark 64 Tex 56 NC 68 V		Tex 58 Ark 62 Ark 70 VI

	VII	VIII		IX
Nonsegregationist	Ga 66 *La 67* Ala 70	*Tex 60* NC 64 Ark 68	Ga 70 Miss 71 La 71-72	Tex 62 *Tex 64* *Tex 66* Tex 68 Tex 72 *Tenn 62* *Tenn 66* *Tenn 70* Fla 66 Fla 70 Va 69 *Ark 72* NC 72

aItalicized elections are those in which the Democratic nomination was settled in the first primary.

segregation, agreed that the council was itself the state's principal bulwark against integrationists and other undesirables, and advocated outlawing the NAACP.[4]

For Charles Sullivan, a young delta lawyer making his first attempt for the governorship, the essential issues were the relationship of Mississippi Democrats to the national party, the ending of statewide prohibition, retention of the right-to-work law, and legislative reapportionment. More of a conservative ideologue than Barnett, Sullivan advanced the notion, a heresy at a time when integration was commonly viewed as the issue, that the AFL-CIO was a greater threat to Mississippi than the NAACP. The question of integration, he argued, was but a subterfuge for the creation of a "socialistic labor dictatorship." If the national Democrats continued to support a "strong central government," Mississippi Democrats should make plain their disagreement with the national tendencies of the party. The state's most urgent problem, he explained on Independence Day, was to preserve the ideal of "state sovereignty." "We are the last state that stands by the Southern way of life," he said days before the election, "and I am the man to lead Mississippi in this fight."[5]

Neither his desire for industrial development nor his belief in the advantages of racial segregation differentiated Gartin from the rest of the field. As the only candidate with statewide political experience, Gartin considered prior office holding an important issue. Because he was considered the protégé of Governor J. P. Coleman, Gartin was frequently attacked as a "moderate" on segregation. This accusation was denied. A "proud" member of the Citizens' Council, he felt the "successful maintenance of total segregation" constituted Mississippi's greatest challenge. The Mississippi statutes, he explained, were filled with "protective legislation designed to defend our cherished Southern way of life," legislation which Gartin had helped write. There was no ambiguity, only redundancy, concerning Gartin's commitment to the racial status quo. Describing himself as a "total and complete advocate of absolute segregation," he promised that, if elected, "there ain't gonna be no integratin'." "Carroll Gartin," he claimed, "is a successful, total and absolute segregationist."[6] Statements along these lines made it difficult to portray Gartin convincingly as a moderate.

Although he waged the most segregation-oriented campaign of any candidate in 1959, Ross Barnett was not a single issue politician. At various times he discussed such problems as economic development, prohibition, and labor unions.[7] Nonetheless, Barnett's appeal rested at bottom on his reputation for intransigent opposition to racial change. Fundamentalist theology was invoked to justify the caste system. "I don't believe God meant for the races to be integrated," Barnett said. "God placed the black man in Africa and separated the white man from him with a body of water." God particularly discouraged racial intermarriage. "The good Lord made you white because he wanted you white," Barnett reasoned, "and he intended for you to stay that way." Far from being a racial "moderate," the candidate characterized himself as a "firm and un-wavering believer in the complete segregation of the races." His commitment to white supremacy explicitly entailed opposition to black political participation. Barnett attacked a proposal for a constitutional convention on the ground that blacks would probably have to be represented: "Ross Barnett is not ready to let the Negroes into a convention nor the legislature of the state of Mississippi." To Barnett racial desegregation was an unmitigated evil. "Integration has ruined every community in which it has been practiced," he declared. "I would rather lose my life than to see Mississippi schools integrated."[8]

Gartin might have more political experience, Barnett conceded, but his defense of segregation was open to serious criticism. According to Barnett, his opponent, though a member of the State Sovereignty Commission, "never lifted a finger" to aid Faubus in his struggle at Little Rock or to support a group of Clinton, Tennessee, segregationists (defended by Barnett) who had been cited for contempt of court for obstructing school desegregation. "I submit to you," Barnett asserted, "that I am the only candidate with actual court experience, in state, federal and even the United States Supreme Court, fighting the leftwingers and NAACP leaders who have attempted to ram integration down our throats." White Mississippians could have confidence that Barnett would never compromise on the principle of racial segregation.[9] In an election-eve television address, his words encouraged segregationists throughout the state:

> I have tangled with these NAACP and leftwing agitators and I know how they maneuver. I have been on the firing line against moderates and integrationists. You will never find Ross Barnett giving a blessing to [Arkansas Congressman] Brooks Hays. As governor, I want to unite the governors of other southern states to take a firm stand against integration while we crystallize public sentiment in our favor in the North.[10]

Barnett led Gartin by a small margin (35 to 34 percent of the state vote) in the first primary and increased his lead in the runoff.[11]

Campaigns such as the above, though numerous in the Deep South in the years before token compliance with the *Brown* decision was achieved, have not persisted in southern electoral politics. With the exception of the 1958 primary in Tennessee and the 1963 primary in Mississippi, elections held after some school desegregation had taken place, the militant segregationists in these contests essentially sought to persuade the electorate that they were better qualified than their rivals to maintain total segregation in the public schools. Federal intervention in the Deep South states to enforce court orders requiring school desegregation, along with the revival of black voting, undermined the type of primary in which strong segregationists faced each other. Militant segregationists continued to seek the governorship, but beginning in the 1960s they were typically opposed by moderate segregationists or nonsegregationists. Reflection on the winners of these first primaries suggests another conclusion. Even among competing militant segregationists, the more extreme segregationists of the two candidates tended to lead the first primary field. Putting aside two elections (Mississippi 1955 and South Carolina 1958) where there appeared to be little difference in the degree of militancy between the candidates, the more strident of the two strong segregationists placed first in four (South Carolina 1954, Alabama 1958, and Mississippi 1959 and 1963) out of six cases. Only in Tennessee and Georgia (both 1958) were the relatively less extreme of the militant segregationists successful.

Militant Segregationists and Moderate Segregationists

One quarter of the Democratic first primaries between 1954 and 1973 were contests between a militant segregationist and a moderate segregationist. Nine states experienced these campaigns, but they were far more common in the Peripheral South than in the Deep South (see Cells II and IV of Table 29). Although moderate segregationists did compete on fairly even terms with strong segregationists in the first primary, examination of Cell IV of Table 29 suggests that the success of the moderate segregationists was due in large measure to the timing of their campaigns. A majority (four of seven) of the moderate segregationist victories were achieved before the Little Rock crisis of 1957, the event which enormously increased the salience of the school desegregation issue in southern campaigns. Moreover, in each of these pre-Little Rock primaries the winning moderate segregationist was an incumbent governor seeking a second term. (Deaths of previous governors in North Carolina and Florida had created this abnormal situation.) Under these circumstances Frank Clement of Tennessee, Orval Faubus of Arkansas, Luther Hodges of North Carolina, and LeRoy Collins of Florida, all of whom favored school segregation, won first primary majorities against militant segregationists. If these pre-1957 victories are set aside, the competitiveness of the moderate segregationists is considerably diminished. To illustrate the seg-regation-oriented appeals found in these campaigns two post-Little Rock victories for moderate segregationists (Georgia 1962 and Mississippi 1967) and two first primaries in which strong seg-regationists defeated moderate segregationists (Texas 1954 and Arkansas 1958) will be discussed. Two other militant segregation-ist-moderate segregationist contests—North Carolina 1960 and Alabama 1962—will be considered in the next chapter.

Texas 1954. The "modified class politics" that Key identified in Texas[12] reached a new level of explicitness in the 1954 first primary. Incumbent Governor Allan Shivers, the leader of the conservative Democrats who was seeking a third term, was opposed for a second time by a liberal attorney from Austin, Ralph Yarborough. Shivers ran as a champion of States' Rights and as a foe of various un-Texan organizations. The critical issue for Texans, he believed, was whether or not their governor would be chosen by "the CIO-PAC, the ADA, NAACP and [George] Parr combine." Yarborough's campaign themes were corruption in state government—a "cesspool of corruption bubbles all around this [Shivers] administration," he asserted—and redistributive economic policies. His "good will for farmers and the average working man" was contrasted with Shivers' solicitude for the prosperity of his "Cadillac-driving . . . yacht-sailing cronies."[13]

As the campaign drew to a close, Shivers emphasized his hostility to school desegregation. While the governor did not want Texas schools "run by Washington, by the Supreme Court or by the NAACP," Shivers complained that Yarborough's position on desegregation was unclear. Campaigning in East Texas, Shivers attacked the *Brown* decision as "the greatest invasion of local rights in the history of the Supreme Court," asserted that "We're going to keep segregated schools in Texas," and promised to "smoke out" Yarborough, whom he characterized as a "captive" of the NAACP, on the issue. "No court can pass an edict," Shivers informed the electorate, "to change what God Almighty made."[14]

Yarborough's stance on school desegregation was ambiguous. He had hoped to avoid the issue and concentrate on have-not economic questions, but his equivocal stance enabled Shivers to portray him as unreliable on the segregation issue. For obvious political reasons Yarborough never advocated school desegregation, and his position became more conservative as the election approached. After first refusing to comment because he had not read the *Brown* decision, he later suggested that schools should continue to be segregated for a year to enable a solution to be devised "in Texas by Texans in the Texas way." When the State Board of Education ruled that Texas schools would remain segregated during the 1954-55 school year, he supported the decision without taking a stand on the merits of desegregation. A week before the election, with Shivers constantly raising the issue, Yarborough came out against compulsory desegregation. He did not favor "the forced mingling of children where they don't want to go." This pronouncement was accompanied by a demand that blacks be provided equal facilities and by a denunciation of Shivers for "preaching a hymn of hate between the races."[15] His final position, which gave some comfort to segregationists, was meant to be as noncontroversial as possible. Shivers led Yarborough by less than 25,000 votes and was forced into a runoff (see Chapter 8) because he lacked a majority. Yarborough defeated Shivers in rural Texas but Shivers had majorities in the urban areas.

Although the segregation issue did not dominate the campaign, Shivers used it to Yarborough's disadvantage. The election was held two months after the *Brown* decision, so that Yarborough could be linked to the NAACP as well as to "labor bosses" and the Americans for Democratic Action. Yarborough's difficulty in addressing the segregation question illustrates the general dilemma of southern moderate segregationists matched against strong segregationists. Politicians who failed to defend segregation explicitly risked their careers, yet the support of blacks (where they voted in force) and white liberals (where they existed) might be lost should the status quo on race be praised too vigorously. Faced with an exceedingly sensitive issue, candidates disinclined to race-bait frequently attempted to ignore the issue if at all possible and tended to be on the defensive against pressure from militant segregationists.[16]

Arkansas 1958. The 1958 Arkansas primary, the first election following Governor Orval Faubus's efforts in 1957 to prevent school desegregation in Little Rock, was not a close race. Faubus's triumph was thoroughly predictable, but the campaign merits scrutiny as an example of the political advantages that accrued from time to time after 1954 to southern politicians who engaged in spectacular feats (whether successful or not) to thwart desegregation. In running for his third term against two comparatively obscure opponents, Chris Finkbeiner and Lee Ward, the governor campaigned sparingly.

Finkbeiner, a Little Rock businessman, thought Faubus was already too powerful to be entrusted with a third term. He supported segregation but condemned Faubus's actions in Little Rock. There would be, he told Negro leaders, no repetition of that crisis because he would "never do anything contrary to the courts." Whites were reassured that Finkbeiner would preserve segregated schools.[17] Ward, who was a judge from Paragould, proved to be a stronger critic of Faubus. He urged an "absolute reversal of the reckless and destructive course" of Arkansas race relations since Little Rock. Emphasizing his own "strong preference" for segregation, Ward argued that no public official should act to "destroy the very fabric of law and order." It was the governor's responsibility to "seek reconciliation not chaos," but Faubus, a "dedicated demagogue," had manufactured the Little Rock crisis with "studied duplicity." If Ward were governor, desegregation policy would be established by local school boards rather than by the governor, and under no circumstances would he lead Arkansas "into insurrection or rebellion against the federal government." Suggesting that political expediency rather than any authentic opposition to desegregation lay at the root of Faubus's behavior, Ward accused the governor of appealing "to the lowest instincts of human nature." In his opinion the *Brown* decision was wrong, but Faubus's response to desegregation had "brought disgrace to Arkansas."[18]

One month before the primary, Faubus formally began his campaign. Presenting a "program of progress," the governor spent much of his opening address discussing his efforts to raise welfare benefits. Little attention was paid to his opponents or to the Little Rock controversy, though Faubus emphasized that he would continue to oppose school desegregation. "I have taken my position in the protection and defense of the people of Arkansas, in your constitutional right to govern yourselves in state and local affairs," Faubus said. "From this position I shall not recede nor yield." Even though his battle with the Eisenhower administration had made him a target of abuse from enemies of Arkansas within and outside the state, his daily conduct would continue to demonstrate that "it's Courage That Counts." Faubus would never "surrender" to the demands of the NAACP. Throughout the 1958 campaign Faubus carried on a running attack against his Little Rock critics, particularly the *Arkansas Gazette* and its publisher, Harry Ashmore, former Governor Sidney McMath, and Mrs. Daisy Bates, an NAACP leader. Outside "do-gooders" and "meddlers" who connived to destroy the state's racial traditions were denounced with regularity.[19]

The other candidates strove, without appreciable success, to overcome Faubus's contention that he was only a man of principle beset by misguided enemies. Talk of "outsiders," Finkbeiner suggested, was a bogus issue intended to distract attention from the "dictatorial powers" that a third term would give Faubus. Ward believed Faubus had made a "cynical and potentially destructive decision" to run as a militant opponent of desegregation. Freedom of speech was threatened within Arkansas; according to Ward, some citizens were afraid to criticize Faubus's handling of school desegregation because "they say that they will be called 'nigger lovers' or threatened with loss of business if they speak out." Faubus, in firm control of the situation, ignored Ward and Finkbeiner and continued to assail his detractors. "High labor moguls" as well as the NAACP were fighting him, but their efforts would be wasted. If the circumstances warranted another call-up of the National Guard as in Little Rock, Faubus would not hesitate to "do it again."[20] With Faubus's performance as governor the central issue, the Arkansas electorate responded by giving Faubus 69 percent of the vote. This showing was a full ten percentage points more than he had received in the 1956 first primary. His landslide victory, moreover, demonstrated to other southern politicians the utility of conspicuously defying a national administration.

Figure 18, which displays the geography of the Faubus vote for two first primaries before and after Little Rock, reveals Faubus's massive electoral support in the late 1950s and early 1960s. Strong support for Faubus was originally concentrated in the mountain counties of northwestern Arkansas, the section of the state least preoccupied with the segregation issue. Faubus received large majorities in the counties of western and northern Arkansas in his reelection campaign of 1956, but he achieved impressive support in southeastern Arkansas, the most tradition-bound region, only after he emerged as a national symbol of resistance to school desegregation.[21] Arkansas citizens gave Faubus a truly overwhelming vote in the 1958 first primary. Seventy-three of 75 counties supplied majorities, and he won landslide victories—over 60 percent—in more than 90 percent of the state's counties. Faubus again ran exceedingly well in southern and eastern

Figure 18. The Faubus vote in Arkansas before and after the Little Rock crisis: support for Orval Faubus in Democratic first primary elections for governor, 1954-60

1954 First Primary

1956 First Primary

1958 First Primary

1960 First Primary

Over 60%: shaded
50-59%: striped
45-49%: dotted

Arkansas when he sought an unprecedented fourth consecutive term in 1960. While rural counties with low black populations contributed the greatest percentage support for Faubus in the 1954 and 1956 primaries, his strongest vote in the late 1950s was derived from rural counties with high black concentrations. As Thomas Pettigrew and Ernest Campbell have shown, the "mountain candidate" of 1954 and 1956 became the "delta favorite" after Little Rock.[22]

Georgia 1962.   Racial segregation was the dominant theme of the 1962 Georgia first primary, one of the few southern primaries after Little Rock in which a moderate segregationist defeated a militant segregationist. The election matched former Governor Marvin Griffin, a rural strong segregationist in the Gene Talmadge tradition, against a young and urban-oriented state senator from Augusta, Carl

Sanders. Griffin's strategy was straightforward; he ran his usual racist campaign. Sanders, a far more sophisticated politician, developed several themes, the most important of which were Griffin's extremist views on civil rights, corruption in Griffin's previous administration, and the need for new industry in Georgia. The 1962 primary was the first election for governor held after federal courts had invalidated Georgia's county unit system of nominations, and Sanders was particularly interested in attracting an urban vote.

Unlike many moderate segregationists who faced strong segregationists, Sanders never became defensive on the segregation issue, continually asserting that only he could bring racial peace to the state. "Whether it be Marvin Griffin or Martin Luther King," Sanders declared early in the contest, "I will not tolerate agitators nor permit violence or bloodshed among our citizens regardless of color or creed."[23] From the beginning Sanders attempted to appease whites who hated King for his leadership of the civil rights movement while obliquely indicating to blacks that their rights, at least some of them, would also be protected. He proposed to follow a middle course between supporting desegregation efforts and actively defying the federal government over civil rights. "I will not stand with George Wallace or Martin Luther King," Sanders would say. "I'm going to stand with the people of Georgia." In a speech at Albany, where King had been leading sit-in demonstrations protesting racial segregation, Sanders promised to help local law enforcement agencies keep the peace and criticized King for advocating the violation of "unjust" laws. He hoped "the work of agitators and rabble rousers seeking to arouse and divide the people who live in this community is over or soon will be over." Although he would "use every legal means to preserve segregation of the races in Georgia," Sanders promised to govern with dignity. "I won't cause you and your state to be spread across the headlines all over the nation, and cause you embarrassment," he declared.[24]

If Griffin deserved repudiation because of his violence-prone posture on segregation, past experience had demonstrated that he was also uninterested in providing an honest administration. Corruption was a major issue for Sanders because an unseemly number of Griffin's appointees had subsequently served prison terms for plundering state accounts. "I still say you couldn't trust Marvin Griffin then," Sanders charged, "and you can't trust him now."[25] Finally, Sanders stressed industrial development (and substantially increased appropriations for education) and his ability to entice outside business into the state. Improvement in Georgia's industrial position was essential if the state wished to "keep our young people at home and employed." Compared to Griffin's efforts, Sanders accurately described his campaign as an attempt to "move Georgia forward."[26]

Griffin's campaign, a less elaborate affair, consisted above all of exacerbating the racial fears and antagonisms of white Georgians. Martin Luther King, Jr., was Griffin's favorite target, and the former governor suggested that Sanders' "right-hand supporter" be lodged "so far back in the jail you will have to pipe air back to him." When Sanders visited Albany, Griffin denounced his rival as a "weeping willy" who had begged "Martin Luther King to quit it." If he won the election, he continued, "I can promise you next January I'll nip this unhealthy and ungodly thing in the bud!" His defeat, on the other hand, would mean that whites might "not have a chance to elect anybody [Atlanta banker] Mills B. Lane, King, and [Atlanta *Constitution* publisher] Rastus McGill don't select."[27]

While Sanders was determined to prevent racial violence, Griffin's public attitude toward violence was, at best, irresponsible. His most notorious remarks on the control of "Negro agitators" were made before a responsive rural audience, where he disclosed that the most persuasive way to discourage racial protests was to "cut you a black-jack sapling and brain 'em and nip 'em in the bud."[28] With the election less than a month away, Griffin began to call attention to the Negro "bloc vote" that would surely be cast against him. "I am not a bigot. I am not prejudiced," he announced to the Georgia electorate. "But I do not intend, if I can help it, to let the NAACP divide the good white folks and control this state by a bloc vote." Although he had personally aided blacks in many ways when he was governor, Griffin would not let "Martin Luther King and his rabble rousers take over" Georgia.[29]

The segregation issue assumed a new and more ominous dimension in the final days of the primary. Observing with scorn that Ku Klux Klan leaders had endorsed Griffin, Sanders promised to control the Klan and to prosecute any group that "demonstrates for the purpose of violence." He did not anticipate massive Negro support because "Carl Sanders is not committed to the NAACP or to anybody else." Nightrider terrorism seemed to be increasing, and Sanders blamed Griffin in part for violence against blacks. His opponent's behavior was convincing Klansmen that "if they support him they can go out carrying guns and have the backing of the state."[30] Two days before the election a pair of black churches in a rural county were burned. Griffin, dismissing evidence to the contrary, argued that the fires were probably faked. "There's too much of this going on," he reasoned, "for it not to be a put up job."[31] Sanders responded with a denunciation of lawlessness and race-baiting politicians:

> There is no act more cruel and more destructive to American ideals than the burning of a church. Such despicable acts are caused by the preaching of hatred. The decent people know that the days of the Ku Klux Klan and masked night riders are over. They know that we must take a sensible approach to our problems—and that approach is law and order.[32]

Griffin ended his campaign with a shrill attempt to arouse a white "bloc vote." Jackie Robinson, the first black major league baseball player and a visitor to Georgia, had the audacity to urge blacks to vote against Griffin. "If this isn't enough to electrify the white people of Georgia to go to the ballot box Wednesday and vote for me, then what does Georgia want?"[33]

A substantial majority (58 percent) of the Georgians who voted in 1962 apparently did not want a rural, hard-lining segregationist as governor, at least not one whose past administration had established the contemporary record for financial corruption. The abolition of the county unit system gave urban voters genuine political strength for the first time, and there was a perfect inverse rank ordering between demographic traditionalism and the Sanders vote. Sanders received 72 percent of the vote in metropolitan Atlanta, had majorities in the medium urban and low black counties, and failed to carry the high black counties. Griffin obtained over half the vote in the black belt counties but only 25 percent in the Atlanta SMSA, which cast over a quarter of the total state vote. Geographically, the vote divided roughly along north-south lines. Griffin had majorities in most of the rural counties of southern Georgia, especially those in the southwestern quarter of the state, while Sanders carried most of the counties north of the fall line and several counties in southeastern Georgia. Despite Sanders' impressive victory, it would be a mistake to interpret the 1962 Georgia primary as in any significant sense a vote against racial segregation. Sanders was a fresh, dynamic political figure and a voice of reason compared to Griffin, but he did not campaign (nor could he pragmatically have been expected to do so in the early 1960s) as a nonsegregationist. "I am a segregationist," he told audiences. "I believe in equal opportunity but if I am elected governor I will not tolerate race-baiting or race-mixing."[34] Many voters apparently considered a moderate segregationist committed to economic development preferable to a militant segregationist of questionable integrity.

Mississippi 1967. In contrast to previous Mississippi practice, leading candidates for governor in the 1967 first primary campaigned less regularly and less explicitly as advocates of white supremacy. No major candidate repudiated racial segregation or openly sought black votes, but the growth of a sizable black electorate (up from 30,000 in 1963 to 200,000 four years later), the fact that some desegregation had been achieved, and an increasing awareness within the business community that racial turmoil was bad for business all provided incentives for campaigns relatively less oriented toward race baiting.[35] State Treasurer William Winter ran as a moderate segregationist, while Congressman John Bell Williams, former Governor Ross Barnett, and Jimmy Swan, a country music singer and broadcaster, campaigned as strong segregationists.

Barnett, unlike his past campaigns, made industrial development a more central issue than even States' Rights. With only scattered exceptions, his strong segregationist position had to be inferred from his opposition to "The Lyndon Johnsons, the Bobby Kennedys, the Hubert Horatio Humphreys and other left-wing liberals in Washington who seek to dominate this nation." Like the Wallaces in 1966 (see below), Barnett had come to understand that the days of unfeigned and uninhibited racism were largely past. The self-styled "Tried and True Conservative" denounced Winter as a "liberal" and Williams as a "middle-of-the-road" candidate, but his advanced age (69) and the publicity given to his efforts to compromise with the Justice Department during the Ole Miss crisis of 1962 diminished his appeal among militant segregationists. Barnett often attacked the school desegregation guidelines and Negro riots, yet his "racial integrity" address, a commonplace in previous races, was rarely delivered. Barnett's views on segregation had not changed. He still believed that segregation was "the only sensible basis for racial integrity," and he could describe Senator Theodore G. Bilbo's *Separation or Mongrelization of the Races—Take your Choice*, a racist concoction he had studied "from cover to cover," as a book for "all the people of America." Running as a sporadic militant segregationist, the former hero of Ole Miss finished fourth with only 11 percent of the vote.[36]

By far the most vociferous segregationist in 1967, Swan viewed the governor's race in stark, apocalyptic terms, as a final chance to save white children in Mississippi from "the massive integration experiment by the communistically oriented HEW guidelines." The catastrophe of full-fledged desegregation could be averted, he argued in daily speeches, by the creation of a statewide system of free yet private schools. Other candidates merely assailed the guidelines. Swan proposed to "DO SOMETHING about the integration of our children in the public schools. Swan has pledged [a campaign advertisement continued] that within twelve months from the day he takes office, his plan for FREE, private, SEGREGATED SCHOOLS for every white child in the State of Mississippi will be in operation . . . or he will resign his office of Governor and apologize publicly to every citizen in Mississippi." With Swan in the governor's chair, local peace officers could anticipate full cooperation "against the attacks by communists, federal agents, federal judges and long-haired beatniks." A political amateur, Swan nonetheless placed third with 18 percent of the vote.[37]

Williams, who had been stripped of his seniority by Democrats in the House of Representatives for supporting Barry Goldwater in 1964, campaigned as a "sensible conservative." He had placed his principles above party loyalty, and the basic issue, in his view, was whether Mississippians were "willing to surrender to Lyndon Johnson and the Great Society rather than stand up for our principles with John Bell Williams." Although he spent little time enumerating the merits of the caste system, his segregationist racial views were evident in his numerous attacks on the HEW desegregation guidelines and in his unwillingness to countenance Negro riots. Winter might want the school desegregation guidelines "rewritten," but Williams thought they should be "erased and completely repealed." Nor would blacks be permitted to burn and loot. "We are not going to have any band of marauders marching through Mississippi throwing brick bats and destroying your property," he declared. His opponents were ridiculed as inept or controlled by national Democrats. "Mississippi cannot stand another four years of Ross Barnett," he commented, nor did the state need the liberalism of William Winter. Offering himself as a "middle-of-the-road" alternative, Williams promised that "peace and tranquility" would prevail under his leadership.[38]

Winter ran an unusually constructive campaign which stressed state problems, particularly Mississippi's inadequate public school system, and the disadvantages of "uncertain leadership" in the governor's office. He believed the voters were tired of the "arm waving and bombast that excites emotion but fails to get the job done" and would welcome a politician who could "handle our affairs in a way that our enemies can't have the opportunity to come in here and interfere." Though he opposed the HEW desegregation guidelines and "federal encroachment into state affairs" generally, Winter spent less time denouncing Washington than he did outlining his solutions to the state's underfinanced educational system, lack of job opportunities, and inadequate highway program. His political record, he contended, refuted the accusation that he was a "liberal," and the reputed "Kennedy candidate" claimed that he had never met Robert Kennedy. Except for criticizing Williams as one who had "left his post in a time of trial," Winter did not directly attack his opponents. In his final pre-election statement, he suggested that the state needed a chief executive who "remains cool in hot situations, exercises sober judgment and is willing to fight." Should he be elected, he would strive to "raise the sights of the people of this state."[39] With the strong segregationist vote split among three candidates, Winter led Williams by less than 25,000 votes (33 percent to 29 percent) in the first primary. Although Mississippians had rejected the most conspicuous segregationists (Swan and Barnett together polled only slightly more votes than Williams), Winter's narrow margin made his defeat in the runoff highly probable.[40]

Contests between a militant segregationist and a moderate segregationist, although the most frequent type of primary between 1954 and 1965, rarely occurred in the post-Voting Rights Act period. Apart from several pre-Little Rock primaries involving incumbent governors of Peripheral South states, strong segregationists tended to place first in these elections. Moderate segregationists defeated militants only in Georgia (1962), where the strong segregationist was attacked as corrupt, and in North Carolina (1960), a campaign that will be considered in the following chapter. In the 1967 Mississippi first primary a moderate segregationist led the field when the militant segregationist vote was divided three ways, but in the second primary the surviving militant segregationist won without difficulty. Particularly in the years between the Little Rock crisis and federal intervention to reform southern racial practices, first primaries which matched militant segregationists against moderate segregationists were generally resolved in favor of the candidate who offered the greatest opposition to racial change. These elections declined after 1965 as the growth of black electorates and the achievement (in varying degrees) of racial desegregation made the adoption of a segregationist campaign stance less functional to political success than it once was.

Militant Segregationists and Nonsegregationists

Only 10 percent of the contested Democratic first primaries in the post-*Brown* period featured a militant segregationist and a nonsegregationist among the two leading candidates. Five of the six primaries of this nature came after 1965, a reflection of the creation of constituencies (mainly black voters) supportive of candidates less tied to southern racial norms. Although nonsegregationists led as many of these first primaries as strong segregationists (see Cells III and VII of Table 29), the competitiveness of the nonsegregationists should not be overstated. In the 1966 Georgia and 1970 Alabama campaigns, the first of which will be considered in the next chapter, nonsegregationists won the first primary but were defeated in the runoff. Moreover, the single first primary in which a nonsegregationist won a majority against a militant segregationist was highly atypical. In the 1967 Louisiana primary Governor John McKeithen, benefiting from a reform of the state constitution which permitted an incumbent governor to seek a second term, drew virtually no serious opposition. The absence of a vigorously contested primary in Louisiana, a state with a reputation for hard-fought campaigns, may be inferred from the fact that McKeithen received 81 percent of the vote. In the remaining militant segregationist versus nonsegregationist matches (Florida 1964, Arkansas 1966, and Alabama 1966), the strong segregationists were victorious. The 1966 Alabama first primary, which will serve to illustrate this type of campaign, offered voters an unusually clear-cut choice with respect to race.

Despite the outcome, the 1966 Democratic primary in Alabama began a new era in that state's electoral politics. For the first time in modern Alabama history, a major candidate for governor campaigned as a nonsegregationist; the black vote reached an impressive total, exceeding 200,000; and blatant appeals to racial prejudice all but disappeared, to be replaced by a new, euphemistic vocabulary. Having failed to amend the state constitution to allow himself to run for reelection, Wallace encouraged his wife to seek the governorship. Lurleen Wallace was opposed by a large field, but Attorney General Richmond Flowers was the only candidate besides Mrs. Wallace to obtain at least 10 percent of the vote. Wallace's stormy career as governor provided the campaign's main issue.

Flowers was the first significant white candidate for governor to campaign as an aggressive advocate of black rights. During his term as attorney general he had frequently disagreed with Wallace's approach to civil rights issues. Flowers began his campaign by urging local rather than federal responsibility for maintaining law and order. He described Wallace as a "Pied Piper of defiance" and predicted that the Wallace administration's "present attitude of defiance and discord" would culminate in additional federal court orders concerning school desegregation and in more civil rights legislation. Flowers freely admitted that his own campaign, which emphasized industrial development and improved educational opportunities, was designed in particular (though not exclusively) to attract black support. "Sure, I solicit the Negro vote," he said. "I'm promising equal opportunity, equal education and good jobs for every citizen in this state." Negro political activists, not "just a few Uncle Toms," would be appointed to state jobs if he became governor. Flowers was endorsed by two major black political organizations, largely because he was the sole candidate willing to shake hands and campaign personally in Negro districts. Among other suggestions, Flowers argued that "our shanty, one-room schools must go," urged the creation of an interracial commission to help resolve racial conflicts, and hailed the 1965 Voting Rights Act as a "rival of the emancipation proclamation." Several days before the election Dr. Martin Luther King, Jr., toured the black belt and advocated massive black support for Flowers. "So when your boss asks you how you're going to vote, you tell him you're going to vote for Wallace, then go on down and vote for Flowers," King advised black voters. Although Flowers received the bulk of the black vote, he was outpolled nearly 3 to 1 by Mrs. Wallace.[41]

After four turbulent years as Alabama's governor, George Wallace was firmly established in 1966 as the strongest state politician in the South since the *Brown* decision. During the primary Wallace emphasized the neo-Populist economic policies of his administration and promised to resist further federal intervention in the area of race relations. In contrast to his previous campaigns, however, Wallace did not explicitly defend the principle of racial segregation. Indeed, most references to blacks pertained to the benefits (for example, free textbooks, improved educational facilities) which Wallace claimed they had received during his tenure as governor. "I am proud that you, as Alabamians, have done something for them that no other administration has ever done," the governor said.[42] The disappearance of unambiguous references to segregation did not signify that the

Wallaces had changed their attitudes on segregation. An Alabama journalist has well summarized Wallace's racial stance in 1966:

> An outsider might be astonished to find that nowadays Wallace never deals with the race issue per se in his campaign oratory. Pugnacious outcries such as "segregation today, segregation forever" in his inaugural speech as Governor have now given way to a more sophisticated approach: "We will awaken the nation to the liberal-Socialistic-Communist design to destroy local government in America."
> This approach is not too subtle for rural Alabama "red-necks" who understand that he means to preserve segregation, nor is it so crude that it entirely robs him of respectability elsewhere in Alabama and the nation . . . To the Southerner, Wallace's philosophy means keeping the status quo; to a small-businessman in Peoria, it might mean an outcry against Washington bureaucracy.[43]

As the Wallaces carefully pointed out, Alabamians could expect the same type of administration when Mrs. Wallace assumed office. The themes of the campaign were indicated in Wallace's opening speech, in which he pledged to defend "the free enterprise and property ownership system throughout the country," promised four more years of honesty, integrity and progress, and denounced the national government, Flowers, national news media, and the metropolitan Alabama press. On another occasion he suggested that the primary was of national importance because it tested the popularity of two "fearless, outspoken critics of the liberal beatnik mob." Despite attacks by the "socialist, liberal, beatnik, Communist conspiracy in these United States," Wallace assured the electorate that he would stand up for "constitutional government." As he said in one speech, "I'm not against the federal government . . . but I'm not going to cooperate with a bunch of liberal pinkos."[44]

Some 54 percent of the voters accepted the Wallaces' invitation to "Stand Up for Alabama," and Mrs. Wallace thus became the first Alabamian since James Folsom in 1954 to win the Democratic nomination with a first primary majority. The magnitude of the Wallace victory in 1966 is suggested by Figure 19, which maps the evolution of the core Wallace first primary vote from 1958 through 1970. Wallace's support base in his initial gubernatorial campaign was limited to a cluster of "friends and neighbors" counties in southeastern Alabama including and adjacent to his home county of Barbour.[45] In the 1962 first primary, with Wallace clearly the strong-

Figure 19.   The evolution of the Wallace vote in Alabama: support for George Wallace in Democratic first primaries for governor, 1958-70

1958 First Primary

1962 First Primary

1966 First Primary

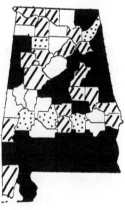

1970 First Primary

Over 60%: shaded
50-59%: striped
45-49%: dotted

est segregationist in the race, the localism of 1958 broadened into sectionalism. A majority of the counties of southern Alabama, the region with the largest black population and hence the greatest stake in the preservation of the caste system, provided Wallace with at least 45 percent of their first primary vote. In the 1966 first primary, with the election amounting to a referendum on Wallace's performance as governor, Wallace obtained strong support from a statewide constituency. Three quarters of the state's 67 counties gave Mrs. Wallace a majority, and she received over 60 percent of the vote in numerous northern Alabama counties as well as southern Alabama counties. Demographically, rural counties with medium black concentrations (62 percent) and low black concentrations (60 percent)—the rural counties with white population majorities—furnished the highest Wallace vote. Black voting limited Mrs. Wallace's success in the black belt counties, yet even there she drew a heavier vote than Flowers (47 to 41 percent). The 1970 first primary, while revealing a considerable decline in the size of the Wallace vote compared to 1966, demonstrates the persistence of core Wallace support in a minority of the counties of northern Alabama.

The reelection of Wallace in 1966 supports the proposition that—other things being equal—governors who have cultivated antagonistic relationships with national administrations over civil rights have often won a measure of white support out of proportion to the success of their efforts. If spectacular exhibitions of defiance such as "standing in the schoolhouse door" seemed to focus national attention on racial discrimination and thereby increase the probability of presidential and congressional action against racial segregation, a governor's prestige was generally unaffected by these consequences. In some southern states, what has apparently counted is less the success of an attempt to prevent desegregation than the defiant act itself.[46]

Moderate Segregationists

In ten of the post-*Brown* first primaries (16 percent) the two leading candidates were both moderate segregationists. These campaigns, as with the primaries involving only strong segregationists or matching strong segregationists against moderate segregationists, occurred mainly in the years preceding federal intervention. The 1968 North Carolina primary, the only contest of this sort held after 1965, was a borderline case. Repeated appeals for law and order resulted in the classification of Robert Scott and Melville Broughton as moderate segregationists. In the general election, however, Scott ran a nonsegregationist campaign. Half of the primaries in which moderate segregationists placed first and second were completed prior to Little Rock (see Cell V of Table 29), and these campaigns generally resembled the pre-*Brown* primaries in which candidates expressed their commitment to segregation in a more or less routine manner. Two points should be mentioned about these contests. First, the victories of James Folsom in Alabama (1954) and Earl Long in Louisiana (1955-56), both by first primary majorities, represented the last major successes for moderate segregationists who were also redistributives. The combination of mildly redistributive economic policies (have-not politics) with a reluctance to engage in race baiting did not survive the intensification of the segregation controversy in the late 1950s. Second, as will become more apparent in the next chapter, the commitment of several politicians to a moderate segregationist stance was not durable. It was not uncommon for moderate segregationists in the first primary to move to a strong segregationist position once they qualified for the runoff. Both these points are illustrated by the Louisiana primaries of 1959-60.

There were five major candidates in the 1959-60 Louisiana first primary.[47] Bill Dodd and James Noe, who finished fifth and fourth, represented the Long faction;[48] deLesseps Morrison championed the "good government," anti-Long forces; Jimmie Davis ran as a middle-of-the-road, "peace and harmony" candidate; and William Rainach campaigned as a militant segregationist.

Rainach was a state senator from North Louisiana. As the candidate of the Citizens' Council, Rainach stressed his unblemished record as a foe of integration, attacked the NAACP, and denounced his opponents as weak on segregation. Louisiana needed a segregationist governor with the ability and imagination to join with other southern chief executives and persuade presidents not to enforce the *Brown* decision, but none of his rivals appeared interested in this responsibility. Morrison, he charged, was controlled by

> ... the national Democrats, and he won't stand up for Louisiana rights. Jimmie Davis won't stand up for anything, and Jimmie Noe is already on record as opposing the segregation states' rights people. I got into this race to preserve peace between the races. It's a country club radical like Morrison with the NAACP backing who will get us into racial trouble.[49]

Racial peace was predicated, of course, on black acceptance of the status quo; none of Louisiana's elementary and secondary public schools were desegregated at the time. Rainach advanced a romanticized version of post-Reconstruction southern history in which racial harmony had existed for 80 years, until the whites "went to sleep and let the NAACP and the Communist Party bring pressure on the Supreme Court." Politicians who betrayed southern principles must be removed from office. Earl Long, for example, had "deserted the white people after the big Negro vote put him in office last time" and was "through in Louisiana politics." "States rights and segregation" were Rainach's constant preoccupations, and his militant segregationist posture enabled him to finish third, out of the running but well situated, with 17 percent of the state vote, to influence events in the second primary.[50]

In the first primary, former Governor Jimmie Davis of Shreveport campaigned in the same innocuous manner that had won him the governorship in 1944.[51] Harmony and unity were the goals of the candidate who wished to befriend "all the people" and who was "not prejudiced against any political faction or group." Under his direction a "favorable climate for industry" would be established, and "prosperity engineering," said to be a Davis specialty, would return to Louisiana. Davis occasionally supplemented this open-arms approach to the electorate with declarations of support for segregation, but the segregation issue was a relatively minor theme in Davis's first primary campaign. Schools would continue to be segregated and there would be no "compromise on the issue of states' rights." No federal agency would be permitted to interfere "with the rights that the Constitution specifically reserves to Louisiana." Davis claimed to be one thousand percent for segregation. Largely ignoring his opponents and speaking in generalities about noncontroversial subjects, Davis finished second, some 65,000 votes behind Morrison but considerably ahead of Rainach.[52] Once in the second primary (see Chapter 8) Davis suddenly became a vehement defender of segregation.

Morrison faced several difficulties as a candidate for the governorship. As Catholic mayor of New Orleans and leader of the anti-Longs, Morrison had a strong political base. Yet these qualities, added to his reputation as a moderate segregationist, made him vulnerable against a single opponent, however impressive his first primary showing might be. Morrison argued that Earl Long had embarrassed the state as governor and that it was time for South Louisiana to elect a chief executive, but sectional and anti-Long arguments were secondary to his main campaign issue, economic development. Rather than attempt to redistribute further the state's limited resources, Morrison proposed to raise per capita income through industrial expansion and job creation. Toward this end he pledged to work closely with the state's oil and gas industries. To the charge that he was soft on segregation, Morrison contended that he was actually a successful segregationist. Of the major southern cities, he said, New Orleans alone had experienced "no real trouble over segregation—and more important, no appreciable mixing." "Look at Little Rock; it's had mixings and bombings," he remarked on another occasion. "Certainly we don't want to go down that road." His was a record of "peaceful segregation," a record he vigorously defended the night before the primary. Opponents had smeared him as a Communist and an integrationist, but he believed "if every city in the South and in the nation could have handled its race problem as well as New Orleans there would not be any problem."[53] Segregation was a peripheral issue for Morrison, of little interest compared to his program for economic development. Although Morrison led the first primary field with 33 percent of the vote, his unwillingness to adopt a clearly militant stand on segregation contributed to his defeat by Davis in the second primary.

Moderate Segregationists and Nonsegregationists

An additional 10 percent of the first primaries have matched moderate segregationists against nonsegregationists. Nonsegregationists and moderate segregationists won an equal number (three apiece) of these primaries (see Cells VI and VIII of Table 29), all of which were held in the Peripheral South. Moderate segregationists placed first in two elections involving incumbent governors (Texas 1958 and Arkansas 1962) and in the 1970 Arkansas primary when Orval Faubus came out of retirement to again seek the governorship. Victories were achieved by nonsegregationists in Texas, where Governor Price Daniel in 1960 conducted a borderline nonsegregationist campaign in winning his third term; in North Carolina, where the nonsegregationist in 1964 did not survive the runoff; and in Arkansas, where the moderate segregationist in 1968 was handicapped by her sex as well as by a lack of political experience. The North Carolina primary will serve as an example of this type of campaign.

Three men, representing differing racial stances, sought the 1964 Democratic nomination in North Carolina. Richardson Preyer, a federal judge from Greensboro, was the most progressive candidate, while Dan Moore, a state supreme court judge from Canton, campaigned as a middle-of-the-roader. Raleigh lawyer Beverly Lake ran as a militant segregationist. In the first primary references to segregation usually concerned the inadequacies of the 1964 Civil

Rights Bill, a measure then before Congress. No candidate supported the proposed legislation and Lake denounced it with particular vigor.

Although his efforts in 1964 were not based as exclusively on hostility to racial change as they had been in his 1960 campaign against Terry Sanford, Lake was still the leading segregationist candidate. Fiscal conservatism and opposition to Communism (expressed by defending a ban on Communist speakers at state universities) were two additional crucial issues for Lake. A politician who was proud to be "called the conservative candidate," Lake attacked the Civil Rights Bill as a "very unwise and unconstitutional" measure and promised to work for its repeal should it become law. Unlike his opponents, he would refuse as governor to "enforce any unconstitutional law of the federal government." Twenty-eight percent of the voters opted for Lake's version of conservatism, but he failed to qualify for the runoff.[54]

Moore campaigned in the first primary as a man of common sense surrounded by racial and economic extremists. Voters were urged to repudiate equally "the siren song of the liberal with his promise that government can do all and the dark mutterings of the extreme rightist who insists that yesterday is better than today and tomorrow is unthinkable." Moore frequently assailed Preyer, his stronger opponent, but he was careful not to embitter Lake by unduly harsh personal attacks. In Moore's view Preyer was too radical for North Carolina. "Rich Preyer," he asserted, "is not only backed by tremendous financial interests but he is backed by other special interests, including the high leadership of the AFL-CIO and the NAACP." Although he would enforce any law passed by Congress, Moore considered the Civil Rights Bill a "mixed bag of legalistic nonsense" and an unparalleled threat to "individual freedom." Questions of civil rights should not be decided by politicians with extremist viewpoints, he declared. "As the middle of the road candidate for governor, I will bring to this problem the calm, moderate approach."[55] When Moore finished second with 34 percent, he was in excellent position to pick up Lake's conservative following in the second primary.

Running with the support of Governor Sanford, Preyer wanted to move North Carolina "into the space age." While not as dynamic or experienced a politician as Sanford, Preyer's interests—educational improvement, economic development, and a higher minimum wage—were similar to those of the governor. He assailed Moore as the candidate of "lobbyists and special interest groups" and contended that both his opponents rejected "the North Carolina way in civil rights." It was obvious to him that a national civil rights bill was unnecessary. In contrast to his opponents, however, he refused to align himself with people "whose attitudes would only stir up trouble and result in closed schools, federal troops and violence and encouragement of the Ku Klux Klan." Throughout his campaign he contrasted North Carolina's approach to civil rights with that of the more intransigent Deep South states. "We don't want to slip back and be another Alabama or Mississippi filled with fear and disorder," he suggested. "That kind of attitude hurts industry, hurts our tourism program, and hurts our people and our State." The type of society he advocated and would try to preserve was grounded on "respect for law and order and respect for each other."[56] After leading the first primary field with 37 percent of the vote, Preyer was thoroughly defeated in the second primary when the great bulk of Lake's support went to Moore.[57]

The impact of federal intervention can be inferred from the history of the moderate segregationist versus nonsegregationist primaries. Moderate segregationists had little difficulty in defeating nonsegregationists prior to 1965. Daniel's victory in the 1960 Texas primary was scarcely a triumph of racial liberalism, for the governor merely chose to avoid the issue; and Preyer's success in the 1964 first primary in North Carolina did not extend to the runoff. In the years following the Voting Rights Act, as many politicians adapted to a new status quo on race, segregationist rhetoric generally declined and segregationist candidates experienced more difficulty in winning. The only contests of this type after 1965 occurred in Arkansas, where the moderate segregationists represented a fading tradition. Both Virginia Johnson and Faubus failed to win Democratic nominations in the post-1965 primaries.

Nonsegregationists

If major candidates for governor before the *Brown* decision and for some years after 1954 typically acknowledged their acceptance of the caste system, one of the most arresting changes that has transpired in southern electoral politics has been the rise of nonsegregationist campaigners. Of the six possible combinations of racial segregation classifications among first and second place finishers in Democratic first primaries, the most common type in the period 1954-73 was the campaign in which both of the leading candidates were nonsegregationists. Twenty-six percent of the post-*Brown* primaries were of this variety, with most of the nonsegregationist primaries occurring in the Peripheral South states and in the years following federal intervention to protect the right to vote and to enforce desegregation in schools and public accommodations (see Cell IX of Table 29). Three fifths of the contested first primaries from 1966 through 1973 matched nonsegregationists against each other, compared to less than a tenth of the primaries before 1966. While Texas (five) and Tennessee (three) witnessed more nonsegregationist primaries than other states, these primaries occurred at least once after 1965 in every southern state except Alabama and South Carolina. (The latter, it will be remembered, did not have a contested Democratic first primary in 1966 or 1970.) As an example of a nonsegregationist versus nonsegregationist campaign, consider the 1966 Tennessee primary.

The Tennessee primary between former Governor Buford Ellington and Nashville attorney John Jay Hooker, Jr., though far less publicized in 1966 than the victories of the Wallaces in Alabama and Lester Maddox in Georgia, is of considerable significance as a gubernatorial campaign in which both major candidates explicitly repudiated racial segregation. Hooker, widely identified as a Democrat with ties to Robert Kennedy, was the more liberal candidate on race and economics. A "new day," he declared in his opening address, "has dawned in Tennessee." The moment had come to cast aside "worn-out prejudices, [and] over-used and mis-used ideas." Hooker denounced Ellington as a do-nothing governor and urged that Tennessee accept more responsibility for its problems. "The philosophy of the Ellington years," in his view, "produced federal action because of state inaction," and Hooker proposed to fight for a state minimum wage, increased spending for education and mental health, and completion of the interstate highway system. None of this implied that he favored a state income tax. Hooker formulated his liberal racial views in general terms. What he envisioned for Tennessee was an affirmative attitude toward civil rights, a "rededication to the ideal that all men are created free and equal, a resolve that prejudice, racism and hatred lie in the past and in the hearts of all the forces of the past, and that equal opportunity, human dignity and full partnership are ahead of us all the way."[58]

In his own initial speech, Ellington promised the state an era of "progress and responsibility." He advocated a larger investment in education and increased efforts for industrial development, and he refused to support a payroll tax or raise the sales tax. Hooker was attacked, as he would be throughout the campaign, for advocating a minimum wage after having previously lobbied in Washington "against the little man" by seeking to exempt certain types of businesses from minimum wage legislation.[59] Ellington's statement on civil rights gives this address considerable importance, but to appreciate his position in 1966 his views on segregation in 1958 should be reviewed. By his own estimation, Ellington was no "fence-straddler" on racial segregation in the 1958 primary. "I am a segregationist," he asserted. "I am an old-fashioned segregationist. And I am unalterably opposed to the integration of our public schools." Black Tennesseans should be satisfied with "the same high standards and the same fair opportunities" that they were already enjoying. Ellington had sponsored legislation to rest desegregation policy with local school boards, and he would propose new laws to prevent desegregation if the need arose. The impact of Little Rock was evident in his pledge to "close a school in order to prevent violence or bloodshed." There was no need to explain that this maneuver was aimed less at preventing violence than at forestalling school desegregation. As the campaign ended, Ellington reaffirmed his support of segregation. "I firmly believe our Southern way of life is the best for all peoples," he said, "and I pledge to you to make every effort to insure that our Southern traditions will not be altered."[60] Eight years later the "old-fashioned segregationist" of 1958 announced that he had changed his mind concerning racial segregation:

Change is an ever constant factor in men's culture. Values change. Standards change. Convictions change. Change is the theme of social growth.

I say this by way of making a frank face-up to the matter of discrimination on account of race and color. I am sure that all Americans are agreed that the word segregation . . . based on race . . . is a term that is obsolete.

Times have changed.

Wise men change with the times.

A combination of factors in our environment shapes our views. In fact, our American heritage has been forged by such factors. So it is not surprising nor strange that many Americans . . . black and white . . . at one time accepted total racial segregation as a way of life.

That arrangement is not in keeping with our concept of human justice or the laws of the land.

And frankly and unashamedly we say to you, we no longer see black and white . . . but we see each person as an American.

Let's bury the word and practice of segregation. Let's stay in step with the times.[61]

Ellington's confession of error on segregation is without parallel among southern governors in the post-*Brown* era.

Since both candidates had taken positive stands on civil rights and were actively organizing black support, the campaign turned on nonracial issues. Hooker, younger and less well known than Ellington, used television effectively but was successfully attacked as a "fat cat lobbyist" and a "high-tax" candidate, as well as a candidate excessively influenced by out-of-state Democrats. When Hooker suggested that Tennessee might emulate "progressive" states like New York, California, and Illinois, Ellington quickly declared that he was "proud to be a Tennessean." Nor was Hooker aided by rumors that he was a "stand-in candidate" for Robert Kennedy. "My opponents can hold Mr. Bobby Kennedy's hand if they want to," Ellington remarked, but he had "no obligation to New York."[62] Ellington won with nearly 54 percent of the vote.

The increase in nonsegregationist versus nonsegregationist campaigns after the Voting Rights Act represents a considerable departure from the historical identification of southern politicians with segregationist perspectives. Should this trend persist through the 1970s, a new era in southern electoral politics would be clearly established. Nonetheless, two qualifications concerning the significance of these contests should be emphasized. First, campaigns which have matched nonsegregationists against each other have not necessarily involved explicitly liberal policy orientations on race. While some nonsegregationists have advocated liberal views on civil rights, others have simply avoided the rhetoric of segregation. In many cases the issue of segregation has essentially disappeared. Thus the 1966 Tennessee primary, although revealing as a concrete example of changed elite attitudes, is not representative of the typical nonsegregationist campaign, for the candidates' discussion of the segregation issue was unusually forthright. Second, most of the nonsegregationist primaries were won by the relatively more conservative of the two leading nonsegregationists. In two elections (Mississippi 1971 and North Carolina 1972) the racial stances of the first and second place finishers were indistinguishable. Of the 14 remaining nonsegregationist primaries, the more conservative candidates placed first in ten. These contests included primaries in Texas (1962, 1964, 1966, and 1972), Tennessee (1962 and 1966), Florida (1966 and 1970), Virginia (1969), and Georgia (1970). The more liberal politicians won four primaries (Texas 1968, Tennessee 1970, Louisiana 1971-72, and

Arkansas 1972), but the Texas and Tennessee candidates either lost the second primary (Don Yarborough in Texas) or were defeated in the general election (John Jay Hooker, Jr., in Tennessee).

Conclusions

Racial segregation was an issue of significance, a question arousing frequent discussion, in roughly three out of every four Democratic primaries in the period 1954-73. A militant stand against racial change, nevertheless, was no guarantee of success in the first primary. Slightly more first primaries were led by nonsegregationists and moderate segregationists than by strong segregationists, and the positions of both militant segregationists and moderate segregationists deteriorated over time. In the years following federal intervention (1966-73), nonsegregationists placed first in more than three quarters of the primaries.

Nearly half of the contested first primaries produced a Democratic nominee for governor, either by a majority of the vote or (far less common) by the capitulation of the second place finisher. Table 30, which cross-tabulates the campaign racial stances of winners and losers in those first primaries which settled the question of nomination, shows that moderate segregationists won a larger percentage (41) of the decisive first primaries than strong segregationists (31) or nonsegregationists (28). The data indicate that moderate segregationists and, with fewer cases, nonsegregationists were competitive when matched against candidates more committed than they to southern racial traditions. Their success, however, was less impressive

Table 30. Position on racial segregation of southern politicians who won the Democratic nomination for governor in a contested first primary, 1954-73, by racial segregation position of second place finishers ($N = 29$)

First Primary Nominees	Second Place Finishers				
	SS	MS	NS	T	%
Strong Segregationist	3	5	1	9	31
Moderate Segregationist	5	5	2	12	41
Nonsegregationist	1	1	6	8	28
Total	9	11	9	29	100

than it might seem. During the interval between the announcement of the *Brown* decision in 1954 and the use of federal troops at Little Rock to implement school desegregation in 1957, the segregation issue was less pervasive than it became after Little Rock. Four of the five moderate segregationist victories over militant segregationists were achieved prior to Little Rock, and the successful candidates were all incumbent governors of Peripheral South states. The only instance in which a moderate segregationist defeated a militant segregationist with a first primary majority in the years after Little Rock and before federal intervention was the 1962 Georgia primary, and that campaign matched a moderate segregationist who was explicitly committed to the defense of segregation against a strong segregationist who was vulnerable to charges of corruption in his previous administration. Two primaries in which nonsegregationists achieved first primary majorities against segregationists were borderline cases. In both campaigns (Texas 1960 and Louisiana 1967) the nonsegregationists were incumbent governors who faced comparatively weak opposition, and the classification of Price Daniel and John McKeithen as nonsegregationists was due far more to their avoidance of segregationist oratory than to any overt support for racial change.

8

The Democratic Second Primary

Southern primaries (Tennessee excepted) are distinguished from primaries elsewhere in the nation by the provision for a runoff between the two leading candidates in the first primary when no individual obtains a majority of the first primary vote. Students of southern politics have explained the creation of the dual primary system basically as a democratic innovation necessary to prevent minority rule. "Under one-party conditions," Key suggested, "the logic of majority decision makes the run-off primary a concomitant of the direct primary."[1] According to Cortez Ewing, "The essential reason for [the second primary's] adoption comes from the very obvious fact that, without a real party battle in the general election, public officials might be elected with the support of nothing more than a small bloc of the dominant Democratic Party membership."[2] The democratic character of the dual primary system should not be overstated, however, because historically blacks were deliberately prevented from voting. As C. Vann Woodward has emphasized, "The joker in the Southern primaries was the fact that they were *white* primaries."[3] A more important point for my purposes concerns the latent function of the second primary. If "attachment to the abstract idea of majority nomination"[4] stimulated the institutionalization of the runoff, the use of this electoral device, as contrasted to nomination by a plurality of the vote in a direct primary, served a more subtle objective as well: the protection of the region's commitment to white supremacy.[5] In the improbable event that a white candidate insufficiently reliable on racial segregation qualified for the runoff, that fact could be exploited by his opponent in the second primary. As this chapter will demonstrate, the revival of racial segregation as an explicit campaign issue after 1954 made it exceedingly difficult, particularly in the years preceding federal intervention, for moderate segregationists and (where they could be found at all) nonsegregationists to survive the second primary. In the years after 1965, however, changes in the racial composition of southern electorates and the reality of desegregation have produced an altered political environment, one in which the second primary has become less conclusively a screening device for candidates who did not campaign as militant segregationists.

A Sweep for the Militant Segregationists before Federal Intervention

While there was a rough balance of strength between the three racial segregation categories in the first primary, this pattern did not persist in the second primary. Militant segregationists were far more successful than either nonsegregationists or moderate segregationists in gubernatorial runoffs in the post-*Brown* South. Slightly more than half (53 percent) of the 32 second primary campaigns in the period 1954-73 were won by militant segregationists, an increase of 22 percentage points over the proportion of contested first primaries in which strong segregationists placed first (see Table 31). In the first primaries, it will be remembered, militant segregationists led the field in fewer elections than moderate segregationists or nonsegregationists. Moderate segregationists, although competitive in the first primary campaigns, were thoroughly routed when they participated in runoffs. They won only 9 percent of the runoffs, a decline of 24 percentage points from their performance in first primaries; and two of their three victories came against other moderate segregationists. Nonsegregationists, in contrast to the other two classifications, were equally successful in both first and second primaries. Thirty-eight percent of the runoffs were won by nonsegregationists, a gain of two percentage points over their first primary showing. Only one quarter of the nonsegregationist victories, however, were achieved against segregationist opponents.

The degree to which militant segregationists succeeded in the second primary is suggested by Table 31, which compares the racial segregation stances of first and second place finishers in first primaries which did *not* settle the Democratic nomination with the positions of winners and losers in the second primaries. Strong segregationists, who had placed first in ten of the 32 first primaries which required a runoff,

Table 31. Racial segregation position of first place finishers in contested Democratic first primaries requiring runoffs and in Democratic second primaries for governor in the South, 1954-73, by racial segregation stance of second place finishers

| First Place Finishers | Second Place Finishers | | | | | | | | | | % SPW minus % FPL |
| | First Primaries Requiring Runoffs | | | | | Second Primaries | | | | | |
	SS	MS	NS	T	%	SS	MS	NS	T	%	
Strong Segregationist	5	3	2	10	31	5	7	5	17	53	+22[a]
Moderate Segregationist	2	5	1	8	25	1	2	0	3	9	-24
Nonsegregationist	2	2	10	14	44	1	2	9	12	38	+2
Total	9	10	13	32	100	7	11	14	32	100	-

[a]Percentage point difference between percentage of second primary winners contributed by a given racial segregation category and the percentage of first primary leaders (including both candidates who received a majority in the first primary and those who led the field but did not obtain a majority) contributed by the same racial segregation classification.

won 17 of the second primaries. Their improved showing in the second primary was due to two factors. First, in several cases militant segregationists finished second in the first primary but won the second primary. Second, candidates who had run as moderate segregationists or (in one instance) as nonsegregationists in the first primary sometimes shifted to a strong segregationist position in the second primary. Militant segregationists clearly dominated the second primary campaigns in which they faced moderate segregationists or nonsegregationists. While strong segregationists established only a slight edge (5 to 4) over moderate segregationists and nonsegregationists in the first primaries which failed to produce a nomination, they almost invariably (12 to 2) defeated candidates less militant than themselves on segregation in the second primaries.

Militant segregationists in both subregions led a higher proportion of second primaries than of first primaries, but the Deep South and the Peripheral South differed enormously (see Table 32) in terms of support for strong segregationists in the second primary. In the Deep South militant segregationists won four fifths (79 percent) of the post-*Brown* second primaries, a compelling demonstration of that subregion's attachment to the racial status quo. In the Peripheral South, by contrast, strong segregationists captured no more than one third of the runoffs while nonsegregationists won half of them. Yet it should be stressed that when militant segregationists were matched in the second primary against moderate segregationists or nonsegregationists, the results were similar. Strong segregationists won each of these contests in the Deep South (6 to 0) and all but two in the Peripheral South (6 to 2). The impressive showing of the nonsegregationists in the Peripheral South was less a reflection of their ability to compete against militant segregationists than of the decline of the strong segregationist campaigner.

When the racial positions of winners and losers in the second primaries are controlled in Table 33 for the effect of federal intervention, it is evident that fundamental changes occurred in the period following passage of the 1965 Voting Rights Act. Although militant segregationists defeated moderate segregationists and nonsegregationists after (4 to 1) as well as before (8 to 1) the Voting Rights Act, militants dominated second primary campaigns only in the years preceding federal intervention. Seventy-six percent of the 1954-65 runoffs, an increase of 32 percentage points over the militants' first primary showing, were led by strong segregationists. Militants continued to have more success in second primaries than in first primaries

Table 32. Racial segregation position of winners in Democratic second primaries for governor in the Deep South and Peripheral South, 1954-73, by racial segregation stance of losers

| | Losers | | | | | | | | | | | |
| | Deep South | | | | | | Peripheral South | | | | | |
Winners	SS	MS	NS	T	%	% SPW minus % FPL	SS	MS	NS	T	%	% SPW minus % FPL
Strong Segregationist	5	4	2	11	79	+36a	0	3	3	6	33	+9
Moderate Segregationist	0	0	0	0	0	-30	1	2	0	3	17	-17
Nonsegregationist	0	0	3	3	21	-5	1	2	6	9	50	+8
Total	5	4	5	14	100	-	2	7	9	18	100	-

aPercentage point difference between percentage of second primary winners contributed by a given racial segregation category and the percentage of first primary leaders (including both candidates who received a majority in the first primary and those who led the field but did not obtain a majority) contributed by the same racial segregation classification.

Table 33. Racial segregation position of winners in Democratic second primaries for governor in the South, before and after the Voting Rights Act, by racial segregation stance of losers

	Losers											
	1954-65					% SPW minus % FPL	1966-73					% SPW minus % FPL
Winners	SS	MS	NS	T	%		SS	MS	NS	T	%	
Strong Segregationist	5	6	2	13	76	+32a	0	1	3	4	27	+18
Moderate Segregationist	1	2	0	3	18	-26	0	0	0	0	0	-14
Nonsegregationist	0	0	1	1	6	-7	1	2	8	11	73	-4
Total	6	8	3	17	100	-	1	3	11	15	100	-

aPercentage point difference between percentage of second primary winners contributed by a given racial segregation category and the percentage of first primary leaders (including both candidates who received a majority in the first primary and those who led the field but did not obtain a majority) contributed by the same racial segregation classification.

after 1965, but they won only slightly more than a quarter of the 1966-73 second primaries. In the absence of federal intervention to encourage black participation and to enforce racial desegregation, the salience of the segregation issue after 1954 operated to benefit those politicians who adopted the most uncompromising stand against racial change. The reduction of the first primary field to two candidates encouraged the more militant campaigner to emphasize the segregation issue, generally by attacking his opponent as "weak" or "ineffective" on race. In the years prior to federal intervention, strong segregationists won 100 percent of the runoffs in the Deep South (an increase of 40 percentage points over their performance in first primaries) and 56 percent of the second primaries in the Peripheral South (a gain of 23 percentage points over the first primaries).

A new and unprecedented pattern emerged after 1965. Nonsegregationists, who had won an insignificant 6 percent of the second primaries from 1954-65, were victorious in nearly three quarters of the 1966-73 runoffs. Perhaps more indicative of important change, given the ease with which the segregation issue had been raised in the past, was the fact that more than half of the second primaries matched nonsegregationists against each other. The changes that occurred after federal intervention, however, have been far more apparent in the Peripheral South than in the Deep South. Nonsegregationists won 89 percent of the Peripheral South's second primaries after 1965, but runoffs in the Deep South were divided between militant segregationists and nonsegregationists (50 percent each). In contrast to the Peripheral South, where nonsegregationists after 1965 were more successful in the second primary than in the first primary (a rise of ten percentage points), strong segregationists in the Deep South continued to have substantially greater success in the second primary (a gain of 37 points) than in the first primary. Strong segregationist appeals in second primary campaigns did not disappear in the Deep South following federal intervention, though they occurred less frequently than in the past.

The success of the militant segregationists in the pre-1965 second primaries and the rise of the nonsegregationists in the runoffs after 1965 are depicted in Figure 20, which supplies a longitudinal comparison of the racial stances of first primary nominees, candidates who placed first in first primaries which required a runoff to determine the nomination, and second primary winners. With the exception of the post-Little Rock years (1958-61), when anti-desegregation sentiment was exceptionally strong across the South, moderate segregationists

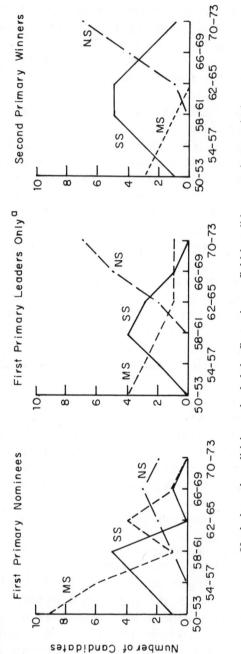

Figure 20. Comparison of racial segregation position of southern politicians who won the Democratic nomination for governor in the first primary, those who led the first primary field but failed to win a majority, and those who were nominated in the second primary, 1950-73

aIncludes only politicians who led the first primary field but did not receive a majority.

SS Strong Segregationist   MS Moderate Segregationist   NS Nonsegregationist

(1950-57, 1962-65) and nonsegregationists (1966-73) won more nominations by first primary majorities than did strong segregationists. In those first primaries which did not settle the nomination for governor, militant segregationists led the field in a greater number of campaigns during the years 1958-65, with moderate segregationists more successful in the early 1950s and nonsegregationists increasingly dominant after 1965. A comparison of the racial stance of the eventual second primary winners with that of the candidates who had led the first primaries suggests that militant segregationists were virtually assured of nomination once they qualified for the second primary. In every four-year period a larger number of strong segregationists won the second primary than led the first primary, and militants were particularly strong in the second primaries of the late 1950s and early 1960s. In the years preceding the Voting Rights Act, militant segregationists clearly controlled the second primary campaigns. The trend after 1965, however, represents a striking departure from the pattern that had previously existed. Put briefly, federal intervention in the mid-1960s helped create a political environment in which nonsegregationists could compete successfully for southern governorships. The initial impact of federal intervention on the second primary results (1966-69) was less than overwhelming, yet all but one of the second primaries of the early 1970s were won by nonsegregationists. If nonsegregationists should continue to win a large majority of the second primaries of the 1970s, one of the basic unwritten rules of southern electoral politics—raise the segregation issue in the second primary if the opposition may plausibly be attacked as weak on segregation—will have been abandoned.

The above generalizations may be illustrated by case studies of selected second primary campaigns. As in the previous chapter, special attention will be given to contests which involved pronounced differences between the candidates on segregation.

Militant Segregationists

Militant segregationists competed against each other in five second primaries (see Cell I of Table 34). These runoffs, all of which were held in Deep South states prior to federal intervention, accounted for nearly 30 percent of the second primaries between 1954 and 1965 but only 16 percent of the total number of post-*Brown* runoffs. The amount of attention paid by candidates to the segregation issue varied from campaign to campaign, yet generally each office seeker attempted to persuade the voters that he was better qualified in some way to preserve total segregation or, if the unimaginable had occurred, to limit desegregation as much as possible. The Mississippi campaign of 1963 represents this type of runoff.

Office holding has occasionally conferred advantages on particular candidates for governor. Lieutenant Governor Paul Johnson, Jr., an unsuccessful gubernatorial candidate in 1947, 1951, and 1955, significantly improved his chances for the 1963 Mississippi governorship by his efforts in the previous year to prevent James Meredith from desegregating the University of Mississippi. Substituting at one point for the absent governor, Johnson had personally confronted Meredith and refused to let him enter the campus. The incident was widely publicized, but Johnson modestly explained during the campaign that he had only done "what any red-blooded Mississippian should have done."[6] Opposed in the first primary by Charles Sullivan[7] and former Governor J. P. Coleman, Johnson campaigned as a militant segregationist determined to resist "federal encroachment upon . . . state sovereignty" and as an experienced promoter of new industry. Although he could no longer promise, as Ross Barnett had done in 1959, to maintain complete racial segregation, Johnson shared Barnett's opinions and concerns and, like Barnett, made resistance to desegregation a central theme of his campaign. According to Johnson, President John F. Kennedy was "out to put the Negro's heel on the white man's back." Because integration would undoubtedly undermine the "racial integrity of future generations," Mississippians needed to determine which gubernatorial candidate "the Kennedys," the instigators of the Ole Miss crisis, feared most. The obvious answer was Johnson, a politician who had dedicated his life to Mississippi and to the maintenance of a segregated social order. Johnson argued that his election would demonstrate to the Kennedy administration that it had not "broken the back of Southern resistance." The Negro "does not want equality," Johnson said. "He wants to dominate. He might dominate in other places; but he won't do it in Mississippi." Johnson used the possibility of legal action against him for his defiance of federal court orders at Oxford as an argument for his election. "If I go down in defeat," he warned, "they are going to take Ross Barnett and me to make an example of for the rest of the world to see—to make them sit up and take notice—and to show what will happen to those who resist federal encroachment. They know that if I had been jailed I would poke my head through the bars and announce for governor and then never have to make a speech to get elected." Total

Table 34.   Campaign racial stances of winners and losers in Democratic second primaries for governor in the South, 1954-73, by sub-region ($N = 32$)

Winners	Losers					
	Strong Segregationist		Moderate Segregationist		Nonsegregationist	
	DS	PS	DS	PS	DS	PS
Strong Segregationist	Miss 55[a] Miss 59 Miss 63 Ala 58 SC 58 I		La 59-60[ab] La 63-64[ab] Ala 62 Miss 67[a] II	Tex 54 Tex 56[b] Fla 60	Ga 66[a] Ala 70[a] III	NC 64[ab] Fla 64 Ark 66
Moderate Segregationist		NC 60 IV		Ark 54[a] Fla 54[a] V		VI
Nonsegregationist		Fla 66[ab] VII		Ark 68 Ark 70[a] VIII	Ga 70 Miss 71[a] La 71-72 IX	Tex 62 Tex 68[a] Tex 72 Va 69 Fla 70[a] NC 72

[a] Second primaries in which the candidate who placed second in the first primary won the runoff.
[b] Second primaries in which a candidate classified as a moderate segregationist or nonsegregationist in the first primary campaigned as a strong segregationist in the runoff.

segregation had ended in Mississippi, but Johnson perceived meaningful progress toward industrial development. "Our people are moving forward," he observed. "In the past few years we lost 270,000 good-for-nothing lazy Negroes and got in their place 78,000 wonderful industrious Yankees with technical know-how."[8]

Although Coleman was comparatively less militant a segregationist than Johnson, in his campaign he clearly expressed an abiding preference for segregation and tried to avoid identification with the Kennedy administration. A "big reason" for his candidacy was his fear that Mississippi might abolish public education if the "present situation" of turmoil and uncertainty persisted. Coleman frequently argued that he had a superior record in opposing desegregation. During his term as governor Mississippians "had no anxiety" over the possibility of integration, whereas Johnson "completely failed his first test at Ole Miss." There would be "no surrender and no invasion" while the state was led by the only segregationist "with any successful experience at all." Far from agreeing with Johnson that the national government and black Mississippians could "take over and control the state," Coleman suggested that more responsible leadership by elected state officials would deny Washington any "opportunity to take us over." His message, deliberately ambiguous, did imply a reversal of the Barnett-Johnson posture of perpetual defiance. "Kennedyism," the charge of his opponents, was considered an irrelevant issue. "If you really want to do something against the Kennedys," he maintained, "you will elect a governor they can't take advantage of," not a shouter who would focus national attention on Mississippi's Jim Crow traditions.[9]

By capitalizing on white resentment of the Kennedy administration, Johnson framed the segregation issue to his advantage. A repudiation of him, he insisted, amounted to an affirmation of Kennedy's civil rights program. "Let the world know you will stand up against Kennedy," he urged. Advertisements featured photographs of the Johnson-Meredith confrontation and described the lieutenant governor as a national symbol of "Mississippi's resistance to the Kennedy-dominated federal government." Against Johnson's argument that his defeat would be interpreted "an an endorsement of the invasion of this state by integrationist forces, outside agitators and demonstrators," Coleman could reply only that the nation was curious to know whether Mississippi would "defend itself in statesmanship and experience or stay in the woods of distress and defeat four more years."[10] In the first primary balloting, Johnson received

39 percent of the vote, compared to 33 percent for Coleman and 28 percent for Sullivan.

During the second primary Johnson continued to run as a militant and Coleman became more emphatic in his support of Mississippi's racial customs. At various times Coleman confessed that he had erred in voting for Kennedy in 1960, emphasized that he had always considered himself a segregationist, and pledged to fight the Kennedys as best he could. This more militant stance was accompanied by his judgment that Johnson's activities at Ole Miss "were partially responsible for giving the Federal Government an excuse" to invade Mississippi. Johnson's effectiveness as a segregationist was questioned. Newspaper advertisements for Coleman used a photograph of the lieutenant governor shaking hands with a U.S. marshal who was escorting Meredith. "When the fist came down, the hand went out, and Meredith went in!" read the caption.[11] Johnson stressed the same issues he had discussed in the first primary. "Appeasement only encourages the Kennedys and the NAACP to move in upon us," he asserted. "We can't be moderates and segregationists at the same time." Johnson denied that he had failed at Ole Miss, contended that the "southern way of life" was at stake in the runoff, and criticized Coleman as "the Judas goat who would lead Mississippi into the Kennedy corral." Attacking the Kennedys and urging Mississippians to "Stand Fast," Johnson won convincingly. He received 57 percent of the state vote and had majorities in every demographic category. In the opinion of the Democratic nominee, the results indicated that the "dark forces of federal control" had been thoroughly routed and that "constitutional, conservative government" would continue to prevail in Mississippi.[12] Johnson's victory over a former governor furnishes another illustration of the proposition that acts of defiance, apart from their effect on the maintenance of segregation, occasionally contributed to the victory of otherwise lackluster candidates. Johnson had been running for governor since 1947. In the years before federal intervention limited the use of segregationist appeals, candidates less given to spectacular public displays of intransigence generally did not defeat more extreme segregationist opponents by arguing that a calm approach to the segregation issue might be a more effective strategy to limit desegregation than a posture of unrestrained defiance.

Second primaries in which strong segregationists competed against each other were characteristically won by the more extreme candidate. With the exception of two campaigns (1955 Mississippi and 1958 South Carolina) where the racial stances of the participants were indistinguishable, these runoffs were won by the more militant (Ross Barnett and Paul Johnson in Mississippi and John Patterson in Alabama) of the two strong segregationists. Second primaries of this type have declined with the mobilization of black voters, presumably because at least one white candidate in a given runoff has found himself in no position to ignore totally that fraction of the electorate now composed of blacks.

Militant Segregationists and Moderate Segregationists

During the years which preceded federal intervention, the most common second primary was the match between a militant segregationist and a moderate segregationist. Two fifths of the runoffs between 1954 and 1965 were of this nature, and for the post-*Brown* period as a whole, strong segregationist versus moderate segregationist contests accounted for 25 percent of the second primaries. Examination of Cells II and IV of Table 34 shows that militant segregationists customarily prevailed, winning seven of the eight runoffs in which they faced moderate segregationists. Second primary campaigns in which the candidates differed on segregation furnish excellent examples of conflict situations where "the ability of one participant to gain his ends is dependent to an important degree on the choices or decisions that the other participant will make."[13] With respect to the militant segregationist-moderate segregationist runoffs, moderate segregationists operated at a serious disadvantage because their decisions on racial strategy normally carried far less weight than those of strong segregationists. When militant segregationists (or first primary moderate segregationists who were nonetheless more hostile toward racial change than their opponents) decided to isolate their rivals as undependable on segregation, defeat for the moderate segregationists commonly ensued. Neither silence on the segregation issue, warnings that outright defiance of the *Brown* decision would lead to political and economic chaos, nor praise of the South's racial traditions—the main responses of the moderate segregationists —proved to be effective against the militants' charges. Because of the opposition of white voters to desegregation, unless the moderate segregationist were an unusually talented politician or there were compensating factors, to be labeled the NAACP candidate or the bloc vote candidate ensured defeat.

Strong segregationists, on the other hand, possessed a wider range of alternatives with regard to segregation. Depending on the seriousness of the threat, a militant segregationist who led the first primary field might continue to campaign as he had in the first primary, possibly ignoring his opponent if his lead were substantial and if he could assume that his segregationist posture was established beyond question. Another line of attack, often employed in close elections, involved increasing the number of references to segregation and citing first primary returns to demonstrate that an opponent was the overwhelming choice of black voters. A third strategy, used occasionally by candidates who finished second in the first primary, was to switch from a moderate segregationist stance to a strong segregationist position. The success of these various approaches is beyond question. No militant segregationist who led the first primary field was subsequently defeated by a moderate segregationist in the runoff, and one militant segregationist (John Bell Williams in the 1967 Mississippi campaign) moved from second to first place as a result of the second primary. In two Louisiana runoffs (1959-60 and 1963-64), a change from ostensible moderation to militancy on the segregation issue was instrumental to the victories of candidates who had placed second in the first primary. To illustrate concretely the effectiveness of militant segregationist appeals in both the Peripheral South and the Deep South after the field had been narrowed to a pair of candidates, the segregation issue in four contests will be described. The 1954 Texas, 1959-60 Louisiana, and 1962 Alabama second primaries all resulted in strong segregationist victories, while the 1960 North Carolina runoff culminated in the single second primary defeat of a militant segregationist by a moderate segregationist.

Texas 1954. When Ralph Yarborough finished by fewer than 25,000 votes behind Governor Allan Shivers in the 1954 Texas first primary (see the preceding chapter for a discussion of the first primary), the Shivers forces "mustered all the racial and economic fears they could find" in order to preserve conservative control of Texas politics. Communists, Negroes, and labor unions, all negative reference groups in Texas, were portrayed as the sources of Yarborough's electoral strength through a widely distributed documentary film (and pamphlet) entitled "The Port Arthur Story."[14] In the film, which depicted in sensational terms what the Shivers faction believed to be the effects of a CIO-led strike against retail stores in a Texas city, black men were shown sharing a picket line with white women and local businessmen were quoted asserting that Communists were responsible for the strike. The Port Arthur situation, Shivers explained in campaign speeches, was nothing less than a "testing ground selected by the Communist inspired plot to paralyze Texas business and industry." "My opponent does not have to look under the bed to find the people who are sponsoring, supporting and sympathizing with· the Communist launched war against Port Arthur," Shivers claimed. "These people are right in the bed with him." Farmers in the El Paso area were warned that Yarborough would encourage the CIO to organize farm workers; and Yarborough was attacked as "subservient to the CIO-PAC and every left-wing group," the kind of radical politician who would probably appoint "one of those CIO redhots as Labor Commissioner."[15]

At a time when McCarthyism was rampant, Yarborough was unable to refute the accusation, however fanciful, that he was soft on communism. Yarborough argued that photographs of Port Arthur strikers carrying Yarborough signs were faked, but he was unable to convince a majority of voters that the election did not match loyal, God-fearing Texans against untrusted out-of-state organizations like the CIO, the NAACP, and the ADA. Class issues continued to be the basis of Yarborough's campaign. One of his newspaper advertisements declared that Yarborough was for "all the people and not just the Big Shots" and that his opponent was supported by every major business interest in the state. "The big gas pipe line companies, the big oil companies, big corporations, the big banks, the big newspapers," it was stated, "want Shivers in as Governor." As Yarborough summarized his candidacy, it was a struggle of "big money against the people."[16]

Though Shivers adopted a militant segregationist position, racial segregation was an issue of secondary importance in the runoff as it had been in the first primary. Shivers promised to retain segregated schools and quoted precinct tabulations from the first primary to bolster his contention that blacks were giving Yarborough firm support. In his view forced integration would "blight the education" of whites and blacks alike, and he believed Yarborough was losing support in East Texas because the voters were "disgusted by his double-talk on the question of mixing white and Negro children in classrooms." Predicting a crisis with the national government over school desegregation, Shivers said he would furnish "independent and fearless leadership."[17] Despite the customary rebukes to the NAACP and the appeal to racial prejudice contained in Shivers' Port Arthur literature, the governor did not appreciably increase his reliance on the segregation issue in the runoff. Yarborough, having gone on record against "forced integration," avoided the issue as much as possible and, when pressed, denounced Shivers for conducting a "hate war" against blacks. Negroes could support him despite his pro-segregation stand because he treated them fairly and believed in equal opportunity, he explained; but Shivers had no reason to anticipate black votes. "With all the abuse heaped on the Negroes by the Governor," Yarborough said, " . . . it would truly be remarkable if they supported him." Whatever Shivers might allege, Yarborough maintained that he had made no private deals with the NAACP. The effect of Shivers' "Port Arthur Story" campaign was to increase participation in the second primary by more than 100,000 voters over the first primary, the bulk of which went to Shivers.[18] Shivers' victory with 53 percent of the vote, which came before the implications of the *Brown* decision were fully apparent, suggested that the segregation issue, along with attacks on Communists and the CIO, could be used advantageously by conservative Democrats in Texas to repel a strong challenge to their control of state government by the liberal faction of the Democratic Party.

Louisiana 1959-60. If segregation were one of a cluster of issues which served to discredit Yarborough with many white voters in 1954, it was the central element in the 1959-60 Louisiana second primary.[19] Although deLesseps Morrison was a New Orleans Catholic, a considerable handicap in statewide elections in Louisiana, his reputation as a moderate segregationist was probably the most important cause of his defeat. Jimmie Davis, who had finished 65,000 votes behind Morrison by advocating harmony in the first primary, altered his strategy and began his runoff campaign by attacking the NAACP:

> As for the NAACP, I hope not one of them votes for me because I don't want their vote. I'm not a hater but there comes a time when you must stand on your principles. We know what is good for the country and we don't want someone from New York running our state.[20]

Davis announced that he intended to "lay it on the line—support the principle [total racial segregation in the public schools] we stand for down here in the South." Anticipating this line of attack, Morrison vigorously defended his record as a segregationist and charged that his opponent's sudden concern for southern traditions was a flagrant example of political expediency. "Who is Davis fooling?" Morrison asked. "Where was he before election day, and what was his stand on these issues then? You know as well as I do—he had no stand." In Morrison's opinion, segregation was an irrelevant issue because both candidates supported the racial status quo.[21]

Charges and countercharges based on the segregation issue persisted throughout the runoff. By portraying Morrison as a captive of the NAACP, Davis seized the initiative and forced Morrison to spend considerable time assuring whites that he could be trusted to preserve segregation. Morrison might pledge to maintain school segregation, accuse Davis of running an "integrated honky-tonk in California," and denounce him as a "hypocrite" for exacerbating racial tensions, but these points were less credible to numerous voters than Davis' assurances that he was "unqualifiedly for segregation" and that he would lead the state into an era of "peace, harmony and progress." Morrison replied to the charge that he had received "the Negro bloc vote" in the first primary by denying any ties to the NAACP and by accusing Davis of soliciting black support by advertising in a black newspaper. Davis ignored Morrison's charge that Davis had Negro support (a sprinkling of NAACP leaders had endorsed Davis) and refused to debate Morrison. "He could argue his case now and until judgment morning and he could never . . . sell me on the NAACP and [Teamsters President] Hoffa," Davis explained. In Louisiana's political climate, particularly outside the urban areas, Davis's straightforward appeal for white votes carried more weight than Morrison's complaint that Davis was preaching racial hatred simply because blacks had rejected him in the first primary despite the fact that Davis had spent "more money advertising for their vote in the Negro press than any other candidate."[22]

As the success of Davis's race baiting became apparent, Morrison warned workers that Davis was surrounded by vehemently anti-labor people and, borrowing from Earl Long, he criticized Davis for having written such songs of dubious taste as "Organ Grinder Blues" and "Sewing Machine Blues." The Davis campaign ended with a final appeal to elect a man who owed nothing to the NAACP or to Jimmy Hoffa and with a proposal to establish a state sovereignty commission.[23] Davis's ability to associate Morrison with the NAACP was a prime factor in his second primary victory. Morrison received a slight majority (52 percent) of the large metropolitan vote, but Davis won majorities in each of the other demographic categories. Davis' strongest vote (62 percent) came from rural parishes with high black populations, a pattern of support consistent with his militant stand against racial desegregation.

The Davis strategy, a combination of a comparatively mild stand against desegregation in the first primary followed by a militant segregationist posture in the runoff, was generally effective in the post-*Brown* decades when the first primary field also included an extreme segregationist (for example, Rainach) and a candidate relatively unconcerned with segregation (for example, Morrison). In these elections the extreme segregationist usually (for an exception, see below) failed to qualify for the second primary, and it was a simple task for the "first primary moderate" (for example, Davis) to become more vocal on race, attack the consistent moderate segregationist as the "Negro candidate," and attract the bulk of the hard core segregationist vote from the first primary. The candidates who were least sympathetic to racial change ordinarily seized the initiative in second primary campaigns by explicitly dramatizing the segregation issue, and moderate segregationists remained competitive only under exceptional circumstances.

North Carolina 1960.   Terry Sanford's victory over Beverly Lake in the 1960 North Carolina second primary provides the single example of a post-*Brown* runoff in which a moderate segregationist defeated a militant segregationist. The extremism (by North Carolina standards) of his opponent, as well as Sanford's greater craftsmanship as a politician, helps account for Sanford's win. Although he represented the liberal faction of the Democratic Party in North Carolina, Lake's "racial radicalism" prompted "the remnants of the 'progressive plutocrats' " to favor Sanford in the second primary.[24] Judged by any standards, Lake's campaign was highly eccentric. A political amateur who combined fiscal conservatism with an obsessive fear of desegregation, Lake's campaign was poorly financed and ill organized. What success he achieved was largely due to his ability to arouse Negrophobia among white voters. Sanford, by comparison, made effective personal appearances, had been organizing throughout the state for years in anticipation of the election, presented innovative policy alternatives, especially in education, and never became defensive on the segregation issue. Forced to choose between a politician who stood for social progress and segregation and a candidate who advocated economic retrenchment as well as militant opposition to racial change, a majority of the North Carolina electorate rejected the extremist.

Having led Lake in the first primary by 87,000 votes, Sanford announced at the outset of the runoff that Lake had introduced a "false issue," segregation, into the campaign. The Fayetteville lawyer said his own position was clear. "I am and have been on the solid ground of being in favor of the North Carolina approach," Sanford remarked. "No other workable solution has been suggested."[25] While

Sanford thus accepted token desegregation, he denied sympathizing with the NAACP and warned that Lake's bellicosity would actually hasten integration:

> I have been [opposed to] and will continue to oppose domination or direction by the NAACP. If Professor Lake is sincere in wanting the kind of climate which will prevent integration, he will quit fanning up the kind of bitterness which makes this kind of climate impossible. Professor Lake is bringing on integration when he stirs it up.[26]

Sanford refused to pit "race against race or group against group," preferring to outline his plans for more industry, higher farm incomes, and better educational facilities, all important components of his "positive program for progress." Unlike most moderate segregationists who faced strong segregationists, Sanford carried the fight to his opponent and attacked Lake directly. An extremist in the governor's chair would "lead to bloodshed, and integration or closed schools," he predicted. "The people of North Carolina do not want integration and we cannot afford to close the schools, but this is where the Professor would lead us." Sanford opposed "mixing the races in the schools" and argued that the basic difference between Lake and himself on integration was that "I know how to handle it, and he doesn't." Lake's speeches might amount to an unworthy appeal to "blind prejudice" against Negroes,[27] but it was difficult for Lake to denounce Sanford convincingly as soft on segregation when Sanford was explaining the segregation issue in these terms:

> Nobody likes the Supreme Court decision and nobody intends to let the NAACP dominate North Carolina, but it is not going to serve any constructive purpose to keep saying this over and over. The more we stir it up, the harder it is going to be to keep the Supreme Court out of North Carolina's affairs. The Professor's approach is leading us to closed schools or mixed schools, and we have got to stop his approach.[28]

While Sanford's position begged the question of the inevitability of increased school desegregation whatever a state's approach might be on the matter, his argument did have the tactical advantage of blaming the strong segregationist for integration yet to come.

Compared to Sanford's efforts, Lake's campaign was highly disorganized. Lake, a former law professor who resided in Raleigh, stressed two issues in his speeches. As he said in a televised debate with

Sanford, he ran primarily to oppose "the NAACP's program of complete integration and Sanford's program of spend and spend and tax and tax." When Sanford pressed him about his position on closed schools, Lake asserted that he could both prevent integration and keep the schools open, a feat to be accomplished by changing public opinion within the state against even token school desegregation. Sanford, while maintaining his opposition to school integration, attacked Lake for making a "naked and immoral appeal to race prejudice and nothing more." North Carolina could do without the "climate of hate" that Lake was encouraging. Sarcasm was used to discredit Lake. The state needed "massive intelligence" rather than "massive resistance," and Sanford suggested that Lake's election would bring "thunderclouds of court orders and lightning bolts of federal troops." Against these charges, Lake warned that Sanford's school improvement program was too expensive and would culminate in a "new day of bankruptcy" for the state. Schools would not be closed while he was governor. "What I would close," he asserted, "is the NAACP." Previously Lake had suggested that "with the power of public opinion, positively but peacefully expressed, we will drive the NAACP from our state." Precisely how public opinion would peacefully deal with the NAACP was left to the imagination.[29]

The magnitude of Sanford's victory is indicated by the fact that his 75,000 vote majority represented only a slight decline from his first primary lead. Sanford's firm commitment to the "North Carolina way" in school desegregation placed him squarely in the tradition of Luther Hodges in state politics and made him acceptable to an electorate accustomed to a relatively calm approach to token integration. Across the state Sanford won 56 percent of the vote, with his strongest support coming from the urban areas and the low black rural counties. Lake received a slight majority (52 percent) in the high black rural counties.

Alabama 1962.   The 1962 Democratic primaries in Alabama are of unusual significance.[30] They marked the decline of former Governor James Folsom, a moderate segregationist whose emphasis on have-not economic programs had made him a major figure in state politics since the mid-1940s, and the rise to power of George Wallace, a former state representative and judge whose distinctiveness lay in uniting progressive economics with an uncompromising stand against racial change. In the first primary the important candidates were Wallace, Folsom, and Ryan deGraffenried, a state senator from Tuscaloosa. Eight years after the *Brown* decision Alabama had yet to begin even token school desegregation, but lawsuits were being contested and the primary was waged in an atmosphere of increasing apprehension concerning the preservation of complete racial segregation in Alabama public schools.

Indeed, Folsom's willingness to emphasize his acceptance of segregation was itself a significant indicator of the salience of the segregation issue in 1962. Laboring under the handicap of being considered soft on the issue, Folsom referred to Negroes as "niggers" in the early stages of his campaign. Folsom complained that "a bunch of professional nigger cussers" were creating racial tension and proposed a solution to the desegregation issue based on his experience as governor. The former chief executive claimed that he had resolved an attempt to integrate the University of Alabama in 1956 by "working with nigger leaders," and he was convinced that he could again discourage the filing of school desegregation suits. At the same time, he unequivocally condemned violence and promised to stop "night floggings of our citizens." Although Folsom soon reverted to his practice of saying Negro or colored people rather than nigger, his habitual reliance upon redistributive economic programs was supplemented by an unprecedented (for Folsom) concern with the segregation issue. "I can't promise you we won't have integration," he said, "but I'll tell you one thing—Alabama will be the last state to get it."[31] If Folsom was less a hard-lining segregationist than Wallace, his comprehension of the aspirations of black Alabamians was grotesque:

> All the Negro wants from the white people [he told a rally] is leadership. All the Negro wants is separate but equal schools.
> There are three things which a Negro wants to do with his own kind. On Sunday he wants to go to a Negro church; on Monday he wants to take his kids to a Negro school; and on Saturday night, when his hair gets kinky, he wants to go honky tonkying with his own kind.
> They tell me that if any of us could be a nigger for just one Saturday night we would never want to be white folks again.[32]

Patronizing buffoonery of this sort seriously limited Folsom's ability to moderate a racial crisis of the first magnitude.

DeGraffenried, who disassociated himself from Folsom's and Wallace's have-not politics and from Wallace's defiant position on segregation, considered himself the single candidate representing "any hope of any change in politics in Alabama." While his platform stressed improvements in old-age benefits, better schools and roads, more health facilities, and the like, he declined to make specific economic pledges. Under his leadership Alabamians could expect a concerted effort to acquire new industry, but there would be "No pie in the sky, no great glorious promises, just good government." A convinced segregationist, his approach to the prevention of school desegregation differed substantially from that of Wallace. "What's the use of all this talk about segregation?" he asked. "We all agree on it. We're all for segregation." Yet shouting defiance of the federal government seemed an ineffective strategy to deGraffenried. "This loud mouth talk, instead of thinking and planning, has gotten us into a lot of trouble," he argued. DeGraffenried claimed to have a "positive plan to protect State's Rights," a plan that involved the establishment of a "State Department of State Rights," but he also believed that the segregation issue would have to be won essentially at the national level.[33]

As would be expected from a past supporter of Folsom, Wallace promised to raise state expenditures in a variety of areas, especially schools and old-age assistance. Have-not politics was secondary, however, to the candidate's militant stand on segregation. In his speeches Wallace often contended that he had "called the bluff" of the federal courts in connection with an attempt to compel him, as a state judge, to release certain voter registration records to federal officials. There was controversy over whether Wallace had obeyed the federal court orders (Federal District Judge Frank Johnson, a frequent target of Wallace, asserted that Wallace had complied but refused to elaborate on the issue), but Wallace himself had no doubts. "I would like to remind anyone who says I didn't back down the federal court," Wallace said, "that he is an integrating, race-mixing, scalawagging liar." Wallace promised to challenge the federal government personally if school desegregation were ordered in Alabama, and he asserted that his uncompromising defense of segregation was compatible with industrial development. Little Rock's experience to the contrary, Alabama could "move forward with new business and industry, and at the same time retain our Southern way of life because it is the right way." There was no need, therefore, for voters to weigh the advantages of segregation against the prospect of a partially desegregated society with better jobs and higher income.[34]

Wallace's position on racial segregation in 1962 was set forth at length in his campaign platform:

I will continue to fight for segregation because it is based on firm conviction of right, and because it serves the best interests of all our people.

I shall react vigorously to outside meddling. We shall fight in the arena of an increasingly sympathetic national public opinion. We shall fight them in the arena of our courts by interposing constitutional prerogatives of its chief executive.

I pledge to stand between you and the efforts of a "force cult" to impose on you doctrines foreign to the concepts of our constitutional government, foreign to our way of life and disruptive of the peace and tranquility of our citizens. I will face our enemies face to face, hip to hip and toe to toe and never surrender your governor's office to these 1962 carpetbaggers, scalawags and polywags. Right will prevail if we fight. We can have peace and progress in Alabama if we stand firm. There is no other way.[35]

The federal courts were attacked as "utterly irresponsible," and Wallace promised to "stand up against that crowd when I'm governor." Advertisements left the impression that Wallace had discovered a new technique to circumvent school desegregation. After claiming that Wallace had *"risked up to five years Federal Prison* by refusing to turn over records to the Civil Rights Commission in 1959," the advertisement promised that Wallace would "place himself in a position so that Federal Court Orders must be directed against *him, the governor,* rather than some lesser official." While this maneuver might appear to have no practical bearing on the ultimate enforcement of a federal court order, the Wallace forces said that their candidate would "refuse to abide by any illegal Federal Court Order . . . *as he has in the past!"* If a particular Alabama school were ordered to desegregate, Wallace commented after the first primary election, "I'm going to stand there and transfer the white children to another school."[36]

There was little interaction between the candidates in the first primary. Wallace placed first (33 percent) and led deGraffenried by 45,000 votes. Folsom was eliminated when he trailed deGraffenried by approximately 1,000 votes. A multiplicity of factors—Folsom's reputation for weakness on the segregation issue, the withdrawal of a lesser candidate whose vote was calculated to go to candidates other than Folsom, and Big Jim's peculiar performance on statewide television the night before the primary—contributed to Folsom's poor showing.[37] Wallace was stronger in rural counties than in urban counties, and his greatest support (49 percent) came from the black belt.

Once established as the front runner, Wallace had little incentive to publicize his opponent by attacking him as unreliable on segregation, although he occasionally used this argument; deGraffenried, by comparison, frequently criticized Wallace's approach to the segregation issue by asserting that defiance would be counterproductive. "This is no time for someone going around making a lot of noise and trying to stir up trouble about segregation," he said. Confident that the Alabama legislature was sufficiently ingenious to devise legal means to "preserve our traditions," he advocated a more subtle approach to the maintenance of the caste system. "We've got to get out of court, get off the front pages, stop having violence," he argued, "because every time we do [the integrationists] gain a little more." For his part, Wallace gave the law and order argument, usually advanced at this time by moderate segregationists against strong segregationists, a reverse twist by contrasting Mississippi's racial "peace" with the results—"riots and killings and sit-ins and kneel-ins"—of a "little integration" in Georgia. "I'll go by Mississippi's plan when I'm governor," he announced. Wallace continued to promise not to obey desegregation court orders as governor, and he rejected deGraffenried's idea that his position on segregation was too extreme. "To those who go about the state saying 'George Wallace's stand for segregation is too strong,' my reply is that on anything as important as segregation you are for it or you are not. And if you are for it how can you be too strong for it?" Once the situation had been defined in these terms, other implications followed. Some southern politicians who claimed to be segregationists might actually be "moderates." Even in Alabama, Wallace observed, people could be found who advocated "moderation or 'creeping integration' and that is exactly what certain people in Georgia stood for when Atlanta was integrated recently." It was perfectly clear to Wallace whom the moderates favored in the governor's race. "My stand on segregation is known to the people of Alabama," he said shortly before the election. "The moderates, the liberals and the NAACP know how I stand and my opponent is going to get their vote."[38]

Against Wallace's refusal to differentiate between means to perpetuate the accepted, uncontroversial end of segregation, deGraffenried suggested that "chaos and turmoil and threats," the essence of the Wallace approach, "would only serve to speed that which we dread most—integration of our schools." Segregation could best be preserved by acting "in a sound, sane and sensible manner like we have done up to now, by adopting sane, sound and sensible laws"; Wallace's "loud threats and dares" merely invited the ridicule of the national news media. His opponent to the contrary, deGraffenried feared that an attitude of defiance in the governor's office would cripple Alabama's efforts to win new industry. "A rabble-rousing governor can't go out and bring in new industry," he said. "Who would listen to a rabble-rouser, a preacher of chaos and turmoil. And neither can a state preserve segregation by rabble-rousing." By the final days of the campaign, deGraffenried was frequently assailing Wallace as a "loud-mouthed rabble-rouser," and on election eve he predicted, with considerable foresight, that Wallace's stand on civil rights would "destroy segregation in Alabama and bring us to wreck and ruin."[39]

Wallace won the second primary comfortably, with 56 percent of the vote. Figure 21, which maps out the evolution of the Wallace second primary vote from 1958 to 1970, indicates that the geographic center of the Wallace vote in 1962 was southern Alabama, the region with the largest concentration of blacks. While Wallace carried most of the rural counties of northern Alabama, his heaviest vote—in excess of 60 percent—was found in southern Alabama. As the most militant segregationist in the campaign, Wallace achieved a measure of voter acceptance in 1962 which had eluded him in his original 1958 campaign. In both of the 1962 primaries the Wallace vote increased steadily along a demographic continuum from large metropolitan areas to rural counties with black population majorities. Seventy-two percent of the black belt votes were cast for Wallace in the 1962 run-off, compared to 46 percent in the Birmingham and Mobile SMSAs. In the election for governor preceding the massive entry of blacks into

Figure 21. The evolution of the Wallace vote in Alabama: support for George Wallace in Democratic second primaries for governor, 1958-70

1958 Second Primary   1962 Second Primary   1970 Second Primary

Over 60%: shaded
50-59%: striped
45-49% dotted

the Alabama electorate, support for Wallace was most pronounced in the demographically traditional counties.

Wallace's victory in 1962, achieved without resort to daily attacks on deGraffenried as a pawn of the NAACP, illustrates the point that strong segregationists, particularly front runners in the first primary, have not invariably needed to intensify their opposition to desegregation in order to win runoffs. Had Wallace run second in the first primary, the situation would have been different.

Second primaries in which moderate segregationists faced strong segregationists were won almost invariably by the candidate who expressed the most unqualified opposition to racial change. These campaigns, common as they were prior to 1965, virtually disappeared in the years following federal intervention. The single example of a militant versus moderate segregationist runoff was the 1967 Mississippi second primary (see note 40 of Chapter 7), and that contest occurred while levels of school desegregation were still relatively low. As with the second primaries that matched strong segregationists against each other, runoffs involving moderate segregationists and militant segregationists diminished after 1965 because a certain degree of desegregation was achieved and because one or both of the second primary participants found it inexpedient to disregard the black vote.

Militant Segregationists and Nonsegregationists

To a large degree, the strong segregationist-moderate segregationist campaign so characteristic of the pre-Voting Rights Act runoffs was replaced after 1965 by second primaries in which militant segregationists competed against nonsegregationists. Approximately one fifth of the post-*Brown* second primaries matched strong segregationists against nonsegregationists, but four of the six runoffs of this variety (some 27 percent of the 1966-73 second primaries) were held after federal intervention. Whether they came before or after 1965, however, the results of these runoffs were similar. Nonsegregationists were defeated five out of six times, and in three cases the successful militant segregationists were campaigners who had finished second in the first primary (see Cells III and VII of Table 34). Strong segregationists enjoyed the same strategic advantages against nonsegregationists that they possessed against moderate segregationists, except that against nonsegregationists the militants generally had to assume that they could draw sufficient white support to offset the opposition of expanded black electorates after 1965. The nonsegregationists, much like the moderates who faced strong segregationists, tended to deemphasize race-oriented questions and to be defensive about their racial stances. With the exception of Robert King High of Florida, the nonsegregationists in these runoffs did not adopt explicitly liberal positions on civil rights. Consideration of the 1964 and 1966 Florida second primaries and the 1966 Georgia runoff should provide a sense of the racial views expressed in these campaigns.

Florida 1964 and 1966.   A comparison of the leading candidates' racial stances in the 1964 and 1966 Florida primaries illustrates both the impact on campaign rhetoric of the civil rights legislation of the mid-1960s and the tendency of some southern politicians to resort to segregationist attacks when all else fails. In 1964 the eventual runoff participants were two mayors, Haydon Burns of Jacksonville and Robert King High of Miami. High, who was clearly the most liberal politician to seek the Florida governorship in the 1960s, ran on a platform that attacked "special interests," advocated a state minimum wage of $1.25 per hour, and supported the Civil Rights Bill of 1964, including the public accommodations section. High promised to appoint a biracial committee to prevent "mobs in the streets and law by ax-handles," and he advocated a wholesale change in the tone of state government, an end to the political influence of "special interests that have grown too mighty while morals have sunk too low." Inadequately financed and not well known in North Florida, High relied upon large metropolitan (especially Miami) and black votes to qualify for the runoff.[40] In the first primary Burns promised a "businessman's approach" to government, strenuously opposed the Civil Rights Bill, and emphasized his ability to preserve law and order. While his references to civil rights were comparatively restrained at this stage of the campaign, he declared that Floridians should not let the Civil Rights Bill "steamroller over us." Free enterprise was said to be threatened by this "monstrous" bill, and Burns promised to utilize "every legal means" to prevent its implementation in Florida. As observers had predicted, Burns led the first primary field easily, carrying 56 of 67 counties with pluralities or better and building a lead of some 100,000 votes over High.[41]

During the runoff Burns repeatedly attacked High's position on civil rights. The public accommodations issue was an "absolutely dividing line" between the candidates, according to Burns. "He's broadly in support of this civil rights bill before the Congress and I'm diametrically opposed," Burns explained. "I think it's a clear cut issue, right down the middle." Burns described himself as the "candidate of the majority" and referred to High as the "candidate of the NAACP." High proposed to match his record as mayor of Miami against Burns' achievements in Jacksonville and argued that his opponent's "racial extremism" would "lead us down the road to economic ruin." In High's opinion, "Any man who is willing to stir up racial strife by reckless appeals to violence in order to satisfy his own ambitions is unworthy to become governor of Florida." Although he termed himself a racial moderate, High's support for the 1964 Civil Rights Bill and his willingness to discount racial considerations when appointments were made were liberal positions. "I'm not a hater," High said. "I believe a man ought to have an opportunity to improve himself, to better his economic lot, have the right to get an education and to vote." Burns asserted that he was a "moderate" rather than a "hard core segregationist." "I am not a radical or extremist on either side of this or any question," he contended, "and I will denounce anybody who so tries to characterize me." Nevertheless, Burns' efforts to increase the salience of the segregation issue were evident in his frequent attacks on High as the "NAACP candidate," in his belief that he and High were "as far apart as the North Pole and the South Pole" on the Civil Rights Bill, and in his pledge to "stop the inroads of the federal government" with respect to southern racial practices.[42]

High attempted, without appreciable success, to minimize his black support by showing that individual Negroes favored Burns. In one face to face encounter, High asserted that Burns had also received Negro support, in particular from a former president of the Ft. Lauderdale NAACP. Burns responded as follows: "What promises did you make to get their endorsement? You're certainly not a Negro. I can't see where you came to be the Negro's candidate in Florida in every Negro precinct." A newspaper poll indicated that most white voters perceived High as too liberal on civil rights, and Burns made High's alleged ties to the "sinister" NAACP a theme of his runoff campaign. North Florida audiences in particular were informed that High had requested NAACP support. "He has it," Burns said. "He is their candidate." Burns was confident that the election would demonstrate to civil rights advocates that they were "in the gross minority." High responded to these attacks by denouncing Burns as the candidate of the DuPont "financial colossus" and by warning that Burns' election would adversely affect tourism and industry.[43] Burns won a comfortable (58 percent) victory. High received a narrow majority (52 percent) of the large metropolitan vote, but Burns took 65 percent of the medium urban vote and over 70 percent of the vote in rural Florida.

Two years later High defeated Burns in a second primary despite the latter's appeals to white racial prejudice against High. The victory of a nonsegregationist over a militant segregationist in the 1966 Florida runoff did not, however, indicate public support for High's racial liberalism; it was basically the result of dissatisfaction with Burns' performance in office. Passage of the Civil Rights Act of 1964 and the Elementary and Secondary Education Act of 1965, as well as the more effective organization of the black electorate, removed such issues as public accommodations desegregation and school desegregation from consideration, and in the first primary all the major candidates— Burns, High, and Scott Kelly[44]—freely cultivated black support.

Frequently attacking Burns' ethics and predicting a "revolt of conscience and character" that would retire Burns from public life, High made "integrity in government" the principal issue of his campaign. "A vote for Haydon Burns is a vote for bossism and the iron fist in government," he charged. State expenditures were up because of Burns' "cronyism—that ancient practice of dealing with your friends." Although High spent less time discussing civil rights in 1966 than he had in 1964, he questioned the authenticity of his opponents' newly professed commitment to equal opportunities for blacks. Both Kelly and Burns had sought the governorship in 1964 "with one plank—segregation," he reminded an audience of black teachers. Burns had attacked him as the "NAACP candidate," and Kelly had pledged to "veto, veto, veto" any civil rights bills that might emerge (the danger was purely hypothetical at the time) from the Florida legislature. Blacks were encouraged by High to repudiate the candidates who had recently "deliberately exploited the race question for political advantage."[45]

Challenges to his integrity put Burns on the defensive. He accused High and Kelly of distorting his record and attempted to focus attention on public education, which he considered Florida's most important problem. In contrast to his 1964 campaigns, Burns did not run as a segregationist. It was true that blacks gave him "very little support" in 1964, but the governor attributed his unpopularity to "vicious propaganda which was nothing more than just that." "Now we've got a new ballgame," he advised black teachers. "I have been able to project the image that I have had in all my 17 years in public office." Blacks had been appointed to state offices, including a seat on the Board of Regents, and Burns predicted late in the first primary campaign that blacks would prefer him to High. The results of the first primary were generally interpreted as a repudiation of the Burns administration. The incumbent governor led the field with 35 percent of the vote, but High polled 32 percent and trailed Burns by less than 35,000 votes. A change of campaign strategy was clearly indicated for Burns, and the governor, remarking that he had "worn gloves up to now," promised a fighting second primary campaign against his "ultra-liberal" opponent.[46] Floridians had witnessed their first Democratic primary in a decade in which segregation was not an explicit issue, but in view of Burns' inability to refute convincingly attacks on his integrity, the most expedient solution to the governor's loss of public confidence appeared to lie in the revival of race-baiting appeals.

To High the first primary returns indicated that nearly two thirds of the electorate had rejected Burns. Burns interpreted the results differently. "We saw a recurrence of bloc voting Tuesday," he announced. While he solicited the vote of any individual Floridian, he would "make no appeal for bloc-vote support." Voters could opt for a home-grown, middle-of-the-road "progressive conservative" or they could select an "ultra-liberal candidate of the Boston-New York-Washington axis." Expressed with a space-age metaphor, the runoff would determine whether Florida would "hold fast to sound, safe and proven conservative fiscal and philosophical principles, or go into orbit with strange and terrifying theories of dreamers from Harvard's ivory towers." High gained the runoff, in Burns' opinion, solely because he bought the "Negro bloc vote." When asked for evidence of vote buying, Burns simply asserted that various black leaders had been paid off. "I say that High had delivered to him the Negro bloc vote," he said. "He had it in 1964. He had it again last Tuesday and if he had not had it he would not be in the second primary." Burns was confident that the public would not "accept an ultra-liberal candidate or permit a paid Negro bloc to decide the election."[47]

In his speeches High deplored the tone and substance of Burns' charges and assailed his opponent as a practitioner of "hog pen morality in politics," a wheeler-dealer who "seems to consider integrity positively un-American." High was satisfied that "even prejudice cannot save him now." Roy Wilkins and Martin Luther King, Jr., joined Robert Kennedy on Burns' list of outside meddlers who favored High. While Burns contended, "I'm not a racist," he specifically urged Floridians to "do as the people of Alabama did [in nominating Lurleen Wallace for governor]—beat down the Negro bloc vote." As the campaign drew to a close, the candidates' attacks and counterattacks became particularly vituperative. The charge that he was controlled by blacks and prominent outsiders was dismissed by High as the product of "a tortured mind in the throes of a mortal political wound." High accused Burns of reducing the campaign to "mud slinging and race baiting," while Burns warned the voters that "radical extremists are trying to take control of the state." Unable to cope with High's integrity issue, Burns was defeated by a margin of 54 to 46 percent, and High became the first Democratic nominee in recent history to win without the backing of major business lobbies, as well as the first gubernatorial nominee from Dade County.[48] Heavy urban support, especially from the large metropolitan SMSAs which gave him 60 percent of the vote, was the key to High's nomination.

High was the only nonsegregationist to defeat a strong segregationist in a post-*Brown* second primary, and even this single victory was short-lived. High's subsequent failure to win the general election strongly suggests that his success was due far less to any genuine public approval of his economic and racial liberalism than to a compelling desire to reject Burns. "During his short term Burns angered many voters by an arrogant use of his patronage powers and by influencing purchases from those who had given him campaign contributions," Manning Dauer has concluded. "By alienating some of the conservative Democrats, he lost the 1966 [second] primary to Mayor High."[49] The Burns-High second primary was reminiscent of the 1962 Griffin-Sanders campaign in Georgia. There too charges of corruption and unethical conduct during a governor's term were a major factor in the defeat of a militant segregationist. Some subjective standard of public trust must normally be met, it would appear, before even so potent an issue as that of Negro bloc voting becomes effective.

Georgia 1966. The 1966 Georgia second primary is a final example of a runoff campaign which matched a nonsegregationist against a militant segregationist.[50] Participating in the runoff were Ellis Arnall, a former governor who had earned a reputation as a reformer in the 1940s, and Lester Maddox, an Atlantan long identified with the struggle to preserve white supremacy and with other conservative causes. In the first primary Arnall stressed economic issues. Industrial development and expanded state spending, particularly in education, were the main components of his program to "Move Georgia Forward." Arnall defended the policies of the Johnson administration and the national Democratic party, but he generally avoided comment on racial issues until rioting erupted in Atlanta during the closing days of the first primary. His reaction to the riots was to denounce "black power, racial violence and insurrection." The Klan, the John Birch Society, and SNCC were "brothers under the skin," he believed. "They have one thing in common, the preachment of hate, violence and bloodshed." In his opinion "Georgia is no place for Stokely Carmichael or for SNCC."[51] Arnall led the first primary field with 29 percent of the vote.

Widely known for his pistol-waving but unsuccessful attempt to avoid desegregating his Atlanta restaurant in 1964, Maddox waged a grassroots campaign which emphasized "outspoken opposition to integration, civil rights, and the United States Supreme Court and . . . homespun fundamentalism on morals and religion."[52] His candidacy was enlivened by flippant remarks, such as his promise to autograph ax handles in the governor's mansion, and Maddox was always prepared to denounce civil rights advocates like Martin Luther King, Jr., and President Lyndon Johnson. Deportation or jail was recommended for King. When Georgia's Nobel Prize winner left the state during the campaign to lead demonstrations for open housing in Chicago, Maddox discerned a causal relationship between his campaign and King's absence. Once governor, Maddox confided, "we're going to run him out of the state for good." Johnson was advised to "change his policy that is geared for Negroes and against whites. Surely he is not so stupid as to think 180 million white Americans are not going to demand their rights." Since the public accommodations controversy had largely been settled by the Civil Rights Act of 1964, Maddox focused attention on HEW's "communistic" school desegregation guidelines and offered a simple, direct solution to this threat to Georgia's sovereignty. "When I get in the office of governor," he informed the electorate, "I'm going to throw them out or they're going to throw me in jail." In the first primary the self-proclaimed "only segregationist candidate" placed second. Maddox received some 24 percent of the vote and trailed Arnall by 45,000 votes.[53]

In the second primary Maddox continued to run a hard-lining segregationist campaign, while Arnall relied more on press releases and television appearances than on face-to-face campaigning to press his belief that Maddox was far too erratic and irresponsible to serve as governor. The central question for Arnall was whether the voters would elect a man who was able to "move the state dramatically ahead, or one who will allow our state to slip backward into stagnation and confusion." Georgians could choose either "responsible government or ax-handle government," and Arnall felt the state had experienced "too much strife, too much pistol waving and too many ax handles" to be impressed by a candidate who "advocates defiance of law." The election of Georgia's most flamboyant "preacher of fear, distrust and radical extremism" would also embarrass the state nationally by de stroying its image of moderation, an image essential for economic and social development. "We can make progress and promote prosperity," Arnall said, "as we maintain law and order in Georgia, as we condemn violence, pistol-waving, ax-handle lawlessness, fear, hate and strife." As governor, Maddox would combine extremism with incompetence; "business development would stagnate . . . , chaos and confusion would replace activity and hate would replace reason." On television Arnall exhibited pistols and ax handles and asked voters to weigh these symbols of defiance against the Georgia and United States Constitutions. Considering the background of his opponent, Arnall thought the second primary was "the most critical election ever held in the history of our state."[54]

An exponent of "states rights, free enterprise, and honesty and efficiency in government," Maddox announced that he would "stand up for the people of Georgia and say 'no' to Washington and the edicts of the federal government." If Arnall deplored Maddox's penchant for dispensing ax handles, Maddox warned whites that his opponent was a "wild Socialist who is the grandaddy of forced racial integration in the Georgia sellout, a candidate who would never raise his voice or a finger—much less an ax handle—to protect the liberty of Georgia children and all Georgians." Blacks would not have rioted in Atlanta had he been governor, because riots occur "only where we're ready to surrender, appease and compromise." The candidates exchanged accusations concerning past or present Klan support, with Arnall denying previous membership in the Klan; and Arnall issued a statement claiming that Maddox was running with SNCC's support. SNCC favored Maddox, he said, because "any creator of civil disobedience, lawlessness and violence is a direct help to SNCC in . . . perpetuat[ing] disorder for fund-raising and public attention." As in the first primary, Arnall repudiated "the theory of black power and all of the hate and defiance of the law that are inherent in it." The day before the election he reiterated his charge that Maddox interpreted law and order in terms of the "use of ax handles and pistols, violence and defiance." Although Arnall was considered a slight favorite, Maddox won the second primary by 70,000 votes (54 to 46 percent) in what the Atlanta *Constitution* described as "perhaps the most smashing political upset in Georgia's history."[55]

Maddox won by combining a landslide vote in rural Georgia, where

52 percent of the state vote was cast, with a substantial minority of the urban vote. Arnall ran successfully only in the cities. He received 57 percent of the vote in the Atlanta SMSA and 53 percent of the medium urban vote; blacks and (less heavily) upper income whites accounted for most of his urban support.[56] Outside the major urban centers Arnall was simply no competition for Maddox, who polled 64 percent of the low black rural vote and 62 percent of the high black rural vote. (Since by 1966 blacks constituted a considerably larger fraction of the total electorate in the high black than in the low black counties, it is apparent that Maddox's support among whites was greatest in the rural counties which had high black populations.) The magnitude of the Maddox vote in rural Georgia is clearly revealed in Figure 22. Eighty-six percent of the state's counties gave Maddox a majority, and in 40 percent of the counties Maddox defeated Arnall by a margin of better than two to one. As Figure 22 shows, Maddox obtained more than two thirds of the vote in a large number of southern Georgia counties and in a smaller number of counties in northern Georgia. The 22 Arnall counties included urban areas, a few high black counties where blacks were well organized, and several low black counties in extreme northern Georgia. Maddox's victory, achieved after federal intervention and in the state that many observers—extrapolating from Carl Sanders' election in 1962 against Marvin Griffin—had considered to be comparatively more progressive than other Deep

Figure 22.   Maddox country: geography of the vote for Lester Maddox in the Democratic second primary for governor in Georgia, 1966

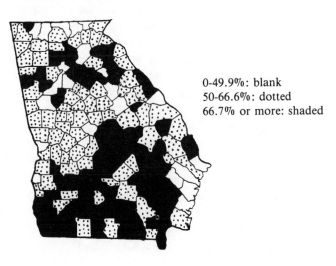

0-49.9%: blank
50-66.6%: dotted
66.7% or more: shaded

South states, illustrated both the continuing strength of the rural areas in Georgia electoral politics despite the abolition of the county unit system and, more generally, the inability of nonsegregationists to survive second primary campaigns against militant segregationists.

Although the strong segregationist versus nonsegregationist runoffs accounted for 27 percent of the post-Voting Rights Act second primaries, structural changes in southern electoral politics—principally the organization of black voters and the desegregation of schools and public accommodations—should make this type of runoff a declining phenomenon. Future runoffs between militants and nonsegregationists will probably be limited, by and large, to campaigns in which the strong segregationist established such a firm segregationist posture with whites prior to federal intervention that he could rationally expect enough white support to overcome the opposition of blacks. Among segregationist governors George Wallace best survived the reentry of blacks into southern political systems. When Wallace finished second in the 1970 first primary, for example, he intensified his efforts to increase the salience of racial cleavages, and an analysis of the 1970 Wallace votes indicates that his efforts to associate his opponent with black militants were instrumental to his victory in the second primary.[57]

Nonsegregationists

The final variety of second primary campaign which occurred fairly often in the post-*Brown* decades (see Cell IX of Table 34) was the runoff in which neither participant ran as a bona fide segregationist.[58] Although more than a quarter of the total second primaries between 1954 and 1973 matched nonsegregationists against each other, these runoffs became common only after federal intervention resolved the principle of racial desegregation and strengthened the South's black electorates. Eight of the nine nonsegregationist versus nonsegregationist runoffs were held after 1965. More of these campaigns occurred in the Peripheral South than in the Deep South, yet even a majority of the Deep South states (Georgia, Mississippi, and Louisiana) experienced second primaries in the early 1970s in which the explicit segregationist appeals so apparent in prior runoffs were absent. If it is correct to assume that the second primary functioned for decades to screen potential Democratic nominees who might be untrustworthy on the segregation issue, the spread of the nonsegregationist second primary represents a significant change in southern electoral politics. By and large, campaigns between competing nonsegregationists were characterized less by emphatic presentations of racially liberal viewpoints than by sporadic and general references to racial matters. In most cases the historic issue of racial segregation was essentially avoided, and both candidates endeavored to acquire a share of the black vote without simultaneously alienating the white electorate. The 1962 second primary in Texas is an example of this type of runoff.

In the 1962 primaries, one of the most significant sets of elections in post-*Brown* Texas politics, neither of the two most successful candidates conducted segregationist campaigns.[59] Both John Connally and Don Yarborough were making their first campaigns for the governorship, and they solicited black votes more openly and vigorously than had generally been the custom in the past. Connally, a protégé of Lyndon Johnson, resigned as Secretary of the Navy in the Kennedy administration to make the race. Backed by virtually every important segment of the state's business community, Connally was the candidate of the conservative faction of the Texas Democratic party. He disassociated himself from the more controversial programs of Kennedy's New Frontier, including Medicare and federal aid to education, and demanded a 10 percent cut in state expenditures. If he were more conservative on economic policy than the other leading candidates, he was not an unequivocal conservative in 1962.[60] Connally declined to "scream States' rights," suggesting instead that when states defaulted on their responsibilities, other levels of government would respond to demands for particular services. Improvement in education and in economic growth generally were considered the state's central problems, yet incumbent Governor Price Daniel had neither the imagination nor the qualities of leadership necessary to attack these problems. In Connally's view, Texas needed a governor who could furnish "the progressive and aggressive leadership it must have for the next two years." Though he was often criticized as a glorified errand boy for Vice-President Johnson, Connally was a sophisticated and well-organized campaigner who knew how to use the mass media effectively. He led the first primary field easily with nearly 30 percent of the vote and established a lead of roughly 110,000 votes over Yarborough.[61]

Yarborough, the representative of the liberal faction of the Texas Democrats, was the only gubernatorial candidate to embrace the New Frontier without reservations. A Houston lawyer with a revivalistic speaking style, he advocated repeal of the state's sales tax and urged voters to "make Texas first" in education and social welfare programs. Yarborough praised John F. Kennedy as a great president and argued that he was the only candidate with the courage to "curb the power of the out-of-state oil and gas monopolies."[62] Although racial justice was not a central theme of his campaign addresses, Yarborough went on record against "both public and private racial discrimination."[63] Not taken too seriously by the other candidates, he finished second with 22 percent of the state vote.

In the runoff campaign neither Connally nor Yarborough ran as segregationists. Yarborough sought the backing of white liberals, organized labor, blacks, and Mexican-Americans, while Connally, in contrast to previous candidates of the conservative Democratic faction like Allan Shivers and Price Daniel, also worked to obtain black and Mexican-American support.[64] Under these circumstances such phrases as bloc vote and NAACP candidate, the staple runoff accusations of the conservative Democrats against Ralph Yarborough in the mid-1950s, disappeared as campaign scarewords. To be sure, other ideological differences remained. As the front runner, Connally called for party unity and insisted that his opponent was controlled by radical (but nonracial) groups like the Americans for Democratic Action. Connally accused Yarborough of being anti-business and promised to be a "business booster and not a business baiter." Yarborough, unable to persuade Connally to debate him, spoke of Texas' need for new industry and more tourism, promised to repeal the sales tax, and described himself as "the only 100 per cent Kennedy New Frontiersman" in the runoff. When he charged that Connally had once lobbied for "big Eastern monopolistic gas companies," Connally retaliated with a different version of the "Eastern interests" issue. "Eastern and Northern influences are at work in this race—hard at work—and against John Connally," he claimed. "One of them—one of the ringleaders—is the ADA. That's the Americans for Democratic Action." According to Connally, the ADA was appealing to religious prejudices by telling Protestants that he was a Catholic while advising Catholics that Connally had resigned from the Kennedy administration because he was anti-Catholic. "The architect of this diabolical plan," Connally asserted, "is the left-wing ADA who stand for everything that Texas doesn't." Voters were informed that an "elite corps of henchmen" had been specially imported to Texas to implement this scheme.[65]

Yarborough dismissed Connally's accusations of support from out-of-state labor leaders as false and said that his opponent's story of religious bias was "a new low" in statewide campaigning. "His whole design," Yarborough contended, "is to bring in irrelevant and unconnected matters so that the people's eye will be taken off the real ball—that is, whether the Eastern lobbyists will continue to hold down the Texas wage scale, teachers' salaries, tourism and industrial growth." Connally emphasized his independence of special interests, especially the ADA, and attacked Yarborough as a chronic over-promiser who offered "something for nothing for everybody." References to blacks were infrequent, but Connally did tell one black audience that he favored improving educational and job opportunities for all Texans and that he repudiated politicians who would "put race against race, religion against religion, class against class." The candidate proposed to create intrastate unity by treating all groups —Anglos, Mexican-Americans, and Negroes—simply as Texans.[66] The results of the runoff were closer than most observers had anticipated. Connally's lead declined to 26,000 votes and he won the second primary by a narrow margin of 51 to 49 percent. The Connally-Yarborough second primary in 1962 was the first instance of a runoff in the post-*Brown* years in which neither candidate identified himself as a segregationist and in which both candidates actively attempted to organize support in black precincts. It is true that Connally and Yarborough did not emphasize civil rights in their speeches, but the 1962 Texas campaign was the first runoff in which the more liberal candidate was not explicitly attacked as the NAACP candidate. The sinister triumvirate so frequently invoked by the conservative Democrats during close campaigns in the 1950s—out-of-state labor bosses, the ADA, and the NAACP—was reduced by one third, presumably because of increased political participation by black Texans. The state's most liberal publication concluded from the 1962 primaries that "racism is dead in statewide Texas politics."[67]

In view of the unwavering support which white politicians have customarily given to the racial traditions of the South, the emergence of second primary campaigns in which neither candidate ran openly as a segregationist constitutes an important development in southern electoral politics. A slight majority (53 percent) of the second primaries between 1965 and 1973 involved nonsegregationists against nonsegregationists, and these runoffs were distributed among seven of the ten southern states which use the dual primary system. Compared to the virtual absence of such campaigns between 1954 and 1965, it seems apparent that the cumulative impact of various changes associated with the intervention of the national government into southern racial practices has encouraged many white office seekers to reconsider the utility of explicitly defending the caste system. As black electorates have grown and schools and public accomodations generally have been desegregated, the principle of racial segregation has been defended less and less in second primaries. If the absence of segregationist campaigning in runoff elections by either candidate is taken as an indicator of significant change in southern politics, the second primaries in the years following federal intervention comprise the first set of runoffs since the adoption of the dual primary system in which a commitment to the norm of racial segregation was not an informal requirement for serious consideration.

The magnitude of the observed changes in elite orientations toward segregation should not be overstated. As has been emphasized previously, the nonsegregationist classification is not synonymous with racial liberalism. Many of the nonsegregationists merely side-stepped the issue of segregation versus desegregation; they have been considered nonsegregationists less because they supported the civil rights of black southerners than because they chose not to identify themselves as segregationists. Indeed, while nonsegregationists no longer defended the principle of racial segregation, most of them continued to oppose changes, such as the busing of schoolchildren to achieve racial balance in the public schools, which would go beyond token or moderate levels of desegregation. Examination of the second primaries in which nonsegregationists faced each other suggests the further conclusion that the more liberal of the two nonsegregationists typically lost the election. Putting aside two runoffs (Mississippi 1971 and North Carolina 1972) in which few differences in the candidates' racial positions were discernible, the more conservative nonsegregationists won five of seven elections. Peripheral South liberals like Don Yarborough (1962, 1968) and Francis Farenthold (1972) in Texas and Henry Howell (1969) in Virginia failed to win the second primary, and in the Deep South Carl Sanders (Georgia 1970) was also defeated. Victories by the relatively more liberal nonsegregationists were achieved in Louisiana and Florida, but even here the stances of the participants were not radically dissimilar. Edwin Edwards was only marginally more liberal than J. Bennett Johnston in the 1971-72 Louisiana runoff, and Reubin Askew's reputation for racial liberalism was acquired more from his performance as governor than from his campaign rhetoric in the 1970 Florida second primary. The spread of the nonsegregationist versus nonsegregationist second primary after 1965, while representing a historic departure from the explicitly segregationist campaigns so common prior to federal intervention, was thus something less than a revolutionary change in southern electoral politics. Few of the nonsegregationists adopted genuinely liberal positions on race relations in the second primaries, and even fewer won the Democratic nomination for governor.

Conclusions

For reasons that are readily apparent and by tactics that were fairly common, militant segregationists dominated the great majority of Democratic second primaries in the first decade (roughly 1954-65) following the *Brown* decision. As long as whites comprised the bulk of the electorate and took seriously the promises of strong segregationist politicians that threatened changes in southern racial traditions could be prevented by determined white leadership, racial segregation was the region's most easily exploitable issue. The second primary campaign, moreover, provided militant segregationists with an excellent opportunity to direct the electorate's attention toward racial considerations. When the first primary field was reduced to two campaigners in the second primary, the more militant opponents of desegregation, at least those with a modicum of political experience, were able to proclaim their own satisfaction with the racial status quo while attacking their rivals as less qualified than they to preserve segregation or, worse yet, as supporters of racial change. If segregation were a volatile issue at the time of the election, extraordinary circumstances were needed to prevent a militant segregationist victory.

The most common argument employed by strong segregationists against either moderate segregationists or nonsegregationists was the charge that an opponent was weak or soft on the maintenance of the caste system, and the standard second primary indicator of such weakness was the bloc vote given by blacks in the first primary to the strong segregationist's opponent. (It will be recognized that in several Deep South states the size of the bloc vote was necessarily limited, since very few blacks were registered voters.) An examination of first primary returns in selected black precincts by the militant segregationist would invariably demonstrate that his opponent was the overwhelming favorite of the blacks, and it would follow, as night the day, that whites should therefore deliver a bloc vote—the argument was not expressed in these terms, of course—in favor of the strong segregationist candidate. Pejorative references to the bloc vote may be traced in virtually every runoff in which militants were challenged by candidates less identified with unqualified opposition to desegregation. The bloc vote charge was used with particular success by several candidates who campaigned as moderate segregationists in the first primary but adopted a strong segregationist posture in the runoff. In these second primaries (Texas 1956; Louisiana 1959-60 and 1963-64; North Carolina 1964; and Florida 1966), the "first primary moderates" usually attempted to win the support of militant segregationists who had been eliminated in the first primary by attacking their opponents as bloc vote recipients. Unless the "second primary militants" were vulnerable on nonracial grounds, as was Haydon Burns in the 1966 Florida runoff, the switchers could expect to win.

If most second primaries prior to 1965 were won by strong segregationists, the years following federal intervention (1966-73) were characterized by a significant decline in the percentage of militant segregationist victories and by the emergence of the nonsegregationist versus nonsegregationist contest as the typical form of second primary competition. Two developments in particular have apparently operated to make southern politicians less willing to campaign as unequivocal advocates of racial segregation. First, the creation of substantial black electorates, which was accomplished by the latter half of the 1960s, has made it more difficult for the average gubernatorial candidate (though not for a George Wallace) to repudiate the black vote in the traditional manner of the militant segregationist. Since the effectiveness of the bloc vote charge always rested on an assumption that the bloc vote was too small to determine the outcome, attacks on the bloc vote may be considered poor campaign strategy once black voters constitute a sufficiently large proportion of the electorate to be able to decide a close election. The second change that has contributed to a lessening of explicit segregationist rhetoric in second primaries is the desegregation of schools and public accommodations in the South. The reality of racial change has tended to shift the argument over segregation from a discussion of the principle of racial segregation to an examination of the degree to which schools (for example) should be desegregated. Inasmuch as white southern politicians in the twentieth century were never reluctant to defend the principle of the caste system, this shift in emphasis amounts to a tacit acceptance on the part of many candidates of the racial change which has occurred. As a growing number of politicians have come to see little advantage in challenging the new status quo on race relations, the result has been an avoidance of the type of segregationist rhetoric which was commonplace in the first decade or so after the *Brown* decision.

On the assumption that the *Brown* decision aroused white fears of racial change and therefore benefited in the short run those politicians who supported most strenuously the preservation of a racially segregated society, it was suggested in the previous chapter that what needed to be explained were the circumstances under which moderate segregationists defeated militant segregationists and nonsegregationists defeated segregationists. Several of the case studies have attempted to explain why particular strong segregationists or moderate segregationists were defeated, but it may be appropriate to summarize the findings of this survey of Democratic first and second primary campaigns. Attention will be limited to decisive first primaries (that is, those which produced a Democratic nominee for governor) and second primaries in which the two leading candidates were a strong segregationist and a moderate segregationist, a strong segregationist and a nonsegregationist, or a moderate segregationist and a nonsegregationist.

Strong segregationists ordinarily won the campaigns in which they faced moderate segregationists. Although the moderate segregationists appeared to be fairly competitive against militant segregationists, winning six elections while losing ten, four of the six moderate segregationist victories occurred prior to the Little Rock crisis of 1957 and thus were achieved before the segregation issue attained its greatest salience. In all these campaigns the successful moderate segregationists were running in Peripheral South rather than Deep South states, had the advantage of being incumbent governors seeking second terms, and characterized themselves as segregationists. In no more than two instances between 1957 and 1973 were moderate segregationists able to defeat militants, and in both cases the weaknesses of the strong segregationists were instrumental to the victories of the moderate segregationists. Terry Sanford faced a strong segregationist in the 1960 North Carolina second primary who was poorly organized and financed and who could be attacked (by the standards of the "North Carolina way") as an extremist on school segregation. In the 1962 Georgia first primary Carl Sanders enjoyed the considerable advantage of running against a former governor whose administration had been egregiously corrupt. Both Sanford and Sanders dismissed their opponents as too extreme on race and pledged their best efforts to preserve racial segregation.

The nonsegregationists were even less successful against the militants than were the moderate segregationists. Nonsegregationists defeated strong segregationists no more than twice in eight contests, and neither of the nonsegregationist victories could be considered impressive triumphs for racial liberalism. The defeat of Governor Haydon Burns by Robert King High in the 1966 Florida second primary was far less an expression of support for High's nonsegregationist posture than a repudiation of Burns' ethics; and High was later defeated in the general election. John McKeithen, the other nonsegregationist winner, was easily renominated for governor in the 1967 Louisiana first primary, but he encountered little serious opposition and deemphasized the segregation issue during his campaign.

Nonsegregationists were more competitive when they were matched against moderate segregationists. In these campaigns the differences between the candidates' racial stances were less explicit than in the strong segregationist versus nonsegregationist campaigns, and the nonsegregationists won slightly more elections (three of five) than they lost. Texas Governor Price Daniel, a borderline nonsegregationist in the 1960 first primary, won a third two-year term against a moderate segregationist, while Marion Crank easily defeated a woman in the 1968 Arkansas second primary. The most significant defeat of a moderate segregationist by a nonsegregationist was Dale Bumpers' victory over Orval Faubus in the 1970 Arkansas second primary. Bumpers, who was previously unknown in Arkansas politics, proved to be an elusive target for an aging politician whose organization had deteriorated and whose public record, as well as his personal life, was controversial.

To generalize from the post-*Brown* Democratic primaries, candidates who were relatively less "safe" on the segregation issue than their opponents tended to win only when one or both of the following conditions were present:

1. The strong segregationist (or moderate segregationist) in the race had conspicuous liabilities as a candidate. A reputation for corruption on the part of the strong segregationist, for example, would give the less militant opponent an advantage that might offset his rival's stronger position on segregation.
2. The nonsegregationist (or moderate segregationist) possessed a situational advantage. Incumbent governors, for example, were in a superior position to campaign against militant segregationists (or moderate segregationists) than candidates who did not hold the governorship.

These conditions did not typically prevail. It is well to recall that most of the nonsegregationist victories in the post-*Brown* South were achieved against other nonsegregationists. Three fourths of the elections won by nonsegregationists, in both the first primary and the second primary, were of this nature. In short, nonsegregationists tended to succeed not because they regularly defeated segregationist candidates, but rather because such changes as increased black voting and the desegregation of schools and public accommodations led to a general reconsideration by white politicians of the wisdom of conducting explicitly segregationist campaigns.

9

The General Election

Few generalizations about twentieth century American politics have been more obvious and more thoroughly documented than the description of the South as a "one-party region." From Key's pioneering analysis in the late 1940s down to a variety of contemporary efforts to measure interparty competition in the American states, there has been general agreement among political scientists on the accuracy of the one-party characterization and on the Deep South states as the source of one-party politics in its most unqualified form.[1] Although it is true that there has been an impressive revitalization of southern Republicanism since the mid-1960s in contests for governor, during the years covered by this study Democratic nominees more often than not regarded their Republican opponents as nuisances rather than genuine competitors.

The dominant position of southern Democrats in the post-*Brown* era as a whole is clearly apparent in Austin Ranney's classification of the 50 states according to degree of interparty competition for major state offices. Employing an index based on average support for Democratic candidates for governor, the average percentage of Democrats elected to both houses of the state legislature, and the proportion of gubernatorial and legislative terms controlled by the Democrats, Ranney found that 28 of the 39 nonsouthern states qualified as two-party states during the period 1956-70. Within the South, however, there were no two-party states. A majority of the southern states (the five states of the Deep South, Texas, and Arkansas) were classified as one-party Democratic, and the remaining four Peripheral South states ranked as modified one-party Democratic.[2] The mean Deep South score on interparty competition was .95, where

an index number of .85 or better was defined as one-party Democratic; and the Peripheral South average (.84) was narrowly within the
range (.70 to .84) established for the modified one-party Democratic
category.

By eliminating the results for state legislative seats and expanding
the time period slightly to include all elections held between 1950 and
1973, Ranney's index may be adapted to measure interparty competition solely for the southern governorship. This modified index,
while less comprehensive than the original, provides a clearer comparison of party strength for the office with which this study is concerned. Index numbers for each state have been determined by taking
the average of two variables: the average Democratic vote in general
elections from 1950 through 1973 and the percentage of general
elections won by Democrats during this period. The findings disclose a
heightened subregional division, with the Deep South states and
(barely) Texas continuing to rank as one-party Democratic, and with
Arkansas joining Tennessee, Florida, and North Carolina in the
modified one-party Democratic classification. When legislative contests are excluded and only the governorship is considered, Virginia
emerges as a two-party state. Compared to Ranney's more complex
index, the Deep South mean for gubernatorial interparty competition
(.92) decreased considerably less than did the Peripheral South mean
(.74). Peripheral South Republicans, it appears, fared relatively better
in elections for governor than in state legislative contests. In the Deep
South, with the exception of Louisiana and Alabama, Republicans
have been more or less equally unsuccessful in both legislative and
gubernatorial elections. Judged by either index, the minority status of
the Republic party in the South is manifest.[3]

Although the basic concern in this chapter, as in the two previous
chapters, is to assess the racial stances of winners and losers at a
specific juncture in the southern electoral process, the increasing
significance of the general election in southern politics first needs to be
examined. Once the status of the general election and of southern
Republican parties has been placed in comparative and historical
perspective, racial segregation as a general election issue will be considered.

Party Competition for the Southern Governorship

In a study of southern general elections published in 1956, Coleman
Ransone observed that "The formalities of the general election are

carried out on the appointed day but the results actually have been known since the victor in the Democratic primary was announced some months previously.''[4] Much has changed, particularly since the mid-1960s, to make Ransone's statement obsolete or partially obsolete. As even a casual comparison of the state chapters in Key's *Southern Politics* with those contained in Havard's *Changing Politics of the South* makes plain, in most southern states it is no longer possible to dismiss the Republican party as a hopeless minority. Key's generalization that "the Democratic primary in the South is in reality the election"[5] might be revised as follows: "The Democratic primary and, increasingly, the general election, are both significant arenas for public choice in southern politics."

To examine comparatively the development of the general election as an authentic component of electoral politics in the South and to provide insight into the strength of the Republican party within each state, Table 35 summarizes general election interest and the Republican vote for governor at three points in time: 1921-47 (a period covered in *Southern Politics* and hence useful for historical perspective on the one-party system), 1950-73 (the time encompassed by this study), and the most recent election, through 1973, for which results are available (to take into account recent changes which may be obscured by averages collected over a large number of elections). General election interest, which Key calculated to demonstrate the relative insignificance of general election voting in the one-party South, is simply the ratio (expressed as a percentage) of total participation in the general election to total turnout in the Democratic first primary.[6] Percentages of less than 100 thus indicate cases in which participation in the primary exceeded participation in the general election. For the years 1921-47, interest in the general election was lowest in the states of the Deep South. Average general election turnout as a percentage of the primary vote was lowest in South Carolina (13) and highest in Alabama (62), and the average general election interest for the Deep South states (34) indicated that approximately three times as many voters in that subregion cast ballots in the Democratic primary as participated in the general election. None of the Peripheral South states ranked as poorly in general election interest as the highest Deep South state; and Virginia, Tennessee, and North Carolina had percentages exceeding 100. The mean for the Peripheral South was 80 percentage points higher than the Deep South mean, suggesting a modest degree of respectability for

Table 35. The growth of party competition for southern governorships: general election interest and the percentage of the general election vote won by Republicans, 1921-47, 1950-73, and most recent election

Political Unit	General Election Interest[a]			Republican Gubernatorial Vote		
	1921-47 Mean	1950-73 Mean	Most Recent	1921-47 Mean	1950-73 Mean	Most Recent[b]
South Carolina[c]	13	45	76	0.1	14.6	45.6
Mississippi	18	46	102	0.4	11.3	0.0
Louisiana	28	52	96	1.1	17.1	42.8
Alabama	62	62	84	12.4	13.0	0.0
Georgia	47	68	131	0.0	14.7	40.7
Tennessee	127	92	188	33.5	17.1	52.0
Texas	69	113	155	14.3	27.6	45.0
Arkansas	72	118	131	14.1	30.6	24.6
Florida	91	136	228	21.6	35.8	43.1
North Carolina	209	208	186	33.5	42.1	51.0
Virginia	114	216	224	16.9	43.0	50.7
Deep South mean	34	55	98	2.8	14.1	25.8
Peripheral South mean	114	147	185	22.3	32.7	44.4
South mean	77	105	146	13.4	24.3	36.0

Sources: General election interest percentages for 1921-47 are taken from V. O. Key, Jr., *Southern Politics in State and Nation* (New York: Knopf, 1949), p. 409. Subregional and regional means were added by me. For the period 1950-73, general election interest is derived from data supplied by southern Secretaries of State and from figures taken from the series *America Votes: A Handbook of Contemporary American Election Statistics*, ed. and comp. Richard M. Scammon (vols. 1-2, New York: Macmillan, 1956, 1958; vols. 3-5, Pittsburgh: University of Pittsburgh Press, 1959, 1962, 1964; vols. 6-10, Washington: Congressional Quarterly, 1966, 1968, 1970, 1972, 1974). Mean Republican support is calculated from data in Paul T. David, *Party Strength in the United States, 1872-1970* (Charlottesville: University Press of Virginia, 1972); the 1972 volume of *America Votes*; and a report on the 1973 general election issued by the Virginia State Board of Elections.

[a]Following Key, general election interest is measured by calculating total participation in gubernatorial general elections as a percentage of total participation in Democratic first primaries for governor. Percentages for nine states in the "Most Recent" column are derived from elections held between 1970 and 1972. The South Carolina figure is for 1962, there being no contested Democratic primaries in 1966 or 1970; and the Virginia percentage is for 1969, because there was no Democratic primary in 1973.

[b]All percentages in this column are taken from general elections held between 1970 and 1973.

[c]States are rank ordered from lowest to highest based on mean general election interest during the years 1950-73.

general elections in the Peripheral South that was missing in the Deep South.

Data on general election interest for 1950-73 reveal substantial improvements in the status of the general election for eight southern states. No change occurred in Alabama, where the Republican resurgence of the mid-1960s was temporarily halted by the presence of George Wallace; nor did relatively greater general election participation characterize North Carolina politics, the state which had already (1921-47) achieved the region's highest degree (209) of general election interest. Tennessee was the only state in which general election interest sharply declined between 1921-47 and 1950-73. The Republican party there, which had competed fairly vigorously in the earlier period, ran candidates intermittently for the governorship (preferring instead to emphasize senatorial elections) until 1970. But if most states increased their general election participation, Table 35 also shows that subregional differences in turnout persisted. In the table the states have been ranked (lowest to highest) by their average general election interest between 1950 and 1973. The highest percentage attained in the Deep South (Georgia, 68) is considerably below the lowest percentage in the Peripheral South (Tennessee, 92), just as the Deep South mean (55) is much lower than the Peripheral South mean (147). In the 1950-73 elections, all the Peripheral South states except Tennessee had general election interest percentages in excess of 100.[7]

Because much of the expanded participation in general elections is of recent origin, figures have also been included for the last campaigns in the period. By the early 1970s even the Deep South states (mean = 98) were experiencing general election voting in excess of or equal to primary turnout. Georgia, with a sizable urban Republican vote, led the Deep South in general election interest with a percentage of 131.[8] All the Peripheral South states exhibited considerable general election interest (mean = 185). Florida and Virginia (1969 data) experienced contests in which more than twice as many voters participated in the general election as in the Democratic primary; percentages in the 180s were recorded in Tennessee and North Carolina; and ratios well in excess of 100 occurred in Texas and Arkansas. General election interest, in short, was high throughout the Peripheral South.

If general election interest has risen to unprecedented levels in most states, how vigorously have Republican candidates competed for the governorship? The second half of Table 35 compares the southern states over time and by subregion concerning the proportion of the general election vote won by Republicans.[9] Between 1921 and 1947 Republicans frequently failed to contest the governorship (particularly in South Carolina, Mississippi, Georgia, and Louisiana) or drew poorly when they did run. Only in Tennessee and North Carolina, states with a tradition of mountain Republicanism, was the average Republican vote (33.5 percent) even moderately high. Republicans in the Peripheral South received, on the average, slightly better than one fifth of the total vote, compared to an abysmal 3 percent in the Deep South. Eight states experienced average Republican gains of ten percentage points or more for the elections between 1950 and 1973. Every Deep South state except Alabama witnessed a substantial increase in the Republican component of the general election vote, but the 1921-47 Republican base in the Deep South states was so low that none of them averaged as much as 20 percent Republican support for 1950-73 elections. In the Peripheral South Republicans have challenged Democrats with considerable success. Virginia and North Carolina led the South in mean Republican support, both providing the average Republican nominee with more than two fifths of the vote. Florida Republicans averaged some 36 percent of the vote, and Arkansas and Texas supplied Republicans with more than a fourth but less than a third of the general election vote. The mean Republican vote in Tennessee, in contrast to the other Peripheral South states, declined to 17 percent. Tennessee Republicans offered only token resistance to the Clement-Ellington organization which dominated gubernatorial politics between 1952 and 1970. The average Republican vote in the Deep South (14) was well less than half the Peripheral South mean (33) for 1950-73.

Figures for the most recent Republican vote, all of which are taken from elections held between 1970 and 1973, provide a convenient supplement to the average Republican votes. The Deep South states divide into two groups. Republican candidates in South Carolina, Louisiana, and Georgia ran creditable but losing campaigns in which they all received at least 40 percent of the vote, a far cry from the typical Republican performance in the past. Yet in Mississippi and Alabama, despite obvious general election interest, the Republican party offered no candidates at all. Opposition to the Democratic nominees came rather from blacks (Charles Evers in Mississippi and John Cashin in Alabama) running as independents. While potential Republican candidates probably viewed Wallace in Alabama and Bill Waller in Mississippi as undefeatable, the reluctance of the Republican parties to field nominees is perhaps better understood as an unwillingness by the Republicans to risk splitting the white vote and possibly allowing a black campaigner to win a plurality of the vote. The extraordinary refusal of Alabama and Mississippi Republicans to contest the governorship in the early 1970s seems explicable only as an additional example of the racial conservatism of those states. By comparison with the Deep South, Peripheral South Republicans enjoyed considerable success in the early 1970s. Republicans won governorships in Tennessee, North Carolina, and (for the second consecutive time) Virginia, and they ran highly competitive races in Texas and Florida. The weak showing of the Arkansas Republicans (25 percent), however, suggests that much of the success of the Arkansas party in the late 1960s was due to the personal influence of Winthrop Rockefeller. By the end of the post-*Brown* years, then, Republicans in the Peripheral South (mean = 44) continued to outpoll their fellow Republican nominees in the Deep South (mean = 26). Several Deep South states, most notably South Carolina, have begun to give Republicans solid backing, yet Republicanism in Alabama and Mississippi has remained underdeveloped. Compared to Republican performances prior to the mid-1960s, however, it is evident that Republican candidates in a majority of southern states have earned the right to be taken seriously by the Democrats.

Table 35 reinforces a theme—the analytic importance of comparing Deep South with Peripheral South patterns—which has recurred throughout this book. The more pronounced racial traditionalism of the Deep South, grounded in the realities and myths of slavery, Civil War, Reconstruction and Redemption, Populism, and, above all, the presence of blacks in large numbers, has been reflected in the campaign racial stances assumed by Democratic candidates for governor and in the greater probability of surviving the dual primary system afforded more racially traditional campaigners. These findings, again and again disclosing sizable subregional differences in general election interest and in the size of the Republican vote, offer new illustrations of the stronger racial conservatism associated with Deep South politics. Precisely because the Republican party was linked historically to the cause of the freedman (however tangential, ineffective, or mythical that relationship may actually have been) and because the Democratic party portrayed itself as the champion of white supremacy, Republicans in the Deep South have found it more difficult than Peripheral South Republicans to win political respectability. Moreover, attaining legitimacy with white voters has often involved an absorption by Deep South Republicans of the prevailing racial stances of Deep South Democrats. While Republicans in the Peripheral South have by no means been conspicuously free of segregationist rhetoric, on the whole they have tended to adopt less traditional racial positions than the Deep South Republicans. The point to be emphasized is that the observed differences between the Deep South and the Peripheral South concerning interparty competition for the governorship are closely related to the differential impact of the racial cleavage from one subregion to another.

A Profile of Democratic and Republican Nominees

Following decades of political futility, the Republican party in most southern states has become a force to be reckoned with in elections for governor. There were no Republican victories between 1954 and 1965, but in subsequent campaigns Republicans won the governorship twice in Arkansas (1966 and 1968), twice in Virginia (1969 and 1973), and once each in Florida (1966), Tennessee (1970), and North Carolina (1972).[10] Yet despite these successes, the most common type of general election in the post-*Brown* decades was the contest in which the victory of the Democratic nominee was a foregone conclusion, an inevitability accepted by Republicans as well as by Democrats. In several elections no Republican appeared on the ballot, while in others the vote given the Republican candidate was nominal. According to criteria to be introduced shortly, approximately three fifths of the general elections waged between 1954 and 1973 were not serious campaigns.

Consequently, any examination of campaign stances on racial segregation in general elections must first determine which general elections merit study, a question involving practical considerations as well as the specification of criteria to distinguish competitive from noncompetitive contests. Until recently satisfactory newspaper accounts of general elections have been more difficult to obtain than of primaries. Sensing certain victory once they won the Democratic nomination, many Democrats have sharply curtailed their public appearances during the general election campaign. Republicans, often relatively obscure political figures, have often been given only sporadic coverage by the news media. Hence the classification of some candidates is rendered highly problematic because of the typically superficial reporting of general elections which prevailed throughout the 1950s and extended well into the 1960s. Even if occasional general elections assume more importance in retrospect than observers had anticipated, they may be difficult to trace in state newspapers.

Two criteria have been employed to narrow the discussion of general elections to those campaigns that were vigorously contested.

First, all general elections were identified in which the Republican candidate won a minimum of 33.3 percent of the total vote. Application of this standard reduced the number of post-*Brown* general elections from 66 to 29. Second, those general elections were eliminated in which, despite a Republican vote of one third or more, relatively little serious campaigning occurred. In four cases a judgment was made that the Republicans conducted token campaigns and were not taken seriously by either their Democratic opponents or the press.[11] These elections were dropped, leaving a total of 25 highly contested general elections. Finally, the 1970 Arkansas general election, in which the Republican candidate received 32.4 percent of the vote, was counted as a competitive race because the Republican was an incumbent governor.

Analyses of campaign stances thus far have necessarily ignored similarities and differences between Republicans and Democrats. Now that 26 competitive general elections have been isolated, it is possible to determine whether or not Republicans have differed appreciably from Democrats on racial segregation and economic development, and whether differences between the political parties have been of greater or lesser magnitude than differences between Deep South and Peripheral South candidates, irrespective of their party affiliation. Table 36 displays the percentage distribution of campaign stances on both policy dimensions by party, subregion, and region. Before inspecting the findings, several limitations of the available data should be made explicit. Since most of the competitive general elections (69 percent) were contested after federal intervention, the results are likely to reveal higher percentages of innovative campaign stances, especially on the racial dimension, than would be the case if a larger number of competitive general elections had occurred prior to 1966. The figures are biased in favor of less traditional campaign orientations in a second way. Approximately two fifths of the possible general elections are represented, but the elections are heavily skewed toward Peripheral South campaigns. Nearly half (46 percent) of the Peripheral South general elections are included, compared to 28 percent of the Deep South elections. All in all, 73 percent of the competitive general elections were held in the Peripheral South states. It should also be kept in mind that the Deep South results rest on a small number of cases and that the addition of a few more elections could alter the findings considerably. These qualifications notwithstanding, a sufficiently large body of campaigns exists to permit a sketch of Republican and Democratic policy views.

Table 36. Campaign stances on racial segregation and achievement of economic development of participants in selected general elections for governor in the South, 1954-73, by party, subregion, and region (percent)

Campaign Stance	Deep South			Peripheral South			South		
	Rep	Dem	Total	Rep	Dem	Total	Rep	Dem	Total
Strong Segregationist	43	29	36	5	11	8	15	15	15
SS-Marginalist	43	0	21	0	5	3	12	4	8
SS-Redistributive	0	0	0	0	5	3	0	4	2
SS-Adaptive	0	14	7	5	0	3	4	4	4
SS-Progressive	0	14	7	0	0	0	0	4	2
Moderate Segregationist	29	29	29	42	16	29	38	19	29
MS-Marginalist	0	0	0	32	5	18	23	4	13
MS-Redistributive	0	0	0	0	5	3	0	4	2
MS-Adaptive	29	29	29	11	5	8	15	12	13
MS-Progressive	0	0	0	0	0	0	0	0	0
Nonsegregationist	29	43	36	53	74	63	46	65	56
NS-Marginalist	14	0	7	11	5	8	12	4	8
NS-Redistributive	0	0	0	0	0	0	0	0	0
NS-Adaptive	14	29	21	42	53	47	35	46	40
NS-Progressive	0	14	7	0	16	8	0	15	8
Totals	100	100	100	100	100	100	100	100	100
Number of Cases	(7)	(7)	(14)	(19)	(19)	(38)	(26)	(26)	(52)

The data presented in Table 36 generally support the proposition that the relationship between party and subregion in southern politics varies according to issue. Stated in bald form, party affiliation (irrespective of subregion) divided the gubernatorial candidates less on racial segregation than did subregion (disregarding party), whereas the converse was true when economic development orientations were analyzed. Considerably higher percentages of Republicans and Democrats in the Deep South adopted militant segregationist stances than did either Republicans or Democrats in the Peripheral South. Nonsegregationists comprised majorities in both the Peripheral South parties (though far more heavily among Democrats) but represented less than half of the Democrats and Republicans in the Deep South. Deep South Republicans, with 43 percent classified as strong segregationists, were the most racially conservative candidates in the general elections. Their racial stances contrasted most strikingly with those of the Peripheral South Democrats, 74 percent of whom ran nonsegregationist campaigns. A moderate segregationist posture was disproportionately found (42 percent) among Peripheral South Republicans. These findings are an illustration of the general argument that American political parties tend to reflect local values and traditions. Seeking office in a highly traditional racial environment, Republicans in the Deep South had more in common on the segregation issue with their Deep South Democratic opponents than they did with Peripheral South Republicans.

In view of the Deep South's heritage of racial conservatism, the results summarized above are hardly surprising. Because the Deep South has never been clearly and unambiguously differentiated from the Peripheral South along economic lines, sharper cleavages on economic development might be anticipated between Republicans and Democrats than between the subregions. Findings contained in Table 36 bear out this expectation. In all four economic development categories, the differences between Democrats and Republicans (whatever their subregion) exceed the differences between subregions (ignoring party affiliation). Republicans, and especially Deep South Republicans, campaigned far more often as marginalists (47 percent), the most traditional economic development category, than did Democrats (12 percent). Moreover, none of the southern Republicans campaigned as redistributives or progressives, thus leaving to a small minority of Democrats the articulation and championship of have-not economic issues. Adaptives constituted majorities in every group except for the Deep South Republicans, but they were more common among Democrats (62 percent) than among Republicans (54 percent). Unlike the other three categories, equal percentages of adaptives (58) were found amond Republicans and Democrats in the Peripheral South.

For the South as a whole the modal participant in a competitive general election was the nonsegregationist and adaptive (40 percent), a combination which has been interpreted as relatively innovative by southern standards. Unidentified with the principle of racial segregation and willing to support additional investment in public education to further economic development, this type of candidate included more Democrats (46 percent) and more Republicans (35 percent) than any other possible combination of racial and economic development stances. Closer examination, however, reveals important subregional differences. Nonsegregationist-adaptives were far less prevalent among Republicans (14 percent) and Democrats (29 percent) in the Deep South than among Republicans (42 percent) and Democrats (53 percent) in the Peripheral South. At the other end of the continuum, the least innovative combination—the strong segregationist and marginalist—included a sizable fraction of total candidates only among Deep South Republicans (43 percent). These candidates, who objected strongly to racial change and were unenthusiastic about increased expenditures for public education, generally viewed themselves as Barry Goldwater conservatives. Among Peripheral South Republicans the strong segregationist-marginalist combination did not appear. The Goldwater tradition there assumed a milder form, most frequently appearing in the fusion of a moderate segregationist stance with marginalist economic views (32 percent); and it was less pervasive than the nonsegregationist-adaptive orientations of Republicans like Linwood Holton of Virginia and James Holshouser of North Carolina.

A more systematic analysis, using indexes of dissimilarity, reinforces the importance of subregion in differentiating campaign racial stances and of party in distinguishing economic development positions. The index of dissimilarity varies from 0 (complete similarity between two groups being compared) to 100 (total dissimilarity). Here it may be interpreted as the minimum percentage of candidates in one group (such as all Republicans) who would need to shift their campaign stance on a particular policy dimension in order to match the percentage distribution of campaign stances within a second group (such as all Democrats).[12] When indexes of dissimilarity are calculated for a series of comparisons (see Table 37), variations by issue in the

Table 37. Indexes of dissimilarity for racial segregation and economic development categories in selected general elections for governor in the South, 1954-73, by party and subregion

Type of Comparison	Index of Dissimilarity for Racial Segregation	Index of Dissimilarity for Economic Development
Inclusive comparisons		
Party: Republicans with Democrats	19	35
Subregion: Deep South with Peripheral South	28	6
Comparisons between subregions		
Deep South Republicans with Peripheral South Republicans	38	15
Deep South Republicans with Peripheral South Democrats	45	41
Deep South Democrats with Peripheral South Democrats	31	27
Deep South Democrats with Peripheral South Republicans	24	42
Comparisons within subregions		
Deep South: Republicans with Democrats	14	57
Peripheral South: Republicans with Democrats	26	26

relationship between party and subregion are delineated rather forcefully. The most inclusive comparisons, those which contrast all southern Republicans with all southern Democrats and all Deep South candidates with all Peripheral South candidates, reveal substantial differences from one issue to the next. Party dissimilarity on racial segregation (19) was less pronounced than subregional dissimilarity (28). The opposite situation prevailed for economic development, where the subregions were quite similar (6) but the parties were fairly dissimilar (35). With the single exception of the comparison between Deep South Democrats and Peripheral South Republicans, there were greater dissimilarities on segregation when Republicans and Democrats were compared across subregions than when Republicans were compared to Democrats within the same subregion. The greatest dissimilarity of all on racial segregation occurred when Deep South Republicans were matched against Peripheral South Democrats (45), while the least dissimilarity involved a comparison of Deep South Republicans with Deep South Democrats (14). The latter finding is entirely consistent with the Deep South's history of racial traditionalism.

When economic development is considered, however, the role of the subregion in structuring campaign stances is diminished. The absence of redistributive or progressive rhetoric among business-minded southern Republicans and their greater affinity for marginalist positions make party affiliation a more sensitive variable than subregion in distinguishing economic development stances. Comparisons between subregions disclose larger dissimilarities between Republicans and Democrats than between Democrats (or Republicans) in one subregion and Democrats (or Republicans) in the other subregion. Deep South Republicans, for example, had much more in common with Peripheral South Republicans (15) than with Peripheral South Democrats (41). In contrast to the similarity which they exhibited on segregation, Republicans and Democrats in the Deep South were more dissimilar on economic development (57) than any other comparison in Table 37. To restate the findings, dissimilarities were rooted in party when the issue was the achievement of economic development; on the racial dimension, candidates irrespective of their political party tended to adopt stances that reflected long-standing subregional differences concerning the salience and disposition of racial conflict.

General Election Winners

Compared to the outcomes of the Democratic primaries, the

winners of competitive general elections campaigned far less often as strong segregationists. Moderate segregationists were victorious 31 percent of the time, but fewer than a tenth of the general elections were won by militant segregationists. Nonsegregationists placed first in slightly more than three fifths of the campaigns. The unusually low percentage of strong segregationist victories represented, moreover, a decline of 15 percentage points for that category compared to the racial stances which the Democratic nominees had assumed in the primaries. Moderate segregationists were relatively more successful in the general elections than in the Democratic primaries; no net change occurred in the success of the nonsegregationists. In line with expectations, the racial stances of the winners varied according to subregion. More than half (57 percent) of the successful candidates in the Deep South were classified as segregationists, though even here moderate segregationists were much more common than strong segregationists. Nonsegregationists, by comparison, captured two thirds of the Peripheral South campaigns (see Table 38).

The location and timing of the competitive general elections account in part for the poor showing of the strong segregationists. Most of the general elections which met the criteria established for competitive races occurred after 1965 in the Peripheral South. Peripheral South electorates could be expected to be less supportive of militant segregationists, and actions taken by the national government in the mid-1960s to change southern racial traditions generally reduced, though they did not eliminate, the advantages previously associated with an aggressive defense of segregation. But additional factors are required to explain why the general election did not become, in effect, a second runoff campaign, an election in which racially conservative Democratic voters could join Republicans in defeating any Democratic nominee (or vice versa) considered weak on segregation.

Perhaps the most significant reason why strong segregationists failed to dominate general elections is that the campaign racial stances of Republicans and Democrats have been fairly similar. Republican nominees, especially in the Peripheral South, have not constituted a monolithic segregationist bloc, waiting for an opportunity to assail nonsegregationist Democrats. Indeed, slightly larger percentages of successful Republicans than Democrats ran as nonsegregationists, and victorious Republicans were far more often nonsegregationists than segregationists (see Table 39). Linwood Holton of Virginia and Winthrop Rockefeller of Arkansas, for example, were more progressive

Table 38. Campaign racial stances of winners in competitive general elections for governor in the South, 1954-73, by subregion and region (percent)

Campaign Stance	Deep South		Peripheral South		South	
	Winners	Net Change[a]	Winners	Net Change	Winners	Net Change
Strong Segregationist	14	-29	5	-11	8	-15
Moderate Segregationist	43	+29	26	+10	31	+16
Nonsegregationist	43	0	68	0	62	0
Total	100		100		100	
Number of Cases	(7)		(19)		(26)	

[a]Net change represents the percentage point difference between the proportion of general election winners holding a particular position on racial segregation and the percentage of Democratic nominees (considering only those Democratic nominees who subsequently took part in a competitive general election) adopting the same position. Democratic nominees who faced no primary competition (South Carolina, 1966 and 1970; Texas, 1970; and Virginia, 1965 and 1973, counting Henry Howell as a Democrat) were assigned their general election stances for purposes of this analysis.

Table 39. Campaign racial stances of Republican and Democratic winners in competitive general elections for governor in the South, 1954-73, by subregion and region (percent)

Campaign Stance	Deep South		Peripheral South		South	
	Republican	Democrat	Republican	Democrat	Republican	Democrat
Strong Segregationist	0	17	0	8	0	11
Moderate Segregationist	100a	33	29	25	38	28
Nonsegregationist	0	50	71	67	63	61
Total	100	100	100	100	100	100
Number of Cases	(1)	(6)	(7)	(12)	(8)	(18)
Percentage of Elections Won	14	86	37	63	31	69

aThe Republican victor in this case (Howard Callaway in the 1966 Georgia general election) did not receive a majority of the state vote and was subsequently defeated by the Democratic nominee when the state legislature met to decide the governorship.

on civil rights than most of the Democrats who were elected governor. In those campaigns (mainly in the Deep South) where Republican candidates did appeal to racial prejudice against Democrats, the Democrats often took advantage of their party label and appealed for support on grounds of party loyalty. The party loyalty argument, which could not be raised during the Democratic primaries, thus on occasion presumably operated to weaken the salience of the segregation issue among many whites who had traditionally supported nominees of the Democratic party. Another factor which contributed to the lack of strength for militants relates to campaign strategy. A small number of Democrats, having themselves waged strong segregationist campaigns in order to win the Democratic nomination, switched to a moderate segregationist posture in the general election in the hope of uniting Democrats (including blacks who might view the Democrat as the lesser of evils) against the Republicans.

Patterns of Conflict

With this overview of competitive general elections, the inquiry moves next to an exposition of selected campaigns. My objectives in describing particular elections are to convey the language which southern politicians have used to address racial questions and to identify the circumstances under which candidates who adopted less traditional racial stances (that is, nonsegregationists and, in some cases, moderate segregationists) survived the southern electoral process. Table 40 classifies the racial positions of winners and losers in competitive general elections from 1954 through 1973, with Democratic and Republican victories also distinguished. All the six possible combinations of segregation categories which might be present in any given campaign will be considered, though some will be discussed more fully than others.

Strong segregationists only. Competitive general elections in which both the Republican and Democratic nominees ran as militant segregationists were rare, largely because of the Republican party's weakness in the Deep South and because Peripheral South candidates (whether Republican or Democratic) ordinarily could not afford to write off the black electorate by assuming militant stances. In all but one of the 26 competitive general elections, at least one of the two major party candidates was either a moderate segregationist or a nonsegregationist. Yet if the 1963 Mississippi general election between Democrat Paul Johnson, Jr., and Republican Rubel Phillips was a

Table 40. Campaign racial stances of winners and losers in selected general elections for governor in the South, 1954-73, by sub-region and party (N = 26)

Winners	Losers					
	Strong Segregationist		Moderate Segregationist		Nonsegregationist	
	DS	PS	DS	PS	DS	PS
Strong Segregationist	Miss 63			Va 57		
	I		II		III	
Moderate Segregationist	*Ga 66*ab SC 66	*Ark 66* NC 68d	La 64c	NC 60 NC 64c		Ark 64 *Fla 66* *Va 73*
	IV		V		VI	
Nonsegregationist	SC 70			Tex 62 Tex 72 Fla 70	Ga 70 La 72	Va 65 *Va 69* Ark 68 Ark 70 Tex 68 Tex 70 *Tenn 70* *NC 72*
	VII		VIII		IX	

aItalicized elections indicate Republican victories.

bThe Republican candidate, Howard Callaway, received more votes than the Democratic nominee, Lester Maddox. Callaway did not obtain a majority, however; and the state legislature, as it was empowered to do under Georgia law, subsequently elected Maddox governor.

cGeneral elections in which the Democratic nominee campaigned as a moderate segregationist in the general election but as a strong segregationist in the second primary.

dA general election in which the Democratic nominee campaigned as a nonsegregationist in the general election but as a moderate segregationist in the first primary.

deviant case, it is nonetheless instructive as an illustration of why national intervention was required in the Deep South to make the right to vote a reality for blacks. The shock of a Democratic President ordering federal marshals to desegregate the University of Mississippi in the fall of 1962 stimulated an extraordinary debate among the state's white political elite over the organization of political conflict. Republican and Democratic politicians disagreed strenuously over the implications of a two-party system as compared to a one-party system for the maintenance of white supremacy. Democrats generally accepted the argument that the creation of a second party would lead to campaigns in which one or both of the parties, seeking additional votes, would favor an expansion of the black electorate. Republicans, however, rejected the proposition that two-party politics would inevitably culminate in the mobilization of nonvoting blacks and instead contended that a second party was needed to protect the interests of Mississippi's white majority. In the course of the 1963 general election campaign the goal of both the Democratic and Republican parties—continued white domination of Mississippi politics—was expressed with exceptional clarity.

A Republican only since early in 1963, Phillips considered himself a Goldwater conservative. His posters carried the message "K.O. the Kennedys," and his hostility to racial change was emphatic. "I was born a segregationist," he announced, "I am for segregation today and I will be for segregation when I die."[13] In his opinion the Ole Miss crisis demonstrated the inadequacies of the one-party system and the necessity of devising a two-party system to defend white Mississippians against racial desegregation. The Republican candidate explained the relationship between party organization and white supremacy as follows:

The one-party system to which Mississippi has been shackled for these many years has failed miserably in preserving our customs and traditions and segregated way of life. The one-party system to which [the Democrats] adhere so strongly gave us John and Bobby Kennedy and the integration of our state university.

Mississippi, under a two-party system, would have a much better chance of maintaining segregation because each party would act as a watch dog over the other. The first party that gave the pro-segregationist [integrationist?] minority bloc any encouragement in an effort to win votes, would be immediately exposed by the other.

I would like to point out that the Democratic party is overwhelmingly the party of the Negro and has been for a number of years. We have strong evidence that the Negro vote in Mississippi has made deals with Democratic candidates in Democratic primaries in the past. This is the sort of thing we would like to do away with.[14]

The fiasco at Ole Miss had shown that the national Democratic party was unable or unwilling to protect Mississippi's racial mores; closer to home, Phillips doubted the authenticity of the Democratic nominee's commitment to segregation. To support his contention that Johnson's history "branded him as an integrationist," Phillips quoted from a 1954 speech in which Johnson suggested that the South had "brought [the *Brown* decision] on ourselves" and accused Johnson of having "made deals for the Negro vote during his three previous gubernatorial races." More embarrassing for the lieutenant governor was Phillips' charge that Johnson had participated in private negotiations with Governor Ross Barnett and Attorney General Robert Kennedy to admit James Meredith to the University of Mississippi after a pro forma display of resistance by Mississippi authorities. "While my opponent was bragging about how he had stood tall," Phillips said, "he had already made a secret agreement with Bobby Kennedy . . . It was a fraud and a disgrace, and he didn't have the courage to tell the people about it." As Phillips summarized the private diplomacy of the Ole Miss crisis, "Johnson and Kennedy played a game of cowboys and niggers to conceal the true facts from the people."[15]

The Democratic candidate, on the other hand, viewed the election of a Republican governor as a catastrophe which "would set this state back 20 years and would please the Kennedys, the left wing liberals of both parties and black racists." Johnson repudiated both national parties and ridiculed Phillips' assertion that blacks belonged in the Democratic party. "I have no use for either of the national parties and the puny leadership they offer," he told a Citizens' Council meeting. "The Republican Party is the true home of the Negro minority groups." Should he be elected, Johnson promised to "stand firm to uphold states' rights and racial integrity and oppose federal encroachment in Mississippi," to expand the duties of the State Sovereignty Commission, and to help organize an unpledged electors movement in the South to prevent the reelection of President Kennedy. A Republican advertisement containing transcripts of private conversations between Barnett and the Kennedys on Ole Miss was dismissed as "libelous" and a "new low in Mississippi campaigning."[16]

If Mississippi Republicans believed segregation could best be defended through the establishment of a second party committed to white supremacy, Johnson and his fellow Mississippi Democrats rejected this argument totally. "Your defense against Mississippi's handful of Republicans and the possibility of a growing Negro vote is the continued unity of our white conservative majority," claimed one Democratic advertisement. "As long as one party controls all of the governmental machinery within Mississippi, and as long as that party is dominated by loyal, white, conservative Mississippians, you and your loved ones and your way of life are as safe as they can be in this troubled world."[17] The Democratic case against two-party competition was elaborated in a joint statement issued by Johnson and Carroll Gartin, the Democratic nominee for lieutenant governor:

> Mississippi stands today as the only state in the American union whose public institutions are totally and completely segregated. The backbone of white control and constitutional government in our state has been and is the one party system. Under this system Mississippi has been able thus far to preserve our customs, traditions, and particular way of life in the South.
>
> The creation and maintenance of a so-called two party system in Mississippi is the most deadly peril facing our nation since reconstruction. The end of the one party system in our state would foretell the abandonment of Mississippi's noble fight for the rights of the states, the integrity of its races, and constitutional government.
>
> . . . Make no mistake about it, the Republican candidates for governor and lieutenant-governor are the instruments of the national Republican Party, whose purposes and ideologies on the race question are as diabolical as those of the Kennedy controlled national Democratic Party.
>
> Paul Johnson and Carroll Gartin owe no allegiance to either national party. We are committed to no one and no group outside of the borders of our beloved state. Our sole obligation is to the people of Mississippi . . . We shall not fail our native people.[18]

Johnson's own advertisements warned whites that the results of a two-party system would be integration and the election of blacks to public office. "The best defense for our way of life," his literature concluded, "is unity of the white conservative majority under Mississippi Democratic leadership."[19] A Democratic advertisement published shortly before the election recapitulated the Republican-Democratic quarrel in language that simultaneously emphasized the intended effects of one-party politics and exemplified without ambiguity the "closed society" mentality of Mississippi's Democratic leadership:

The Republicans claim: The "two-party system" would help preserve segregation.

THE TRUTH: it would divide Mississippi's white conservative majority and give our handful of liberals and our large Negro population a chance—which they do not now have—to become an effective political force.[20]

Thus the bias of Mississippi politics before enforcement of the Voting Rights Act. When Johnson easily defeated Phillips with 62 percent of the vote, he interpreted his election as a "victory for the one-party system of Mississippi, which has afforded all the people of Mississippi the protection we have sorely needed since Reconstruction."[21]

From Johnson's perspective the one-party system had again fulfilled its intended function: the preservation of white supremacy. The debate between Republicans and Democrats over the comparative advantages of two-party versus one-party politics was not as contra-dictory as it might appear. As long as most blacks were deliberately factored out of the electoral process, either party system could be manipulated to protect white political control. Historically, the Mississippi Democratic party had succeeded in defending the caste system, but it was conceivable that a second white-dominated party (a variation on Democratic factions) might be equally successful. But once blacks enter the electorate in force, it becomes less probable in the long run that either a one-party system or a two-party system can maintain virtually unqualified white control. As Phillips' own performance in the 1967 general election suggests, the presence of a large number of uncommitted black voters may occasionally induce under-dog candidates such as Mississippi Republicans to appeal for black support.[22]

Militant segregationists and moderate segregationists. Compared to the results of Democratic second primaries, where strong segregationists almost invariably defeated moderate segregationists, the three competitive general elections of this type were divided more evenly (see Table 40). The expected victory of the more militant candidate occurred unambiguously only in the 1957 Virginia general election, a campaign which coincided with the Little Rock crisis. There the spectacle of a Republican Chief Executive sending federal troops into a southern state to enforce school desegregation court orders contributed to a landslide victory of 63 percent for the Democratic candidate, Lindsay Almond. Different circumstances were involved in the single straightforward victory of a moderate segregationist over a strong segregationist. In the 1966 South Carolina general election Democratic Governor Robert McNair defeated a Republican, State Representative Joseph O. Rogers, Jr., who was far more outspoken on segregation. Rogers' proclamation that he was better qualified than McNair to battle the federal government could not offset McNair's numerous advantages. McNair possessed the Democratic party label in a state with a long tradition of party loyalty in state contests; he was an incumbent and thus was ideally situated to maintain a relatively cohesive organization; and, with the election following the implementation of the Voting Rights Act, he had the expected support of a large bloc of black Carolinians who had little incentive to vote for Rogers. A moderate segregationist, McNair nonetheless promised to preserve the state's "national image," a reputation for peaceful behavior acquired "because we said we weren't going to violate the law in civil rights changes." McNair won a comfortable victory (58 percent) in which the estimated black vote for him exceeded the margin of his statewide majority.[23]

The only strong segregationist versus moderate segregationist campaign which was at all closely contested was the 1966 Georgia general election, a race worth recounting as an example of the persistence of segregationist rhetoric despite black enfranchisement. Opposition to desegregation was an important component of the political reputations of Lester Maddox, the Democratic nominee, and, to a lesser degree, of the Republican challenger, Congressman Howard "Bo" Callaway. Unlike most militant segregationists in 1966, Maddox did not use euphemistic language to convey his opinions on racial issues. "I certainly will espouse segregation in every way possible during the four years that I am governor of all the people," Maddox said. "I will be a segregationist the day I take office and I'll be a segregationist the day I leave office." Segregation, after all, was nothing less than "the Christian and American way." Maddox declined to be described as a "moderate" because to him the term signified "an extreme liberal." At least in terms of campaign style, Callaway articulated a "responsible approach" to civil rights. His opponent might attend Ku Klux Klan rallies and "stand up and fight the federal government in the streets," but Callaway proposed rather to "fight for our way of life in the South in a very reasonable way." Turmoil, rioting, and martial law, followed by a contraction of job opportunities, were the probable results, as the Republican nominee saw them, of a Maddox victory.[24]

For strategic reasons Callaway refused to characterize himself as a segregationist. "I'm not hedging," he replied when asked if he were a segregationist. "But I won't answer that without a definition of segregation." He could say, however, that he was no integrationist. Late in the campaign Callaway professed to be bewildered by charges that he was a racist and again declined to describe himself as a segregationist. "Segregation is a vague term that means different things to different people," he explained. "As a congressman, I have treated people alike regardless of race." This refusal to affirm segregation publicly was practically the sole concrete gesture Callaway made to attract the support of blacks and white moderates or liberals. Nonconservatives of both races were advised, in effect, that the Republican was the lesser of evils. Callaway repeatedly denounced Maddox as a volatile and inexperienced politician, a candidate who "would only enforce the laws he believes in" and "whose only claim to fame is violating the law." Worst of all in Callaway's estimation, Maddox's behavior had generated an "unbelievable" amount of bad national publicity for Georgia.[25]

Fresh from his unanticipated triumph in the Democratic runoff, Maddox claimed that his campaign had "driven [Charles] Weltner out of Congress, Lyndon Johnson out of the country [the President was temporarily visiting Asia] and sent Martin Luther King running north." In spite of his extreme views on segregation, Maddox thought blacks would vote for him. "All Georgians will be treated in a fair and just manner," he promised. "No Georgian regardless of race, creed, color or national origin will be mistreated." Maddox would even appoint blacks to state advisory boards, though he hastened to emphasize that "these colored people won't be involved in our social life." As the election neared, Maddox ridiculed Callaway for his ambiguous position on segregation. "He doesn't know whether he's a Republican or a Democrat," Maddox complained. "He doesn't even know whether he's a segregationist or an integrationist." According to Maddox, his opponent was spending $250,000 to "get the Negro bloc vote." Against all these charges, Callaway maintained that the fundamental issue before Georgians was "responsibility versus irresponsibility."[26]

In fact blacks had little cause to back either candidate. If Maddox was unquestionably the more virulent racist, Callaway's economic conservatism (apart from a willingness to increase expenditures for education) and his "responsible" opposition to civil rights made him unattractive as well. Many blacks, joined by a minority of whites, therefore abstained or voted for Ellis Arnall as a write-in candidate. The state vote broke sharply along urban-rural dimensions. Callaway won large majorities in the large metropolitan (57 percent) and medium urban (58 percent) categories, while Maddox easily carried the high black rural (55 percent) and low black rural (62 percent) areas. Callaway led Maddox by 3,000 votes across the state (46.5 percent to 46.2 percent), but Arnall polled 7 percent and prevented a majority for either of the major candidates. In the absence of a majority, Georgia law required that the state legislature select the governor from the two leading candidates in the general election. Since Democrats dominated the legislature, Callaway forces challenged the law on constitutional grounds. Following extensive litigation, the Supreme Court upheld the Georgia law. Maddox's election by the Democratic-controlled legislature predictably occured in January 1967, and the former pistol waver and ax handle entrepreneur, having gained the confidence of less than a plurality of Georgia's voters, assumed the governorship.[27]

Militant segregationists and nonsegregationists.   If strong segregationists were less successful against moderate segregationists in general elections than in Democratic primaries, they achieved no general election victories at all when they faced nonsegregationists. Nonsegregationists, though they were defeated by militants five out of six times in the runoffs, won the three general elections involving strong segregationists (see Table 40). At least three factors contributed to the nonsegregationist victories. Because all these general elections were held after 1965, nonsegregationists could reasonably anticipate a larger number of votes from newly mobilized blacks to offset the segregationist vote than would have been possible a few years before. Second, none of the nonsegregationists (Winthrop Rockefeller of Arkansas, Robert Scott of North Carolina, and John West of South Carolina) emphasized racially liberal positions in their campaigns; rather, they avoided segregationist oratory and generally attempted to moderate racial controversies.[28] Finally, the nonsegregationists in North Carolina and South Carolina had the considerable advantage of running as nominees of the dominant Democratic party. The 1966 Arkansas general election, which produced the state's first Republican governor since Reconstruction, illustrates the racial cleavages which appeared in these campaigns.

Winthrop Rockefeller's victory in 1966 was due not only to the money, organization, and program of the Republican candidate but also to the nature of his opposition. Rockefeller had the good fortune to campaign against James D. "Justice Jim" Johnson, a fiery stump orator given to Biblical quotations who was Arkansas's answer to George Wallace and Lester Maddox.[29] In the Democratic primaries Johnson had demonstrated his support for southern racial traditions less by specific references to blacks than by stalking past them as though they did not exist. The prospect of a close general election against an able Republican opponent brought about some change —how meaningful is debatable—in Johnson's approach to racial issues. Johnson began to shake hands with blacks and to tell them "You know I need you"; and he became slightly less bellicose in his speeches, even promising at one point not to engage in "any schoolhouse-door stands in Arkansas."[30]

Though Johnson's references to racial matters were comparatively subdued, it was clear that he disassociated himself from efforts to reduce racial discrimination. He unequivocally opposed open housing legislation as "the most dastardly bill that was ever introduced in Congress" and accused Rockefeller of financing "such racial agitators as Martin Luther King and Stokely Carmichael," but late in October he claimed that race had not been a significant issue in the campaign. Hostile to school desegregation guidelines, he pledged to abide by court decisions concerning their legality and did not continually assail the guidelines. Yet there were definite limits to his quasi-moderation, and in the final stages of the campaign he sought to reassure whites of his segregationist views without crudely alienating blacks. He was not persuaded, he said, that merely holding certain convictions on segregation necessarily made one "a bigot and a racist and unworthy of consideration. Friends, Jim Johnson's a Southerner and I have no apologies to the state of Arkansas . . . for being a Southerner." In a television appearance on election eve he both refused to apologize for being a segregationist and promised to protect the legal rights of all, "without regard to race, color or creed." He would not, however, "tolerate the sordid spectacles that you have witnessed . . . in varying degree in practically every state where the chief executive is an integrationist." The former leader of the White Citizens Council could report with a straight face that he had always "treated our colored citizens with fairness and impartiality."[31]

Indisputably a more attractive candidate to blacks than Johnson, Rockefeller deemphasized civil rights and did not court Negro support extensively.[32] Well organized, adequately financed, and a more experienced campaigner than he had been in 1964 against Orval Faubus, the Republican candidate spent most of his time outlining his plans for educational improvement and economic development. Rockefeller promised to give top priority to education and to raise educational standards to the point where "all our boys and girls have equal opportunities"; and he argued that his business connections would enable him to develop new industry within the state. If Rockefeller did not crusade for civil rights, he did attack Johnson as a demagogue and an opportunist. The most significant difference between the two candidates, he told a gathering of ministers, was that "You have never heard me say anything that included the words 'hate' or 'bigot'—and you never will." "Are we going to have a man who preaches hate and bigotry," he asked on another occasion, "or are we going to have a man who is concerned about these young people, their future, the future of Arkansas?" In a final television appearance Rockefeller urged the electorate to reject the "smears and vilification of a badly beaten man" and pledged to bring "the wholesome change for which you have longed."[33]

By Arkansas standards, Rockefeller's position on racial controversies was relatively liberal. When he opposed federal efforts to encourage school desegregation, he couched his opposition in terms of disagreement with federal methods. It was a mistake for the Office of Education to tell localities to achieve specific rates of desegregation, yet he believed "we're making the right move in terms of integration." No federal bureaucrat, he insisted, could be "more dedicated and sincere than I am." From Rockefeller's perspective, an extended discussion of racial issues, much less active support for civil rights legislation, could only have benefited Johnson.[34] Emphasizing education, economic progress, and the advantages of responsible leadership, Rockefeller won the governorship with 54 percent of the state vote. The Republican received 62 percent of the urban vote, carried the black belt counties with 55 percent, and achieved a slight majority of 51 percent in the low black rural areas. Majority support for Johnson was limited to rural counties with medium black populations (52 percent). It would be unwarranted to consider Rockefeller's victory as a repudiation of segregation per se by white voters. Johnson's evangelistic campaign style, his chest-beating harangues patterned after those of George Wallace, alienated many Democratic voters.[35] The threat of renewed federal-state confrontations over school desegregation, measured against Rockefeller's comprehensive approach to Arkansas's economic problems, was probably instrumental to a Republican victory. Toward that victory black voters made an indispensable contribution.[36]

Moderate segregationists only. Three general elections in which moderate segregationists opposed each other may be passed over quickly. These campaigns occurred prior to 1965 and were won by Democrats (see Table 40). The only intriguing aspect of the moderate segregationist versus moderate segregationist general election is that in two cases the successful Democrats had campaigned in the second primary as militant segregationists. Having utilized strong segregationist rhetoric to discredit their opposition within the Democratic party and facing Republicans who were less vulnerable to accusations of softness on racial change, John McKeithen of Louisiana and Dan Moore of North Carolina apparently decided that further segregationist militancy would be superfluous. Appeals to party loyalty, rather than denunciations of the bloc vote, characterized their general election campaigns.

Moderate segregationists and nonsegregationists. In the Peripheral South the persistence of segregationist appeals in post-1965 general elections has been manifest primarily in campaigns between moderate segregationists (mainly Republicans) and nonsegregationists (mainly Democrats). Nearly one in four of the competitive general elections in the South placed moderate segregationists against nonsegregationists, and these contests resulted in an equal number of victories (three) for each classification. In general elections the data in Table 40 thus show that nonsegregationists were more successful against militant segregationists (3-0) than against moderate segregationists (3-3). Two complementary explanations may be offered for the comparative weakness of the nonsegregationists vis-à-vis moderate segregationists. First, in the Peripheral South an undiluted strong segregationist posture would be more likely to encourage the cohesive opposition of blacks and of moderate or liberal whites than would a more subtle and sophisticated evocation of racial divisions. Second, the racial *and* economic liberalism of the nonsegregationists in the 1966 Florida and 1973 Virginia general elections increased those candidates' vulnerability. (I omit for this discussion the 1964 Arkansas general election, where an inexperienced Republican challenger, Winthrop Rockefeller, was easily handled by Orval Faubus, the Democratic incumbent.) Compared to the three nonsegregationists who did defeat strong segregationists (Rockefeller, Robert Scott of North Carolina, and John West of South Carolina), the two nonsegregationists who lost to moderate segregationists were substantially more liberal on both race and economics. Robert King High was unable to unite Florida Democrats under his leadership and was portrayed by Claude Kirk, the Republican candidate, as an ultra-liberal. In Virginia, the neo-Populist Henry Howell was attacked by Mills Godwin as an antibusiness candidate, a tool of "liberals and labor bosses," and an advocate of the "socialistic and welfare programs that so many of us object to so strenuously."[37] The nonsegregationist Democrats who defeated moderate segregationists (John Connally and Dolph Briscoe in Texas and Reubin Askew in Florida) were far less identified with racial and economic liberalism than High or Howell. This distinction is less valid in the case of Askew, whose fight for a corporate sales tax was bold and vigorous. However, Askew's racial liberalism was more evident after he became governor than during his campaign, and his opponent, Governor Kirk, had become a Republican liability by 1970. A review of the 1973 Virginia general election illustrates the continuation of qualified segregationist appeals.

The 1973 campaign featured the most explicit cleavage on racial issues in Virginia since the 1957 "Massive Resistance" debate between Lindsay Almond and Ted Dalton. Former Democratic Governor Godwin, a recent convert to Republicanism, avoided outright segregationist rhetoric but denounced his opponent as a proponent of school busing. Lieutenant Governor Howell, a Democrat who ran technically as an Independent, denied that he supported busing and described Godwin as a school closer. Godwin won an exceedingly narrow victory in which race was but one of many considerations.

When Godwin had first won the governorship in 1965, he had conducted a nonsegregationist campaign (see below). In 1973 he occasionally made statements which suggested a reduction, rather than an intensification, of racial conflict. "We cannot afford an official stance," he said, "that pits large against small, wealthy against poor, business against labor or black against white." Yet far more characteristic of his 1973 campaign was his contention, expressed as part of a broad strategy to disparage Howell's liberalism, that the candidates differed significantly on the issue of school busing. Even though a Supreme Court decision in May 1973 reduced the likelihood of immediate school busing in Virginia, Godwin continued to view busing as a "vital issue in this campaign." He criticized Howell in particular for a 1972 television interview in which Howell had described busing across jurisdictional lines (for example, sending black students from the District of Columbia into northern Virginia) as a possible means to "save our nation from being a divided black-white nation." "The public wants state officials doing everything they can [about busing]," Godwin remarked on one occasion. "No one is advocating turning back the clock, but we've got to fight radical things like school district consolidation, crosstown busing and arbitrary quotas." Godwin's attacks on busing, designed as they were to attract the votes of both white suburbanites and Wallace supporters, intensified as the campaign proceeded.[38]

One of the most racially and economically liberal candidates in post-*Brown* southern politics, Howell attempted to subordinate racial divisions to economic issues. Such issues as repeal of the sales tax on food and nonprescription drugs and consumer protection were emphasized as Howell sought to unite lower-income Virginians across racial lines. "With all this inflation, people are worried most about their pocketbooks," Howell would argue. "Everybody knows a state official can't do anything about desegregation policies handed down by the Federal Government." In addition to stressing economic issues, Howell was more candid about his racial liberalism than were most nonsegregationists who faced segregationist opponents. Godwin's advocacy of massive resistance during the 1950s was assessed as an "unbelievable act of irresponsibility," and sponsors of an antibusing amendment to the Constitution were informed that Howell considered their efforts a "charade." Throughout the general election campaign Howell consistently expressed his opposition to school busing. "I've come out in this campaign totally committed to an integrated school system," he said. "It's what the law requires and what the law should require." Nonetheless, he was well aware that the great majority of Virginians opposed school busing and he agreed with their position: "We can't force people to do but so much." In his opinion there was no real difference between his campaign stance against busing and the views he discussed in the 1972 television interview.[39]

The disparity between his unequivocal opposition to busing in 1973 and his more ambiguous analysis of the problem in 1972 may have cost Howell votes, but it did not produce a Godwin landslide. Godwin received only a 15,000 vote majority (50.7 percent of the state vote) out of more than a million votes. In view of Howell's aggressive, neo-Populist campaign style, what is surprising is not so much Howell's defeat as the closeness of the race. The two candidates split the large metropolitan and low black rural votes almost evenly. Godwin ran slightly ahead of Howell in the medium urban areas (52 percent) and won his strongest support (55 percent) in the medium black rural counties. Howell carried the black belt with 55 percent.[40] Once his victory was assured, Godwin seemed to adopt a more conciliatory posture toward blacks. "As far as the minority races are concerned," he said in a post-election press conference, "they will be treated fairly by me, generously by the next administration."[41]

Nonsegregationists only.   By far the most common type of competitive general election in the South was the campaign between two nonsegregationists (see Table 40). Nonsegregationist Democrats faced nonsegregationist Republicans in slightly less than two fifths of the post-*Brown* competitive general elections, with the Democrats winning a slight majority (6-4) of these elections. Nine of the ten campaigns between nonsegregationists took place after 1965, a fact suggestive of the impact on southern politics of the national government's efforts to reform southern racial traditions. Most of these contests also occurred in the Peripheral South, where Republican candidates tended to be less conservative than Deep South Republicans on a range of policy questions. Georgia and Louisiana were the only Deep South states experiencing such general elections, while Florida was the single Peripheral South state which failed to do so. As in the Democratic primaries, the nonsegregationists did not typically champion racial change. Most of the nonsegregationist candidates avoided explicitly segregationist rhetoric, issued generalities on the order of "I will be governor of *all* the people," and, for the most part, emphasized nonracial matters. However, the candidates did engage in a more or less open and vigorous competition for black votes. Because of their party label Democrats were ordinarily better situated to attract black support, but such Republicans as Winthrop Rockefeller and Linwood Holton campaigned more aggressively than did their Democratic opponents for the votes of blacks.

The 1965 Virginia general election suggests that black mobilization encouraged some militant segregationists to revise their racial stances in order to remain competitive. In this election the major candidates were Mills Godwin, a politician long active in the Byrd Organization, and Linwood Holton, a representative of the moderate wing of the Republican party. Largely because of the contributions black Virginians had made toward the successful election of Lyndon Johnson in 1964, "both parties sought Negro votes in the 1965 gubernatorial race, and for the first time in this century it was done with little fear of being smeared 'party of the Negro.' "[42] With its control of state politics challenged by a Conservative party with roots in the high black rural areas as well as by the Republicans, the Byrd Organization in 1965 appealed to a much broader spectrum of the Virginia electorate than had been its custom. Segregationist oratory, a characteristic of Godwin's earlier political career, was missing in 1965.[43] The man who had supported "a firm policy against integration and [for] maintenance of maximum segregation under the law" when he ran for lieutenant governor in 1961 was now committed in general terms to legal equality for all Virginians. As Godwin explained to an association of black teachers, "I seek to be the Governor of all the people of Virginia." When Godwin discussed his role in the massive resistance movement, it was to argue that massive resistance had actually contributed to long-term racial harmony by giving whites time to adjust to the idea of school desegregation. Godwin attempted to retain conservative backing with reassurances that he would govern "in the Virginia tradition" and would encourage "good, sound, solid, sane, safe government," yet his promises to expand state services, especially education, won support from the state AFL-CIO, many Negro organizations, and liberal Democrats.[44]

Whereas Godwin tended to ignore the segregation issue, Holton constantly reminded audiences that Godwin had been a leading advocate of massive resistance. It was ridiculous, Holton believed, for a "school closer" like Godwin to argue that race relations had been bettered by massive resistance. Five schools had been shut in 1957 as the result of legislation supported by Godwin, and Godwin's unadopted plans in 1959 "would have closed schools throughout the state." Holton solicited black support far more openly than Godwin, advocating poll tax repeal and the appointment of a Negro to the State Board of Education (Godwin refused to make a specific commitment on this point) and agreeing "absolutely" that blacks deserved opportunities to get white collar positions in state government. During the campaign Holton appealed to blacks "like other Virginians" rather than addressing blacks as blacks. Nonetheless, he did describe his opponent to black educators as a politician "who led the fight that closed schools for 13,000 students in Virginia and would have closed all the schools if he could have done so."[45]

Since the Conservative party won 14 percent of the state vote, most of which would otherwise have gone to Godwin, Godwin's ability to capture a majority of the black vote materially aided his candidacy.[46] Godwin's plurality of 48 percent was ten points higher than Holton's performance. The Democrat carried every demographic category but achieved a clear majority of 51 percent only in the low black rural counties. Holton, who drew roughly two fifths of the urban and low black rural votes, received only 20 percent of the rural high black ballots. The Conservative party made its best showing (31 percent) in the rural counties with high black populations, the areas where whites were least willing to accept racial desegregation.

The novelty of general election campaigns involving only nonsegregationists becomes all the more apparent when the southern politician's long-standing commitment to segregation is recalled. General elections of this type have occurred for essentially the same reasons they developed in the post-1965 Democratic second primaries. From the perspective of many white politicians with gubernatorial ambitions, the black vote has become too large to justify policy stands that would concede most black voters to the opposition. While serious conflict may persist over the degree and scope of racial change deemed tolerable, most politicians now accept the irreversibility of school and public accommodations desegregation and of the extension of black voting rights. As a consequence, both Republican and Democratic nominees in many cases have sought to ameliorate racial conflict and to adopt positions that could be construed as comparatively inoffensive to both races.

Further reflection on the racial views of the winners and losers in the nonsegregationist versus nonsegregationist general elections supports a conclusion advanced in the chapter on Democratic second primaries. The winners of these contests were usually less liberal on racial issues than their opponents. Relatively more liberal candidates were victorious in two elections (Arkansas 1968 and Louisiana 1972) but were defeated five times (Virginia 1965; Texas 1968 and 1970; Arkansas 1970; and Tennessee 1970). Appreciable differences between the nonsegregationists could not be detected in the 1969 Virginia, the 1970 Georgia, and the 1972 North Carolina campaigns. In all these general elections, probably no more than three politicians—Holton and Rockefeller, Republicans who succeeded once, and John Jay Hooker, Jr., the unsuccessful Tennessee Democrat—could be judged liberal by national standards. The nonsegregationist stances of most general election participants represented minimal accommodations to racial change.

Conclusions

It is evident that strong segregationists, whether they faced moderate segregationists or nonsegregationists, achieved less success in the general elections than in the Democratic primaries. This finding may be explained away in part by recalling that, compared to the Democratic primaries, more of the competitive general elections occurred in the Peripheral South and after the passage of civil rights legislation and the realization of widespread school desegregation. Had there been additional competitive general elections in the period 1954-65 and in the states of the Deep South, the racial stances of the Democratic primary winners and general election winners would have been more similar.

Yet the timing and the location of the competitive general elections should not obscure other factors—the anchoring effect of Democratic party identification in states that have historically been classified as one-party Democratic or modified one-party Democratic[47] and favorable images of the Democratic party held by southern whites[48]—which have operated under certain conditions to reduce the "normal" appeal of segregationist rhetoric in southern politics. To be specific, Democratic nominees for governor who chose to campaign as nonsegregationists against segregationist Republicans could ordinarily expect to obtain the votes of many white segregationists because of those voters' loyalty to candidates of the Democratic party.[49] General elections between nonsegregationist Democrats and segregationist Republicans generated cross-pressures on segregationist voters who identified with the Democratic party and had positive party images; and, as S. M. Lipset has generalized, "cross pressures resulting from multiple-group affiliations or loyalties account for much of the 'deviation' from the dominant pattern of a given group."[50] The argument is not that nonsegregationist Democrats necessarily received the bulk of the segregationist-Democratic vote, for that is an empirical question well beyond the scope of this study. Rather, the point is that the Democratic party label functioned to divide the segregationist vote at the expense of the segregationist Republican candidates. In addition, if the nonsegregationist stance of the Democratic candidate were essentially mild and noncommittal rather than emphatically pro-civil rights, voters who preferred both segregation and the Democratic party would presumably feel less compelled to vote against their party identification or image. There is no hard evidence in either direction on this hypothesis, but it seems plausible that segregationist-Democratic voters would tend to give the Democratic nominee the benefit of the doubt. As we have seen, the nonsegregationist Democrats who defeated segregationist Republicans were less explicit (frequently much less so) on civil rights than were the nonsegregationist Democrats (counting Howell as a Democrat) who lost to segregationist Republicans. Finally, with the exception of Reubin Askew, none of the victorious nonsegregationist Democrats could be described as economic progressives. Accordingly, they were less open to the charge of being consistently liberal or ultraliberal on race and economics.

The circumstances have now been outlined under which candidates who were comparatively less traditional on racial segregation defeated opponents with a demonstrably stronger commitment to southern racial customs. If the 1966 general election in Georgia is set aside because the popular vote did not determine the winner, the less traditional candidates succeeded against their more traditional opponents in nearly two thirds of the campaigns. Of the seven general elections won by the less traditional candidates, the typical victory was achieved in the Peripheral South, during the period 1966-73, and by a nonsegregationist Democrat. The nonsegregationist postures of these Democrats were more implicit than explicit, and their stances on economic development did not leave them vulnerable to attack as excessively liberal on economics.

The first and the final pair of reasons advanced to explain the victories of the less traditional politicians specify the conditions under which party identification and party image—the only unique elements differentiating general elections from Democratic primaries—might be most expected to divide the segregationist vote. Matthews and Prothro's research indicates that the pool of segregationist voters has been proportionately smaller in the Peripheral South than in the Deep South,[51] so that nonsegregationist Democrats in the Peripheral South stood to lose fewer white votes than their counterparts in the Deep South. Federal intervention in the mid-1960s expanded the black electorate significantly and shifted the substance of racial conflict from quarrels over the principle of racial segregation to divisions concerning the scope of racial change. Both these developments aided nonsegregationist Democrats. Bland and perhaps obfuscating stances by nonsegregationists were calculated to attract black support while alienating as few whites as possible, and the avoidance of uniformly liberal orientations represented an effort to remain well within the mainstream of southern politics. All these factors contributed to a political environment in which party identification and party image could function to the advantage of nonsegregationist Democrats.

Because of the strong affinity which many white southerners have felt for the Democratic party, especially the state Democratic party, it seems likely that the Democratic party label constituted the most important resource of the victorious nonsegregationists.

Findings presented in this chapter, though obviously far from conclusive, do not on the whole provide impressive evidence for the hypothesis that the revived general election might function in the southern electoral process chiefly as an alternative to the Democratic second primary, a contest in which those Democratic nominees for governor who were "wrong" on civil rights might be challenged by militant segregationist Republicans. While there have been occasional campaigns of this sort (none of which the Republicans won), they have been much less common than general elections in which racial cleavages were comparatively minor. Fully half of the 18 competitive general elections held between 1966 and 1973 involved only nonsegregationists; and another 22 percent of the competitive elections, those matching nonsegregationist Democrats against moderate segregationist Republicans, exhibited a weaker form of racial division than campaigns which placed nonsegregationists or moderate segregationists against strong segregationists. Largely because nonsegregationist Democrats could evoke the party label and because Republicans themselves were not consistently committed to segregationist stances, the general elections were less easily manipulated by militant segregationists than were the Democratic second primaries.

10

The Governors

Thus far in this survey of the segregation issue in gubernatorial campaigns the outcomes of Democratic primaries and competitive general elections have been examined. To complete the investigation it is necessary to evaluate the racial (and economic development) perspectives of those politicians who were elected governor in the first two decades following the *Brown* decision. Apart from providing an overview of southern politics during the Second Reconstruction, the identification of the governors' stances on these policy dimensions affords an opportunity to compare the findings with Key's assessment of the competence and effectiveness of the southern political elite of the 1940s. As Key emphasized, a multitude of factors made the job of the southern politician exceptionally difficult:

> Southern politics labors under the handicaps common to all states. Southern politicians are also confronted by special problems that demand extraordinary political intelligence, restraint, patience, and persistence for their solution. The South's heritage from crises of the past, its problem of adjustment of racial relations on a scale unparalleled in any western nation, its poverty associated with an agrarian economy which in places is almost feudal in character, the long habituation of many of its people to nonparticipation in political life—all these and other social characteristics both influence the nature of the South's political system and place upon it an enormous burden.[1]

The South's political leadership, Key argued, was generally incapable of ameliorating the enormous social and economic problems of the region. "When all the exceptions are considered, when all the justifications are made, and when all of the invidious comparisons are drawn," Key concluded, "those of the South and those who love the South are left with the cold, hard fact that the South as a whole has developed no system or practice of political organization and leadership adequate to cope with its problems."[2]

Pessimistic about meaningful political change in the short run, Key suggested that such "fundamental trends" as a "decline in the Negro population, the growth of cities, and the dilution of an agricultural economy by the rise of industry and trade" would facilitate—though not "automatically" produce—long-term political change.[3] Over the past quarter century the South has urbanized considerably, its economy has become more industrial and commercial, and the relative size of the black population has decreased. These social and economic trends, when combined with such spectacular political events as the *Brown* decision, the civil rights movement, the Civil Rights Act of 1964, and the Voting Rights Act of 1965, have reshaped the milieu of southern electoral politics. In view of the manifest public policy failures of the old southern politics and of the unprecedented social, economic, and political changes that have taken place since 1950, it is essential to determine the extent to which significant changes in attitudes toward racial segregation and the achievement of economic development are discernible among winning candidates for the governorship. Because of the centrality of racial conflict in southern history, primary attention will be given to this policy dimension.

An investigation of the racial stances of politicians who survived southern campaigns also focuses attention on the bias of the region's electoral institutions with regard to racial traditions. Since the one-party system was deliberately structured to ensure white supremacy, the most conspicuous bias of the old electoral process was the exclusion as serious candidates of any politicians who opposed the caste system.[4] As the review of pre-*Brown* campaigns indicated, acceptance of the principle of racial segregation was a minimal requirement for electoral success.

In attempting to conceptualize systemic bias, it is useful to distinguish a broader from a narrower variation. The more inclusive indicator of this standing bias in favor of the racial status quo is simply the percentage of governorships won by segregationists. If the electoral system worked as its planners intended, presumably few if any nonsegregationists would obtain high office in the South. However, inferences of systemic bias which rest solely on the racial attitudes of the winners lack precision, for such estimates include the bias resulting from the historical discouragement of nonsegregationists as potential campaigners as well as the bias attributable to the net impact of the electoral process in screening or filtering out "deviant" (that is, nonsegregationist) candidates. The narrower concept of systemic bias refers to differences between the racial positions of all the major contestants for the governorship and the campaign stances of the winners. In an attempt to estimate the systemic bias that may be attributed to net change within the electoral process itself, the proportion of governors furnished by a given racial category may be compared with the percentage of major candidates in that classification. By subtracting the percentage of strong segregationists among first primary contestants from the proportion of militant segregationist governors, for example, it is possible to determine whether or not strong segregationists improved their relative strength over the course of the electoral process. A comparison of net internal changes between the racial categories before and after 1965 should serve as a rough test of the effect of national intervention upon electoral outcomes in the South.

What follows in this chapter is essentially a descriptive account of the winners' policy orientations on segregation, with little systematic explanation of why particular observed changes may have occurred. The decision to separate description from analysis, while partly a matter of organizational convenience, reflects a belief that sustained description of the governors' campaign attitudes should contribute to an improved understanding of continuity and change in recent southern politics. Compared to the stability of southern politicians' racial positions in the first half of the twentieth century, the post-*Brown* years constitute a period of relative discontinuity and stand unquestionably as the most eventful decades in the history of the South since the founding of the one-party system. Because established patterns of race relations were challenged during the Second Reconstruction, an intensive study of elite attitudes appears justified. If racial traditions in the South have changed significantly since the *Brown* decision, measurable differences should be visible over time in the racial stances of the region's governors.

The Post-*Brown* Governors: An Overview

Deferring until later the question of change within the post-*Brown* era, I will begin by considering the outcomes of the 66 governorships decided between 1954 and 1973. Tables 41 and 42 display the required information. During this 20-year period, a slight plurality (38 percent)

Table 41.   Campaign racial segregation stances of southern governors, 1954-73, by economic development position and subregion (percent)

Campaign Stance on Racial Segregation	Campaign Stance on Achievement of Economic Development																	
	Deep South						Peripheral South						South					
	M	R	A	P	T	NC	M	R	A	P	T	NC	M	R	A	P	T	NC
Strong Segregationist	100	0	33	67	60	+9	50	33	0	0	24	+2	67	25	11	57	38	+5
Moderate Segregationist	0	100	33	0	20	-11	38	67	17	0	32	+1	25	75	22	0	27	-4
Nonsegregationist	0	0	33	33	20	+1	13	0	83	100	44	-3	8	0	67	43	35	-1
Totals	100	100	100	100	100		100	100	100	100	100		100	100	100	100	100	
Number of Cases	(8)	(2)	(9)	(6)	(25)		(16)	(6)	(18)	(1)	(41)		(24)	(8)	(27)	(7)	(66)	

Symbols: M = Marginalist; R = Redistributive; A = Adaptive; P = Progressive; T = Totals; NC = Net Change (percentage of winners holding a given position on racial segregation minus percentage of major candidates in Democratic first primaries holding the same position)
Tau beta values: Deep South = .33; Peripheral South = .66; South = .43

Table 42. Campaign economic development stances of southern governors, 1954-73, by racial segregation position and subregion (percent)

Campaign Stance on Achievement of Economic Development	Campaign Stance on Racial Segregation														
	Deep South					Peripheral South					South				
	SS	MS	NS	T	NC	SS	MS	NS	T	NC	SS	MS	NS	T	NC
Marginalist	53	0	0	32	-16	80	46	11	39	-6	64	33	9	36	-10
Redistributive	0	40	0	8	-3	20	31	0	15	-3	8	33	0	12	-3
Adaptive	20	60	60	36	+7	0	23	83	44	+16	12	33	78	41	+12
Progressive	27	0	40	24	+12	0	0	6	2	-7	16	0	13	11	0
Totals	100	100	100	100		100	100	100	100		100	100	100	100	
Number of Cases	(15)	(5)	(5)	(25)		(10)	(13)	(18)	(41)		(25)	(18)	(23)	(66)	

Symbols: SS = Segregationist; MS = Moderate Segregationist; NS = Nonsegregationist; T = Totals; NC = Net Change (percentage of winners holding a given position on economic development minus percentage of major candidates in Democratic first primaries holding the same position)
Tau beta values: Deep South = .66; Peripheral South = .33; South = .43

of the South's governors campaigned as militant segregationists, another 27 percent were moderate segregationists, and 35 percent were classified as nonsegregationists. Although the figures reveal the predominance of segregationist governors for the period as a whole, a comparison of the 1954-73 findings with the pre-*Brown* elections (given in Table 4, above) demonstrates that the consensus on racial segregation which white politicians had maintained in the early 1950s did not survive the revival of the desegregation controversy. The appearance of an appreciable number of successful nonsegregationists marks a significant change in southern electoral politics. Yet if the post-*Brown* governors as a group were less tradition-oriented than their predecessors, it is equally apparent that nonsegregationist winners were largely restricted to the Peripheral South. Three fifths of the Deep South governors, more than twice the percentage of Peripheral South winners, were militant segregationists. Nonsegregationists won a plurality (44 percent) of the Peripheral South governorships but only a fifth of the Deep South contests. In both subregions a majority of the winners adopted segregationist positions. Inspection of the "net change" columns in Table 41 reveals that shifts in the distribution of major candidates and governors generally benefited the strong segregationists. The percentage of southern governorships won by militants was five points higher than their share of major candidates, and the systemic bias in favor of militant segregationists was especially pronounced in the Deep South (+9).

The post-*Brown* governors also differed from the successful politicians of the early 1950s in terms of their views on the achievement of economic development. In the pre-*Brown* years, it will be recalled, traditional economic development positions were the norm: nearly four fifths of the winners were marginalists and less than 10 percent were adaptives. During the Second Reconstruction, innovative economic development stances became much more common. A slightly larger proportion of adaptives (41) than of marginalists (36) were elected, and the redistributive and progressive categories both contributed slightly more than a tenth of the South's governors. While the progressives were much more successful in the Deep South than in the Peripheral South (24-2), subregional differences in the percentage of winning adaptives were fairly modest. Over the course of the electoral process the adaptives, a comparatively innovative type, improved their presence considerably (+12) while the opposite was true for marginalists (-10).

Separate examinations of the segregation and economic development dimensions, two fundamental components at the elite level of the South's "slow-moving social revolution,"[5] have shown that important changes have taken place within each policy area since the *Brown* decision. If white politicians are beginning to respond to a vastly more complex socioeconomic and political environment, these changes in elite orientations should be complementary. As an empirical question, have traditional and innovative positions on one policy dimension generally been matched by respectively traditional and innovative stances on the second dimension? Cross-tabulation of the variables indicates that, despite subregional differences, the dimensions of racial segregation and economic development are associated. Across the South in the years 1954 through 1973, 64 percent of the successful militant segregationists were marginalists and 78 percent of the winning nonsegregationists were adaptives. Reversing the comparisons, 67 percent of the victorious marginalists were strong segregationists and an equal percentage of adaptives were nonsegregationists.

The data in Tables 41 and 42 disclose basic subregional variations in the economic development positions associated with particular stances on racial segregation. In the tradition-bound Deep South, the most significant differences with respect to the achievement of economic development are those separating militants from moderate segregationists and nonsegregationists. Over half of the Deep South strong segregationists were marginalists, but none of the successful moderate segregationists or nonsegregationists campaigned as marginalists. By contrast, in the comparatively more open political culture of the Peripheral South, differences are more apparent between segregationists (of whatever variety) and nonsegregationists. While four fifths of the Peripheral South militants and 46 percent of its moderate segregationists were marginalists, adaptives comprised 83 percent of the nonsegregationists there.

Consideration of the economic development dimension suggests similarities as well as differences between the subregions. Governors in both the Deep South and the Peripheral South who adopted traditional (marginalist or redistributive) positions on economic development characteristically assumed traditional stances on racial segregation (strong or moderate segregationist). Clear subregional differences are evident, however, when the racial positions associated with the innovative economic development categories (adaptives and progressives) are examined. Adaptives were mainly segregationists and progressives typically campaigned as strong segregationists in the Deep

South, but in the Peripheral South the relation between innovative orientations on economic development and segregationist stances was reversed: 83 percent of the Peripheral South adaptives were nonsegregationists. Aside from the extremely poor showing of the progressives in the Peripheral South, economic development categories succeeded about as well in one subregion as in the other. Primarily because racial segregation has been the inherently more controversial and divisive issue, distinctive subregional patterns have been more apparent for segregation than for economic development.

The changing policy stances of southern governors are presented in Table 43, which shows the distribution of the combinations of racial segregation and economic development categories by region and subregion for the entire post-*Brown* era and for the elections which preceded and followed federal intervention. While the typical pre-*Brown* governor (71 percent from 1950 through 1953) campaigned as a moderate segregationist and marginalist, in the 20 years which followed the *Brown* decision the modal southern governor was the nonsegregationist-adaptive (27 percent), followed closely by the strong segregationist-marginalist (24 percent). Subregional patterns, of course, were widely divergent. The modal winning candidate in the Deep South (32 percent) was the militant segregationist-marginalist. In the Peripheral South, nonsegregationist adaptives were elected more frequently (37 percent) than any other combination. Over the region moderate segregationists who were marginalists, redistributives, or adaptives each accounted for approximately one tenth of the governorships. Other combinations theoretically possible occurred rarely or not at all. For example, a handful of strong segregationist-adaptives (all from the Deep South) and nonsegregationist-marginalists (both from Texas) were elected governor. Of greater significance for understanding the "breadth" of southern politics, very few politicians who ran as nonsegregationists and as redistributives or progressives won governorships during the Second Reconstruction. Reubin Askew of Florida, Jimmy Carter of Georgia, and Bill Waller of Mississippi were exceptions, and the latter two politicians were far from genuinely liberal on civil rights. A white politician might succeed either as a nonsegregationist or as a neo-Populist (whether redistributive or progressive), but the combination was considered radical by southern standards. Such politicians as Don Yarborough of Texas, Robert King High of Florida, Henry Howell of Virginia, and Richmond Flowers of Alabama were repeatedly assailed as ultra-liberal and defeated.

The magnitude and timing of changes in the governing elite's

Table 43. Campaign stances on racial segregation and achievement of economic development of southern governors, before and after Voting Rights Act of 1965 and 1954-73, by region and subregion (percent)a

Campaign Stance	Pre-Voting Rights Act 1954-65			Post-Voting Rights Act 1966-73			Post-*Brown* 1954-73		
	DS	PS	Reg	DS	PS	Reg	DS	PS	Reg
Strong Segregationist	73 (14)	40 (4)	53 (7)	40 (5)	0 (-2)	15 (2)	60 (9)	24 (2)	38 (5)
SS-Marginalist	47	32	38	10	0	4	32	20	24
SS-Redistributive	0	8	5	0	0	0	0	5	3
SS-Adaptive	20	0	8	0	0	0	12	0	5
SS-Progressive	7	0	3	30	0	12	16	0	6
Moderate Segregationist	27 (-14)	40 (-2)	35 (-6)	10 (-2)	19 (4)	15 (2)	20 (-11)	32 (1)	27 (-4)
MS-Marginalist	0	20	13	0	6	4	0	15	9
MS-Redistributive	13	16	15	0	0	0	8	10	9
MS-Adaptive	13	4	8	10	13	12	12	7	9
MS-Progressive	0	0	0	0	0	0	0	0	0
Nonsegregationist	0 (0)	20 (-2)	13 (-1)	50 (-4)	81 (-2)	69 (-4)	20 (1)	44 (-3)	35 (-1)
NS-Marginalist	0	8	5	0	0	0	0	5	3
NS-Redistributive	0	0	0	0	0	0	0	0	0
NS-Adaptive	0	12	8	30	75	58	12	37	27
NS-Progressive	0	0	0	20	6	12	8	2	5
Totals	100	100	100	100	100	100	100	100	100
Number of Cases	(15)	(25)	(40)	(10)	(16)	(26)	(25)	(41)	(66)

Symbols: DS = Deep South; PS = Peripheral South; Reg = Region

aFigures in parentheses in the body of the table are percentage point differences between the proportion of governors holding a given racial position and the proportion of major candidates in Democratic first primaries holding the same stance. Because of rounding, net changes do not always sum to 0.

campaign attitudes are brought into sharper focus by comparisons of the distribution of winners' views during the period 1954-65, the years which generally preceded national intervention into the South's racial practices, with the 1966-73 elections, a time span encompassing two waves of elections following federal intervention. Highly traditional postures on both racial segregation and economic development were common for the governors who were elected between the *Brown* decision and the Voting Rights Act. Thirty-eight percent of the southern governors (47 percent in the Deep South and 32 percent in the Peripheral South) were militant segregationist-marginalists, the least innovative combination of segregation and economic development categories. Unreservedly supportive of the status quo on race relations and unconvinced that the state's economic development could be advanced by substantially increased state spending for education, the militant segregationist-marginalists succeeded more often than any other type of southern office seeker prior to federal intervention.

The differences between the governors' pre-1965 and post-1965 campaign stances are remarkable. In the elections that followed national legislation to desegregate public accommodations, encourage school desegregation, and enforce the right to vote, militant segregationist-marginalists declined rapidly as a force in southern politics. No militant segregationist-marginalist was elected governor in the Peripheral South between 1966 and 1973, and in the Deep South this combination was far less successful than the strong segregationist and progressive. Victorious militant segregationists after 1965, in brief, were more likely to be innovative than traditional on the economic development dimension. The modal southern governor in the late 1960s and early 1970s, in clear distinction to his predecessors, campaigned as a nonsegregationist-adaptive. Nearly three fifths of the South's governors (and 75 percent of the Peripheral South chief executives) were of this variety; and even in the Deep South, where racial conservatism was still more pronounced, there were as many nonsegregationist-adaptive winners as there were strong segregationist and progressives. Furthermore, when nonsegregationists who were progressives are added to the nonsegregationist-adaptives, half the Deep South governors and an overwhelming majority of the Peripheral South governors (81 percent) held relatively innovative positions on both policy dimensions. Thus as the principle of racial segregation was increasingly repudiated (tacitly or explicitly) and as the necessity for a more skilled labor force became better appreciated, the campaign stances of southern governors resembled less and less those of the 1954-65 winners. Although the indicator is less subtle than would be desirable in principle, examination of the net changes in the comparative positions of the three racial classifications before and after 1965 strongly suggests the impact of national intervention on the outcomes of southern elections. Systemic bias against racial change was substantial (especially in the Deep South) in the years before national intervention but declined considerably in both subregions after 1965. The net gain for militant segregationists fell from + 14 to + 5 in the Deep South, while in the Peripheral South the advantage which strong segregationists had earlier enjoyed (+ 4) became a slight disadvantage (- 2). With black political participation greatly enhanced and with some measure of racial segregation a *fait accompli* in many aspects of southern life, militant stands on segregation were no longer as associated with electoral success as they once were.

Indexes of dissimilarity (see Table 44) support the proposition that elite orientations have shifted appreciably and (though not entirely) the argument that subregional differences on racial segregation have exceeded subregional differences on economic development. Comparisons of 1954-65 with 1966-73 campaign positions yield indexes of dissimilarity ranging from 50 to 78 and hence indicate that important changes occurred over time. The 1966-73 contests excepted, racial segregation produced greater subregional dissimilarity than did

Table 44. Indexes of dissimilarity on racial segregation and achievement of economic development dimensions for southern governors, by region and subregion and before and after passage of the Voting Rights Act

Type of Comparison	Racial Segregation Dimension	Economic Development Dimension
Comparisons between subregions		
Deep South with Peripheral South, 1954-65	33	24
Deep South with Peripheral South, 1966-73	40	47
Deep South with Peripheral South, 1954-73	36	22
Longitudinal comparisons, 1954-65 with 1966-73		
Deep South	50	50
Peripheral South	61	78
South	57	67

economic development. In the elections held after 1965, racial dissimilarity increased between the Deep South and Peripheral South governors (as more Peripheral South governors campaigned success-fully as nonsegregationists and no strong segregationists were elected) but was exceeded by a heightened dissimilarity on economic develop-ment (largely a product of subregional differences in the proportions of victorious progressives and adaptives). For the pre-1965 campaigns and for the entire set of post-*Brown* elections, however, the sub-regions were more alike on economic development than on racial segregation.

To conclude this overview of southern elections, Tables 45 and 46 report the winners' campaign stances for individual states. Because of the limited number of elections occurring in any single state, the findings are presented for the post-*Brown* era as a whole. Changes over time in elite orientations are obscured by summary data, to be sure, but it is still possible to contrast central tendencies in the out-comes of gubernatorial elections from one state to another. A comparison of the racial stances of the Deep South winners reveals the extreme traditionalism of Alabama and Mississippi, both of which awarded the governorship to militant segregationists in four fifths of the elections, and of Georgia. Alabama was the single southern state in which no nonsegregationist became governor. Louisiana, by virtue of choosing nonsegregationists in both of its post-1965 contests, ranks as the most change-oriented state in the Deep South. Net changes in the distribution of the various racial categories over the course of the electoral process benefited strong segregationists in three states (note particularly Alabama) but failed to do so in Mississippi and South Carolina.[6] If the most common combination of racial and economic development views is used as an indicator of variations in state politi-cal cultures, a rank ordering of the Deep South states in terms of over-all campaign traditionalism may be devised. In Mississippi (60 percent) and Georgia (40 percent), the most successful politicians were the strong segregationist-marginalists. Highly traditional on the achievement of economic development as well as on racial segrega-tion, these states were the most consistently change-resistant political units in the South. Although Alabama's governors were as dedicated to the racial status quo as those of Mississippi, the Alabama electorate preferred militant segregationists who were simultaneously progres-sives. In three out of five elections Alabama's chief executives (that is, George and Lurleen Wallace) combined racial traditionalism with innovative, neo-Populist stances on economic development. The

Table 45. Campaign stances on racial segregation and achievement of economic development of governors in the Deep South states, 1954-73 (percent)a

Campaign Stance	Alabama	Georgia	Louisiana	Mississippi	South Carolina
Strong Segregationist	80 (40)	60 (7)	40 (14)	80 (-2)	40 (-16)
SS-Marginalist	20	40	20	60	20
SS-Redistributive	0	0	0	0	0
SS-Adaptive	0	0	20	20	20
SS-Progressive	60	20	0	0	0
Moderate Segregationist	20 (-20)	20 (0)	20 (-33)	0 (-6)	40 (7)
MS-Marginalist	0	0	0	0	0
MS-Redistributive	20	0	20	0	0
MS-Adaptive	0	20	0	0	40
MS-Progressive	0	0	0	0	0
Nonsegregationist	0 (-20)	20 (-7)	40 (19)	20 (8)	20 (9)
NS-Marginalist	0	0	0	0	0
NS-Redistributive	0	0	0	0	0
NS-Adaptive	0	0	40	0	20
NS-Progressive	0	20	0	20	0
Totals	100	100	100	100	100
Number of Cases	(5)	(5)	(5)	(5)	(5)

aFigures in parentheses in the body of the table are percentage point differences between the proportion of governors holding a given racial position and the proportion of major candidates in Democratic first primaries holding the same position.

remaining Deep South states were relatively less supportive of candidates with highly traditional policy orientations. In comparative
perspective South Carolina falls in an intermediate position. The
modal winning combination there (40 percent) was the moderate
segregationist-adaptive. Louisiana, with 40 percent of its governors
running as nonsegregationist-adaptives, was less closed to innovative
positions on segregation and economic development than the other
Deep South states.

Examination of the Peripheral South states (see Table 46) discloses
the comparative weakness of militant segregationists except in Virginia (40 percent) and Florida (33 percent), and, equally as important, isolates Texas and Tennessee as the only states in which more
than half the governors were nonsegregationists. Seventy percent of
the Texas governors and 60 percent of the Tennessee winners ran nonsegregationist campaigns. Although the victors in these elections
typically were not the most racially liberal candidates available, in
comparison to other southern states the chief executives of Texas and
Tennessee were not greatly preoccupied with the preservation of racial
segregation. Arkansas and Virginia elected a substantial proportion of
nonsegregationists (40 each), while North Carolina and Florida, like
three of the Deep South states, chose only one nonsegregationist
governor in the post-*Brown* period. Net changes within the electoral
process, while tending to favor militant segregationists, did not
universally do so. Strong segregationists accounted for a larger percentage of winners than major candidates in North Carolina, Texas,
and (especially) Virginia but declined in strength in Tennessee and
Florida. It is more difficult to rank the Peripheral South states on
overall campaign traditionalism (because of ties in modal combinations of racial and economic development stances), but three groups
of states—those relatively less innovative, those strongly innovative by
regional standards, and those in between—may be distinguished
without doing excessive violence to the data. Although none of the
Peripheral South states was as unambiguously traditional on both
segregation and economic development as Mississippi and Georgia,
Florida and North Carolina were the Peripheral South's least innovative states. Moderate segregationist-marginalists supplied half of
Florida's governors, and moderate segregationist-adaptives, a slightly
more innovative combination, were elected more frequently than any
other type of candidate in North Carolina. Virginia and Arkansas
present mixed patterns. Equal percentages of Virginia's governors (40)
were found in the most traditional (militant segregationist-marginalist) and in one of the least traditional (nonsegregationist-adaptive)

Table 46. Campaign stances on racial segregation and achievement of economic development of governors in the Peripheral South states, 1954-73 (percent)[a]

Campaign Stance	Arkansas	Florida	North Carolina	Tennessee	Texas	Virginia
Strong Segregationist	20 (0)	33 (-8)	20 (5)	20 (-3)	20 (9)	40 (15)
SS-Marginalist	0	33	20	20	20	40
SS-Redistributive	20	0	0	0	0	0
SS-Adaptive	0	0	0	0	0	0
SS-Progressive	0	0	0	0	0	0
Moderate Segregationist	40 (0)	50 (25)	60 (6)	20 (-3)	10 (-9)	20 (-5)
MS-Marginalist	0	50	20	20	10	0
MS-Redistributive	40	0	0	0	0	0
MS-Adaptive	0	0	40	0	0	20
MS-Progressive	0	0	0	0	0	0
Nonsegregationist	40 (0)	17 (-17)	20 (-11)	60 (6)	70 (0)	40 (-10)
NS-Marginalist	0	0	0	0	20	0
NS-Redistributive	0	0	0	0	0	0
NS-Adaptive	40	0	20	60	50	40
NS-Progressive	0	17	0	0	0	0
Totals	100	100	100	100	100	100
Number of Cases	(10)	(6)	(5)	(5)	(10)	(5)

[a]Figures in parentheses in the body of the table are percentage point differences between the proportion of governors holding a given racial position and the proportion of major candidates in Democratic first primaries holding the same position.

combinations, and in Arkansas the moderate segregationist and redistributives were as successful as nonsegregationist-adaptives (40 percent). In Texas and Tennessee the winners' campaign views were innovative on both policy dimensions. Three fifths of the Tennessee and half the Texas governors were nonsegregationist-adaptives. Outcomes in these two Peripheral South states were substantially different from the results of elections in Mississippi, Georgia, and Alabama.

A final comment should be added concerning the victorious neo-Populists (whether redistributives or progressives) in the Second Reconstruction. The few advocates of have-not economics who survived the electoral process tended to be concentrated in a small number of states. Only in Arkansas (where Orval Faubus accounted for all the neo-Populist victories), Alabama, and Georgia were neo-Populists elected more than once between 1954 and 1973, and there were no successful neo-Populists in South Carolina, North Carolina, Tennessee, Texas, and Virginia. Of the neo-Populists who did succeed, the candidates who emphasized traditional racial values simultaneously with neo-Populist economics (that is, the Wallaces and Faubuses) demonstrated more staying power (though Faubus's career ended in futility) than did the older agrarian politicians who stressed economic issues over racial cleavages (the Folsoms and Longs). The victories of several nonsegregationist and neo-Populist politicians in the early 1970s (Reubin Askew, Jimmy Carter, and Bill Waller) should not obscure the fact that the South's most racially and economically liberal candidates—for example, Ralph Yarborough and Don Yarborough in Texas—characteristically were defeated in elections for governor. This inability of the consistently liberal candidates to win represents a significant qualification to the general argument suggested here that there has been a broadening of choice since 1954 on both racial segregation and the achievement of economic development in southern electoral politics.

Regional and Subregional Trends, 1950-73

By graphing the results of successive waves of elections, the shifts in elite attitudes described above may be fixed more precisely in time and space. Data on the governors' campaign stances have been gathered for one set of pre-*Brown* elections, three sets of post-*Brown* but pre-Voting Rights Act campaigns, and two sets of post-Voting Rights Act contests. By including all the region's governors over a reasonably lengthy and highly eventful period in southern history, the trend lines thus generated for the Deep South, the Peripheral South, and the region as a whole should provide insight into the policy differences between the old and the new southern politics. The particular question I am asking may be expressed as follows: among those white southern politicians who have won governorships, what changes in attitudes toward racial segregation and the achievement of economic development have become apparent since 1950?

Longitudinal changes in the economic development stances of the governors may be treated briefly. Figure 23 graphs the economic development position of successful gubernatorial candidates by region and subregion from 1950 to 1973. Roughly three quarters of the southern governors chosen during the 1950s campaigned as marginalists, politicians who believed the state could best encourage economic growth by limiting its own spending and, using tax advantages as bait, by energetically recruiting new industry. Redistributives won all but one of the remaining governorships, and campaigners like Long and Folsom were less interested in economic development per se than in redividing existing resources to benefit have-not groups directly. Price has summarized the policy consequences of this situation: "The politics of black belt vs. non-black belt or of agrarian protest vs. Big Mules is fascinating to behold, but essentially a Merry-go-round. The most interesting thing is the campaign itself, not any substantive policy results. Such politics is cyclic, if not plain static."[7] White politicians in the 1950s were generally more interested in defending racial segregation in the public schools than in proposing or supporting any innovative, expensive role for the state's long-term economic development. At a time when many politicians contemplated closing the public schools to prevent desegregation, it made little sense politically to advocate substantially higher investments in public education.

During the 1960s and early 1970s, as the region's need for a better educated, more skilled labor force became more obvious, and as the school desegregation controversy waned, at least in the Peripheral South, southern campaigns grew somewhat less "static." Adaptives emerged as a relatively innovative voice in southern politics, winning a majority of the governorships contested between 1962 and 1973. Marginalists won less than a fifth as many elections from 1962 to 1973 (13 percent) as they had in the previous twelve years (73 percent). In the Deep South, progressives were victorious in two fifths of the 1962-73 campaigns and accounted for more victories in the 1970-73 wave of elections than did adaptives. The growth of the adaptives and the dwindling of the marginalists occurred in both subregions but were most evident in the Peripheral South.

Figure 23. Southern governors' campaign stances on achievement of economic development, 1950-73, by region and subregion (percent)

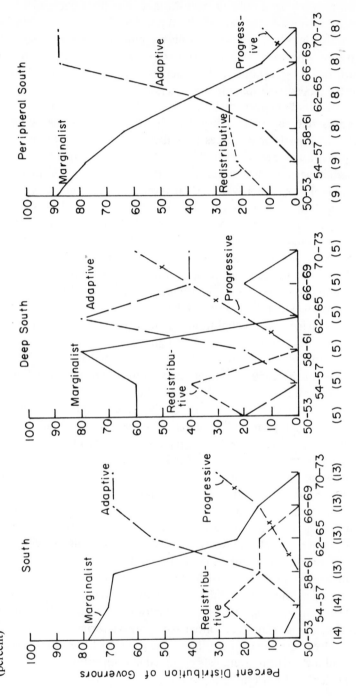

The rise and partial decline of the segregation controversy in the Second Reconstruction is clearly shown in Figure 24, which graphs the campaign racial stances of governors by region and subregion over time. For most governors in the pre-*Brown* years, racial segregation was a latent or, at most, a secondary issue. No one was elected governor who questioned the merits of the caste system, yet only a small minority, unevenly distributed even within the Deep South, campaigned as militant segregationists. The average governor (86 percent) ran as a moderate segregationist. These politicians would affirm their loyalty to southern racial customs if circumstances required it; otherwise, they ignored the topic or minimized the relevance of the segregation issue by arguing that the status of blacks was a closed question.

Southern campaigners responded predictably once the Supreme Court ordered school desegregation. Ambitious politicians, to put it mildly, perceived few incentives to advocate compliance. In the mid-1950s, blacks were generally ill organized politically; whites did most of the voting and preferred racial segregation; and neither the Eisenhower administration nor the Congress appeared anxious to help the Supreme Court implement the *Brown* decision. Militants won 43 percent of the southern governorships from 1954 to 1957, again outnumbered by moderate segregationists (57 percent). Had the Supreme Court ordered immediate desegregation, instead of compliance "with all deliberate speed," the percentage of strong segregationists would doubtless have been considerably higher. Militant segregationists reached the height of their regional influence in the late 1950s and early 1960s, often in direct response to the 1957 school desegregation crisis in Little Rock. The political rewards of conspicuously defying national authority were demonstrated to white politicians across the South by Arkansas Governor Orval Faubus's landslide reelection in 1958. Seventy-seven percent of the gubernatorial contests from 1958-61 were won by militants, a showing exceeded in the post-*Brown* South only by the nonsegregationists' performance in the early 1970s. Only two moderate segregationists were successful between 1958 and 1961, and, for the first time, a borderline nonsegregationist was elected.[8] In the third wave of post-*Brown* elections, the commanding position of the militants became less pronounced. Despite the Wallace movement and other manifestations of reaction in the South, the consensus among white southern politicians concerning racial segregation began to evaporate in the early 1960s. Half as many strong segregationists (38 percent) were elected in the South from 1962 to

Figure 24. Southern governors' campaign stances on racial segregation, 1950-73, by region and subregion (percent)

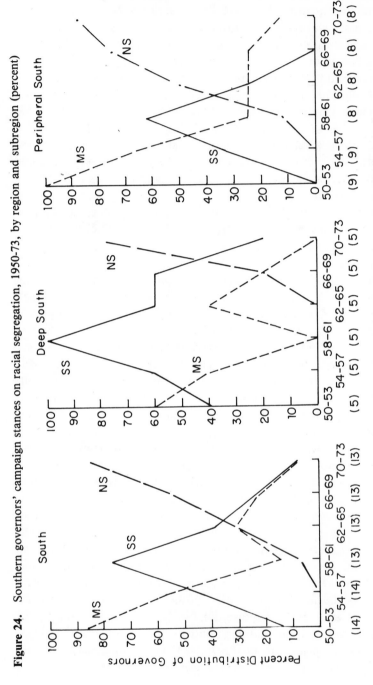

SS Strong Segregationist   MS Moderate Segregationist   NS Nonsegregationist

1965 as were chosen during the previous four years. The percentage of moderate segregationists doubled (31 percent), and, more significantly, there was a fourfold increase (31 percent) among nonsegregationists. To an inordinate degree, elections for governor during the first 12 years after the *Brown* decision reflected the white South's determination to perpetuate racial segregation. As Table 43 shows, 53 percent of the 1954-65 governorships were captured by strong segregationists, another 35 percent went to moderate segregationists, and the remaining 13 percent were won by nonsegregationists. Militancy was particularly evident in the Deep South, where 73 percent of the governors from 1954 to 1965, compared to 40 percent in the Peripheral South, campaigned as strong segregationists.

The regional trend toward fewer winning segregationists (whether militants or moderates), a change that may properly be viewed as historic, accelerated in the last half of the 1960s and became genuinely regional in scope in the early 1970s. Data on the 13 governorships decided from 1966-69 clearly indicate the erosion of the white South's traditional solidarity regarding racial segregation. Militant segregationists won 23 percent of the elections, less than one third of their victories in the late 1950s, and moderates accounted for another 23 percent. For the first time in the history of the modern South, half of the region's governors campaigned as nonsegregationists. In the final set of elections available for classification (1970-73), nonsegregationists were dominant throughout the South. Eighty-five percent of the governorships contested in the early 1970s were taken by nonsegregationists, and the only victorious militant segregationist was George Wallace. The ability of an increasing number of nonsegregationists to survive the electoral process is one indication that significant political change was occuring in the South.

For the entire post-Voting Rights Act period, nonsegregationists won a heavy majority (69 percent) of the region's elections, while moderate segregationists and strong segregationists each succeeded in only 15 percent of the 26 campaigns. Subregional differences in electoral outcomes were, of course, substantial. Until the early 1970s the rise of the nonsegregationist governor was limited primarily to the Peripheral South. Four fifths of the Peripheral South governorships between 1966 and 1973 were won by nonsegregationists, compared to half of the Deep South contests. The principle of racial segregation is now virtually dead as an explicit campaign issue in the Peripheral South. No politician campaigning as a militant segregationist has been elected governor in that subregion since 1964. On the other hand, racial segregation tended to persist much longer as a significant campaign issue in the Deep South. The nonsegregationist trend lines in Figure 24 show that the Deep South lagged two waves of elections behind the Peripheral South in electing sizable fractions of nonsegregationist governors. Nonsegregationists succeeded in such Peripheral South states as Texas and Tennessee prior to federal intervention, but there was little evidence of changed outcomes in Deep South campaigns until the second wave of post-1965 elections (1970-73). Presumably in the Deep South a longer period of time was required to organize the potential black electorate and to persuade white politicians of the practicality of nonsegregationist approaches. In the early 1970s four of the five Deep South governorships were won by candidates who were not public advocates (whatever their private convictions may have been) of the principle of racial segregation. Although the results of a single set of elections do not establish a trend, they indicate at the minimum a significant discontinuity in the Deep South's accustomed pattern of resistance to racial change.

As a final attempt to describe the changing racial stances of white southern politicians, consider the graphs presented in Figure 25. The charts display, by region and subregion, the proportions of major candidates and winners contributed over time by militant segregationists and nonsegregationists, the polar orientations on racial segregation. It is apparent that systemic bias, which may be defined as the tendency of the South's electoral institutions to benefit those campaigners who were more strenuously opposed to racial change than their competitors, has varied considerably over the past quarter century. Across the South, however, higher percentages of strong segregationists were ordinarily elected governor than were represented among the major candidates. As the total field of candidates was reduced, the screening process associated with the South's electoral institutions tended regularly to favor the militant segregationists.[9] In view of the region's commitment to racial segregation, it is not surprising to discover that net change beneficial to the militants was greatest in the post-Little Rock years (1958-61), following a dramatic demonstration of the seriousness of the Supreme Court's challenge to the Jim Crow system. With the exception of the 1958-61 elections (when there were very few nonsegregationists) and the 1970-73 campaigns (after federal intervention had altered the old rules of southern politics), nonsegregationists tended to decline relative to their initial strength as they proceeded through the electoral process. Comparison of subregional patterns indicates that systemic bias was

Figure 25. Comparison of major candidates and winners who campaigned as strong segregationists and nonsegregationists in southern elections for governor, 1950-73, by region and subregion (percent)

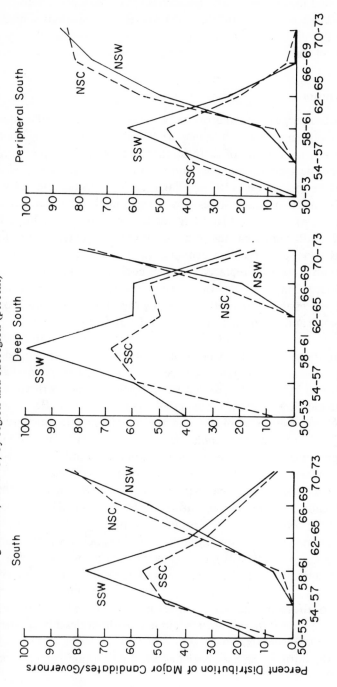

SSC Strong Segregationist Candidates   SSW Strong Segregationist Winners
NSC Nonsegregationist Candidates   NSW Nonsegregationist Winners

greater and more consistently beneficial to the strong segregationists in the Deep South, with the 1958-61 results for that subregion providing a classic example of a political system closing ranks against threatened change to local traditions.

Conclusions

It has been argued that a growing percentage of successful contenders for southern governorships may be described as nonsegregationists and that the appearance of these candidates is an indication of meaningful political change in the South. Compared with the political atmosphere of the late 1950s and early 1960s, considerable progress has been made, in many states, toward eliminating or reducing the explicitness of the more blatant forms of race baiting. In most Peripheral South campaigns the principle of racial segregation is a dead or dying issue, and truculent demands for the preservation of racial segregation have been replaced by more euphemistic language in the Deep South. Since the *Brown* decision, the spectrum of politically feasible expression on matters concerning the caste system has broadened significantly, especially in the Peripheral South.

At the same time, it must be emphasized that the decline of segregationist oratory, where it has occurred, has not been accompanied by much specific attention to the socioeconomic needs of black southerners. Progress in civil rights, as measured by the campaign rhetoric of white politicians, has been more verbal than substantive. Because of the minority position of blacks and the indifference or hostility of many whites, it seems improbable that many white candidates will use campaigns to articulate fundamental problems—employment, education, housing, law enforcement, and welfare—of blacks in the South. Black gains have been associated more with "liberty" than with "equality."[10] The right to participate in politics has largely been won, but the concept of "equal results" has not been seriously raised in state campaigns. Moreover, the decline of explicitly segregationist rhetoric does not necessarily mean that white politicians have given up race as a campaign issue. My concern has been to trace changing elite attitudes toward racial segregation, an important but not the sole indicator of the race issue. Many white candidates have found and will find ways to appeal to anti-black prejudices without describing themselves as segregationists.

While the shifts which have been discerned in the campaign rhetoric of many governors are thus less than monumental and fall exceedingly short of the region's needs, they should not be dismissed as trivial. As Leslie Dunbar has suggested, southern history provides a perspective for evaluating the events of the Second Reconstruction:

> We can note that any government has but three possible postures toward the question of racial equality: in favor, opposed, or neutral. The political theory of the South has for more than three centuries been grounded on the principle of white supremacy. It has been the cardinal doctrine. If . . . southern state governments were to follow the lead already given by some municipalities, and move from opposition to neutrality, this would be a truly historic change.[11]

A systematic analysis of racial segregation as a campaign issue indicates that, particularly in the Peripheral South, signs of a shift by white elites from opposition to neutrality have become more and more visible.

During the 1960s and early 1970s many governors also reached a new understanding of the state's role in promoting economic development. Numerous white politicians have become less concerned with the size of the state's budget and more willing to support substantially higher state spending for public education as a long-range investment in economic development. In the period following federal intervention into southern race relations, then, many southern governors could be differentiated from their predecessors by a comparatively reduced preoccupation with the principle of racial segregation and by a heightened interest in innovative economic development policies. An appreciable number of white politicians, in short, were beginning to frame issues of greater relevance to the needs of the contemporary South.

PART FOUR

Conclusion

11

Explaining Racial Change
in Southern Electoral Politics

Measured against the historical subordination of the South's black minority, the most significant aspect of recent southern politics has been the rapidity of racial change, the suddenness with which traditional white assumptions concerning the "place" of black southerners have been discredited. Two decades after the Supreme Court first ruled segregated public schools unconstitutional, state governments openly premised upon white supremacy have become obsolete or are in the process of becoming so, and a partial accommodation of black and white objectives is being pursued in the more progressive southern states.

Yet in the initial years following the *Brown* decision, it was far from apparent that substantial school desegregation could be achieved. Neither the Eisenhower administration nor Congress gave the Supreme Court appreciable political and moral support in enforcing desegregation, and voluntary compliance with the decision by local school boards, which was minimal to begin with, virtually ended after the Little Rock crisis. Control over desegregation policy rested primarily at the state level, and the central tendency of southern chief executives and legislators was resistance rather than compliance. Law after law was enacted to circumvent the *Brown* decision and, in general, to make it difficult for blacks to exercise their constitutional rights safely and expeditiously.[1] But eventually the segregationists' tactics of intimidation, obfuscation, and delay failed, for the white southern leadership could not contain the civil rights movement which erupted in 1960. The use of fire hoses, cattle prods, and tear gas against nonviolent civil rights demonstrators, as well as occasional murders, proved counterproductive in an age of national television coverage; and national legislation followed to protect the civil rights of black southerners. Five years after widespread sit-in demonstrations began, school districts throughout the South were desegregating in order to qualify for federal aid-to-education grants, public accommodations were increasingly open to all southerners, and thousands of previously excluded blacks were entering the electorates of the Deep South. Campaigns for the governorship were less frequently rituals for the reaffirmation of white supremacy, and an explicit and fervent commitment to racial segregation was less instrumental to political success than it had recently been.

If southern politics prior to 1954 can be accurately regarded as closed even to the possibility of meaningful structural change in race relations, the era of the Second Reconstruction, considered in broad historical perspective, witnessed the opening of southern electoral politics to racial change. Some southern states were clearly more receptive to pressures for reform than others, and the purpose of this final chapter is twofold: first, to measure the degree to which politicians in the different states adopted less traditional views on racial segregation; and second, to explore as systematically as the available data permit several factors which appear to be theoretically useful in explaining variations in racial change.

In order to compare the states and subregions with respect to the changing racial stances of white politicians, an index of racial change has been devised which can be interpreted as the ratio of nonsegregationist to segregationist strength. Index numbers based on all post-*Brown* campaigns have been calculated for each state by dividing the percentage of nonsegregationist governors (or major candidates, as the case may be) by a weighted percentage of segregationist governors (or major candidates). The segregationist proportions have been weighted, with militant segregationists counted at full strength and moderate segregationists at half strength, to adjust for differences from state to state in the intensity of the white politicians' commitment to racial segregation.[2] Index numbers in excess of 1.00 represent states in which nonsegregationists won more governorships or were more numerous as major candidates than segregationists (as weighted). Index numbers of less than 1.00 identify states in which segregationist winners or candidates were more common than nonsegregationists. The lower the index number, the less the racial change among white politicians.

The opening of southern politics to comparatively innovative stances on segregation is portrayed in Figure 26, which plots indexes

Figure 26. The "opening" of southern electoral politics: indexes of racial change for gubernatorial candidates and winners, by state, subregion, and region, for the post-*Brown* era[a]

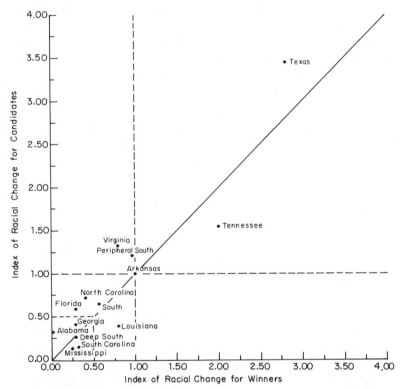

[a]Subregional and regional indexes are computed from means of the states included within each political unit.

of racial change by state, subregion, and region for candidates and winners. Texas and Tennessee are the only states in the post-*Brown* period in which nonsegregationists consistently exhibited greater strength than segregationists. Nonsegregationists and segregationists were equally successful in Arkansas, a result made possible, however, only because the moderate segregationists' strength has been halved; and Virginia achieved an index of racial change in excess of 1.00 for candidates but not for governors. In the remaining states more segregationists than nonsegregationists ran for governor and were elected. Racial change was least evident, of course, in the Deep South states. In Alabama, Mississippi, South Carolina, and Georgia, no index of racial change reached 0.50. Although seven states (the Deep South plus Florida and North Carolina) were uniformly more supportive of segregationists than nonsegregationists, their limited racial change should be evaluated against the historical commitment of southern politicians to the racial status quo. It is highly unlikely that many candidates for governor in the half century or so between the development of the one-party system and the *Brown* decision could be described as nonsegregationists. If indexes of racial change were computed and graphed for elections held between 1900 and 1950, they would probably cluster as the intersection of the *x*-axis and *y*-axis (0.00, 0.00). The fact meriting emphasis is less the modest amount of racial change in many states (most of the elections occurred before federal intervention) than the existence of some racial change among governors or major candidates in all southern states. Alabama alone rejected all nonsegregationist campaigners and thus maintained a perfect segregationist score (0.00) on the index of racial change for winners.

From Figure 26 it is apparent that openness to racial change has varied considerably from one state to another, with the Peripheral South states generally having higher indexes of racial change. Given these variations, the final task is to explain the observed differences in racial change. A number of factors—the demographic environment of electoral politics, the structure of factional and party competition, the willingness of the national government to enforce desegregation court orders in certain situations and, more generally, the significance of national decisions which have altered particular norms of southern politics, the role of black voting, limited but perhaps important attitudinal shifts among white southerners, and the emergence of a post-1965 generation of white politicians—need to be examined in understanding why southern politicians no longer speak with a united voice on the principle of racial segregation.

The Constraints of Demography

"If the whites of the black belt give the South its dominant political tone," Key wrote, "the character of the politics of individual states will vary roughly with the Negro proportion of the population."[3] Key's emphasis on the significance of demographic factors—particularly black population and rural-urban composition—in conditioning southern racial politics suggests a starting point for explaining racial change. In previous chapters a classification of southern counties (large metropolitan, medium urban, low black rural, and high black rural) has been used to compare and contrast the demographic setting of electoral politics in the southern states. To probe the relationship between political demography and racial change, these categories may be reduced to an index of demographic traditionalism. This index represents the ratio of the less traditional components of the state vote (the two urban categories and the low black rural classification) to the most traditional component of the state electorate (the rural areas with high black populations).[4] The higher the index number, the less "southern" the state's demography.

A ranking of the states according to demographic traditionalism (see Table 47) suggests three types of electoral settings. An index number of less than 1.00 signifies an extremely traditional environment for electoral politics, one in which a larger proportion of the state vote originates in the high black rural counties than in the three less tradi-

Table 47. Ranking of southern political units on index of demographic traditionalism (IDT)[a]

Interpretation of IDT	Political Unit	IDT
Qualitatively Less Traditional Setting (over 5.00)	Tennessee	16.50
	Texas	14.00
	Florida	11.16
Traditional Setting (1.00-4.99)	Peripheral South Mean	4.05
	Virginia	3.39
	South Mean	2.08
	Alabama	2.05
	Louisiana	1.91
	Arkansas	1.45
	Georgia	1.43
	North Carolina	1.40
	Deep South Mean	1.19
	South Carolina	1.07
Extremely Traditional Setting (0.00-0.99)	Mississippi	0.40

[a]Each state's index is calculated from the mean percentage distribution of the state vote in Democratic first primaries for governor, 1950-73. Subregional and regional indexes are based on means of the states included within each classification. The index of demographic traditionalism is defined as the following ratio: percent large metropolitan vote plus 0.5 percent medium urban vote plus 0.33 percent low black rural vote divided by percent high black rural vote.

tional categories (as weighted). Mississippi, with an index of demographic traditionalism of 0.40, has offered the least auspicious setting for racial change in the South. States with indexes of demographic traditionalism ranging from 1.00 to 4.99 may be considered to exhibit traditional settings. Because the black belt whites successfully "impressed on an entire region a [racial] philosophy agreeable to [their] necessities," it would be misleading to interpret an index number of 1.00 or 2.00 as indicating a loose balance between the less traditional and the traditional votes.[5] Hence index numbers up to 4.99 have been considered representative of tradition-saturated demographic settings. The four remaining Deep South states, North Carolina, Arkansas, and Virginia have been characterized by traditional demographies, social settings unfavorable to racial change. Campaigns in Tennessee (IDT = 16.50), Texas (14.00), and Florida (11.16), by comparison, have occurred in qualitatively less "southern" demographic environments. These states have all contained a multiplicity of large metropolitan centers and insignificant high black rural votes. On the basis of their demography, Tennessee, Texas, and Florida would be expected to be less resistant to racial change than states with low scores on the index of demographic traditionalism.

Figure 27 demonstrates compellingly the constraints of demography on southern racial change in the Second Reconstruction. None of the eight states with "southern" demographic settings achieved indexes of racial change in excess of 1.00, while two of the three states with relatively "nonsouthern" demographies led the region in degree of racial change. Stated differently, significant racial change was limited to two states where big cities were prominent and where minimal fractions of the electorate resided in rural counties with sizable black populations. Presumably the comparatively small audience for old-fashioned segregationist rhetoric in Texas and Tennessee indirectly encouraged a milder form of racial politics than was found elsewhere in the South. As the highly deviant case of Florida illustrates, however, a "nonsouthern" demography was not invariably associated with racial change.

Racial change in the three states which fall at opposite ends of the demographic traditionalism scale can largely be understood in terms of their demography. Texas and Tennessee on the one hand, and Mississippi on the other, are situated where they "should" be, given the demographic setting in which their campaigns take place. Yet in several states racial change is less satisfactorily accounted for by demographic considerations alone. Florida and Alabama experienced less racial change than their demographies would predict, and Arkan-

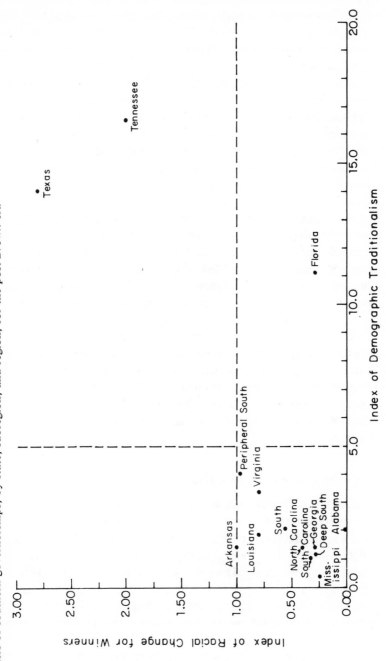

Figure 27. The constraints of demography: relationship between index of demographic traditionalism and index of racial change for winners of southern governorships, by state, subregion, and region, for the post-*Brown* era

sas and Louisiana had higher indexes of racial change than states with similar demographic settings. Political variables, including the impact of specific personalities such as Wallace in Alabama and Winthrop Rockefeller in Arkansas, seem important in clarifying these variations in racial change.

Although the generally close fit between demographic traditionalism and racial change should be kept in mind as relationships are explored between explicitly political factors and white elite attitudes on segregation, it should be stressed that political variables are considerably more susceptible to short-term manipulation than are such environmental variables as black population size and urbanism.[6] As Price has argued in a different context, "Political factors may be less potent *predictors* of state or city spending than economic factors. But the political factors are much more subject to short-run human control. Mississippi voters can turn to a Republican candidate overnight—as they did in 1964, when Mississippi became *the* banner GOP state for Goldwater. But Mississippi *cannot* become as wealthy as Connecticut overnight."[7] Likewise, South Carolina will not shortly come to resemble Tennessee in demographic composition. Only in three states have indexes of demographic traditionalism for Democratic first primaries for governor measurably risen over the past quarter century, and these states were the ones which already possessed "nonsouthern" demographies. Eight states, including all the Deep South states, have continued to be highly "southern" in their demographic settings; if racial change if evident in these states, it should be attributed to political factors rather than to demographic change.

Factional and Party Competition

Campaigns for governor are embedded in patterns of intraparty and interparty competition (patterns of varying stability, to be sure) as well as demographic environments, and these political structures might plausibly be expected to exert some bearing on the degree of racial change experienced by individual states. Yet, as we shall see, it is doubtful that variations in the degree of factionalism within the Democratic party or in the extent of Republican-Democratic competition furnish valid general explanations for differences in racial change.

Conflicting hypotheses concerning the relationship between Democratic factionalism and racial politics may be extracted from the research of Key and Matthews and Prothro. In his analysis of the one-party system, Key distinguished those states that had a "tightly organized majority faction within the Democratic party" from states whose "factional organization approximates a bi-factional division" and from states which exhibited "varying degrees of multifactionalism."[8] Writing several years before the *Brown* decision restored the segregation issue to the agenda of southern politics, Key argued that the "nature of political organization" had implications for "the question of race." "A cohesive faction has the power to discipline wild-eyed men," he concluded. "A chaotic factionalism provides no block to unscrupulous and spectacular personalities. The kinds of individuals thrown into positions of state-wide leadership in North Carolina and Virginia [states with dominant majority factions at the time] over the past thirty years contrast markedly with many of those who have risen to power in states with more loosely organized politics."[9] According to this analysis uninhibited defenses of the racial status quo should be more characteristic of multifactional than unifactional systems.

Matthews and Prothro's work, although not strictly comparable to Key's research, comes to different conclusions. Studying black voter registration as of the late 1950s, they found that rates of black mobilization were *lower* than predicted by a set of socioeconomic variables in states with "one dominant faction" than in states characterized by "multifactionalism" and that black registration was higher than expected in states with "two competitive factions." More interestingly for our purposes, while neither of the states classified by Matthews and Prothro as "one dominant faction" typically produced "major candidates favorable to Negroes," politicians judged relatively acceptable to blacks regularly appeared in two of the four bifactional states and in three of the five multifactional states.[10] While Matthews and Prothro were not explicitly concerned with the relationship between factional systems and the racial positions of successful candidates, their research implicitly challenges Key's argument that unifactional systems should produce fewer extremists.

Against these diverse findings,[11] alternative hypotheses can be proposed which deprecate linkages between degree of factionalism and extent of racial change for the post-*Brown* era. The timing of federal intervention and differences in subregional political cultures, it is suggested, offer better keys to comprehending racial change than does factional structure. If the principle of racial segregation again became a live issue (as it was not during the period covered by Key's study and during half the years which Matthews and Prothro used to classify state factional systems), opposition to racial change could be expected to prevail, with intensity of resistance greatest in the Deep South, irrespective of a state's factional structure. Furthermore, if a national decision to desegregate southern institutions were made and effectively administered, changed elite orientations on the segregation issue should be evident (especially in the Peripheral South) across all types of Democratic factionalism. Political organization per se would be less crucial to racial change than the presence or absence of national intervention.

If individual states could be accurately classified for the 1954-73 Democratic primaries as unifactional, bifactional, or multifactional, it would be a simple matter to test whether or not differences in factional structure have been related to variations in racial change among southern governors. The unfortunate reality is that, as Havard has written, "The taxonomy of southern politics cannot now be reduced to a single major classification of the eleven states of the South, with subspecies being identified in categories of factional competitiveness."[12] Factional patterns over the past twenty years have simply been too unstable in too many states to allow meaningful categorization. To quote Havard again:

> The structures of the factional systems of the various states have been greatly affected by the disintegration of the Democratic Party structures and the tentative rise of Republican organizations. Strong statewide organizations based on rural versions of urban machine politics have all but disappeared; the friends-and-neighbors tendency still prevails to some extent in several states, but it is less clearly identifiable than it once was; and bifactionalism seems to have gone by the board, except possibly in Texas, and even here the growth of Republicanism has confused the lines of this form of intraparty competitiveness.[13]

The decline of the Longs in Louisiana, the Byrd Organization in Virginia, and the Talmadge faction in Georgia, as well as the rise and fall of the Faubus wing of the Democratic party in Arkansas, all of which occurred during the Second Reconstruction, suggest the difficulty of reducing factional competition to a single term for many of the states.

Two simplifications have been necessary, given the transitional character of the period, to operationalize the concept of intraparty factionalism. First, individual primaries rather than states have been classified as unifactional, bifactional, or multifactional.[14] If the complexity and instability of factional structures precludes the use of states as units of analysis, the relationship between factionalism and racial change may still be examined at the levels of subregion and region. A second simplification employed to facilitate classification is that the primaries are distinguished solely in terms of the division of the first primary vote between competing factions. Factionalism as conceived here refers only to factions as organizations, with no consideration given to factions in the electorate.[15]

Table 48, which compares indexes of racial change by region and subregion for each type of Democratic primary, fails to show persistent relationships between factional structure and racial change. Remembering that types of primary and not state factional systems are being contrasted, in no instance is there support for Key's hypothesis that "tightly organized majority factions" would be less supportive of extremists than more disorganized factions. After 1954 unifactional primaries frequently permitted the dominant faction to capitalize on the Supreme Court's threat to the racial status quo. Virginia's Byrd Organization, previously noted for its rejection of unrestrained segregationists, turned out to harbor "wild-eyed men" of its own once the threat to white supremacy materialized. Indeed, leadership for the massive resistance movement of the mid-1950s came from the South's most durable political organization. The southwide results for 1954-73, showing racial change to be greatest in bifactional

Table 48. Indexes of racial change for Democratic gubernatorial nominees in the South by degree of factionalism in Democratic first primaries, controlling for subregion and federal intervention

Political Unit	Type of Primary[a]			Total
	Multifactional	Bifactional	Unifactional	
South, 1954-73	0.51	0.80	0.36	0.55
South, 1954-65	0.13	0.17	0.00	0.11
South, 1966-73	2.00	3.32	-[b]	2.73
Deep South, 1954-73	0.17	0.29	-[b]	0.24
Peripheral South, 1954-73	1.00	1.25	0.29	0.90

[a]Unifactional primaries are defined as those in which the leading candidate received a minimum of 60.0 percent of the vote. Primaries in which the leader received less than 60.0 percent but in which the two highest candidates obtained 75.0 percent or more of the vote are considered bifactional. The remaining primaries are classified as multifactional.

[b]Omitted because of small number of cases.

primaries, are more in line with Matthews and Prothro's findings. However, when controls are applied for federal intervention and for subregional differences, the initial relationship between bifactionalism and racial change is much reduced. Very little racial change occurred prior to 1966 in any type of primary, whereas indexes of racial change were fairly high in both multifactional and bifactional primaries (especially the latter) after federal intervention. Putting aside the unifactional category, similarities in degree of racial change were more apparent within subregions than between them. Primaries in which the vote essentially divided between two factions have been slightly more likely to be associated with higher indexes of racial change, but the overall impact of factional structure has been modest compared to national intervention and to subregional political cultures.[16]

If a stable and fairly balanced division of the white vote would enhance the political leverage of black southerners, then the growth of competitive Republican parties would seem to encourage, over the long run, nonsegregationist campaigning.[17] But with the unsettled conditions of the immediate past and with some Republican parties deliberately ignoring the black vote and seeking to establish themselves as a second party of white supremacy, party competition as such could not be expected to exert any pervasive moderating effect upon the racial positions of white nominees. It is hardly surprising, then, that Figure 28 reveals no discernible positive association between interparty competitiveness for the governorship and indexes of racial change.[18] Deep South states have been solidly one-party Democratic in gubernatorial politics and highly supportive of segregationists, but in the Peripheral South, where Republican competitiveness has risen, the variables are unrelated. Interparty competition was least advanced in the state (Texas) that scored highest on racial change, while the South's only two-party state (Virginia) elected nonsegregationists less frequently than segregationists. Because interparty competition (though increasing over time) was so poorly developed in the post-*Brown* years, Figure 28 does not necessarily refute the hypothesis that, other things being equal, stable party competition should improve the bargaining advantages of the black minority and thereby reduce the likelihood of segregationist campaigning. A meaningful test of that proposition must await the institutionalization of two-party politics.

For the present, two generalizations about southern Republican parties deserve emphasis. Republican nominees in the post-*Brown*

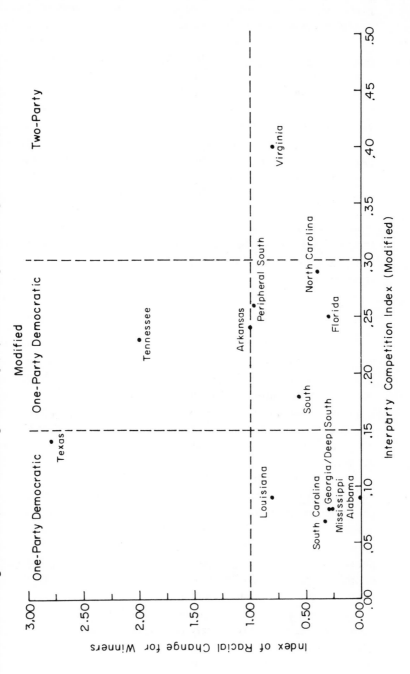

Figure 28. The limitations of party competition: relationship between interparty competition index (modified from Ranney) and index of racial change for winners of southern governorships, by state, subregion, and region, for the post-*Brown* era

general elections adopted a variety of stances on segregation, and their positions commonly but not invariably reflected subregional differences in the salience of racial cleavages. Peripheral South Republicans tended to be nonsegregationists or moderate segregationists; Republicans in the Deep South were more likely to run as militant segregationists or moderate segregationists. Second, most of the Republicans who were elected governor—especially Rockefeller in Arkansas, Holton in Virginia, and Holshouser in North Carolina—were nonsegregationists who perceived the inclusion of blacks into the Republican party as essential to the long-term strength of southern Republicanism. Although considerable time and money were expended in the Deep South from the 1964 Goldwater campaign onwards to make the Republican party an alternative center of racial conservatism, this strategy produced no Republican governors in the Deep South through 1973. Even in the Deep South, it is far from a certainty that a Republican party based primarily on opposition to desegregation has much future.[19]

Federal Intervention as the Sine Qua Non of Racial Change

The decline of segregationist campaign rhetoric cannot be explained without reference to federalism. If the political demography of most states implied a politics of white supremacy, and if satisfaction with the racial status quo pervaded all categories of Democratic factionalism after 1954, national decisions in the mid-1960s nonetheless produced significant changes in the racial stances of white politicians. These national actions, which will be considered shortly, were largely the consequence of pressures for reform generated by the southern civil rights movement. The enduring achievement of the civil rights movement was less the reforms won in particular local confrontations (sometimes there were no immediate victories) than the successful dramatization, before a national audience, of the injustice and inhumanity of the Jim Crow system. In the absence of effective national intervention to protect the civil rights of blacks, it is highly improbable that segregationist campaigning would have diminished in more than a small minority of states.

A comparison of indexes of racial change for 1954-65 and 1966-73 campaigns (see Table 49) strongly supports the argument that national intervention was the sine qua non of significant change in the racial stances of white politicians. Prior to federal intervention little racial change was apparent in the Peripheral South and no racial change at

Table 49. The impact of federal intervention on the racial stances of campaigning southern politicians: comparison of indexes of racial change for candidates and winners in elections for governor before and after passage of the Voting Rights Act of 1965, by subregion and region

Political Unit	Pre-Voting Rights Act 1954-65		Post-Voting Rights Act 1966-73	
	Candidates	Winners	Candidates	Winners
Deep South	0.00	0.00	1.33	1.11
Peripheral South	0.39	0.33	8.86	8.65
South	0.20	0.18	3.60	3.00

all was evident in the Deep South. The one-party system functioned smoothly, in accordance with the intentions of its designers, to ensure that political leadership remained totally in the hands of segregationist whites. But when national intervention finally occurred in the mid-1960s, its impact on campaign rhetoric was substantial. Nonsegregationist stances became more or less routine after 1965 in the Peripheral South, and even in the Deep South, there were more nonsegregationist candidates and governors than segregationists (as weighted). A review of the national government's role in the segregation controversy is needed to explain why federal intervention, by indirect as well as direct means, altered the racial positions of many campaigners.

Meaningful federal support for racial change in the South developed slowly and reluctantly. After a survey of southern efforts to resist the *Brown* decision, one scholar concluded in 1961 that "school boards acting in bad faith did not have to fear federal pressure."[20] Putting aside Little Rock, where the issue could be defined in abstract terms as the supremacy of national law, President Eisenhower maintained a public position of "aloofness from the battle against racial injustice."[21] Under the leadership of President Kennedy, the executive branch gradually became a more energetic advocate of black civil rights. In 1963 racial conflicts in Alabama culminated in a sustained drive by the Kennedy administration to legislate against some forms of racial discrimination. When protracted civil rights demonstrations in Birmingham were followed by George Wallace's "shabby little minuet" in a schoolhouse door at the University of Alabama, Kennedy responded with a nationally televised address which defined the civil rights problem as a "moral crisis" and promised legislation to outlaw discrimination in public accommodations and government employment, permit the Justice Department to intervene in local desegregation suits, and prohibit racial discrimination in programs financed by the national government. A year later, with the active support of President Johnson, the Civil Rights Act became law.[22]

The Civil Rights Act of 1964 desegregated public accommodations throughout the South and authorized administrators to withhold federal funds from segregated state and local programs. It was the first of three laws which comprised, in their totality, an unprecedented (in this century) intervention by the national government into southern race relations. Passage of the Elementary and Secondary Education Act of 1965 enormously encouraged racial change in public education, for the new grants were contingent upon a showing of some desegregation. During the 1964-65 school year, it is estimated that no more than 2.25 percent of the South's black students attended public schools with whites. This figure rose to 6.1 percent the following year and climbed to 15.9 percent in 1966-67.[23] The increased desegregation was unimpressive compared to the magnitude of the problem, but it represented the beginning of widespread compliance with the *Brown* decision. When the threat of federal pressure was balanced by the prospect of federal dollars, the result was a "quiet social revolution in the schools of the South after 1964."[24] As Gary Orfield has argued, "The existing social order could not be preserved when Federal officials had both strong financial leverage and a clear congressional mandate to use the power of that money to challenge the tradition of unrestricted localism in education and to force recognition of the rights of black students."[25] Voting rights was a third area in which national policy became more protective of black interests. Although civil rights organizations had struggled for years to overcome obstacles to voter registration in the Deep South, no comprehensive and effective voting rights legislation was introduced by the Johnson administration until after the nation had witnessed the spectacle of Alabama state police clubbing down defenseless and nonviolent demonstrators on a Selma bridge. The Voting Rights Act of 1965 provided for the appointment of federal voting examiners to supersede local registrars in areas where restrictive suffrage requirements (such as literacy tests) were in effect and less than half of the voting age population had participated in the 1964 presidential election.[26]

Thus as the federal executive intervened on occasion to impose school desegregation and as the activities of the civil rights movement in the early 1960s gradually expanded the arena of racial conflict from small, isolated southern constituencies to Washington, local whites found it more difficult to preserve total racial segregation.[27] A series of federal-state confrontations, all lost by the militant segregationists, ultimately suggested to many politicians the futility of continued defiance on the principle of racial desegregation; and passage of the Civil Rights Act and the Voting Rights Act meant that white southerners could no longer claim that racial change lacked a congressional mandate. With the enactment of federal aid to education in 1965, funds being contingent upon some degree of desegregation, local school districts were given a strong economic incentive to integrate. Once public accommodations were desegregated, once increasing proportions of blacks came to exercise the franchise, and once widespread (though generally token) school desegregation began, most campaigners (especially outside the more recalcitrant Deep South states) accepted some measure of racial integration as a political reality.

The laws mentioned above affected the campaign stances of white politicians both directly and indirectly. By simplifying voter registration in states which had previously suppressed black participation, the Voting Rights Act helped convert meager and vulnerable bloc votes into much larger entities and thus gave campaigners a tangible incentive to avoid explicitly segregationist rhetoric. Indirectly, the success of national intervention in desegregating schools and public accommodations put most segregationist politicians on the defensive. Their message tacitly shifted from "let's protect our segregated institutions" (a commitment to maintain an existing state of affairs which required no sustained sacrifices on the part of white voters) to "let's resegregate our institutions" (an invitation to reverse a *fait accompli* which was supported in principle by all branches of the national government and to which many white southerners were adapting). The reality of racial change reduced the credibility of traditional segregationist rhetoric. Orfield's conclusions about federalism and school desegregation are pertinent to an understanding of the implications of national intervention for changes in the racial attitudes of southern politicians:

The institutions of American federalism and the popular beliefs associated with them make long-term national intervention in local race relations possible only under the most extraordinary conditions. The best that can be expected within the normal pattern of political relationships is a temporary use of Federal power against the local status quo. Temporary intervention, however, is no small accomplishment, particularly when it exposes the fallacy of the extreme racial stereotypes used to justify local segregation. Even a brief exercise of national authority can relieve local leaders of the political burdens of implementing a deeply resented change and can create a new status quo which some local leaders will defend.[28]

Applying Orfield's interpretation to electoral politics, the significance of federal intervention was that it created a "new status quo" based on extensive desegregation of schools and public accommodations. National intervention indirectly affected campaign stances by forcing the remaining segregationists to run increasingly as disturbers of this "new status quo" while allowing other office seekers to portray changes in race relations as a *fait accompli* of the national government. Simultaneously, the expansion of black electorates conditioned campaign rhetoric more directly by increasing the political risks of defending segregation.

The Black Vote

While national legislation generally reduced the salience of the segregation controversy, the single most important consequence of federal intervention for campaign behavior was probably the encouragement it gave to the mobilization of black voters. With several conspicuous exceptions, post-1965 elections for governor have confirmed the prediction that "Negroes, when they vote, can cause a startling change in the style, if not the substance, of Southern politics. Segregationists will have to choose between abandoning race-baiting as a political tactic or getting out of politics."[29] The vote, whatever its other limitations may be, has at least provided a partial check on segregationist campaigning. To understand why this has been the case, analyses of black mobilization are required which are sensitive to changes in the level of white participation.

The rise in black political participation, though one of the most dramatic accomplishments of the civil rights movement, must be seen in the perspective of white participation patterns. During the 1960s far more additional whites than blacks registered to vote in the South,[30] and much of the increased white registration is best viewed as a reaction—a white countermobilization—to black participation.[31] To the extent that black registration was matched or exceeded by a surge of new white voters, the impact of the black vote would be lessened. Although there is evidence of considerable countermobilization by whites in the Deep South, particularly in Alabama where Wallace symbolized die-hard resistance to black participation, Table 50 shows substantial gains in the relative mobilization of blacks during the 1960s.[32] Ratios of estimated black registration rates to white registration rates typically increased over the decade, with the most striking

Table 50.   Patterns of black voter mobilization I: ratios of black to white voter registration rates, before and after federal intervention, by state, sub-region, and region[a]

Political Unit	Pre-1965		Post-1965		
	1960	1964	1966	1968	1970
Alabama[b]	0.22	0.33	0.58	0.59	0.67
Georgia[b]	0.42	0.67	0.62	0.66	0.71
Louisiana[b]	0.40	0.40	0.57	0.67	0.70
Mississippi[b]	n.a.	0.10	0.52	0.64	0.78
South Carolina[b]	0.29	0.49	0.64	0.74	0.78
Arkansas	0.62	0.64	0.85	0.90	0.89
Florida	0.56	0.85	0.76	0.74	0.71
North Carolina[b]	0.41	0.51	0.62	0.70	0.69
Tennessee	0.77	0.95	0.93	0.89	0.87
Texas	0.66	1.64	1.16	1.15	1.15
Virginia[b]	0.50	0.58	0.76	0.87	0.77
Deep South Mean	0.34	0.40	0.59	0.66	0.72
Peripheral South Mean	0.58	0.79	0.83	0.87	0.84
South Mean	0.49	0.60	0.71	0.77	0.79

Sources of voter registration estimates upon which ratios have been calculated: U.S. Commission on Civil Rights, *Voting,* Vol. I of *1961 Report* (Washington, D.C.: U.S. Government Printing Office, 1961); U.S. Commission on Civil Rights, *1959 Report* (Washington, D.C.: U.S. Government Printing Office, 1959); Pat Watters and Reese Cleghorn, *Climbing Jacob's Ladder: The Arrival of Negroes in Southern Politics* (New York: Harcourt, Brace & World, 1967), Appendix 2; *Voter Registration in the South, Summer, 1966* (Atlanta: Voter Education Project, Southern Regional Council, 1966); *Voter Registration in the South, Summer, 1968* (Atlanta: Voter Education Project, Southern Regional Council, 1968); Chester W. Bain, "South Carolina: Partisan Prelude," in William C. Havard, ed., *The Changing Politics of the South* (Baton Rouge: Louisiana State University Press, 1972), pp. 598-599; and William C. Havard, "The South: A Shifting Perspective," in Havard, ed., *Changing Politics of the South*, p. 21.

[a]Each cell is computed by dividing the estimated percentage of the black voting age population registered to vote by the estimated percentage of the white voting age population registered to vote.

[b]State covered by the Voting Rights Act of 1965. Not all North Carolina counties were affected.

changes occurring in Arkansas and in the seven states covered by the Voting Rights Act. Black mobilization in Arkansas, a state not placed under the Voting Rights Act, was stimulated by the organizational efforts of Winthrop Rockefeller. In two additional states, Texas and Tennessee, blacks have registered at approximately the same rates as whites. (If Mexican-Americans were removed from the white voting age population in Texas, it is likely that the Texas ratios would drop below 1.00.) Florida is the only deviant case, and the results there are partly an artifact of the state's rapid growth in population.[33] Prior to federal intervention blacks were far better mobilized in relation to whites in the Peripheral South than in the Deep South. Subregional differences declined after the Voting Rights Act went into effect, but they were not completely eliminated as of 1970. By the late 1960s black electorates across the South were "approaching the critical level at which [they] can no longer be safely ignored."[34]

On the assumption that a higher level of black voter registration as compared with white registration indirectly reflects the strength of black political organization within a state, differences in statewide voter registration rates have been calculated by subtracting the estimated percentage of eligible Negroes registered to vote in a given year from the comparable white figure. As Table 51 indicates, the magnitude of these differences in registration rates is strongly associated (gamma = .80 and lambda b = .41) with the campaign racial stances of governors elected in the post-*Brown* era. The more blacks have been mobilized in rough proportion to whites, the more likely candidates have been to avoid militantly segregationist postures. In elections where the difference in registration rates was less than 15 percentage points, 82 percent of the winners were nonsegregationists. Where whites have registered at significantly higher rates than blacks, successful campaigners have commonly emphasized traditional segregationist views. Sixty-eight percent of the elections in which differences exceeded 30 percentage points were won by strong segregationists. If blacks within a state become sufficiently well organized to approximate white registration rates, they may influence campaign rhetoric (by raising the costs of race baiting) even while constituting a small percentage of the total electorate.[35] Yet a qualification needs to be recognized. An explanation of changed campaign stances on segregation based on equivalent black and white registration rates (an indicator of black political organization) fits the Peripheral South reasonably well. However, it cannot account adequately for the decline of segre-

Table 51. Southern governors' campaign stances on racial segregation and differences in white and black voter registration rates, 1954-73 (percent)

Campaign Racial Stance	Differences in Registration Rates[a]				
	High	Medium	Low	Totals	(N)
Strong Segregationist	68	20	12	37	(23)
Moderate Segregationist	28	40	6	26	(16)
Nonsegregationist	4	40	82	37	(23)
Totals	100	100	100	100	(62)
Number of Cases	(25)	(20)	(17)	(62)	
Index of Racial Change	0.05	1.00	5.57	0.74	

Sources of voter registration estimates: Same as for Table 50, and Donald R. Matthews and James W. Prothro, *Negroes and the New Southern Politics* (New York: Harcourt, Brace & World, 1966), p. 148; and Tilman C. Cothran and William M. Phillips, Jr., "Expansion of Negro Suffrage in Arkansas," *Journal of Negro Education,* 26 (Summer 1957), 290.

[a]High = 30 or more percentage points difference between percentage of eligible whites registered to vote and percentage of eligible blacks registered; Medium = 15-29.9 percentage points difference; Low = less than 15 percentage points difference. Where data were not available for the election year, the average of the preceding and succeeding years was used. Estimates for 1971-73 elections were based on 1970 data. Four elections were omitted for lack of data: Arkansas, 1954; Tennessee, 1954 and 1958; and Texas, 1954.

gationist language outside the Peripheral South, for registration gaps in the Deep South (despite narrowing over time) have remained sizable. The mean difference between the registration rates of whites and blacks in the Deep South states fell from 43.7 percentage points in 1964 to 24.0 points in 1970. Comparable figures for the Peripheral South states are 13.7 in 1964 and 13.2 in 1970.[36]

A more promising hypothesis to explain changed campaign rhetoric in the Deep South states centers on the political leverage that may be derived from the sheer size of the black vote in relation to the entire electorate. Even if whites have continued to register at higher rates than blacks, gains in the black proportion of total voters may give campaigners an incentive to avoid segregationist stances. Table 52, which reports changes over time in the estimated proportion of registered voters who were black, suggests that federal intervention helped transform small bloc votes in the Deep South into much greater and less vulnerable fractions of the total electorate. Prior to federal inter-

Table 52. Patterns of black voter mobilization II: estimated percent black of total registered voters, before and after federal intervention, by state, sub-region, and region

| Political Unit | BVAP/ TVAPa | Pre-1965 | | Post-1965 | | | Net Changeb |
		1960	1964	1966	1968	1970	
Alabamac	26.2	7.1	10.6	17.1	17.5	19.2	12.1
Georgiac	25.4	12.5	18.6	17.4	18.4	19.5	7.0
Louisianac	28.5	13.8	13.7	18.4	21.2	21.9	8.1
Mississippic	36.1	n.a.	5.2	22.8	26.6	30.5	25.3
South Carolinac	29.4	10.7	17.0	21.0	23.5	24.5	13.8
Arkansas	18.5	12.3	12.6	16.1	16.9	16.8	4.5
Florida	15.2	9.2	13.3	12.0	11.7	11.3	2.1
North Carolinac	21.6	10.2	12.2	14.5	16.2	15.9	5.7
Tennessee	15.0	14.0	14.4	14.1	13.6	13.3	-0.7
Texas	11.7	8.1	17.9	13.3	13.3	13.3	5.2
Virginiac	18.9	10.4	11.9	15.0	16.9	15.3	4.9
Deep South mean	29.1	11.0	13.0	19.3	21.4	23.1	12.1
Peripheral South mean	16.8	10.7	13.7	14.2	14.8	14.3	3.6
South mean	22.4	10.8	13.4	16.5	17.8	18.3	7.5

Sources: Same as for Table 50.

a1960 black voting age population as a percentage of the total 1960 voting age population.

b1970 percent black of total registered voters minus 1960 (1964 for Mississippi) percent black of total registered voters.

cState covered by the Voting Rights Act of 1965. Not all North Carolina counties were affected.

vention blacks contributed slightly more than a tenth of the Deep South's registered voters; enforcement of the Voting Rights Act and additional voter registration campaigns systematically expanded the percentage of blacks among registered voters in the last half of the 1960s. By 1970 blacks accounted for an estimated 30 percent of the electorate in Mississippi, for one quarter of South Carolina's registered voters, and for one fifth of the Alabama, Georgia, and Louisiana electorates. These figures were still below the estimated (1960) percentage of blacks among the total voting age population for each state (compare the 1970 data with the percentages listed in the first column), but they obviously represented the development of a substantial minority of votes.

What are the consequences for campaign strategy of black electorates in the range of 20 to 30 percent of total registered voters? The short answer—nonsegregationist campaigning by at least some ambitious politicians and a switch to euphemisms by segregationists—is widely appreciated, but the reasoning behind changed racial stances needs to be elaborated. Table 53 has been devised in an effort to clarify, in hypothetical terms, the relationship between the size of the black vote and the racial composition of successful electoral coalitions. To construct the table it is necessary to assume that a campaign is limited to two candidates, with one candidate totally repudiating the black vote and the other candidate being relatively acceptable to blacks (either as the lesser of evils or as someone who is viewed positively). If blacks constitute a fixed percentage of the entire state vote and cast their ballots unanimously against the unacceptable candidate (or in favor of the acceptable candidate), what percentage of the white vote is needed by each candidate in order to win a majority of the total state vote and how many white votes are needed at the minimum by each candidate to offset successfully each white vote captured by his opponent?

Table 53 reveals that a politician who could obtain a unanimous black vote amounting to 10 percent of the entire state vote would still need about 45 percent of the total white vote in order to achieve a winning coalition. However, if blacks were able to supply 20 percent of the state vote, their candidate would need the support of only 38 percent of the white vote. Stated in ratio terms, the acceptable politician would require for victory a minimum of no more than three white votes for every five white votes secured by his opponent. Conversely, campaigners who wrote off the black vote completely would need only 56 percent of the white vote if blacks accounted for 10 percent of the state electorate, but they would be required to win more than 62 percent of the white vote once the black vote exceeded 20 percent of the total state vote.[37]

As we saw in Table 52, as of 1970 the proportion of blacks among total registered voters ranged from 19 to 30 in the Deep South and from 15 to 17 percent in Arkansas, North Carolina, and Virginia. In all these states, a politician who totally alienated the black vote would require between 59 and 72 percent of the white vote to survive. Although obtaining white majorities of that magnitude on the basis of segregationist campaigning is not an impossible task (witness the success of George Wallace), the number of southern gubernatorial campaigners who might realistically anticipate such overwhelming white support has diminished rapidly.[38] Second primary defeats suffered by Orval Faubus of Arkansas (1970 and 1974) and by Lester Maddox of

Table 53. Understanding the new southern politics: size of the black vote and the racial composition of successful electoral coalitions

Hypothesized Size of Black Vote[a]	Minimum Share of White Vote Required for Majority of Total Vote[b]		Minimum Number of White Votes Required to Offset Each White Vote Won by Opponent[c]	
	By Candidate "Acceptable" to Blacks	By Candidate "Unacceptable" to Blacks	By Candidate "Acceptable" to Blacks	By Candidate "Unacceptable" to Blacks
0.0	50.1	50.1	1.00	1.00
5.0	47.5	52.7	0.90	1.11
10.0	44.6	55.7	0.80	1.25
15.0	41.3	58.9	0.70	1.43
20.0	37.6	62.6	0.60	1.66
25.0	33.5	66.8	0.50	1.99
30.0	28.7	71.6	0.40	2.49
35.0	23.2	77.1	0.30	3.32
40.0	16.8	83.5	0.20	4.97
45.0	9.3	91.1	0.10	9.80
50.0	0.002	100.002		

[a]Hypothesized black vote as a percentage of the total state vote.

[b]These columns give the percentage of the white vote needed to win a majority of the state vote by the unacceptable and acceptable candidates, if the black vote is cast unanimously against the unacceptable candidate. For example, if blacks comprise 25 percent of the total state vote and ballot completely against the unacceptable candidate, the acceptable candidate would need one third of the white vote and the unacceptable candidate would need two thirds of the white vote to achieve 50.1 percent of the state vote. The equation used to determine the white vote required by the acceptable candidate is: $b + (100 - b)(x) = 50.1$, where b = percent black of the total state vote; $100 - b$ = percent white of the total state vote; and x = percent of the white vote needed to produce 50.1 percent of the total state vote. For the unacceptable candidate the equation is: $(100 - b)(x) = 50.1$, where b = percent black of the total state vote; $100 - b$ = percent white of the total state vote; and x = percent of the white vote needed to produce 50.1 percent of the total state vote.

[c]These columns report ratios between the percentage of white votes required for victory, given hypothesized levels of black participation, by the acceptable candidate as compared with the unacceptable candidate, and vice versa. For example, if blacks cast 25 percent of the state vote and voted unanimously against the unacceptable candidate, the acceptable candidate would need, in order to win a majority of the state vote, a minimum of one white vote for every two white votes secured by the unacceptable opponent.

Georgia (1974) illustrate the difficulty of overcoming segregationist reputations under conditions of extensive black participation.

The assumptions necessary to build Table 53 are clearly oversimplifications as applied to specific campaigns. Nevertheless, by directing attention to the properties of electoral coalitions formed under hypothetical circumstances of extreme racial polarization, the findings help explain why unvarnished segregationist campaigning has diminished in the Deep South. Furnished accurate information on the size of the black vote, politicians who lacked established statewide constituencies would be less likely than their predecessors to gamble that unambiguous attacks on the new racial status quo would unite whites sufficiently to overcome the opposition of blacks. But if blacks in the Deep South are increasingly positioned to defeat most strong segregationists in campaigns for governor, electing politicians with whom they feel genuine rapport is by no means assured. The lesser of evils will often be the only alternative to abstention; and even in races where no politician openly campaigns as a segregationist, the nonsegregationists may be vague and noncommittal on many issues of concern to black voters. Nonsegregationists, as has often been said, are not necessarily racial liberals. Hence impressive as the advances in black voter registration have been, serious limitations remain concerning what the vote is likely to accomplish for black southerners. One widely recognized constraint bears repetition: since blacks are far from constituting a majority of the voting age population in any southern state (see the first column of Table 52), the black vote by itself cannot elect a governor.[39]

Assuming that the black vote is here to stay and will become better organized over time, it seems probable that candidates for southern governorships will become less prone to insult, attack, and dismiss this fraction of the electorate. If the black vote accomplishes nothing else, it has already produced significant changes in the tone of southern politics. Stem-winding race baiting has definitely waned. Superficially, the absence of pejorative references to blacks and unambiguous defenses of segregation might resemble the pre-*Brown* era when segregation was a latent issue. But where pre-1954 candidates did not need to discuss the caste system because unanimity on the subject was taken for granted, the contemporary decline in overt segregationist rhetoric is rooted in a reluctance to antagonize needlessly an organized minority and in an inclination to project less bellicose political images. Important as black participation may be, it remains true that "the vote for southern Negroes is a necessary but not a sufficient condition for racial progress in the South.''[40] For if whites were united on the principle of segregation, black voting would be insufficient to alter the racial tone of southern politics, no matter how cohesively blacks participated. It is necessary, therefore, to examine trends in the racial attitudes of white southerners.

The Changing Racial Attitudes of White Southerners

The distribution of opinions among voters and the intensity with which opinions are held, particularly on matters related to race, affect the campaign stances politicians adopt.[41] Candidates for governor are unlikely to respond affirmatively to black demands when those demands are opposed by solid majorities of whites; nonsegregationist campaigning becomes an alternative for politicians only when a significant portion of white voters find other issues—the maintenance of open schools, economic development, and fear of the consequences of federal-state confrontations are examples—more relevant for voting purposes than race. Is there reason to believe that the segregationist attitudes of white southerners have significantly moderated since 1954? Available survey data, which apply to the region as a whole and do not take into account differences between subregions or between states, permit no more than an incomplete and sketchy answer to this question,[42] and the following paragraphs are not meant to suggest that white southerners have experienced wholesale changes of opinion on issues involving race relations since the *Brown* decision. The evidence would not support such a contention.[43] Regional surveys do indicate, nonetheless, that segregationist norms have declined over time on some racial issues, and it is plausible to hypothesize that this increasing division of white attitudes, presumably more characteristic of the Peripheral South than the Deep South, has reduced the need for segregationist rhetoric among candidates and expanded the range of politically feasible alternatives on race-related matters. In reviewing white attitudes toward selected racial questions, it will be useful to distinguish between what whites prefer and what they are willing to accept.

Over the years white resistance to the principle of school desegregation, the single most controversial racial issue in recent southern politics, has diminished considerably. Only 14 percent of white southerners agreed in 1956 that it would be a good idea to teach black and white students in the same classroom, an extremely skewed distribution of opinion that virtually precluded support of the *Brown* decision by politicians seriously interested in winning public office. By the time of federal intervention in 1965, though, 36 percent of the whites supported school desegregation, and by 1970 "almost half of them" favored it.[44] A narrow majority of white southerners still preferred segregated schools, but the growth of a large minority of whites willing to accept the principle of the *Brown* decision has presumably given politicians in many states a degree of maneuverability on the issue of school desegregation which campaigners did not have in the past.

White southerners have been less resistant to some forms of public accommodations desegregation than to school integration. One year after the Civil Rights Act went into effect, 47 percent of the region's whites agreed that blacks should have equal access to restaurants, hotels, theaters, parks, and related facilities, an increase of 38 percentage points over the 9 percent who agreed in 1944 that "some restaurants in town should serve Negroes and whites." Andrew Greeley and Paul Sheatsley found that, as of 1970, white southerners typically accepted the desegregation of public transportation, restaurants, hotels, and parks.[45] The percentage of whites favoring desegregation of public transportation, for example, climbed from 27 percent in 1956 to 49 percent in 1963 and further increased to 67 percent in 1970.[46] More broadly, a comparison of 1963 with 1970 results on a "pro-integration" scale devised by the National Opinion Research Center provides additional evidence of increasing white accommodation to racial desegregation. The average "pro-integration" score for white southerners rose from 2 (on a 0 to 6 scale) in 1963 to nearly 3 in 1970. Declines in segregationist attitudes, while greatest among young southerners, were observed at each age level. As Greeley and Sheatsley conclude, "The changing attitudes in the South entail not only the influx of a new generation but also an actual change of position by many older white Southerners."[47]

Allowing for subregional differences and granting that the data are hardly comprehensive, the above figures suggest that southern politicians have encountered, over the years, less constituency pressure to resist racial desegregation. Further and perhaps better evidence for this hypothesis comes from questions that explore white beliefs concerning the inevitability of racial change. Whites resigned to desegregation probably would be less inclined to expect their leaders to continue fighting for a lost cause than whites who were confident that the caste system could be successfully defended. Questions designed to measure white sentiment regarding the probability of desegregation disclose striking changes over time. Fifty-five percent of white southerners believed in 1956 that the region's schools, restaurants, and public accommodations would "eventually" be desegregated. Five years later fully three quarters of the whites thought integration was unavoidable, and, in 1963, a year before the Civil Rights Act was passed, an overwhelming majority of the whites (83 percent) anticipated desegregation.[48] Fragmentary as the data may be, the widespread recognition by whites of the inevitability of some desegregation has probably given politicians in some states a measure of leeway on the segregation issue. Modest attitudinal shifts and a general recognition by white voters of the likelihood of racial change have contributed to a situation in which politicians who were predisposed to de-emphasize racial conflict could sometimes do so without ensuring their own defeat.

Generational Change within the Southern Political Elite

The rise of nonsegregationist governors reflects in part a generational change within the southern political elite, a change which may be attributed primarily to the success of national actions calculated to redefine critical "rules of the game" in the South. Many factors determine the length of political careers, but one requisite is the continuing relevance to voters of the political agenda which was predominant when the politician first began his effort to win major office. If assumptions concerning what issues are important and how those issues should be addressed prove to be inaccurate, a politician may be too identified with the concerns and conflicts of his formative years to adapt successfully to changed circumstances. In the recent history of the South, the exercise of national authority to encourage black participation and to desegregate a wide range of institutions has expedited the transfer of political leadership from an old to a new generation.

Many members of the "Little Rock generation" of southern politicians, as those office seekers may be designated whose statewide or national careers antedated 1966, by and large staked their political careers on the perpetuation of traditional racial conflict. A defense of the caste system, whether by militant or by moderate rhetoric, was perceived as a political necessity. When they eventually failed to resist federal pressures for desegregation, however, segregationists of the Little Rock era were forced either to become nonsegregationists (no easy task for many of them considering their past enthusiasm for the Jim Crow system), to continue championing segregation while softening their language, or to retire from electoral politics. In any event, the

Little Rock generation discovered that the issue once assumed essential for victory had become problematic in its net impact. George Wallace might survive as a strong segregationist, but his victories would be exceptions to the central tendency. Politicians of the "New South generation," defined here as individuals who did not seek statewide office or win election to Congress before 1966, reached maturity as campaigners after the principle of desegregation had been settled. Consequently, as a collectivity the New South generation has had little incentive to view explicitly segregationist rhetoric as instrumental to long-term political success. Since they had not committed themselves on the segregation controversy in statewide campaigns prior to 1966, they were in a much better position than were representatives of the Little Rock generation to adjust their campaign behavior to the new racial status quo.

The significance of national intervention for changed campaign stances is emphasized anew when southern governors elected after 1965 are grouped by the timing of their original entry into statewide or national politics (see Table 54). Differences between the Little Rock generation of politicians and the New South generation appear as expected. All but one of the candidates who began their pursuit of the

Table 54. Generational change within the southern political elite: campaign racial stances of southern governors elected after federal intervention (1966-73), by timing of original entry into statewide or national politics (percent)

Campaign Racial Stance	Little Rock Generation[a]	New South Generation[b]	All Winners	(N)
Strong Segregationist	19	10	15	(4)
Moderate Segregationist	25	0	15	(4)
Nonsegregationist	56	90	69	(18)
Total	100	100	100	(26)
Number of Cases	(16)	(10)	(26)	
Percentage of Total Cases	62	38	100	
Index of Racial Change	1.80	9.00	3.00	

[a]Winners active before federal intervention; defined as politicians who won or were major candidates for statewide office before 1966 or who were elected to Congress prior to 1966.

[b]Winners active after federal intervention; defined as politicians who did not seek statewide office prior to 1966 or who were not elected to Congress prior to 1966.

governorship after 1965 (90 percent) campaigned as nonsegregation-ists, while the successful segregationists were typically politicians of the Little Rock generation. The single deviant case for the New South generation is purely a technical exception, for Lurleen Wallace was widely viewed as a surrogate for her husband. Most of the nonsegrega-tionists among the Little Rock generation were Peripheral South candidates who entered statewide competition in the early 1960s (for example, John Connally and Preston Smith of Texas, Winthrop Rockefeller of Arkansas, and Linwood Holton of Virginia); John McKeithen of Louisiana and Buford Ellington of Tennessee were the only members of the Little Rock generation who successfully switched from a strong segregationist position in their original gubernatorial campaign to a nonsegregationist stance in their second campaign. The New South generation was a minority (38 percent) of the governors elected between 1966 and 1973, but its size will grow over time. With blacks relatively well organized in many Peripheral South states and comprising large fractions of the electorate in the Deep South and several Peripheral South states, with white attitudes less overwhelm-ingly pro-segregation than in the past, and with desegregation—of varying scope—a reality for approximately a decade by 1973, whites who aspired to southern governorships had compelling reasons to avoid the rhetoric associated with the Little Rock generation of cam-paigners.

Generational considerations aside, the commitment of important segments of southern business to economic development has contribu-ted to the decline of segregationist campaigning. Business-oriented candidates and their financial supporters in the business community, when forced by the national government to make a choice, have generally valued economic stability and growth over the principle of racial segregation.[49] Although the willingness of business to take the initiative in moderating racial conflict has been exceedingly slight, the business community (particularly in the urban South) tended to accept desegregation once the Civil Rights Act went into effect.[50] And as major business institutions adapted to national legislation on race relations, it is plausible to surmise that campaign funds were less read-ily available to support politicians who threatened to disrupt the new status quo on race.

Explaining Racial Change: A Recapitulation

Now that several factors have been discussed that help explain why many candidates for the southern governorship have ceased to run as segregationists, it is appropriate to review the behavior of white politicians over the course of the Second Reconstruction. Figure 29 provides a focus for the recapitulation by graphing regional and subregional indexes of racial change for each of the six waves of elections utilized in this study.

Prior to the Supreme Court's school desegregation decision of 1954, segregation was largely a latent issue in southern elections for governor. In the early 1950s the principle of racial segregation was not seriously challenged from within or without the South, and many campaigners apparently believed there was no need to agitate an issue that was assumed to be irrevocably settled. If there were politicians who had reservations about the caste system, they had no electoral incentive to publicize their doubts. Constraints of history and demography made internal opposition to the racial status quo improbable; educational systems were controlled by localities and by state agencies which accepted the legitimacy of separate educational facilities and socialized the youth of the region into the "southern way of life"; and white attitudes at both elite and mass levels were highly supportive of segregation. Despite the Supreme Court's abolition of the white primary in 1944, blacks did not have enough political leverage to bargain with white candidates over the principle of racial segregation. Under these circumstances approval of the Jim Crow system was routinely acknowledged by major candidates. If racial discrimination in the South were to be challenged, the initiative for change would clearly have to come from outside the region.

That initiative came, of course, with the Supreme Court's 1954 ruling that segregation in public education was unconstitutional. The *Brown* decision reopened the broad question of race relations and made segregation a highly salient campaign issue. Each southern state, at some point after 1954 and for varying lengths of time, experienced a period in which strident opposition to desegregation became the central motif of statewide elections. Opposition to racial change was virtually universal in the first two waves of elections following the school desegregation decision (see Figure 29). Although candidates frequently differed with regard to the intensity of their commitment to segregation (some were obviously more extreme than others in their defense of southern racial traditions, and moderate segregationists supported both segregation and the rule of law), they all pledged to fight vigorously against racial change. With whites disinclined to compromise on the principle of segregation, with blacks still dispro-

Figure 29. The timing of racial change in southern electoral politics: indexes of racial change for successful candidates for governor, 1950-73, by region and subregion

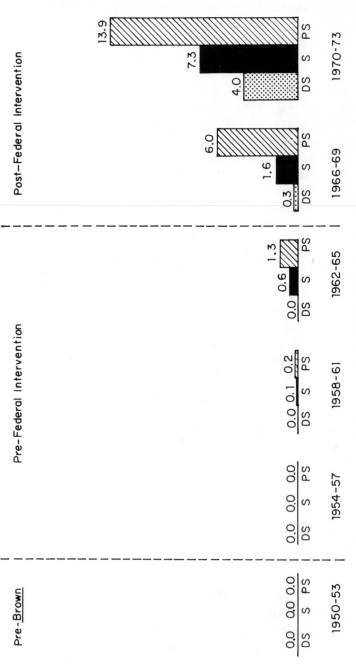

DS Deep South   PS Peripheral South   S South

portionately unregistered to vote, and with Congress and the Chief Executive reluctant (to understate the situation) to help the Supreme Court enforce its decision, an unambiguous stand against desegregation was instrumental to political victory. Strong segregationists, especially following the Little Rock controversy, were highly successful, while moderate segregationists fared poorly once they were matched against militant segregationists in second primary campaigns. Support for segregation prevailed without exception in the Deep South through the early 1960s. In the Peripheral South, however, slight changes in the segregation issue appeared before federal intervention, and more nonsegregationists than segregationists were elected governor in the 1962-65 campaigns. Racial change in electoral politics was first evident in Texas, Tennessee, and Virginia, states where blacks developed considerable strength in urban areas.

For reasons previously discussed at length, since the mid-1960s explicit segregationist rhetoric has increasingly been replaced by campaign oratory that may be characterized as nonsegregationist. Despite their campaign promises, in practice militant segregationists failed to resist pressures for desegregation. Strong segregationists were unable to reverse the *Brown* decision through constitutional amendment, and their highly publicized acts of resistance (Little Rock, Ole Miss, the University of Alabama, and so forth) did not prevent desegregation and sometimes frightened away new industry. Further, by the early 1960s an indigenous civil rights movement was revealing, through one confrontation after another, the injustice of the Jim Crow system. At length the Kennedy and Johnson administrations and the Congress responded with civil rights legislation which, when enforced, defined a new racial status quo. As black voting increased and as many white southerners adjusted to desegregation, opportunities were created for politicians who were not identified with the "fight to the last ditch" mentality of the Little Rock generation. Most of the New South politicians were not racially liberal by national standards, but they accepted token to moderate desegregation as a given. Figure 29 suggests that the long-term impact of federal intervention—an impact transmitted directly through the mobilization of black voters and indirectly through the desegregation of schools and public accommodations—has been substantial. Indexes of racial change for the 1970-73 elections, unlike those of the five previous waves, were high in both the Deep South (4.0) and the Peripheral South (13.9). With regard to the principle of segregation, a large majority of southern governors in the early 1970s did not adopt traditional campaign stances.[51]

Conclusions

Through an analysis of campaign rhetoric over the past quarter century, I have attempted to demonstrate that one important consequence of national intervention in southern race relations has been the cumulative abandonment of old-fashioned segregationist oratory by white politicians. My findings, like those of several other studies, argue against the unqualified proposition that "stateways cannot change folkways."[52] At the time of the *Brown* decision, politicians in the South had few incentives to conduct nonsegregationist campaigns. Since segregationist whites cast most of the votes and neither Congress nor the President was willing to support the Supreme Court, southern office seekers had much to gain and little to lose by urging resistance to the *Brown* decision. But 20 years later, following actions by the national government which altered the structure of southern electoral politics in critical ways, the distribution of incentives vis-à-vis the segregation issue was no longer one-sided. Indeed, with the growth of black electorates and with desegregation an accomplished fact in schools and public accommodations, nonsegregationist campaigning had become astute politics in many states.

The thrust of this work has been to describe and document, at the level of campaigns for the governorship, the emergence of a new southern politics less identified than in the past with segregation per se and based on the reentry of blacks into electoral politics. I have interpreted the observed changes in campaign stances as significant but less than revolutionary, for the following reasons. If the principle of racial segregation was rarely championed by the early 1970s, and if most white candidates have accepted the necessity of soliciting black support, the rise of nonsegregationist campaigners has generally not meant that southern politicians have become discernibly pro-black in their campaign rhetoric. The nonsegregationist category was deliberately constructed to capture the point at which the region's politicians tacitly or explicitly discarded their historical commitment to a segregated social order. A failure to defend the caste system has been interpreted as a significant change in white campaign behavior, one sharply at variance with established norms of white supremacy. While nonsegregationists have clearly dominated recent elections, few of them could be classified as racial liberals by the standards of national politics. In addition, the nonsegregationists who were most sympathetic to black demands for equal treatment were ordinarily defeated. These generalizations should be kept in mind as a hedge against exaggerating the magnitude of racial change in southern campaigns. On the other hand, it would also be a mistake to interpret the shift from segregationist to nonsegregationist campaigning as superficial and unimportant. White politicians have increasingly begun to treat blacks less as second-class citizens and more as constituents whose support should be cultivated, and the decline of unadulterated race baiting, though a negative achievement, has nonetheless elevated the tone of electoral politics and ended one form of verbal oppression against black southerners.

A final qualification concerning the scope of racial change should be emphasized to prevent misinterpretation. Because the caste system has long been perceived as the principal manifestation in the South's social structure of white supremacy values, this study has been confined to white elite attitudes on segregation. The decline of overt segregationist rhetoric does not mean that race is a dead issue in the politics of the South. Controversy over the principle of segregation has diminished; yet other issues may be vehicles for racial conflict. Most southern politicians, for example, have taken racially conservative positions on the issue of busing. In the larger perspective of southern history, however, what is more significant is that the busing controversy has typically involved disagreements over the degree of desegregation and the means used to accomplish desegregation rather than arguments over the principle of desegregated education. Cleavages based on "primordial attachments" such as race are rarely if ever completely eliminated from politics but under the right circumstances conditions may be established to moderate and perhaps contain them.[53] Recent southern history provides evidence that some forms of racial discrimination may be legislated against, and black southerners were assuredly in a much better position to protect their group interests through politics in the early 1970s than they were in 1954.

Two decades after the *Brown* decision, the issue of segregation versus desegregation, as it applies to schools, public accommodations, and programs financed by the federal government, has been resolved in principle against the southern segregationists. Any fundamental reversal of national policy in these areas, any attempt to reinstate the old Jim Crow system, seems highly improbable. Though campaigns may well display racial overtones in varying degree, the black vote should restrain most tendencies toward uninhibited race baiting. Progress is by no means inevitable, but the odds are that the South will continue its reluctant journey toward a more open and just society. That journey was actively opposed by the region's political leadership for much of the twentieth century, and white politicians have acquiesced to it largely because national authority prevailed in the field of civil rights. Structural changes associated with the national government's Second Reconstruction ensure that the South of the future, its many deficiencies notwithstanding, will not be the Arkansas of Orval Faubus, the Mississippi of Ross Barnett, or the Alabama of George Wallace writ large.

Appendixes
Notes
Index

Appendix A

Classification
of Individual Candidates

Tables in this appendix list the racial segregation and achievement of economic development positions adopted by candidates for the southern governorship at successive stages of the electoral process, 1950-73. For each election the candidates are ranked (highest to lowest) according to the size of their state vote. Candidates are eliminated who received less than 10 percent of the vote in any election.

Table A-1. Campaign stances on racial segregation and achievement of economic development of major candidates for governor in Democratic first primaries

Candidate	Year	Classification	Candidate	Year	Classification
Alabama			M. Gallion	1962	SS M
G. Persons	1950	MS M	L. Wallace	1966	SS P
P. Hamm	1950	MS R	R. Flowers	1966	NS P
E. Boozer	1950	MS M	A. Brewer	1970	NS A
J. Folsom	1954	MS R	G. Wallace	1970	SS P
J. Faulkner	1954	MS M	C. Woods	1970	NS A
J. Allen	1954	MS M			
J. Patterson	1958	SS M	*Arkansas*		
G. Wallace	1958	SS P	S. McMath	1950	MS R
J. Faulkner	1958	MS A	B. Laney	1950	SS M
G. Wallace	1962	SS P	S. McMath	1952	MS R
R. deGraffenried	1962	MS A	F. Cherry	1952	MS M
J. Folsom	1962	MS R	B. Tackett	1952	MS M

(continued)

Table A-1 continued.

Candidate	Year	Classification	Candidate	Year	Classification
J. Holt	1952	MS M	S. Lowry	1956	SS M
F. Cherry	1954	MS M	F. Bryant	1956	SS M
O. Faubus	1954	MS R	F. Warren	1956	SS R
G. Jones	1954	MS R	F. Bryant	1960	SS M
O. Faubus	1956	MS R	D. Carlton	1960	MS M
J. Johnson	1956	SS R	H. Burns	1960	SS M
J. Snoddy	1956	SS M	J. McCarty	1960	SS M
			F. Dickinson	1960	SS M
O. Faubus	1958	SS R	H. Burns	1964	SS M
C. Finkbeiner	1958	MS M	R. High	1964	NS R
L. Ward	1958	MS M	S. Kelly	1964	SS M
O. Faubus	1960	SS R	F. Dickinson	1964	SS M
J. Hardin	1960	MS M	J. Mathews	1964	MS A
B. Bennett	1960	SS R	H. Burns	1966	NS A
O. Faubus	1962	MS R	R. High	1966	NS P
S. McMath	1962	NS R	S. Kelly	1966	NS A
D. Alford	1962	SS M	E. Faircloth	1970	NS M
O. Faubus	1964	MS R	R. Askew	1970	NS P
O. Dorsey	1964	MS M	J. Mathews	1970	NS A
J. Hubbard	1964	NS M	C. Hall	1970	NS M
J. Johnson	1966	SS R	*Georgia*		
F. Holt	1966	NS M	H. Talmadge	1950	SS R
B. Hays	1966	NS R	M. Thompson	1950	MS M
D. Alford	1966	MS M			
S. Boyce	1966	NS M	M. Griffin	1954	SS M
			M. Thompson	1954	MS M
M. Crank	1968	NS A	T. Linder	1954	SS M
V. Johnson	1968	MS M	F. Hand	1954	SS M
T. Boswell	1968	NS A	C. Gowen	1954	MS M
B. Bennett	1968	NS P	E. Vandiver	1958	SS M
F. Whitbeck	1968	NS A	W. Bodenhamer	1958	SS M
O. Faubus	1970	MS R	C. Sanders	1962	MS A
D. Bumpers	1970	NS A	M. Griffin	1962	SS M
J. Purcell	1970	NS A	E. Arnall	1966	NS P
H. McClerkin	1970	NS A	L. Maddox	1966	SS P
D. Bumpers	1972	NS A	J. Carter	1966	NS A
B. Hurst	1972	NS M	J. Gray	1966	SS M
M. Harbour	1972	MS M	J. Carter	1970	NS P
Florida			C. Sanders	1970	NS A
D. McCarty	1952	MS M	*Louisiana*		
B. Odham	1952	MS R	C. Spaht	1951-52	MS R
A. Adams	1952	MS M	R. Kennon	1951-52	MS M
C. Johns	1954	MS M	H. Boggs	1951-52	MS M
L. Collins	1954	MS M	J. McLemore	1951-52	MS M
B. Odham	1954	MS R	W. Dodd	1951-52	MS R
L. Collins	1956	MS M			

Table A-1 continued.

Candidate	Year	Classification	Candidate	Year	Classification
E. Long	1955-56	MS R	L. Hodges	1956	MS M
D. Morrison	1955-56	MS M	T. Sanford	1960	MS A
F. Preaus	1955-56	SS M	B. Lake	1960	SS M
D. Morrison	1959-60	MS M	M. Seawell	1960	MS M
J. Davis	1959-60	MS M	J. Larkins	1960	MS M
W. Rainach	1959-60	SS M	R. Preyer	1964	NS A
J. Noe	1959-60	MS R	D. Moore	1964	MS M
W. Dodd	1959-60	MS R	B. Lake	1964	SS M
D. Morrison	1963-64	MS A	R. Scott	1968	MS A
J. McKeithen	1963-64	MS A	M. Broughton	1968	MS A
G. Long	1963-64	MS A	R. Hawkins	1968	NS P
R. Kennon	1963-64	SS M	H. Bowles	1972	NS A
S. Jackson	1963-64	SS M	P. Taylor	1972	NS A
J. McKeithen	1967-68	NS A			
J. Rarick	1967-68	SS M	**South Carolina**		
E. Edwards	1971-72	NS A	J. Byrnes	1950	MS A
B. Johnston	1971-72	NS A	L. Bates	1950	MS M
G. Long	1971-72	NS A	G. Timmerman	1954	SS M
J. Davis	1971-72	MS M	L. Bates	1954	SS M
Mississippi			E. Hollings	1958	SS A
H. White	1951	MS M	D. Russell	1958	SS M
P. Johnson	1951	MS R	W. Johnston	1958	SS R
S. Lumpkin	1951	MS M	D. Russell	1962	MS A
R. Barnett	1951	MS M	B. Maybank	1962	MS M
P. Johnson	1955	SS M	R. McNair	1966	MS A
J. Coleman	1955	SS M	J. West	1970	NS A
F. Wright	1955	SS M			
R. Barnett	1955	SS M	**Tennessee**		
R. Barnett	1959	SS M	G. Browning	1950	MS M
C. Gartin	1959	SS M	C. Allen	1950	MS R
C. Sullivan	1959	SS M	F. Clement	1952	MS M
P. Johnson	1963	SS A	G. Browning	1952	MS M
J. Coleman	1963	SS M	C. Allen	1952	MS R
C. Sullivan	1963	SS M	F. Clement	1954	MS M
W. Winter	1967	MS A	G. Browning	1954	SS M
J. Williams	1967	SS M	B. Ellington	1958	SS M
J. Swan	1967	SS R	A. Taylor	1958	SS M
R. Barnett	1967	SS A	E. Orgill	1958	MS M
C. Sullivan	1971	NS A	F. Clement	1962	NS A
W. Waller	1971	NS P	R. Olgiata	1962	NS A
J. Swan	1971	SS R	W. Farris	1962	NS A
North Carolina			B. Ellington	1966	NS A
W. Umstead	1952	MS M	J. Hooker	1966	NS P
H. Olive	1952	MS M			

Table A-1 continued.

Candidate	Year	Classification	Candidate	Year	Classification
J. Hooker	1970	NS A	D. Yarborough	1964	NS P
S. Snodgrass	1970	NS A	J. Connally	1966	NS A
R. Taylor	1970	MS M	S. Woods	1966	NS P
	Texas		D. Yarborough	1968	NS P
A. Shivers	1950	MS M	P. Smith	1968	NS A
C. March	1950	MS R	W. Carr	1968	NS M
			D. Briscoe	1968	NS A
A. Shivers	1952	MS M	E. Locke	1968	NS M
R. Yarborough	1952	MS R	P. Smith	1970	NS A
A. Shivers	1954	SS M	D. Briscoe	1972	NS A
R. Yarborough	1954	MS R	F. Farenthold	1972	NS P
P. Daniel	1956	MS M	B. Barnes	1972	NS A
R. Yarborough	1956	MS R		*Virginia*	
W. O'Daniel	1956	SS R	T. Stanley	1953	MS M
P. Daniel	1958	MS M	C. Fenwick	1953	MS M
H. Gonzales	1958	NS R	L. Almond	1957	SS M
W. O'Daniel	1958	SS R	H. Carwile	1957	MS M
P. Daniel	1960	NS M	A. Harrison	1961	SS M
J. Cox	1960	MS M	A. Stephens	1961	MS A
J. Connally	1962	NS M	M. Godwin	1965	NS A
D. Yarborough	1962	NS P	W. Battle	1969	NS A
P. Daniel	1962	NS M	H. Howell	1969	NS P
W. Wilson	1962	NS M	F. Pollard	1969	NS A
J. Connally	1964	NS A			

No Democratic primary held in 1973.

Key: SS = Strong Segregationist; MS = Moderate Segregationist; NS = Nonsegregationist; M = Marginalist; R = Redistributive; A = Adaptive; P = Progressive

Table A-2. Campaign stances on racial segregation and achievement of economic development of participants in Democratic second primaries for governor (winners listed first)

Candidate	Year	Classification	Candidate	Year	Classification
	Alabama		S. McMath	1952	MS R
J. Patterson	1958	SS M	O. Faubus	1954	MS R
G. Wallace	1958	SS P	F. Cherry	1954	MS M
G. Wallace	1962	SS P	J. Johnson	1966	SS R
R. deGraffenried	1962	MS A	F. Holt	1966	NS M
G. Wallace	1970	SS P	M. Crank	1968	NS A
A. Brewer	1970	NS A	V. Johnson	1968	MS M
	Arkansas		D. Bumpers	1970	NS A
F. Cherry	1952	MS M	O. Faubus	1970	MS R

Table A-2 continued.

Candidate	Year	Classification		Candidate	Year	Classification	
	Florida			R. Barnett	1959	SS	M
				C. Gartin	1959	SS	M
D. McCarty	1952	MS	M				
B. Odham	1952	MS	R	P. Johnson	1963	SS	A
				J. Coleman	1963	SS	M
L. Collins	1954	MS	M				
C. Johns	1954	MS	M	J. Williams	1967	SS	M
				W. Winter	1967	MS	A
F. Bryant	1960	SS	M				
D. Carlton	1960	MS	M	W. Waller	1971	NS	P
				C. Sullivan	1971	NS	A
H. Burns	1964	SS	M				
R. High	1964	NS	R		*North Carolina*		
R. High	1966	NS	P				
H. Burns	1966	SS	A	T. Sanford	1960	MS	A
				B. Lake	1960	SS	M
R. Askew	1970	NS	P				
E. Faircloth	1970	NS	M	D. Moore	1964	SS	M
				R. Preyer	1964	NS	A
	Georgia						
				H. Bowles	1972	NS	A
L. Maddox	1966	SS	P	P. Taylor	1972	NS	A
E. Arnall	1966	NS	P				
					South Carolina		
J. Carter	1970	NS	P				
C. Sanders	1970	NS	A	E. Hollings	1958	SS	A
				D. Russell	1958	SS	M
	Louisiana						
					Texas		
R. Kennon	1951-52	MS	M				
C. Spaht	1951-52	MS	R	A. Shivers	1954	SS	M
				R. Yarborough	1954	MS	R
J. Davis	1959-60	SS	M				
D. Morrison	1959-60	MS	M	P. Daniel	1956	SS	M
				R. Yarborough	1956	MS	R
J. McKeithen	1963-64	SS	A				
D. Morrison	1963-64	MS	A	J. Connally	1962	NS	M
				D. Yarborough	1962	NS	P
E. Edwards	1971-72	NS	A				
B. Johnston	1971-72	NS	A	P. Smith	1968	NS	A
				D. Yarborough	1968	NS	P
	Mississippi						
				D. Briscoe	1972	NS	A
H. White	1951	SS	M	F. Farenthold	1972	NS	P
P. Johnson	1951	MS	R		*Virginia*		
J. Coleman	1955	SS	M	W. Battle	1969	NS	A
P. Johnson	1955	SS	M	H. Howell	1969	NS	P

Key: SS = Strong Segregationist; MS = Moderate Segregationist; NS = Non-segregationist; M = Marginalist; R = Redistributive; A = Adaptive; P = Progressive

Table A-3. Campaign stances on racial segregation and achievement of economic development of participants in selected general elections for governor (winners listed first)

Candidate	Year	Classification		Candidate	Year	Classification	
Arkansas				R. Scott (D)	1968	NS	A
				J. Gardner (R)	1968	SS	A
O. Faubus (D)	1964	MS	R	J. Holshouser (R)	1972	NS	A
W. Rockefeller (R)	1964	NS	M	H. Bowles (D)	1972	NS	A
W. Rockefeller (R)	1966	NS	A				
J. Johnson (D)	1966	SS	R	*South Carolina*			
W. Rockefeller (R)	1968	NS	A	R. McNair (D)	1966	MS	A
M. Crank (D)	1968	NS	A	J. Rogers (R)	1966	SS	M
D. Bumpers (D)	1970	NS	A	J. West (D)	1970	NS	A
W. Rockefeller (R)	1970	NS	A	A. Watson (R)	1970	SS	M
Florida				*Tennessee*			
C. Kirk (R)	1966	MS	M	W. Dunn (R)	1970	NS	A
R. High (D)	1966	NS	P	J. Hooker (D)	1970	NS	A
R. Askew (D)	1970	NS	P	*Texas*			
C. Kirk (R)	1970	MS	M				
Georgia				J. Connally (D)	1962	NS	M
				J. Cox (R)	1962	MS	M
H. Callaway (R)	1966	MS	A	P. Smith (D)	1968	NS	A
L. Maddox (D)a	1966	SS	P	P. Eggers (R)	1968	NS	A
J. Carter (D)	1970	NS	P				
H. Suit (R)	1970	NS	A	P. Smith (D)	1970	NS	A
Louisiana				P. Eggers (R)	1970	NS	M
J. McKeithen (D)	1963-64	MS	A	D. Briscoe (D)	1972	NS	A
C. Lyons (R)	1963-64	MS	A	H. Grover (R)	1972	MS	M
E. Edwards (D)	1971-72	NS	A	*Virginia*			
D. Treen (R)	1971-72	NS	M	L. Almond (D)	1957	SS	M
Mississippi				T. Dalton (R)	1957	MS	M
P. Johnson (D)	1963	SS	A	M. Godwin (D)	1965	NS	A
R. Phillips (R)	1963	SS	M	L. Holton (R)	1965	NS	A
North Carolina				W. Story (C)	1965	SS	M
T. Sanford (D)	1960	MS	A	L. Holton (R)	1969	NS	A
R. Gavin (R)	1960	MS	M	W. Battle (D)	1969	NS	A
D. Moore (D)	1964	MS	M	M. Godwin (R)	1973	MS	A
R. Gavin (R)	1964	MS	A	H. Howell (I)	1973	NS	P

aElected governor by state legislature but received fewer popular votes than opponent.

Key: SS = Strong Segregationist; MS = Moderate Segregationist; NS = Nonsegregationist; M = Marginalist; R = Redistributive; A = Adaptive; P = Progressive; D = Democrat; R = Republican; C = Conservative; I = Independent

Appendix B

Determining the Core Segregationist Vote

The identification of core segregationist counties for each of the southern states was accomplished by the following procedures. A number of militant segregationist candidates for governor were distinguished for each state. If a given election (whether Democratic first primary, Democratic second primary, or general election) involved a single militant segregationist, his vote was considered the segregationist vote for that contest. Where two or more militants opposed each other, the vote of the more extreme candidate was selected; and, in a few first primaries, a composite segregationist vote was created by combining the votes of two militant segregationists. In this manner a total of 62 separate segregationist votes was acquired for study. While the number of votes per state ranged from two (Tennessee) to nine (Mississippi), in every case except Tennessee at least five segregationist votes were analyzed. For each vote all counties within a state were scored according to whether or not they ranked in the upper half of the vote (in percentage terms) for a particular militant segregationist. Scores were summed across the total number of elections available for a state, and counties which were in the upper half of the vote at least 75 percent of the time were classified as core segregationist counties. This criterion is designed to be fairly lenient (upper half of the vote) in identifying counties which gave relatively strong support to any single militant segregationist yet comparatively rigorous (75 percent of the elections) in distinguishing core segregationist counties. Since I am primarily interested in examining the core segregationist vote for the post-*Brown* period as a whole, a second criterion was employed to control for the impact of the Voting Rights Act of 1965. The effect of the Voting Rights Act was to mobilize blacks in many counties with large black populations which previously had resisted black voting and had provided strong support for militant segregationists. All counties that were in the upper half of the militant vote at least 75 percent of the time before 1965 but that did not rank in the upper half after 1965 have also been designated core segregationist. Counties that met either of the above criteria comprise the total number of segregationist counties for a given state.

By utilizing as many votes for governor as possible and by setting a high threshold for classification as segregationist, those counties may be isolated which have constituted the core of electoral resistance to racial desegregation in the post-*Brown* South. It must be emphasized that this selection procedure is designed to identify the counties within each state which gave relatively consistent support to a variety of militant segregationists. Since the elections are unique to each state and include primaries as well as general elections, the southern states cannot be compared in terms of the level of segregationist voting. Despite this limitation, the approach does permit a synthesis of voting patterns within and between the states of the South for an era of protracted racial conflict. The following table lists the candidates and elections used to determine core segregationist counties.

Table B-1. Selected militant segregationist candidates for governor in the post-*Brown* South

Candidate	Election	Candidate	Election
Alabama		J. Johnson	1966 GE
J. Patterson	1958 FP	*Florida*	
J. Patterson	1958 SP		
G. Wallace	1962 FP	S. Lowry	1956 FP
G. Wallace	1962 SP	F. Bryant	1960 FP
L. Wallace	1966 FP	F. Bryant	1960 SP
G. Wallace	1970 FP	H. Burns-S. Kelly	1964 FP
G. Wallace	1970 SP	H. Burns	1964 SP
Arkansas		H. Burns	1966 SP
J. Johnson	1956 FP	*Georgia*	
O. Faubus	1958 FP	M. Griffin	1954 FP
O. Faubus	1960 FP	W. Bodenhamer	1958 FP
O. Faubus-D. Alford	1962 FP	M. Griffin	1962 FP
J. Johnson	1966 FP	L. Maddox-J. Gray	1966 FP
J. Johnson	1966 SP	L. Maddox	1966 SP

Table B-1   continued.

Candidate	Election	Candidate	Election
L. Maddox	1966 GE	*South Carolina*	
Louisiana		J. Timmerman	1954 FP
		E. Hollings	1958 FP
W. Rainach	1959-60 FP	E. Hollings	1958 SP
J. Davis	1959-60 SP	J. Rogers	1966 GE
R. Kennon	1963-64 FP	A. Watson	1970 GE
J. McKeithen	1963-64 SP	*Tennessee*	
J. Rarick	1967-68 FP		
Mississippi		G. Browning	1954 FP
		A. Taylor	1958 FP
F. Wright	1955 FP	*Texas*	
R. Barnett	1959 FP		
R. Barnett	1959 SP	A. Shivers	1954 FP
P. Johnson	1963 FP	A. Shivers	1954 SP
P. Johnson	1963 SP	W. O'Daniel	1956 FP
J. Williams-J. Swan	1967 FP	P. Daniel	1956 SP
J. Williams	1967 SP	W. O'Daniel	1958 FP
J. Williams	1967 GE	*Virginia*	
J. Swan	1971 FP		
North Carolina		L. Almond	1957 FP
		L. Almond	1957 GE
B. Lake	1960 FP	A. Harrison	1961 FP
B. Lake	1960 SP	A. Harrison	1961 GE
B. Lake	1964 FP	W. Story	1965 GE
D. Moore	1964 SP		
J. Gardner	1968 GE		

Key: FP = Democratic First Primary; SP = Democratic Second Primary; GE = General Election

Notes

1 The Scope of the Study

1. V. O. Key, Jr., *Southern Politics in State and Nation* (New York: Knopf, 1949), p. ix.

2. Clifford Geertz, "The Integrative Revolution: Primordial Sentiments and Civil Politics in the New States," in Clifford Geertz, ed., *Old Societies and New States: The Quest for Modernity in Asia and Africa* (New York: The Free Press, 1963), pp. 109-110.

3. C. Vann Woodward discusses the concept of a "Second Reconstruction" in "From the First Reconstruction to the Second," in Willie Morris, ed., *The South Today* (New York: Harper & Row, 1965), pp. 1-14; and in his own volume, *The Burden of Southern History,* rev. ed. (Baton Rouge: Louisiana State University Press, 1968), pp. 167-186. The single best introduction to southern politics remains Key, *Southern Politics.* Among the more useful general books dealing with the South since *Southern Politics* are: William C. Havard, ed., *The Changing Politics of the South* (Baton Rouge: Louisiana State University Press, 1972); Numan V. Bartley, *The Rise of Massive Resistance: Race and Politics in the South during the 1950's* (Baton Rouge: Louisiana State University Press, 1969); Donald R. Matthews and James W. Prothro, *Negroes and the New Southern Politics* (New York: Harcourt, Brace & World, 1966); and Allan P. Sindler, ed., *Change in the Contemporary South* (Durham: Duke University Press, 1963).

4. 347 U.S. 483.

5. For assessments of efforts to implement school desegregation in the South, see Gary Orfield, *The Reconstruction of Southern Education: The Schools and the 1964 Civil Rights Act* (New York: Wiley, 1969); Bartley, *Rise of Massive Resistance;* Benjamin Muse, *Ten Years of Prelude: The Story of Integration Since the Supreme Court's 1954 Decision* (New York: Viking, 1964); and Harrell R. Rodgers, Jr., and Charles S. Bullock, III, *Law and Social Change: Civil Rights Laws and Their Consequences* (New York: McGraw-Hill, 1972), pp. 69-111.

6. Key, *Southern Politics,* pp. 674-675.

7. James G. Maddox et al., *The Advancing South: Manpower Prospects and Problems* (New York: Twentieth Century Fund, 1967), p. 22. Statistics cited in the remainder of this paragraph are drawn from this source, pp. 23-27.

8. *Ibid.,* p. 19. The changing socioeconomic structure of the South is also examined in John C. McKinney and Edgar T. Thompson, eds., *The South in Continuity and Change* (Durham: Duke University Press, 1965); and John C. McKinney and Linda Brookover Bourque, "The Changing South: National Incorporation of a Region," *American Sociological Review,* 36 (June 1971), 399-412.

9. As a secondary consideration, I shall also investigate candidate perceptions of the role of state government vis-à-vis economic development. Typologies of campaign stances on segregation and economic development will be introduced in Chapter 2.

10. Key, *Southern Politics,* p. 4. Emphasis added.

11. V. O. Key, Jr., *Public Opinion and American Democracy* (New York: Knopf, 1961), p. 558.

12. Key, *Southern Politics,* p. 675.

13. White politicians are discussed in varying degree in the state chapters in Havard, ed., *Changing Politics of the South*; and in Neal R. Peirce, *The Deep South States of America: People, Politics, and Power in the Seven States of the Deep South* (New York: Norton, 1974). Bartley's *Rise of Massive Resistance* is the most detailed history of white political activists in the 1950s; and Neil R. McMillen recounts the growth and decline of the South's most important segregationist group in *The Citizens' Council: Organized Resistance to the Second Reconstruction, 1954-64* (Urbana: University of Illinois Press, 1971). There are a number of useful but more specialized studies of white southern politicians. See, for example, Robert Sherrill, *Gothic Politics in the Deep South: Stars of the New Confederacy* (New York: Grossman, 1968); William D. Barnard, *Dixiecrats and Democrats: Alabama Politics, 1942-1950* (University, Ala.: University of Alabama Press, 1974); Marshall Frady, *Wallace* (New York: World, 1968); James R. Soukup, Clifton McCleskey, and Harry Holloway, *Party and Factional Division in Texas* (Austin: University of Texas Press, 1964); J. Harvie Wilkinson, III, *Harry Byrd and the Changing Face of Virginia Politics, 1945-1966* (Charlottesville: University Press of Virginia, 1968); James W. Silver, *Mississippi: The Closed Society,* new enlarged ed. (New York: Harcourt, Brace & World, 1966); Walter Lord, *The Past That Would Not Die* (New York: Harper & Row, 1965); Numan V. Bartley, *From Thurmond to Wallace: Political Tendencies in Georgia, 1948-1968* (Baltimore: Johns Hopkins Press, 1970); Howard H. Quint, *Profile in Black and White: A Frank Portrait of South Carolina* (Washington: Public Affairs Press, 1958); William C. Havard, Rudolf Heberle, and Perry H. Howard, *The Louisiana Elections of 1960* (Baton Rouge: Louisiana State University Press, 1963); Perry H. Howard, *Political Tendencies in Louisiana,* rev. and exp. ed. (Baton Rouge: Louisiana State University Press, 1971); and A. J.

Liebling, *The Earl of Louisiana* (New York: Simon and Schuster, 1961).

14. See, among others, Matthews and Prothro, *New Southern Politics;* Harry Holloway, *The Politics of the Southern Negro: From Exclusion to Big City Organization* (New York: Random House, 1969); H. D. Price, *The Negro and Southern Politics: A Chapter of Florida History* (New York: New York University Press, 1957); Frederick M. Wirt, *Politics of Southern Equality: Law and Social Change in a Mississippi County* (Chicago: Aldine, 1970); Chandler Davidson, *Biracial Politics: Conflict and Coalition in the Metropolitan South* (Baton Rouge: Louisiana State University Press, 1972); Everett Carll Ladd, Jr., *Negro Political Leadership in the South* (Ithaca: Cornell University Press, 1966); William R. Keech, *The Impact of Negro Voting: The Role of the Vote in the Quest for Equality* (Chicago: Rand McNally, 1968); I. A. Newby, *Black Carolinians: A History of Blacks in South Carolina from 1895 to 1968* (Columbia: University of South Carolina Press, 1973); Andrew Buni, *The Negro In Virginia Politics, 1902-1965* (Charlottesville: University Press of Virginia, 1967); Stokely Carmichael and Charles V. Hamilton, *Black Power: The Politics of Liberation in America* (New York: Random House, 1967); Pat Watters and Reese Cleghorn, *Climbing Jacob's Ladder: The Arrival of Negroes in Southern Politics* (New York: Harcourt, Brace & World, 1967); and Howard Zinn, *SNCC: The New Abolitionists* (Boston: Beacon Press, 1964).

15. Nine of the eleven southern states elected governors to four-year terms during the post-*Brown* era. In Texas and Arkansas, however, chief executives served two-year terms, and hence for these states twice as many campaigns have been available for analysis as in the typical state.

16. For discussions of black disfranchisement, see Key, *Southern Politics,* esp. pp. 531-554; J. Morgan Kousser, *The Shaping of Southern Politics: Suffrage Restriction and the Establishment of the One-Party South, 1880-1910* (New Haven: Yale University Press, 1974); and Paul Lewinson, *Race, Class, and Party: A History of Negro Suffrage and White Politics in the South* (New York: Oxford University Press, 1932). The proliferation of segregation statutes is treated in C. Vann Woodward, *Origins of the New South, 1877-1913* (Baton Rouge: Louisiana State University Press, 1951); C. Vann Woodward, *The Strange Career of Jim Crow,* 3d rev. ed. (New York: Oxford University Press, 1974); and George B. Tindall, *The Emergence of the New South, 1913-1945* (Baton Rouge: Louisiana State University Press, 1967).

17. See, for example, Douglas W. Rae, *The Political Consequences of Electoral Laws,* rev. ed. (New Haven: Yale University Press, 1971); and Maurice Duverger, *Political Parties: Their Organization and Activity in the Modern State* (New York: Wiley, 1954), esp. pp. 216-228, 239-255.

18. Examples of this literature are Orfield, *Reconstruction of Southern Education;* Wirt, *Politics of Southern Equality;* and Rodgers and Bullock, *Law and Social Change.*

2 The Analytic Framework

1. Donald R. Matthews and James W. Prothro, *Negroes and the New*

Southern Politics (New York: Harcourt, Brace & World, 1966), p. 169. Key made a similar distinction, though without using the identical terms. See V. O. Key, Jr., *Southern Politics in State and Nation* (New York: Knopf, 1949), p. 669.

2. Matthews and Prothro, *New Southern Politics,* pp. 355-357.

3. Bernard Cosman, *Five States for Goldwater: Continuity and Change in Southern Presidential Voting Patterns* (University, Ala.: University of Alabama Press, 1966), pp. 120-125 and throughout.

4. In addition to the New York *Times,* the following newspapers were used: Birmingham *News* and Montgomery *Advertiser* (Alabama); *Arkansas Gazette* (Arkansas); Miami *Herald,* Tampa *Tribune,* and St. Petersburg *Times* (Florida); Atlanta *Constitution* and Atlanta *Journal* (Georgia); New Orleans *Times-Picayune* (Louisiana); Jackson *Clarion-Ledger* (Mississippi); Raleigh *News and Observer* and Charlotte *Observer* (North Carolina); Columbia *State* and Charleston *News and Courier* (South Carolina); Nashville *Banner,* Nashville *Tennessean,* and Memphis *Commercial Appeal* (Tennessee); Dallas *Morning News,* Houston *Post,* and *Texas Observer* (Texas); and Richmond *Times-Dispatch* and Washington *Post* (Virginia).

5. Ulrich B. Phillips, "The Central Theme of Southern History," *American Historical Review,* 34 (October 1928), 31.

6. A number of studies have interpreted southern race relations as a caste system, with whites comprising the "superior" caste and blacks constituting the "inferior" caste. See, for example, John Dollard, *Caste and Class in a Southern Town* (New Haven: Yale University Press, 1937); Hortense Powdermaker, *After Freedom: A Cultural Study in the Deep South* (New York: Viking, 1939); Allison Davis, Burleigh B. Gardner, and Mary R. Gardner, *Deep South: A Social Anthropological Study of Caste and Class* (Chicago: University of Chicago Press, 1941); Gunnar Myrdal, *An American Dilemma: The Negro Problem and American Democracy,* 20th anniversary ed. (New York: Harper & Row, 1962); and Gerald D. Berreman, "Caste in India and the United States," *American Journal of Sociology,* 66 (September 1960), 120-127.

7. Washington *Post,* October 20, 1957; Richmond *Times-Dispatch,* October 2, 9-10, 1957.

8. Miami *Herald,* April 7, 24, 27, 1956.

9. Nashville *Banner,* June 24, 1966.

10. Leslie W. Dunbar, "The Changing Mind of the South: The Exposed Nerve," *Journal of Politics,* 25 (February 1964), 20.

11. James G. Maddox et al., *The Advancing South: Manpower Prospects and Problems* (New York: Twentieth Century Fund, 1967), p. 208.

12. In an earlier presentation of this typology neo-Populist/marginalist was used instead of redistributive and neo-Populist/adaptive was employed instead of progressive. See Earl Black, "Southern Governors and Political Change: Campaign Stances on Racial Segregation and Economic Development, 1950-69," *Journal of Politics,* 33 (August 1971), 719-726. The new labels have been adopted to make the terminology less confusing and cumber-

some; definitions of the categories have not changed. It must be emphasized that the typology attempts to classify elite perspectives concerning the achievement of economic development rather than elite views on economic development per se. Precisely because economic development has been a goal desired by practically all politicians, a direct approach to the classification of elite stances on economic development fails to produce interesting variations among the campaigners. Of necessity, therefore, I have tried to devise indicators of strategies that candidates have advocated (sometimes only implicitly) to achieve economic development. For reasons of style, the qualifying phrase "the achievement of" will not always precede the term "economic development" in the text.

13. Richmond *Times-Dispatch,* June 6-7, 1961.

14. Dallas *Morning News,* April 25, 1964.

15. On Faubus's career, see Roy Reed, "Another Face of Orval Faubus," *New York Times Magazine,* October 9, 1966, p. 44 ff.; and Robert Sherrill, *Gothic Politics in the Deep South: Stars of the New Confederacy* (New York: Grossman, 1968), pp. 110-114.

16. Atlanta *Constitution,* October 11, 15, 17; November 1, 1966.

17. See, for example, the discussion of "neobourbons," "neopopulists," and "business conservatives" in Numan V. Bartley, *The Rise of Massive Resistance: Race and Politics in the South during the 1950's* (Baton Rouge: Louisiana State University Press, 1969), pp. 17-24.

18. No attempt will be made to link the positions candidates adopted on the achievement of economic development to the demography of their votes. Research concerning economic development will be limited to the question of whether or not significant changes in elite orientations have occurred since the early 1950s.

19. Key, *Southern Politics,* p. 5.

20. *Ibid.,* p. 315.

21. *Ibid.,* p. 5.

22. *Ibid.,* pp. 5-10, 317-344. See also Alexander Heard, *A Two-Party South?* (Chapel Hill: University of North Carolina Press, 1952), esp. pp. 251-278.

23. For the sake of convenience Key's argument will be referred to as the "black belt hypothesis." The phrase is intended to connote ruralism as well as large black populations.

24. Key, *Southern Politics,* pp. 664-675.

25. On the black belt hypothesis and southern voting behavior, see William J. Keefe, "Southern Politics Revisited," *Public Opinion Quarterly,* 20 (Summer 1956), 405-412; David M. Heer, "The Sentiment of White Supremacy: An Ecological Study," *American Journal of Sociology,* 64 (May 1959), 592-598; Thomas F. Pettigrew and Ernest Q. Campbell, "Faubus and Segregation: An Analysis of Arkansas Voting," *Public Opinion Quarterly,* 24 (Fall 1960), 436-447; William F. Ogburn and Charles M. Grigg, "Factors Related to the Virginia Vote on Segregation," *Social Forces,* 34 (May 1956), 301-308; Werner F. Grunbaum, "Desegregation in Texas: Voting and Action Pat-

terns," *Public Opinion Quarterly*, 28 (Winter 1964), 604-614; Cosman, *Five States for Goldwater;* Donald L. Fowler, *Presidential Voting in South Carolina, 1948-1964* (Columbia: Bureau of Governmental Research and Service, University of South Carolina, 1966), esp. pp. 35-51; Robert A. Schoenberger and David R. Segal, "The Ecology of Dissent: The Southern Wallace Vote in 1968," *Midwest Journal of Political Science*, 25 (August 1971), 583-586; and Louis M. Seagull, *Southern Republicanism* (Cambridge: Schenkman, 1975).

Black voter registration is investigated in, for example, H. D. Price, *The Negro and Southern Politics: A Chapter of Florida History* (New York: New York University Press, 1957); John H. Fenton and Kenneth N. Vines, "Negro Registration in Louisiana," *American Political Science Review*, 51 (September 1957), 704-713; Donald R. Matthews and James W. Prothro, "Social and Economic Factors and Negro Voter Registration in the South," *American Political Science Review*, 57 (March 1963), 24-44; William R. Keech, *The Impact of Negro Voting: The Role of the Vote in the Quest for Equality* (Chicago: Rand McNally, 1968); Johnnie Daniel, "Negro Political Behavior and Community Political and Socioeconomic Structural Factors," *Social Forces*, 47 (March 1969), 274-280; and Harry Holloway, *The Politics of the Southern Negro: From Exclusion to Big City Organization* (New York: Random House, 1969).

Studies of school desegregation include Thomas F. Pettigrew, "Demographic Correlates of Border-State Desegregation," *American Sociological Review*, 22 (December 1957), 683-689; Thomas F. Pettigrew and M. Richard Cramer, "The Demography of Desegregation," *Journal of Social Issues*, 15 (October 1959), 61-71; Donald R. Matthews and James W. Prothro, "Stateways Versus Folkways: Critical Factors in Southern Reactions to *Brown v. Board of Education*," in Gottfried Dietze, ed., *Essays on the American Constitution* (Englewood Cliffs: Prentice-Hall, 1964), pp. 139-156; James W. Prothro, "Stateways Versus Folkways Revisited: An Error in Prediction," *Journal of Politics*, 34 (May 1972), 352-364; John W. Florin, "The Diffusion of the Decision to Integrate: Southern School Desegregation, 1954-1964," *Southeastern Geographer*, 11 (November 1971), 139-144; and A. B. Cochran and Thomas M. Uhlman, "Black Populations and School Integration—A Research Note," *Phylon*, 34 (March 1973), 43-48.

26. Classifications for each of the southern counties have been assigned on the basis of data contained in U.S. Bureau of the Census, *County and City Data Book* (Washington: U.S. Government Printing Office, 1967). The demographic typology suggested here differs in several respects from that devised by Cosman for his study of presidential Republicanism in the South. Cosman grouped southern counties into four categories: traditionally Republican (ascertained by political data), and metropolitan, nonmetropolitan, and black belt (all determined by demographic data). Only in the case of the black belt category are the two classifications identical. Since my objective is not to study the Republican or Democratic vote per se, counties have been differentiated solely on the basis of demographic criteria. Whereas Cosman grouped as metropolitan all counties with populations exceeding 50,000 and classified

as nonmetropolitan all rural counties which did not qualify as traditionally Republican or have black population majorities, I have attempted to separate larger from smaller urban areas and to stratify rural counties more precisely in terms of the size of their black populations. See Cosman, *Five States for Goldwater,* pp. 48-50.

27. Matthews and Prothro, "Social and Economic Factors," p. 29.

28. Circumstances peculiar to specific campaigns may, however, weaken the expected relationship. For example, first primary contests in which several candidates ran as strong segregationists would be less likely to yield the predicted demographic variations than second primary or general election campaigns which matched a militant segregationist against a moderate segregationist or a nonsegregationist.

29. For a detailed application of this typology to the career of George Wallace, see Earl Black and Merle Black, "The Demographic Basis of Wallace Support in Alabama," *American Politics Quarterly,* 1 (July 1973), 279-304.

30. Two exceptions are Cosman, *Five States for Goldwater;* and Seagull, *Presidential Republicanism.*

31. Hugh Douglas Price, "Southern Politics in the Sixties: Notes on Economic Development and Political Modernization" (paper presented at the annual meeting of the American Political Science Association, Chicago, September 1964), p. 3.

3   Candidates, Campaigns, and Racial Segregation before 1954

1. See V. O. Key, Jr., *Southern Politics in State and Nation* (New York: Knopf, 1949), pp. 329-344, 619-663; Numan V. Bartley, *The Rise of Massive Resistance: Race and Politics in the South during the 1950's* (Baton Rouge: Louisiana State University Press, 1969), pp. 28-46; and Donald S. Strong, "Durable Republicanism in the South," in Allan P. Sindler, ed., *Change in the Contemporary South* (Durham: Duke University Press, 1963), pp. 176-177.

2. Dallas *Morning News,* July 13, 19-20, 1950; Houston *Post,* July 16, 1950.

3. Memphis *Commercial Appeal,* July 2, 1950.

4. Noel E. Parmentel, Jr., "Tennessee Spellbinder," *Nation,* 183 (1956), 115. Alabama's "Big Jim" Folsom, a connoisseur of stump speaking, described Clement's platform style as "cuttin', guttin', and struttin'." *Ibid.,* p. 117.

5. Memphis *Commercial Appeal,* July 10-11, 16-17, 1952.

6. *Arkansas Gazette,* July 27, 30; August 7-8, 1952.

7. H. D. Price, *The Negro and Southern Politics: A Chapter of Florida History* (New York: New York University Press, 1957), p. 97; Miami *Herald,* April 2, 1952.

8. *Arkansas Gazette,* July 31; August 2, 6, 10, 12, 1952.

9. Charleston *News and Courier,* June 2, 8, 1950; Columbia *State,* June 21-23, 1950.

10. Birmingham *News,* April 1, 19, 23, 1950.

11. *Ibid.,* April 15, 23, 1950.

12. Jackson *Clarion-Ledger,* July 13, 17, 20, 26, 1951.

13. Donald R. Matthews and James W. Prothro, *Negroes and the New Southern Politics* (New York: Harcourt, Brace & World, 1966), p. 18.

14. Atlanta *Constitution,* May 21, 27, 1950; Atlanta *Journal,* May 20-21; June 4, 1950. For a sympathetic treatment of Talmadge as a governor, see George McMillan, "Talmadge—the Best Southern Governor?" *Harper's Magazine,* December 1954, pp. 34-40.

15. Atlanta *Constitution,* May 27-28, 1950; Atlanta *Journal,* May 21, 26, 1950.

16. Atlanta *Constitution,* June 6, 8, 1950; Atlanta *Journal,* June 14, 17, 1950.

17. Atlanta *Journal,* June 11, 1950; Atlanta *Constitution,* June 10, 1950.

18. Atlanta *Constitution,* June 21, 23, 30, 1950.

19. *Arkansas Gazette,* June 18, 1950.

20. *Ibid.,* June 25, 30, 1950.

21. *Ibid.,* July 2, 5, 15, 1950.

22. *Ibid.,* July 23, 1950.

23. *Ibid.,* July 19, 23, 27, 1950. On this election, see Harry S. Ashmore, "McMath Enlarges His Beachhead," *Reporter,* April 25, 1950, pp. 22-24.

24. For a discussion of Arkansas's geographic divisions, see Thomas F. Pettigrew and Ernest Q. Campbell, "Faubus and Segregation: An Analysis of Arkansas Voting," *Public Opinion Quarterly,* 24 (Fall 1960), 438-442.

25. The racial stances of the major candidates in this first primary are difficult to classify. They have been categorized as moderate rather than as strong segregationists primarily because the segregation issue was treated in the 1951 first primary in a comparatively routine fashion. However, the rhetoric employed by the Mississippi politicians tended to be more extreme (for example, references to "mongrelization") than that found in most southern states at this time. In the 1951 second primary White campaigned as a militant segregationist.

26. Jackson *Clarion-Ledger,* July 6, 11, 25; August 3, 7, 1951.

27. *Ibid.,* July 6, 19-20, 25, 28; August 2, 5, 1951.

28. *Ibid.,* August 12, 14-16, 19, 1951.

29. *Ibid.,* August 18, 1951.

30. *Ibid.,* August 19, 21, 23, 26, 28, 1951.

31. *Ibid.,* August 26, 1951.

32. Birmingham *News,* April 11, 14, 30; May 11, 1950; Montgomery *Advertiser,* April 5, 11, 13, 19, 21, 1950.

33. Key, *Southern Politics,* p. 261.

34. Dallas *Morning News,* June 27, 1952; Houston *Post,* July 16, 1952.

35. Dallas *Morning News,* July 8, 16, 1952; Houston *Post,* July 24, 1952.

36. Dallas *Morning News,* July 21, 27, 1952.

37. These campaigns are discussed in Allan P. Sindler, *Huey Long's Louisiana* (Baltimore: Johns Hopkins Press, 1956), pp. 233-241.

38. New Orleans *Times-Picayune,* December 3, 1951; January 4-6, 8, 1952.

39. *Ibid.,* January 29; February 13, 1952. See also Kennon's comments in *ibid.,* February 14, 1952.

40. Sindler, *Huey Long's Louisiana,* pp. 233-234.

41. Richmond *Times-Dispatch,* June 22, 27, 1953.

42. *Ibid.,* October 10, 21; November 1, 1953.

43. See Robbins L. Gates, *The Making of Massive Resistance: Virginia's Politics of Public School Desegregation, 1954-1956* (Chapel Hill: University of North Carolina Press, 1964), p. 205.

44. Key, *Southern Politics,* p. 665.

45. Albert D. Kirwan, *Revolt of the Rednecks: Mississippi Politics, 1876-1925* (Lexington: University of Kentucky Press, 1951), p. 314.

4 The Deep South States and Racial Segregation

1. Since similar tables will be utilized for the other southern states, a comment on the purposes of Table 6 may be in order. The table summarizes both the racial positions of successful candidates and the demography of their votes. Data have been collected for all contested Democratic first and second primaries and for those general elections (Alabama had none) in which the Republican candidate received a minimum of 35 percent of the vote and conducted a vigorous (as contrasted to a more or less nominal) campaign. The evolution of the segregation issue may be traced by comparing the racial stances of winners and their closest opponents since 1950. The demographic figures, which report the percentage of the vote received by a winner within a given demographic classification, reveal the demographic structure of the vote for particular winners and facilitate comparisons between winners. To make the results more meaningful, the mean percentage distribution of the state vote between demographic categories has been computed for each type of election. For example, Table 6 shows that, on the average, the large metropolitan areas contributed 25 percent of the entire state vote in Democratic second primaries for governor. In 1958 Patterson won 57 percent of that large metropolitan vote.

2. Birmingham *News,* October 30, 1954; and Douglass Cater, "Governor Folsom: Big Man in a Tight Spot," *Reporter,* April 9, 1956, pp. 30-31. On Alabama politics generally, see V. O. Key, Jr., *Southern Politics in State and Nation* (New York: Knopf, 1949), pp. 36-57; Donald S. Strong, "Alabama: Transition and Alienation," in William C. Havard, ed., *The Changing Politics of the South* (Baton Rouge: Louisiana State University Press, 1972), pp. 427-471; Marshall Frady, *Wallace* (New York: World, 1968); Robert Sherrill, *Gothic Politics in the Deep South: Stars of the New Confederacy* (New York: Grossman, 1968), pp. 255-301; Numan V. Bartley, *The Rise of Massive Re-*

sistance: Race and Politics in the South during the 1950's (Baton Rouge: Louisiana State University Press, 1969), pp. 279-286; and Earl Black and Merle Black, "The Demographic Basis of Wallace Support in Alabama," *American Politics Quarterly*, 1 (July 1973), 279-304.

3. Montgomery *Advertiser,* April 6, 17, 20, 1958.

4. Andrew Kopkind, "Alabama Unbound," *New Republic,* November 27, 1965, p. 13.

5. Montgomery *Advertiser,* April 12, 1962.

6. Birmingham *News,* January 14, 1963.

7. *Ibid.,* March 9, 1966. On this election, see Ray Jenkins, "Mr. and Mrs. Wallace Run for Governor of Alabama," *New York Times Magazine,* April 24, 1966, p. 26 ff.

8. Pat Watters and Reese Cleghorn, *Climbing Jacob's Ladder: The Arrival of Negroes in Southern Politics* (New York: Harcourt, Brace & World, 1967), Appendix 2.

9. Birmingham *News,* March 15, 19; April 30, 1970. For a valuable brief account of the 1970 campaigns, see Ray Jenkins, "Standing for It Again in Alabama," *New South,* 25 (Summer 1970), 26-32.

10. Birmingham *News,* May 24, 1970; Montgomery *Advertiser-Alabama Journal,* May 31, 1970; and Washington *Post,* June 1, 1970.

11. These findings are broadly consistent with Key's research. See *Southern Politics,* pp. 41-46. For a more detailed analysis of socioeconomic regions in Alabama, see Horace Mann Bond, *Negro Education in Alabama: A Study in Cotton and Steel* (New York: Atheneum, 1969), pp. 1-8.

12. On demographic and geographic factors in Mississippi politics, see Albert D. Kirwan, *Revolt of the Rednecks: Mississippi Politics, 1876-1925* (Lexington: University of Kentucky Press, 1951), pp. 40-42; Key, *Southern Politics,* pp. 229-238; and Charles N. Fortenberry and F. Glenn Abney, "Mississippi: Unreconstructed and Unredeemed," in Havard, ed., *Changing Politics of the South,* pp. 472-478 and 481-484.

13. Considerable attention has been given to Mississippi politics. See, for example, Key, *Southern Politics,* pp. 229-253; James W. Silver, *Mississippi: The Closed Society,* new enlarged ed. (New York: Harcourt, Brace & World, 1966); Fortenberry and Abney, "Mississippi: Unreconstructed and Unredeemed"; F. Glenn Abney, "Partisan Realignment in a One-Party System: The Case of Mississippi," *Journal of Politics,* 31 (November 1969), 1102-1106; and Sherrill, *Gothic Politics,* pp. 174-215.

14. Jackson *Clarion-Ledger,* July 22, 26-27, 29, 31, 1955.

15. *Ibid.,* August 12-13, 16, 18-19, 1955.

16. Silver, *Mississippi,* pp. 49-50.

17. Jackson *Clarion-Ledger,* July 29; August 2, 1959. Barnett's close relationship with the Citizens' Council is discussed in Neil R. McMillen, *The Citizens' Council: Organized Resistance to the Second Reconstruction, 1954-64* (Urbana: University of Illinois Press, 1971), pp. 326-347.

18. Jackson *Clarion-Ledger,* January 9, 1964.

19. *Ibid.,* June 16; July 18, 23, 1963.

20. *Ibid.,* January 22, 1964.

21. Silver, *Mississippi,* pp. 269-270, 278, 280, 355.

22. Jackson *Clarion-Ledger,* April 22, 1967.

23. *Ibid.,* July 9, 12, 30, 1967.

24. *Ibid.,* August 6, 1967. For an example of Williams' hostility to HEW school desegregation guidelines, see his advertisement in the *Clarion-Ledger* for July 26, 1967.

25. Voter registration estimates are taken from Watters and Cleghorn, *Climbing Jacob's Ladder,* Appendix 2.

26. Jackson *Clarion-Ledger,* August 3, 1971; New Orleans *Times-Pic-ayune,* July 25; August, 1, 3, 5, 24, 1971; and New York *Times,* August 4-5, 1971.

27. For treatments of Georgia politics, see Key, *Southern Politics,* pp. 106-129; Joseph L. Bernd, "Georgia: Static and Dynamic," in Havard, ed., *Changing Politics of the South,* pp. 294-365; Numan V. Bartley, *From Thurmond to Wallace: Political Tendencies in Georgia, 1948-1968* (Baltimore: Johns Hopkins Press, 1970); and Sherrill, *Gothic Politics,* pp. 37-73.

28. Atlanta *Constitution,* August 13; September 9, 1954.

29. Bodenhamer forces distributed pamphlets picturing Vandiver standing between two blacks. Vandiver found it necessary to attack this kind of handout, with its implication that he was not the militant segregationist he claimed to be, as "the height of absurdity." See *ibid.,* July 22-25, 1958.

30. Atlanta *Journal,* August 17, 1958; Atlanta *Constitution,* September 9-10, 1958.

31. Atlanta *Constitution,* July 13, 27; August 7, 1962; Atlanta *Journal,* August 12, 1962.

32. Atlanta *Constitution,* August 15, 22, 1962; Atlanta *Journal,* September 7, 1962.

33. See, for example, Atlanta *Constitution,* August 16, 1962.

34. Reese Cleghorn, " 'Mr. White Backlash,' " *New York Times Magazine,* November 6, 1966, p. 40.

35. Atlanta *Constitution,* July 1, 6, 15; September 6, 1966.

36. *Ibid.,* October 7, 28; November 1, 1966. Voter perceptions of Maddox and Callaway are analyzed in Anthony M. Orum and Edward W. McCranie, "Class, Tradition, and Partisan Alignments in a Southern Urban Electorate," *Journal of Politics,* 32 (February 1970), 156-176.

37. Atlanta *Constitution,* January 12, 1967.

38. Cleghorn, " 'Mr. White Backlash,' " p. 62. The inaugural's promise of a judicious, relatively dignified approach to the governorship by Maddox was hardly fulfilled. See, for example, Robert Sherrill, "Strange Decorum of Lester Maddox," *Nation,* 204 (1967), 553-556; Joseph H. Baird, "Lester Maddox: Puritan in the Statehouse," *Reporter,* October 5, 1967, pp. 19-22; and Calvin Trillin, "U.S. Letter: Atlanta," *New Yorker,* January 27, 1968, pp. 101-105.

39. Watters and Cleghorn, *Climbing Jacob's Ladder,* Appendix 2.

40. Atlanta *Journal,* July 28, 1970; Atlanta *Constitution,* August 27-28,

1970; Atlanta *Journal and Constitution,* August 30, 1970; and New York *Times,* September 10-11, 1970. Carter's campaign strategy is discussed in James Clotfelter and William R. Hamilton, "Electing a Governor in the Seventies," in Thad L. Beyle and J. Oliver Williams, eds., *The American Governor in Behavioral Perspective* (New York: Harper & Row, 1972), pp. 32-39.

41. Text of inaugural address released by the governor's office, January 12, 1971. See New York *Times,* January 13, 1971.

42. For a brief discussion of Carter's "intentionally ambiguous position on racial questions," see James Clotfelter, "Populism in Office or, Whatever Happened to Huey Long," *New South,* 28 (Spring 1973), 58-59.

43. See also the discussion of Georgia's geographic and demographic characteristics in Bartley, *From Thurmond to Wallace,* pp. 15-21 and 35-41; and Bernd, "Georgia: Static and Dynamic," pp. 304-311.

44. See, for example, Allan P. Sindler, *Huey Long's Louisiana* (Baltimore: Johns Hopkins Press, 1956), p. 256; and T. Harry Williams, *Huey Long* (New York: Knopf, 1969), pp. 701-706. On Louisiana politics generally, see also Key, *Southern Politics,* pp. 156-182; Perry H. Howard, *Political Tendencies in Louisiana,* rev. and exp. ed. (Baton Rouge: Louisiana State University Press, 1971); William C. Havard, Rudolf Heberle, and Perry H. Howard, *The Louisiana Elections of 1960* (Baton Rouge: Louisiana State University Press, 1963); A. J. Liebling, *The Earl of Louisiana* (New York: Simon and Schuster, 1961); and Perry H. Howard, "Louisiana: Resistance and Change," in Havard, ed., *Changing Politics of the South,* pp. 525-587.

45. For excellent discussions of Louisiana's political ecology, see Havard, Heberle, and Howard, *Louisiana Elections of 1960,* pp. 3-16; and Howard, *Political Tendencies in Louisiana,* esp. pp. 3-17.

46. Fenton and Vines have emphasized the significance of "religio-cultural" cleavages in Louisiana. See John H. Fenton and Kenneth N. Vines, "Negro Registration in Louisiana," *American Political Science Review,* 51 (September 1957), 704-713.

47. New Orleans *Times-Picayune,* December 7, 10, 1955; January 11, 18, 1956.

48. Havard, Heberle, and Howard, *Louisiana Elections of 1960,* pp. 36-37. For an assessment of the rise of the hard-lining racists, see William C. Havard and Robert J. Steamer, "Louisiana Secedes: Collapse of a Compromise," *Massachusetts Review,* 1 (October 1959), 134-146.

49. New Orleans *Times-Picayune,* October 8; December 9, 1959.

50. *Ibid.,* Nobember 2; December 4-5, 1963.

51. *Ibid.,* December 12, 19-20, 1963.

52. Suggestions along these lines are contained in John Hamilton Korns II, "Leadership and Followship: Political Activities of the Louisiana AFL-CIO," (Senior Honors thesis, Department of Government, Harvard University, 1967), pp. 21-24, 30-31, and 95-97. As an example of McKeithen's conciliatory activities, see his comments on a black protest rally and Ku Klux Klan counter-rally in Baton Rouge, New Orleans *Times-Picayune,* August 19, 1967.

53. Watters and Cleghorn, *Climbing Jacob's Ladder,* Appendix 2.

54. New Orleans *Times-Picayune,* September 6; November 3, 16, 1967.

55. New York *Times,* March 4-5, 1970; New Orleans *Times-Picayune,* May 11, 1971.

56. See New Orleans *Times-Picayune,* October 1, 20; November 6, 8; December 16, 1971; January 19, 1972; Washington *Post,* November 6, 8; December 18-20, 1971; New York *Times,* November 6, 8, 1971; May 10, 1972.

57. For a more detailed analysis, see Chester W. Bain, "South Carolina: Partisan Prelude," in Havard, ed., *Changing Politics of the South,* pp. 589-593.

58. South Carolina politics is examined in Key, *Southern Politics,* pp. 130-155; Bain, "South Carolina: Partisan Prelude," pp. 588-636; Howard H. Quint, *Profile in Black and White: A Frank Portrait of South Carolina* (Washington: Public Affairs Press, 1958); and Ernest McPherson Lander, Jr., *A History of South Carolina, 1865-1960* (Chapel Hill: University of North Carolina Press, 1960), pp. 175-186.

59. Charleston *News and Courier,* May 1, 19, 26-27, 1954; January 19, 1955; Columbia *State,* May 15, 18, 25-26, 29, 1954; June 2, 5, 9, 1954.

60. Columbia *State,* May 7, 10, 14, 17-18, 20-22, 1958; Charleston *News and Courier,* June 13-14, 20, 23-24, 26, 1958; January 21, 1959.

61. Charleston *News and Courier,* May 25, 31; June 2, 5, 1962.

62. *Ibid.,* January 16, 1963.

63. *Southern School News,* May 17, 1964, p. 16. See also Benjamin Muse, *Ten Years of Prelude: The Story of Integration Since the Supreme Court's 1954 Decision* (New York: Viking, 1964), pp. 257-259.

64. Charleston *News and Courier,* October 11, 14, 1966; Columbia *Record,* October 11, 1966; and Columbia *State,* November 9, 1966.

65. Watters and Cleghorn, *Climbing Jacob's Ladder,* Appendix 2; and "State of the Southern States," *New South,* 22 (Winter 1967), 78-79.

66. Quotations from the inaugural address are taken from the Charleston *News and Courier,* January 19, 1967.

67. New York *Times,* January 28, 1970. For a highly critical account of McNair's performance in the Orangeburg case by southern journalists who covered the story, see Jack Nelson and Jack Bass, *The Orangeburg Massacre* (New York: World, 1970).

68. Columbia *State,* October 7, 9, 25, 30-31; November 3, 1970; Charleston *News and Courier,* October 22, 1970; Washington *Post,* October 18, 30, 1970; and New York *Times,* October 4, 24; November 4, 1970.

69. John C. West, "South Carolina Looks to the Future," in Ernest M. Lander, Jr., and Robert K. Ackerman, eds., *Perspectives in South Carolina History* (Columbia: University of South Carolina Press, 1973), pp. 409-414. See also the New York *Times,* January 20, 1971.

70. Washington *Post,* August 27, 1971. See in addition Atlanta *Journal,* August 23, 1971.

5   The Peripheral South States and Racial Segregation

1. Price's differentiation of North Florida and South Florida counties has been followed. See H. D. Price, *The Negro and Southern Politics: A Chapter of Florida History* (New York: New York University Press, 1957), p. 39. Alternative sectional boundaries are presented in William C. Havard and Loren P. Beth, *The Politics of Mis-Representation: Rural-Urban Conflict in the Florida Legislature* (Baton Rouge: Louisiana State University Press, 1962), pp. 14-16; Herbert J. Doherty, Jr., "Liberal and Conservative Voting Patterns in Florida," *Journal of Politics,* 14 (August 1952), 408-409; and Manning J. Dauer, "Florida: The Different State," in William C. Havard, ed., *The Changing Politics of the South* (Baton Rouge: Louisiana State University Press, 1972), pp. 95-97.

2. See Price, *Negro and Southern Politics,* pp. 47-54; and Havard and Beth, *Politics of Mis-Representation,* pp. 16-19.

3. Miami *Herald,* April 9; May 2, 14, 18, 23, 26, 1954. On Florida politics in general, see V. O. Key, Jr., *Southern Politics in State and Nation* (New York: Knopf, 1949), pp. 82-105; Price, *Negro and Southern Politics;* Havard and Beth, *Politics of Mis-Representation;* Doherty, "Voting Patterns in Florida"; and Dauer, "Florida: The Different State," pp. 92-164.

4. Miami *Herald,* April 26-28, 1956; *Southern School News,* April, 1956. For examples of Lowry's race baiting, see Price, *Negro and Southern Politics,* pp. 84-86. The 1956 campaign is described at length in Helen L. Jacobstein, *The Segregation Factor in the Florida Democratic Gubernatorial Primary of 1956* (Gainesville: University of Florida Press, 1972).

5. *Southern School News,* May 17, 1964, pp. 3, 10. For a brief and laudatory assessment of Collins' career as governor, see Reed Sarratt, *The Ordeal of Desegregation* (New York: Harper & Row, 1966), pp. 8-10. A less favorable view is presented in William L. Rivers, "The Fine Art of Moderation," *Nation,* 185 (1957), 470-473.

6. Collins' speech is printed in Hoke Norris, ed., *We Dissent* (New York: St. Martin's Press, 1962), pp. 103-115.

7. *Southern School News,* March 1956; Tampa *Tribune,* March 29; April 27; May 9, 13, 1960; and Miami *Herald,* May 10, 12-13, 1960.

8. Miami *Herald,* April 3, 29, 1964; St. Petersburg *Times,* May 18, 22, 24, 1964.

9. Pat Watters and Reese Cleghorn, *Climbing Jacob's Ladder: The Arrival of Negroes in Southern Politics* (New York: Harcourt, Brace & World, 1967), Appendix 2.

10. Miami *Herald,* April 22; May 5, 15, 1966. On Burns' loss of favor with the electorate, see Dauer, "Florida: The Different State," p. 136.

11. Kirk would cite the late Senate Minority Leader Everett Dirksen to support his contention that a question of constitutional right rather than racial prejudice motivated his opposition to open housing legislation. Jackson-

ville *Florida Times-Union,* October 31; November 6, 1966; Tampa *Times,* October 10, 1966; Miami *Herald,* November 7, 1966.

12. William C. Havard, "The South: A Shifting Perspective," in Havard, ed., *Changing Politics of the South,* p. 21.

13. St. Petersburg *Times,* September 19, 27; October 18, 25, 30, 1970; Tampa *Tribune and Times,* September 27, 1970; Miami *Herald,* September 27, 1970; Washington *Post,* April 7, 9-10, 12, 14-15, 1970; New York *Times,* April 8, 10-13; November 4, 1970; and Dauer, "Florida: The Different State," pp. 144-146.

14. St. Petersburg *Times,* August 29, 1971; Washington *Post,* September 6, 1971; February 29, 1972; and Robert W. Hooker, "Busing, Gov. Askew, and the Florida Primary," *New South,* 27 (Spring 1972), 23-30.

15. Arkansas regions are taken from Thomas F. Pettigrew and Ernest Q. Campbell, "Faubus and Segregation: An Analysis of Arkansas Voting," *Public Opinion Quarterly,* 24 (Fall 1960), 438-442. For discussions of Arkansas politics, see Key, *Southern Politics,* pp. 183-204; Robert Sherrill, *Gothic Politics in the Deep South: Stars of the New Confederacy* (New York: Grossman, 1968), pp. 74-117; Richard E. Yates, "Arkansas: Independent and Unpredictable," in Havard, ed., *Changing Politics of the South,* pp. 233-293; and Jim Ranchino, *Faubus to Bumpers: Arkansas Votes, 1960-1970* (Arkadelphia, Ark: Action Research, Inc., 1972).

16. See, for example, Roy Reed, "Another Face of Orval Faubus," *New York Times Magazine,* October 9, 1966, p. 44 ff.; Numan V. Bartley, *The Rise of Massive Resistance: Race and Politics in the South during the 1950s* (Baton Rouge: Louisiana State University Press, 1969), pp. 260-262; and Sherrill, *Gothic Politics,* pp. 82-85.

17. *Arkansas Gazette,* June 26; July 28; August 11, 1954. On the campaign, see Reed, "Another Face of Orval Faubus," pp. 62, 66.

18. *Arkansas Gazette,* July 10, 17, 1956.

19. *Ibid.,* June 29; July 3, 5, 30, 1958. The governor's statement should not of course be swallowed whole. It combines bad constitutional law with a misguided and patently self-serving assessment of responsibility for the presence of "federal bayonets."

20. *Ibid.,* July 2, 27, 1960.

21. *Ibid.,* July 12, 29, 1962.

22. *Ibid.,* July 21; November 1, 1964.

23. Reed, "Another Face of Orval Faubus," p. 76. See also Sherrill, *Gothic Politics,* p. 116.

24. *Arkansas Gazette,* May 11, 1966. Johnson's difficulties with the press, particularly the *Arkansas Gazette,* persisted. One *Gazette* editorial referred to him as a "terrible person." According to Johnson's wife, the candidate responded to this characterization by expressing shock at the editorial and by exclaiming spontaneously that he "would rather die on the cross of ridicule and persecution standing for the principles upon which this nation was founded and on which this state came into being than to dwell in Herod's

Court, even if Herod himself were the editor of the *Arkansas Gazette.*" *Ibid.*, July 8, 1966.

25. On Rockefeller's career, see Yates, "Arkansas," pp. 275-291.

26. *Arkansas Gazette,* August 16, 19, 31; September 3, 1970; New York *Times,* July 28; September 6, 9-10, 1970.

27. Quotations from Bumpers' inaugural of January 12, 1971, are taken from a copy of the speech provided by the governor's office.

28. Washington *Post,* August 4, 1971.

29. See Havard, "The South: A Shifting Perspective," p. 21.

30. Ranchino, *Faubus to Bumpers,* p. 13.

31. On North Carolina politics, see Key, *Southern Politics,* pp. 205-228; Preston W. Edsall and J. Oliver Williams, "North Carolina: Bipartisan Paradox," in Havard, ed., *Changing Politics of the South,* pp. 366-423; Gordon B. Cleveland and Donald R. Matthews, "Politics," in Richard E. Lonsdale, dir., *Atlas of North Carolina* (Chapel Hill: University of North Carolina Press, 1967), pp. 70-75; Jack D. Fleer, *North Carolina Politics: An Introduction* (Chapel Hill: University of North Carolina Press, 1968); and Thad L. Beyle and Merle Black, eds., *Politics and Policy in North Carolina* (New York: MSS Information Corporation, 1975).

32. Raleigh *News and Observer,* May 17, 1956; August 30, 1957; Raleigh *Times,* September 4, 1957.

33. Southern Education Reporting Service, *A Statistical Summary, State by State, of School Segregation-Desegregation in the Southern and Border Area from 1954 to the Present* (Nashville: Southern Education Reporting Service, 1967), pp. 41, 43.

34. Raleigh *News and Observer,* May 6, 31; June 1, 1960.

35. *Ibid.,* June 15, 1960.

36. *Ibid.,* January 6, 1961.

37. *Ibid.,* April 6, 26; May 6; June 2, 6, 1964.

38. *Ibid.,* April 17; May 2; October 17, 23; and November 8, 10, 1968.

39. Charlotte *Observer,* March 17, 29; May 21, 28; June 4; October 12-13, 15, 23, 1972; Raleigh *News and Observer,* March 15-16; April 2, 19; May 21-22, 24, 1972; and New York *Times,* October 28, 1972.

40. Registration data have been taken from Havard, "The South: A Shifting Perspective," p. 21.

41. See Key, *Southern Politics,* pp. 217-218.

42. Richmond *Times-Dispatch,* August 28, 1956. The massive resistance movement and Virginia politics generally have received considerable scholarly analysis. See, for example, Key, *Southern Politics,* pp. 19-35; Bartley, *Rise of Massive Resistance;* Robbins L. Gates, *The Making of Massive Resistance: Virginia's Politics of Public School Desegregation, 1954-1956* (Chapel Hill: University of North Carolina Press, 1964); Benjamin Muse, *Virginia's Massive Resistance* (Bloomington: Indiana University Press, 1961); J. Harvie Wilkinson, III, *Harry Byrd and the Changing Face of Virginia Politics, 1945-1966* (Charlottesville: University Press of Virginia, 1968); Ralph Eisenberg,

"Virginia: The Emergence of Two-Party Politics," in Havard, ed., *Changing Politics of the South*, pp. 39-91; and Andrew Buni, *The Negro in Virginia Politics, 1902-1965* (Charlottesville: University Press of Virginia, 1967).

43. On the 1956 special session, see Muse, *Virginia's Massive Resistance*, pp. 28-34.

44. *Ibid.*, pp. 43-44.

45. Richmond *Times-Dispatch*, January 12, 1958.

46. Gates, *Making of Massive Resistance*, p. 210; and Muse, *Virginia's Massive Resistance*, pp. 86-94, 118-126.

47. Bartley, *Rise of Massive Resistance*, pp. 320-327; Muse, *Virginia's Massive Resistance*, pp. 126-139. See also Buni, *Negro in Virginia Politics*, pp. 200-202.

48. Muse, *Virginia's Massive Resistance*, p. 171.

49. Richmond *Times-Dispatch*, June 7; July 2, 11, 1961.

50. For detailed accounts of this campaign, see Wilkinson, *Harry Byrd*, pp. 263-284; and Buni, *Negro in Virginia Politics*, pp. 228-253.

51. Richmond *Times-Dispatch*, July 2, 1961; October 27, 1965; and Buni, *Negro in Virginia Politics*, p. 235. Godwin's appeal for Negro and white liberal votes was implicit in his campaign pledge to work for "progress in Virginia." See Buni, *Negro in Virginia Politics*, pp. 234-235.

52. Richmond *Times-Dispatch*, October 28, 1965; and Buni, *Negro in Virginia Politics*, pp. 233-234, 239-240.

53. Richmond *Times-Dispatch*, January 16, 1966.

54. *Voter Registration in the South, Summer, 1968* (Atlanta: Voter Education Project, Southern Regional Council, 1968), n.p.

55. Washington *Post*, September 21; October 10, 1969. See also *ibid.*, October 26, 31; November 2, 1969.

56. *Ibid.*, January 18, 1970.

57. Atlanta *Journal*, August 24, 1971; Washington *Post*, August 26, 1971; January 2, 1974; Richmond *Times-Dispatch*, September 20, 1973; and Frank Rich, "Decency and Loyalty: Linwood Holton Learns the President's Views," *Washington Monthly*, April, 1973, pp. 47-54.

58. Washington *Post*, October 20, 30, 1973; November 9, 11, 1973; January 2, 13, 15, 1973; Richmond *Times-Dispatch*, November 2, 1973; and New York *Times*, September 27, 1973.

59. See Gates, *Making of Massive Resistance*, pp. 1-12; Wilkinson, *Harry Byrd*, pp. 157-169; and Eisenberg, "Virginia," pp. 60-63.

60. There were only two primaries in which militant segregationists sought the governorship and in both cases the candidates came from West Tennessee; a "friends and neighbors" component is probably included in the core segregationist counties, which additional elections, had they been available, might have filtered out. For discussions of the geography and demography of Tennessee, see Hugh Davis Graham, *Crisis in Print* (Nashville: Vanderbilt University Press, 1967), pp. 12-24; and Lee S. Greene and Jack E. Holmes, "Tennessee: A Politics of Peaceful Change," in Havard, ed., *Changing Politics of the South*, pp. 165-170.

61. On Tennessee politics, see Key, *Southern Politics*, pp. 58-81; Greene

and Holmes, "Tennessee," pp. 165-200; Graham, *Crisis in Print,* pp. 269-291; and Norman L. Parks, "Tennessee Politics Since Kefauver and Reece: A 'Generalist' View," *Journal of Politics,* 28 (February 1966), 144-168.

62. Sarratt, *Ordeal of Desegregation,* p. 4.

63. *Ibid.,* p. 4; and Benjamin Muse, *Ten Years of Prelude: The Story of Integration Since the Supreme Court's 1954 Decision* (New York: Viking, 1964), pp. 116-117.

64. Nashville *Banner,* September 3, 1956; September 9, 1957.

65. *Ibid.,* July 4, 1958; Nashville *Tennessean,* August 3, 1958.

66. Graham, *Crisis in Print,* p. 288.

67. Watters and Cleghorn, *Climbing Jacob's Ladder,* Appendix 2.

68. Nashville *Banner,* June 18, 24, 1966; January 16, 1967.

69. Nashville *Tennessean,* July 2; August 2; October 8, 13, 1970; Nashville *Banner,* July 7, 17, 1970; Memphis *Commercial Appeal,* October 4; November 3, 5, 1970; and New York *Times,* January 27; November 4-5, 1970.

70. Havard, "The South: A Shifting Perspective," p. 21.

71. See, for example, O, Douglas Weeks, "Texas: Land of Conservative Expansiveness," in Havard, ed., *Changing Politics of the South,* pp. 201-203; Clifton McCleskey, *The Government and Politics of Texas,* 4th ed. (Boston: Little, Brown, 1972), pp. 4-18; and Dan Nimmo and William E. Oden, *The Texas Political System* (Englewood Cliffs: Prentice-Hall, 1971), pp. 19-32.

72. Key, *Southern Politics,* pp. 254-255. For a concurring judgment, see the second edition of McCleskey's *Government and Politics of Texas,* pp. 81-82. On Texas politics, in addition to the work of Key and McCleskey, see James R. Soukup, Clifton McCleskey, and Harry Holloway, *Party and Factional Division in Texas* (Austin: University of Texas Press, 1964); Weeks, "Texas," pp. 201-230; and Nimmo and Oden, *Texas Political System.*

73. All but five of the 78 desegregated districts in the region during the school year 1955-56 were in Texas. It should not be supposed that this represented much voluntary integration. Most desegregation occurred in West or South Texas districts which contained only a few blacks. Only 1.13 percent of the state's black students attended desegregated facilities in 1956. This rate of desegregation, however token, was nearly double that of any other southern state. See Southern Education Reporting Service, *Statistical Summary,* pp. 32, 40.

74. The effectiveness of Shivers' strategy at Mansfield was contingent upon a minimal response by the national government, and Shivers succeeded where Faubus failed because President Dwight Eisenhower demonstrated little comprehension of what had actually occurred in Mansfield. Defending Shivers' use of state forces to prevent mob action, the President commented that "when police power is exercised habitually by the Federal Government, we are in a bad way." Shivers converted the controversy into a factional issue. "Without paid agitators we would not have trouble," Shivers asserted. "And it is unfortunate that in the National Association for the [Advancement of] Colored People some white people are the worst offenders—some prominent in the so-called liberal Democratic circles in Texas. The agitators ought to be put in jail, but unfortunately they are sitting back in plush offices." Dallas

Morning News, August 31; September 1, 6-7, 1956. On the episode, see Muse, *Ten Years of Prelude,* pp. 88-92.

75. See, for example, Houston *Post,* July 14, 1954; and August 10, 1956.

76. *Texas Observer,* July 11, 1956; Dallas *Morning News,* July 11, 1956. O'Daniel predicted that desegregation would have catastrophic results. The Supreme Court was "telling us we got to eat together, sit together, sleep together and do everything together. Pretty soon there'll be little parties and social affairs, nature will take its course, they intermarry, and the mongrel race takes over. No! The people of Texas are not going to take that!" *Texas Observer,* July 11, 1956.

77. *Southern School News,* May 17, 1964, p. 14. The legislature's actions effectively slowed the pace of school desegregation. For figures, see Southern Education Reporting Service, *Statistical Summary,* pp. 41-43.

78. Dallas *Morning News,* July 1, 6, 13, 1958.

79. *Texas Observer,* March 11, 1960.

80. *Ibid.,* June 8; August 3, 1962.

81. This and succeeding quotations have been taken from John Connally, "Let Us Do It Our Way," in Bradford Daniel, ed., *Black, White and Gray* (New York: Sheed and Ward, 1964), pp. 14-25.

82. Dallas *Morning News,* April 25, 28, 1964.

83. Houston *Post,* April 25-26; May 15, 1968.

84. Mimeographed text of inaugural address, dated January 21, 1969, furnished by the governor's office.

85. Houston *Chronicle,* March 3, 16; May 1-2; June 1, 4, 1972; Dallas *Morning News,* March 3; April 21, 26; May 2, 5, 24; October 17, 26, 29, 1972. The stock scandal is described in Sam Kinch, Jr., and Ben Proctor, *Texas under a Cloud* (Austin: Jenkins Publishing Co., 1972); and Harvey Katz, *Shadow on the Alamo* (New York: Doubleday, 1972).

86. Havard, "The South: A Shifting Perspective," pp. 20-21.

87. Key, *Southern Politics,* p. 667.

88. Percentages for large metropolitan counties are typically based on a small number of counties. The 50 percent segregationist figure for North Carolina, for example, results from considering Union and Mecklenburg as equals, though the latter is by far the more populous county. When the voting behavior of complete SMSAs was analyzed no SMSA in the Peripheral South qualified as segregationist, while the Shreveport and Charleston SMSAs did so in the Deep South.

89. Compared to Deep South cities like Atlanta and Birmingham, the segregationist large metropolitan SMSAs were marginal cases. The Charleston SMSA contained 255,000 inhabitants in 1960 and the Shreveport SMSA had a population of 281,000.

90. It should be noted that the percentage of segregationist black belt counties in several states (for example, Texas, Florida, and Tennessee) is based on a very small number of counties.

91. Key, *Southern Politics,* p. 673.

92. This point is made through a series of case studies in Harry Holloway, *The Politics of the Southern Negro: From Exclusion to Big City Organization* (New York: Random House, 1969).

93. Price, *Negro and Southern Politics,* pp. 35-44.

94. Until 1965 the militant segregationist candidate had invariably been the choice of the Byrd Organization. In the 1965 general election, however, the militant was a third-party candidate. He ran comparatively well in South-side Virginia, but the "friends and neighbors" of Senator Byrd remained loyal to the organization's man.

95. It is not contended, of course, that these two variables are the only important determinants of southern politics. For good summaries of the literature which deal with additional variables, see Thomas F. Pettigrew and M. Richard Cramer, "The Demography of Desegregation," *Journal of Social Issues,* 15 (October 1959), 61-71; and Joe R. Feagin, "Civil Rights Voting by Southern Congressmen," *Journal of Politics,* 34 (May 1972), 484-499.

96. Compare the general similarity of this grouping to the scale of "Southernism" developed by Price, *Negro and Southern Politics,* pp. 8-9.

6 The Major Candidates

1. Pat Watters and Reese Cleghorn, *Climbing Jacob's Ladder: The Arrival of Negroes in Southern Politics* (New York: Harcourt, Brace & World, 1967), p. 258.

2. James W. Silver, *Mississippi: The Closed Society,* new enlarged ed. (New York: Harcourt, Brace & World, 1966), pp. 154-156 and throughout.

3. *Ibid.,* p. 154.

4. V. O. Key, Jr., *Southern Politics in State and Nation* (New York: Knopf, 1949), p. 36.

5. For suggestive comments, see, for example, Harry Holloway, *The Politics of the Southern Negro: From Exclusion to Big City Organization* (New York: Random House, 1969), pp. 287-300 (on Tennessee); and J. Harvie Wilkinson, III, *Harry Byrd and the Changing Face of Virginia Politics, 1945-1966* (Charlottesville: University Press of Virginia, 1968), pp. 166-167, 182-186, and 345-346 (on Virginia).

6. H. D. Price, *The Negro and Southern Politics: A Chapter of Florida History* (New York: New York University Press, 1957), pp. 82-83. Though Price was writing about one-party systems in general, his conclusion applies with particular force to Florida. For an analysis of Florida's "fluid factionalism," see Key, *Southern Politics,* pp. 82-105.

7. As one of the last specimens in the Peripheral South of the oratory traditionally associated with the rural segregationist politician, Johnson's rhetoric concerning racial change is worth preserving:

> If you want to tell [the Johnson Administration in Washington] that you're tired of these federal controls and the persecution of the majority and the illegal [school desegregation] guidelines and you're tired of the policy that says that any wench that wants to have an illegitimate child can get on your tax rolls even to the point of pre-natal care. If you want to tell them that you're tired of appeasing the mob, that you're tired of letting every mob that wants to parade in Mississippi or Alabama or Arkansas or in Washington—opening the gates up there at the White House to that mess of trash . . .

> If you want to tell them you're tired of these things, then I say join hands with Jim Johnson, because a vote for Jim Johnson will be a repudiation of that kind of policy, and a vote for Jim Johnson will be a vote for a man that's got guts enough to stand and tell them that we don't like it . . .
>
> Don't make me beg you . . . You know I need your prayers. You know I need you standing beside me for freedom so that together we can tell the world that we shall not be overcome.

Arkansas Gazette, September 16, 1966.

8. For a description of the transitional 1965 campaign, see Wilkinson, *Harry Byrd,* pp. 267-276.

9. William C. Havard and Loren P. Beth, *The Politics of Mis-Representation: Rural-Urban Conflict in the Florida Legislature* (Baton Rouge: Louisiana State University Press, 1962), p. 28. On Florida politicians generally, see esp. pp. 25-29.

10. The graphs of campaign stances used in this book are based on six periods of four years, beginning in 1950 and ending in 1973. Because all the southern states except Arkansas and Texas (and Tennessee until 1954) elected governors to four-year terms during this time, each electoral wave includes data on two gubernatorial contests for those states with two-year terms and one gubernatorial contest for the remaining states.

7 The Democratic First Primary

1. V. O. Key, Jr., *Southern Politics in State and Nation* (New York: Knopf, 1949), p. 407.

2. On the dual primary system in the South, see *ibid.,* pp. 406-423; and V. O. Key, Jr., *Politics, Parties, and Pressure Groups,* 5th ed. (New York: Crowell, 1964), pp. 384-385.

3. Five Democratic first primaries in the period 1954-73 were uncontested and have been omitted from the following discussion: Virginia, 1965 and 1973; South Carolina, 1966 and 1970; and Texas, 1970.

4. Jackson *Clarion-Ledger,* June 7, 1959.

5. *Ibid.,* June 11, 18, 24, 28; July 5, 22; August 1, 1959.

6. *Ibid.,* June 9, 11, 14; July 2, 5, 16, 1959.

7. Barnett proposed a system of tax incentives to lure industry into the state, attacked COPE and national labor leaders like Walter Reuther while praising native Mississippi workers, and warned of the evils of strong drink. "I am not a moderate on prohibition just as I am not a moderate on segregation," he said. "I am opposed to any program which would put wide-open whisky stores in front of our school children." *Ibid.,* July 9-10, 12, 22, 1959.

8. *Ibid.,* June 14; July 2, 15-16, 29, 1959.

9. *Ibid.,* June 3; July 22, 29, 1959.

10. *Ibid.,* August 4, 1959.

11. In the second primary segregation was superseded by economics as the most discussed issue. Both Barnett and Gartin, it was clear, were strong segregationists, but Barnett put Gartin on the defensive by attacking his ties to organized labor. According to Barnett, his opponent wore the "scarlet robe of

the left-wing element of the CIO" and was manipulated by "labor bosses, political dictators and moderates." Gartin attempted, without much success, to convince the electorate that it would be folly to repudiate a candidate with a "perfect record" on segregation. "Do you want it to go out to the world," he asked, "that Mississippi was dissatisfied with successful segregation and defeated a man at the polls who had been a part of the successful program?" Barnett won with 54 percent of the vote. *Ibid.,* August 11, 18, 26, 1959.

12. Key, *Southern Politics,* p. 255.

13. Dallas *Morning News,* June 5, 22; July 10, 1954. For a critical analysis of Shivers' career, see D. B. Hardeman, "Shivers of Texas: A Tragedy in Three Acts," *Harper's Magazine,* November 1956, pp. 50-56. A more general study of the issue of corruption in Texas politics at this time is presented in Ronnie Dugger, "What Corrupted Texas?" *Harper's Magazine,* March 1957, pp. 68-74.

14. Dallas *Morning News,* July 14-17, 1954; Houston *Post,* July 16, 1954. Yarborough's deficiencies were not limited to the segregation issue. "While I know my opponent is not a Communist," Shivers remarked, "I feel he is the captive of certain people who do not approve of being tough on Communists." Dallas *Morning News,* July 14, 1954.

15. Dallas *Morning News,* July 14-18, 1954.

16. In the 1956 first primary, Yarborough again expressed opposition to school desegregation. "My position on the Texas situation," he said in his first speech, "is clear and unambiguous: I oppose the forced co-mingling of white and Negro children in the schools. I oppose the use of force in the integration of public schools." Local school districts, he said later, should be permitted to resolve their problems by themselves. Yet Yarborough by no means incited racial hatred, and he implicitly appealed for black support when he told a labor group in Houston that he would "continue to fight for the rights of all Texans—and I do mean all." Austin *American,* June 21, 1956; Dallas *Morning News,* July 14, 25, 1956. Yarborough's stand against "forced integration" drew the NAACP's anger. See the *Texas Observer,* June 6, 1956.

17. *Arkansas Gazette,* June 2, 11, 18, 27, 1958.

18. *Ibid.,* June 15, 17, 1958.

19. *Ibid.,* June 29; July 3, 1958.

20. *Ibid.,* July 4-6, 1958.

21. This argument is emphasized with different data in Thomas F. Pettigrew and Ernest Q. Campbell, "Faubus and Segregation: An Analysis of Arkansas Voting," *Public Opinion Quarterly,* 24 (Fall 1960), 436-447.

22. *Ibid.,* p. 445.

23. Atlanta *Constitution,* July 13, 1962. Pressed to explain his dubious grouping of the future Nobel Prize winner with Griffin, Sanders argued that they had "joined hands in creating confusion, stirring up trouble, agitating our people and inciting violence. To me, that puts them in the same category." *Ibid.,* July 19, 1962. Sanders' reasoning rested of course on a tacit assumption that the prevailing system of racial segregation was just.

24. *Ibid.,* July 18, 31; August 7-8, 1962.

25. *Ibid.,* August 9, 1962. "To hear Marvin Griffin telling the people of

Georgia that he's going to give them an honest administration is like hearing Benedict Arnold or Alger Hiss speak on patriotism,'' Sanders remarked. Griffin was defensive about his administration's record for financial rectitude. He offered to ''salivate'' those who, like the Atlanta newspapers, questioned his integrity, and he attacked Sanders in kind. According to Griffin, Sanders' list of accomplishments was ''about big enough for a tomtit to land on. But if you want to talk about his record in shell houses, he's got a pretty good one for bilking and swindling investors.'' *Ibid.,* July 21; August 9, 16, 1962.

26. *Ibid.,* August 11, 24, 1962.

27. *Ibid.,* July 17, 31; August 7, 1962.

28. *Ibid.,* August 15, 1962. Griffin then explained to the assembled Atlanta reporters that ''cutting a blackjack sapling and braining someone is a figure of speech.'' *Ibid.* Griffin later claimed that he had been misquoted. See Robert Sherrill, *Gothic Politics in the Deep South: Stars of the New Confederacy* (New York: Grossman, 1968), p. 93. At the time Griffin was not conspicuously anxious to clarify his terms.

29. Atlanta *Constitution,* August 22, 30, 1962.

30. *Ibid.,* September 5-8, 1962.

31. *Ibid.,* September 11, 1962. Check the insurance policies, Griffin advised. ''These are Hitler tactics. You remember they burned the Reichstag.'' *Ibid.*

32. *Ibid.*

33. *Ibid.*

34. *Ibid.,* August 16, 1962. On the Sanders-Griffin primary, see also Joseph L. Bernd, ''Georgia: Static and Dynamic,'' in William C. Havard, ed., *The Changing Politics of the South* (Baton Rouge: Louisiana State University Press, 1972), pp. 331-336.

35. For concise accounts of this election, see New York *Times,* May 8; July 9; and August 9, 1967.

36. Jackson *Clarion-Ledger,* June 26; July 9, 13, 26, 31; August 9, 1967.

37. *Ibid.,* July 6, 30, 1967.

38. *Ibid.,* July 6, 22; August 6, 1967. Newspaper advertisements claimed that Williams' service in Washington gave him ''an unequalled insight into the minds and methods of the nameless and faceless Washington Bureaucracy.'' To be specific:

JOHN BELL WILLIAMS KNOWS THE TRAPS AND PITFALLS WHICH LYNDON B. JOHNSON SETS FOR THE WEAK-KNEED AND UNWARY. HE WILL NEVER AGREE TO THE SURRENDER OF ANY PORTION OF OUR CONSTITUTIONAL RIGHTS.

THE CHOICE IS CLEAR AND SOLID: THE LIBERAL PHILOSOPHY OF SURRENDER VS. THE SOUND CONSERVATIVE PHILOSOPHY OF JOHN BELL WILLIAMS.

School desegregation guildelines were ''a trap which must be utterly and completely destroyed.'' *Ibid.,* July 26, 1967.

39. *Ibid.,* June 26, 29; July 5, 10-12; August 9, 1967.

40. In the second primary Williams reemphasized his conservative ap-

proach, drew widespread support from Swan and Barnett backers, and defeated Winter by more than 60,000 votes. Describing himself as a veteran fighter for Mississippi traditions, Williams suggested that first primary returns—Williams, Swan, and Barnett together received nearly three fifths of the state vote—had led Winter to praise George Wallace and to talk like a "lifetime member of the John Birch Society." Mississippi conservatives would not of course be fooled by such a candidate. Winter assailed Williams as a politician with "nothing to offer the people of Mississippi but his own reckless and irresponsible actions," actions which had cost the state his congressional seniority. Although he continued to advocate a "constructive, forward looking program," Winter also attacked a "moral decline which began in Washington and is now spreading like a cancerous growth through the fiber of this country." Winter made no open appeal for black votes, but he was nonetheless considered and denounced as the favorite of the "minority bloc vote." Williams won with approximately 55 percent of the vote. *Ibid.*, August 11, 16; September 6, 1967; New Orleans *Times-Picayune*, August 21, 27; September 10, 1967.

41. Birmingham *News*, March 22, 30; April 8, 12, 27, 30; May 4, 1966; and New York *Times*, April 14, 1966.

42. Birmingham *News*, March 5, 1966.

43. Ray Jenkins, "Mr. and Mrs. Wallace Run for Governor of Alabama," *New York Times Magazine*, April 24, 1966, p. 84.

44. Birmingham *News*, March 9, 19; April 5, 22-23, 1966.

45. For a discussion of the significance of "friends and neighbors" voting in Alabama, see Key, *Southern Politics*, pp. 37-41. A more detailed account of the Wallace vote is contained in Earl Black and Merle Black, "The Demographic Basis of Wallace Support in Alabama," *American Politics Quarterly*, 1 (July 1973), 279-304. For a briefer but more technical discussion, see Earl Black and Merle Black, "The Wallace Vote in Alabama: A Multiple Regression Analysis," *Journal of Politics*, 35 (August 1973), 730-736.

46. Wallace's career is elaborated along these lines in Tom Wicker, "George Wallace: A Gross and Simple Heart," *Harper's Magazine*, April 1967, pp. 47-48; and Robert G. Sherrill, "Wallace and the Future of Dixie," *Nation*, 199 (1964), 266-272.

47. For a comprehensive analysis, see William C. Havard, Rudolf Heberle, and Perry H. Howard, *The Louisiana Elections of 1960* (Baton Rouge: Louisiana State University Press, 1963), pp. 3-54.

48. Dodd, running without Earl Long's support, was the least visible of the major candidates. He pictured himself as a more committed segregationist than Morrison or Davis, yet not a "misguided fanatic" like Rainach. Although Dodd was confident that he could maintain segregated schools, he would not imitate Rainach's efforts to "change segregation from a Southern custom into a national religion." Rainach did not deserve to be governor because he was "preaching hate and intolerance and is setting one race against another." New Orleans *Times-Picayune*, October 18; November 26, 1959.

Retired from active politics for two decades, Noe agreed to run for governor (with Earl Long on his ticket as lieutenant governor) to make certain that the achievements of the Longs did not "fall into the hands of a small group of money grabbers and the big city papers." In reality, Long assumed command of the campaign, defending his record as governor and assailing the opposition, especially "Singin', Flingin' " Jimmie Davis, the candidate with the "sweetness and sunshine" platform. "His pockets are lined with oil money, gambling money and 'Bed Bug Blues' [a song Davis had composed in his younger days] record money," Long charged. "He doesn't get excited over anything unless it's got to do with making money or filthy records or going out to Hollywood and appearing in those cheap, grade B moving pictures." Long and Noe opposed desegregation but generally avoided the civil rights issue. Although he would not "try to be elected by hurting anyone," Noe thought no one in the state could be "more solid for segregation" than he was. On election eve, a Noe-Long advertisement announced that they stood "100% for segregation and the continuance of every southern principle and custom. But [they] will not foster or incite racial or religious unrest." These remarks aside, Long was at a disadvantage in demonstrating his support for segregation because of his efforts in the late 1950s to prevent a wholesale purging of blacks from the voting rolls; and his proxy, Noe, received only 12 percent of the vote. *Ibid.,* October 4, 17, 26; November 25; December 4, 1959. For a fascinating account of Long's career at this time, see A. J. Liebling, *The Earl of Louisiana* (New York: Simon and Schuster, 1961).

49. New Orleans *Times-Picayune,* October 4, 1959. Rainach was persuaded that a group of southern governors united on segregation could "trade the socks off of those radical Yankee politicians." *Ibid.,* October 15, 1959.

50. *Ibid.,* October 16-17; November 25; December 3, 7, 1959.

51. For a brief account of Davis' first term as governor, see Allan P. Sindler, *Huey Long's Louisiana* (Baltimore: Johns Hopkins Press, 1956), pp. 181-183. At this stage of his career Davis was more likely to sing "You Are My Sunshine" and "I'd Rather Have Jesus" than his youthful composition, "Organ Grinder Blues."

52. New Orleans *Times-Picayune,* October 8, 10, 12, 18, 25, 27, 29; November 19; December 7, 1959.

53. *Ibid.,* October 2, 5, 7, 9, 26; November 11; December 4, 1959.

54. Raleigh *News and Observer,* April 6, 8; May 22, 27, 1964.

55. *Ibid.,* April 6, 8, 13, 26; May 9, 1964.

56. *Ibid.,* April 6, 9-11, 30; May 16, 29, 1964.

57. Once the first primary votes were tabulated, Moore became more militant on segregation. "My opponent . . . owes a major part of his entire vote to the bloc Negro vote in North Carolina," he asserted. "That is his 'Go Forward' vote; that is his 'mainstream' vote, and it hangs like a millstone around his neck today." Moore believed he would win because he represented Democrats who favored "free elections as opposed to controlled elections; elections controlled by pressure groups, including the NAACP, CORE and others who attempt to lead voters to the polls like sheep to the shambles." Conservative backers of Lake were assured that Moore also was sympathetic to "the conservative element." Preyer denounced Moore's remarks on the black vote as "shameful" and not in "the North Carolina way." "There is no

difference between Dan Moore and me on civil rights," Preyer said. "But I'm not going to inflame the race issue just to get the nomination." Throughout the second primary Moore emphasized the bloc vote question and Preyer's close ties to Governor Sanford, and Preyer was continually forced to defend his independence. Moore was elected in a landslide (62 percent). *Ibid.,* June 2, 5-6, 22, 27, 1964.

58. Nashville *Banner,* June 18, 1966.

59. *Ibid.,* June 24, 1966.

60. *Ibid.,* July 3-4, 26, 1958; *Southern School News,* July 1958, p. 6.

61. Nashville *Banner,* June 24, 1966. At one point in the campaign Ellington told a Negro rally in Memphis that blacks would benefit from his efforts to "upgrade education for all our people, and through equal opportunities for all." His message had been the same across the state, he said. "I would not seek your support and your help and your influence, and then insult you by trying to be one thing to some of the people and another thing to other people." *Ibid.,* July 27, 1966.

62. *Ibid.,* June 21; July 2, 6, 14, 21, 26, 30, 1966.

8 The Democratic Second Primary

1. V. O. Key, Jr., *Southern Politics in State and Nation* (New York: Knopf, 1949), p. 417.

2. Cortez A. M. Ewing, *Primary Elections in the South* (Norman: University of Oklahoma Press, 1953), p. 6.

3. C. Vann Woodward, *Origins of the New South, 1877-1913* (Baton Rouge: Louisiana State University Press, 1951), p. 373. It is not implied by any means that Key ignored the disfranchisement of blacks.

4. Key, *Southern Politics,* p. 422.

5. McCleskey has suggested that "it is likely that racial considerations were . . . involved [in the adoption of the second primary], for the requirement of an absolute majority made it almost impossible for a black candidate to win in the Democratic party primaries." See Clifton McCleskey, *The Government and Politics of Texas,* 4th ed. (Boston: Little, Brown, 1972), p. 49. Without disagreeing with this conclusion, the use of the runoff to eliminate black office seekers is probably best understood as a special case of the broader proposition that the dual primary made it difficult for any candidate, black or white, to win the Democratic nomination who was considered an unreliable defender of the racial status quo.

6. Jackson *Clarion-Ledger,* July 23, 1963.

7. Sullivan, a Clarksdale lawyer and the presidential nominee of Texas' far-right Constitutional Party in 1960, ran as an outspoken opponent of welfare programs. "I have no moral responsibility to support the subsidy of illegitimacy," he said. He showed film clips of Coleman expressing "abiding confidence" in John F. Kennedy in 1960 and accused Johnson as well of having ties to national Democrats. A militant segregationist who nonetheless believed that centralized government posed an even greater threat to freedom

than "race mixing," he promised to do his best to oppose Kennedy's reelection. *Ibid.,* June 23; July 7, 11-12, 24, 1963.

8. *Ibid.,* June 16, 27, 29; July 9, 14, 17, 25, 1963. Johnson encouraged indigent blacks to leave the state. Mississippi needed "an education program to teach some of our Negroes that they are wasting their time staying in Mississippi. Why should a Negro woman with five illegitimate children stay here and draw $90 a month when she can move to California and get $280 or go to Michigan and get $261?" *Ibid.,* July 27, 1963.

9. *Ibid.,* June 18, 27, 30; July 13, 18, 27, 1963.

10. *Ibid.,* July 17, 21; August 4, 1963.

11. *Ibid.,* August 9, 13, 15, 17, 1963. Johnson accused Coleman of trying to "belittle the stand I made for Mississippi at Oxford." As for shaking hands with a federal marshal, "Doesn't he know," Johnson asked, "that you always shake hands with a man before you knock him down?" *Ibid.,* August 22, 1963.

12. *Ibid.,* August 15, 18, 24-25, 29, 1963.

13. Thomas C. Schelling, *The Strategy of Conflict* (New York: Oxford University Press, 1963), p. 5.

14. Stuart Long, " 'Scared Money' Wins an Election in Texas," *Reporter,* October 21, 1954, pp. 23, 26. Radio and television, billboards, and direct mailings were utilized to tell "The Port Arthur Story," and the impact of this "multimillion-dollar blitz technique was obvious and impressive." *Ibid.,* p. 26. Another journalist has argued that Shivers' "ultimate [runoff] strategy was to link Communism to both the Negro issue and organized labor." See D. B. Hardeman, "Shivers of Texas: A Tragedy in Three Acts," *Harper's Magazine,* November 1956, p. 54. These two sources have heavily influenced the following account of the 1954 second primary.

15. Dallas *Morning News,* August 12, 18, 25, 1954.

16. *Ibid.,* August 24, 27, 1954.

17. Austin *American,* July 30, 1954; Dallas *Morning News,* August 7, 24, 27, 1954.

18. Austin *American,* July 31, 1954; Dallas *Morning News,* August 27, 1954; and Long, " 'Scared Money,' " p. 26. Candidates like Yarborough could expect to be attacked as weak on segregation. In the 1956 runoff, for example, Yarborough again had to contend with charges, this time from Price Daniel, that he was the controlled candidate of the NAACP, the CIO, and the ADA. Yarborough denied these accusations and argued that Daniel had "just copied Allan Shivers' speech of 1954 in saying that I was the tool of radical outside forces and of Walter Reuther and the CIO and the NAACP." Dallas *Morning News,* August 8, 1956. See also *ibid.,* August 9, 23, 1956. An excerpt from one of his newspaper advertisements illustrates Yarborough's defensiveness on the question of NAACP support (Dallas *Morning News,* August 24, 1956):

Despite Price Daniel's claim to the contrary, the NAACP opposes Ralph Yarborough. Their newspaper spokesmen in Texas, the Houston *Informer* and the Dallas *Express,* are busy denouncing Ralph Yarborough for his stand on segregation in every issue of these papers.

Price Daniel knows this, yet he continues to try to mislead the people by falsely telling them over television, over the radio, in the newspapers and in letters that the NAACP is supporting Ralph Yarborough. Price, didn't they teach you in Sunday School that 'Thou shalt not bear false witness?' ''

19. William C. Havard, Rudolf Heberle, and Perry H. Howard, *The Louisiana Elections of 1960* (Baton Rouge: Louisiana State University Press, 1963), p. 46. On the runoff campaign generally, see pp. 45-54.

20. New Orleans *Times-Picayune,* December 8, 1959.

21. *Ibid.*

22. *Ibid.,* December 8-9, 13, 18, 22-24, 28, 1959.

23. *Ibid.,* December 24, 1959; January 3-4, 6-7, 10-11, 1960.

24. Gordon B. Cleveland and Donald R. Matthews, "Politics," in Richard E. Lonsdale, dir., *Atlas of North Carolina* (Chapel Hill: University of North Carolina Press, 1967), pp. 72-73.

25. Raleigh *News and Observer,* May 31, 1960.

26. *Ibid.*

27. *Ibid.,* May 31; June 1, 1960.

28. *Ibid.,* June 3, 1960.

29. *Ibid.,* June 14-17, 19, 21, 1960.

30. On these campaigns see Robert Sherrill, *Gothic Politics in the Deep South: Stars of the New Confederacy* (New York: Grossman, 1968), pp. 272-281; and Marshall Frady, *Wallace* (New York: World, 1968), pp. 131-135.

31. *Southern School News,* February 1962, p. 13; and March 1962, p. 2. Folsom's defensiveness on segregation was grounded on such acts as entertaining Harlem Congressman Adam Clayton Powell in the governor's mansion and dismissing a nullification resolution passed by the Alabama Legislature as functionally equivalent to a "hound dog baying at the moon." *Ibid.,* February 1962, p. 13. Later in the campaign Folsom asserted that the leading issue was "whether you're going to have mob rule, castrating, mutilating, flogging, or law and order. When I'm elected, there will be no Klucking here nor Klucking there." Birmingham *News,* April 25, 1962.

32. Montgomery *Advertiser,* April 24, 1962.

33. Birmingham *News,* April 3, 6, 10, 17, 20, 22, 1962.

34. *Ibid.,* April 10, 15, 1962.

35. *Ibid.,* April 22, 1962.

36. *Ibid.,* April 26-27; May 2, 1962.

37. *Ibid.,* April 20, 25-26; May 3, 1962; Montgomery *Advertiser,* May 5, 1962; and Sherrill, *Gothic Politics,* pp. 272-273.

38. Birmingham *News,* May 9-10, 15, 22, 1962. The Birmingham *News* questioned Wallace's ability to attract industry. "If *you* had money to put in a Southern plant," it asked, "would *you* have doubts about a state where a governor spent most of his time inviting judges to jail him?" *Ibid.,* May 13, 1962.

39. *Ibid.,* May 16, 18, 23-24, 27, 1962.

40. Miami *Herald,* April 3, 21, 27; May 1, 6, 1964.

41. *Ibid.,* April 2, 23, 29; May 6, 1964.

42. *Ibid.,* May 7, 10, 12-14, 1964. The St. Petersburg *Times* concluded that "Burns is basing his campaign almost solely on racial issues, speaking only vaguely about other subjects. He has said over and over again that he is not a racist or a bigot, but he obviously won the support of many people who are." St. Petersburg *Times,* May 18, 1964.

43. Miami *Herald,* May 15-17, 19, 21-23, 26, 1964.

44. Kelly had been the most adamant opponent of desegregation among major candidates in the 1964 first primary. The self-designated "symbol of opposition to civil rights in Florida" promised to test the constitutionality of the Civil Rights Bill should it be enacted. If the Supreme Court upheld the law, he would "let [the Johnson administration] enforce it themselves." Two years later, following passage of the Civil Rights Act, Kelly no longer ran as a militant segregationist. "I believe in equal rights for every man, woman and child in the state of Florida regardless of race, color, religion or national origin," he announced to a meeting of black teachers. "Civil rights is a matter of law, but equal rights comes out of your heart." See Miami *Herald,* April 26, 28, 1964; St. Petersburg *Times,* April 8, 1964; April 24, 1966.

45. Miami *Herald,* April 13, 22-23, 27, 30; May 1, 1966.

46. *Ibid.,* April 14, 22-24; May 1, 4, 1966.

47. *Ibid.,* May 5, 9-10, 1966. Despite his attack on bloc voting, Burns believed his candidacy would be attractive to thinking blacks. "The intelligent Negro knows I'm on his side," he explained. *Ibid.,* May 11, 1966.

48. *Ibid.,* May 11, 15-16, 23, 25, 1966.

49. Manning J. Dauer, "Florida: The Different State," in William C. Havard, ed., *The Changing Politics of the South* (Baton Rouge: Louisiana State University Press, 1972), p. 136.

50. For additional discussions of the 1966 Georgia primaries, see Numan V. Bartley, *From Thurmond to Wallace: Political Tendencies in Georgia, 1948-1968* (Baltimore: Johns Hopkins Press, 1970), pp. 67-75; and Joseph L. Bernd, "Georgia: Static and Dynamic," in Havard, ed., *Changing Politics of the South,* pp. 340-345.

51. Atlanta *Constitution,* July 7, 14, 18; September 1, 9-10, 1966.

52. Bernd, "Georgia: Static and Dynamic," p. 343.

53. Atlanta *Constitution,* July 6, 15; August 13; September 6, 18, 1966.

54. *Ibid.,* September 18, 21-23, 1966.

55. *Ibid.,* September 18, 21, 23-29, 1966.

56. Bartley, *From Thurmond to Wallace,* pp. 74-75.

57. See Earl Black and Merle Black, "The Wallace Vote in Alabama: A Multiple Regression Analysis," *Journal of Politics,* 35 (August 1973), 734-736.

58. Two of the six possible combinations of racial stances—moderate segregationist versus moderate segregationist and moderate segregationist versus nonsegregationist—were highly atypical and do not warrant more than passing notice. Second primaries in which the two candidates were both mod-

erate segregationists were limited to the Arkansas and Florida campaigns of 1954. In these runoffs segregation was essentially a latent issue, much as it had been during the early 1950s. As one or both of the runoff participants began to perceive the advantage of adopting a strong stand against racial change, the moderate segregationist against moderate segregationist campaign disappeared.

Second primaries in which moderate segregationists faced nonsegregationists have been equally rare. The only campaigns fitting this description were the 1968 and 1970 Arkansas runoffs, and in both cases the moderate segregationist was defeated. Both Virginia Johnson in 1968 and Orval Faubus in 1970 represented a generation of Arkansas politicians long identified with hostility to racial desegregation. Johnson faced an electorate less than anxious to have a female governor and was soundly defeated (63 to 37 percent). More significant was the defeat in 1970 (the same year George Wallace recaptured the governorship in Alabama) of Faubus, the nation's leading symbol of opposition to school desegregation in the late 1950s. Faubus had been in political retirement since 1966 and his organization had deteriorated. He was beaten decisively (59 to 41 percent) by Dale Bumpers, an unknown politician who promised fresh leadership.

59. The 1962 Texas primaries are considered in greater depth in James R. Soukup, Clifton McCleskey, and Harry Holloway, *Party and Factional Division in Texas* (Austin: University of Texas Press, 1964), pp. 140-149. See also Willie Morris, "Texas Politics in Turmoil," *Harper's Magazine,* September 1962, pp. 76-87.

60. *Texas Observer,* May 2, 1962; Morris, "Texas Politics," p. 86.

61. Dallas *Morning News,* March 16-17; April 10, 1962.

62. *Ibid.,* March 27; April 18-19, 21, 1962.

63. Morris, "Texas Politics," p. 86.

64. Connally's association with the Kennedy administration, however qualified in terms of his support of particular Kennedy programs, probably increased his appeal among minority voters. For an account of the campaign tactics used by Connally forces to carry Mexican-American precincts in San Antonio, see the *Texas Observer,* May 19, 1962.

65. Dallas *Morning News,* May 18-20, 24, 1962.

66. *Ibid.,* May 25-26, 30-31; June 1, 1962.

67. *Texas Observer,* June 8, 1962.

9   The General Election

1. The most comprehensive description and analysis of one-party politics in the South is, of course, V. O. Key, Jr., *Southern Politics in State and Nation* (New York: Knopf, 1949). Subsequent classifications of the 50 states with regard to interparty competition differ in method and span of time covered but repeatedly identify the southern states among the least competitive states. See, for example, Austin Ranney and Willmoore Kendall, "The American Party Systems," *American Political Science Review,* 48 (June 1954), 477-485; Joseph A. Schlesinger, "A Two-Dimensional Scheme for

Classifying the States According to Degree of Inter-Party Competition,"
American Political Science Review, 49 (December 1955), 1120-1128; Coleman
B. Ransone, Jr., *The Office of Governor in the United States* (University,
Ala.: University of Alabama Press, 1956), pp. 12-37; Robert T. Golembiew-
ski, "A Taxonomic Approach to State Political Party Strength," *Western
Political Quarterly,* 11 (September 1958), 494-513; Richard E. Dawson and
James A. Robinson, "Inter-Party Competition, Economic Variables, and
Welfare Policies in the American States," *Journal of Politics,* 25 (May 1963),
265-289; Richard I. Hofferbert, "Classification of American State Party
Systems," *Journal of Politics,* 26 (August 1964), 550-567; Thomas R. Dye,
Politics, Economics, and the Public (Chicago: Rand McNally, 1966), pp.
54-57; David G. Pfeiffer, "The Measurement of Inter-Party Competition and
Systemic Stability," *American Political Science Review,* 61 (June 1967),
457-467; Austin Ranney, "Parties in State Politics," in Herbert Jacob and
Kenneth N. Vines, eds., *Politics in the American States,* 2nd ed. (Boston:
Little, Brown, 1971), pp. 82-121; and Paul T. David, *Party Strength in the
United States, 1872-1970* (Charlottesville: University Press of Virginia, 1972),
pp. 44-48.

2. Ranney, "Parties in State Politics," pp. 84-89.

3. Specific results of the gubernatorial interparty competition index,
carried to two decimal places and using Ranney's cutting points to define categories, are as follows:

One-Party Democratic (.85 or higher)		Modified One-Party Democratic (.70 to .84)		Two-Party (.35 to .69)	
South Carolina	.93	South	.82	Virginia	.60
Mississippi	.92	Tennessee	.77		
Georgia	.92	Arkansas	.76		
Deep South	.92	Florida	.75		
Louisiana	.91	Peripheral South	.74		
Alabama	.91	North Carolina	.71		
Texas	.86				

Figures for the Deep South, Peripheral South, and South are means of the
state scores included within each classification. The Virginia index number
counts Henry Howell, who was listed on the ballot as an Independent, as a
Democrat. If Howell's vote is excluded, Virginia's party competition score
declines further to .56.

4. Ransone, *Office of Governor,* p. 13. See also Key, *Southern Politics,*
pp. 407-408; and Coleman B. Ransone, Jr., *The Office of Governor in the
South* (University, Ala.: Bureau of Public Administration, University of
Alabama, 1951), pp. 37-38.

5. Key, *Southern Politics,* p. 407.

6. *Ibid.,* p. 409.

7. Although some of the disparity in general election interest between the Deep South and Peripheral South is due to the fact that numerous gubernatorial elections in the Peripheral South (but none in the Deep South) coincided with presidential campaigns, subregional differences do not vanish when nonpresidential year campaigns within each subregion are compared. The mean for the Peripheral South (124) is still more than double the Deep South mean (55), and, once again, the Peripheral South state with the lowest degree of general election interest (Texas, 73) exceeds the highest Deep South state (Georgia, 68). For discussions of the relationship between presidential elections and turnout in state contests, see *ibid.,* p. 409; and Ransone, *Office of Governor,* pp. 20-21.

8. The South Carolina figure actually underestimates general election interest in that state. Data for 1962 were used, since there were no contested Democratic primaries in 1966 or 1970.

9. For additional summaries of the Republican vote in southern elections for governor, see Alexander Heard, *A Two-Party South?* (Chapel Hill: University of North Carolina Press, 1952), pp. 66-69; Coleman B. Ransone, Jr., "Political Leadership in the Governor's Office," *Journal of Politics,* 26 (February 1964), 205-213; and Louis M. Seagull, *Southern Republicanism* (Cambridge: Schenkman, 1975).

10. These results confirmed Walter Dean Burnham's 1964 prediction of a "selective expansion of Presidential Republicanism." See Burnham's article, "The Alabama Senatorial Election of 1962: Return of Inter-Party Competition," *Journal of Politics,* 26 (November 1964), 829.

11. The omitted general elections were: Arkansas, 1954; Virginia, 1961; and Florida, 1960 and 1964. In Arkansas the unusually high Republican vote was less the expression of growing Republicanism than a reflection of disappointment by Democratic followers of an incumbent governor who had been defeated in the Democratic primary. See Richard E. Yates, "Arkansas: Independent and Unpredictable," in William C. Havard, ed., *The Changing Politics of the South* (Baton Rouge: Louisiana State University Press, 1972), pp. 259-260. Virginia Republicans, compared to their previous and subsequent efforts, were still recovering in 1961 from the impact of Little Rock; they mounted their least intensive campaign of the post-*Brown* era. In Florida the votes for little known Republican candidates were inflated by simultaneous presidential elections.

12. This interpretation of the index of dissimilarity is adapted from John C. McKinney and Linda Brookover Bourque, "The Changing South: National Incorporation of a Region," *American Sociological Review,* 36 (June 1971), 401. The index is computed "by taking the absolute differences between the percentages in each category for the two distributions to be compared, summing them, and taking half the difference." *Ibid.*

13. Jackson *Clarion-Ledger,* October 15, 17, 22, 1963.

14. *Ibid.,* October 22, 1963.

15. *Ibid.,* October 22-24, 30, 1963; November 2, 1963. Shortly after the *Brown* decision was announced, Johnson told a service club that the South's

refusal to educate blacks properly had led to the ruling. For a summary of the secret conversations involving Attorney General Kennedy, Governor Barnett, and Lieutenant Governor Johnson, see George B. Leonard, T. George Harris, and Christopher S. Wren, "How a Secret Deal Prevented a Massacre at Ole Miss," *Look,* December 31, 1962, pp. 18-36.

16. Jackson *Clarion-Ledger,* October 18, 26, 29-30, 1963.

17. *Ibid.,* October 20, 1963.

18. *Ibid.,* October 23, 1963.

19. *Ibid.,* October 31, 1963.

20. *Ibid.,* November 3, 1963.

21. *Ibid.,* November 7, 1963. Although Phillips obtained nearly two fifths of the state vote, an impressive achievement for a Republican in Mississippi, analysis of county level voting patterns indicates that "at least some" of the Republican votes were probably cast not by Republicans but by supporters of Democratic candidates who were eliminated in the primaries. See Charles N. Fortenberry and F. Glenn Abney, "Mississippi: Unreconstructed and Unredeemed," in Havard, ed., *Changing Politics of the South,* p. 497.

22. In the 1967 general election, with black voter registration having increased from less than 30,000 in 1963 to some 200,000, Phillips dropped his strong segregationist posture and told a statewide television audience that preoccupation with segregation hindered the state's economy. "The white cannot keep the Negro down without paying the awesome penalty of restricting his own advancement," he said. The Republican advocated a "two-way street in human relations" and argued that the Negro "cannot be expected to become a producer, and to make a significant contribution to Mississippi's progress, until he gets—at our hands—this chance to improve himself." Phillips still considered himself a segregationist, but his message that the state must cease to fight old battles was a step toward moderation by the Mississippi Republican party. Phillips' revised racial stance, which still contained a patronizing strain, did not improve his electoral performance. He won only 30 percent of the vote, a decline of eight points from his original showing. New York *Times,* October 4, 8, 1967. See also New Orleans *Times-Picayune,* October 8, 1967; Washington *Post,* November 5, 1967; and New York *Times,* November 5, 1967.

23. Charleston *News and Courier,* October 11, 19, 1966; Columbia *Record,* October 11, 1966. Estimates of black voting patterns are found in "State of the Southern States," *New South,* 22 (Winter 1967), 79.

24. Atlanta *Constitution,* October 7-8, 12-15, 1966. As an example of his "responsible approach" Callaway argued that school desegregation guidelines had to be fought at their source, in Congress. He denounced Maddox for having passed out ax handles at a Klan rally in 1964. Maddox insisted that blacks would support him if they were familiar with his program and "not just one incident in my life." *Ibid.,* October 12-15, 1966.

25. *Ibid.,* October 26, 28, 1966; November 4, 1966.

26. *Ibid.,* October 15, 26-27, 1966; November 1, 3, 1966.

27. *Ibid.,* November 5, 12, 18, 1966; January 11-12, 1967; New York *Times,* January 4, 7, 11-12, 1967. Shortly before the election a group of black

leaders, including State Senator Leroy Johnson, urged blacks to vote for Arnall. "Georgia's Negroes," they argued, "know that Lester Maddox offers them blood in the streets, indignity, violence . . . Georgia's Negroes also know that Rep. Howard (Bo) Callaway is a silk-stockinged segregationist who is no better than Maddox. Callaway's congressional record, and his acts as a businessman and a politician make it crystal clear that he is a racist who will destroy the working man, undermine his security, and wreck his children's education, all in the name of being a conservative and a state's righter." Atlanta *Constitution,* November 5, 1966. Other Atlanta blacks and the Atlanta *Daily World,* however, were pro-Callaway. See, for example, Atlanta *Daily World,* October 12, 15, 1966; November 8, 1966. For additional discussion of the 1966 general election, see Numan V. Bartley, *From Thurmond to Wallace: Political Tendencies in Georgia, 1948-1968* (Baltimore: Johns Hopkins Press, 1970), pp. 75-81; and Joseph L. Bernd, "Georgia: Static and Dynamic," in Havard, ed., *Changing Politics of the South,* pp. 345-351.

28. See, for example, Raleigh *News and Observer,* October 16, 30, 1968; Washington *Post,* October 18, 1970; and Columbia *State,* October 31, 1970.

29. The structure and the emotional tone of Johnson's campaign speeches were rooted in southern revivalism, with Johnson performing the role of fundamentalist preacher. At the conclusion of Johnson's address the audience was given an opportunity to win its political salvation, to "stand up," not for Jesus, but for "Justice Jim's" concept of freedom. "It'll literally tingle your spine," Johnson predicted, "to be able to stand with people who want to tell the world that they want to stand up for Arkansas, that they want to stand up for freedom, yes, friends, that they want to stand up for America." *Arkansas Gazette,* October 28, 1966. Johnson was addicted to the flamboyant exaggeration, typically expressed in rural idioms. During the Democratic primaries, for example, he solicited the support of organized labor by boasting that he had invariably favored labor's interest during his tenure as a state judge, even when his interpretation of the law "took the hide off, when it dang near meant raping the law in your behalf." *Ibid.,* May 22, 1966.

30. *Ibid.,* October 28, 1966; November 5, 1966; New York *Times,* October 26, 1966.

31. *Arkansas Gazette,* October 20, 1966; November 6, 8, 1966; *Arkansas Democrat,* October 13, 1966.

32. Early in October a Little Rock Negro leader complained that he was unable to confer with either candidate. *Arkansas Democrat,* October 9, 1966.

33. *Arkansas Gazette,* October 16, 18, 25-26, 28, 1966; November 5-6, 8, 1966.

34. *Ibid.,* October 16, 18, 1966. In general, the less said about civil rights, the better Rockefeller liked it. "Rockefeller has opposed Federal civil rights legislation and avoids the issue as much as he can. He speaks of his 'human relations' work as an Urban League member in the same breath as he objects to Federal 'bureaucrats' imposing unrealistic rules on a sovereign state." Washington *Post,* November 4, 1966.

35. If Johnson "had been a calm, responsible segregationist," one

unidentified Democratic politician commented, he would have been elected. Most Arkansas whites still preferred segregation, he continued, but they refused to "tear up their school system over segregation again." New York *Times,* November 10, 1966.

36. One student of Arkansas politics estimates that Rockefeller received 71 percent of the estimated 85,000 black votes cast in 1966. See Jim Ranchino, *Faubus to Bumpers: Arkansas Votes, 1960-1970* (Arkadelphia, Ark.: Action Research, Inc., 1972), p. 74. Blacks thus gave Rockefeller approximately 60,000 votes, a total well in excess of Rockefeller's 49,000 vote majority.

37. Miami *Herald,* October 1, 1966; Richmond *Times-Dispatch,* October 20, 1973; and Washington *Post,* September 21, 1973.

38. Washington *Post,* July 28, 1973; October 14, 20, 26, 1973; Richmond *Times-Dispatch,* September 23, 1973; and New York *Times,* September 27, 1973. For a transcript of Howell's 1972 interview, see the Washington *Post,* October 20, 1973. Howell's statement both recognized the difficulty of persuading white Americans to accept desegregation proposals that entailed significant costs of time and money and argued that "if it's going to be some distribution of the young people of the District of Columbia into Maryland and into Virginia, to save our nation from being a divided black-white nation, then we've got to try this." Godwin forces gave the latter half of Howell's remarks wide distribution.

39. Washington *Post,* May 27, 1973; September 13, 1973; October 14, 20, 30, 1973; Richmond *Times-Dispatch,* October 10, 21, 1973; and New York *Times,* September 27, 1973; October 29, 1973.

40. Inspection of a scatter plot (not shown) relating the percentaged Howell vote by county or independent city to percent nonwhite (as of 1970) of county/city population suggests that the Howell versus Godwin contest did not sharply polarize the state as a whole along racial lines. In all but a handful of counties the Howell vote exceeded the nonwhite proportion of the population, and support for Howell ranged widely among counties and cities with nonwhite populations of less than 30 percent. There was, however, a modest positive association between percent nonwhite and the Howell vote once the size of the nonwhite population exceeded 30 percent. For a concise analysis which argues that factors other than race contributed importantly to Howell's defeat, see Washington *Post,* December 17, 1973.

41. *Ibid.,* November 9, 1973.

42. Andrew Buni, *The Negro in Virginia Politics, 1902-1965* (Charlottesville: University Press of Virginia, 1967), p. 259. For more comprehensive accounts of this election, see *ibid.,* pp. 228-246; and J. Harvie Wilkinson, III, *Harry Byrd and the Changing Face of Virginia Politics, 1945-1966* (Charlottesville: University Press of Virginia, 1968), pp. 263-284.

43. In 1956 Godwin had expressed his opposition to desegregation in unqualified language: "Integration, however slight, anywhere in Virginia would be a cancer eating at the very life blood of our public school system . . . [The *Brown* decision] is either right or wrong. If we think it is right, we should accept it without circumvention or evasion. If it is wrong, we should never accept it at all. Men of conscience and principle do not compromise with

either right or wrong." Richmond *Times-Dispatch,* September 5, 1956, quoted in Robbins L. Gates, *The Making of Massive Resistance: Virginia's Politics of Public School Desegregation, 1954-1956* (Chapel Hill: University of North Carolina Press, 1964), p. 174.

44. Richmond *Times-Dispatch,* July 2, 1961; October 9, 13, 23, 25, 31, 1965; Washington *Post,* October 29, 1965; and Buni, *Negro in Virginia Politics,* pp. 234-235.

45. Richmond *Times-Dispatch,* October 13, 15, 27-28, 30, 1965; Washington *Post,* October 11, 1965; and Buni, *Negro in Virginia Politics,* pp. 233-234.

46. Estimates of the size and distribution of the black vote vary widely, but there is general agreement that Godwin received considerably more black support than Holton. See Buni, *Negro in Virginia Politics,* pp. 243-245; and Wilkinson, *Harry Byrd,* pp. 282-283. If Godwin needed to overcome his advocacy of massive resistance to attract black voters, Holton had the misfortune to campaign one year after Barry Goldwater had been the Republican presidential nominee.

47. The concept of party identification is developed at length in Angus Campbell et al., *The American Voter* (New York: Wiley, 1960), throughout. An obvious qualification to the hypothesized significance of party identification for the success of Democratic nominees should be made explicit. Data collected by the Survey Research Center show that, among white southerners, identification with the (national) Democratic party has diminished considerably since the early 1950s. The percentage of whites in the region classifying themselves as Democrats declined from 75 in 1952 to 46 in 1972. But because the white southerners' sense of identification with the Republican party remained quite low (18 percent in 1972), Democratic candidates still enjoyed in 1972 a large net advantage (28 points) among whites. See Paul Allen Beck, "A Socialization Theory of Partisan Realignment: The South" (paper presented at the annual meeting of the Southwestern Political Science Association, Dallas, March, 1974), Table 5. For additional data and analysis, see E. M. Schreiber, " 'Where the Ducks Are': Southern Strategy versus Fourth Party," *Public Opinion Quarterly,* 35 (Summer 1971), 157-167; and Douglas S. Gatlin, "Party Identification, Status, and Race in the South: 1952-1972," *Public Opinion Quarterly,* 39 (Spring 1975), 39-51.

48. Party images of white and black southerners in the early 1960s have been examined comprehensively in Donald R. Matthews and James W. Prothro, "The Concept of Party Image and Its Importance for the Southern Electorate," in M. Kent Jennings and L. Harmon Zeigler, eds., *The Electoral Process* (Englewood Cliffs: Prentice-Hall, 1966), pp. 139-174; and in Matthews and Prothro, *Negroes and the New Southern Politics* (New York: Harcourt, Brace & World, 1966), pp. 377-404. The caveat placed on party identification as a factor aiding Democratic nominees extends to party image as well, for there has been considerable deterioration in white images of the (national) Democratic party since the early 1960s. In 1968 and 1972 the net Democratic image of white southerners was unfavorable rather than favorable. It is likely, however, that dissatisfaction with the national Democratic

party exceeded dissatisfaction with the state party. The changing images of the national parties are analyzed in Merle Black and George Rabinowitz, "An Overview of American Electoral Change: 1952-1972" (paper presented at the annual meeting of the Southern Political Science Association, New Orleans, November, 1974), pp. 6-24.

49. The position suggested here can be applied as well to situations where moderate segregationist Democrats opposed strong segregationist Republicans. This type of general election was limited to the 1966 South Carolina campaign and resulted in a solid victory (58 percent) for the Democrat. South Carolina Republicans were making their first serious campaign for the governorship since 1876.

50. Seymore Martin Lipset, *Political Man* (New York: Doubleday, 1960), pp. 31-32.

51. Matthews and Prothro, *New Southern Politics,* p. 356.

10   The Governors

1. V. O. Key, Jr., *Southern Politics in State and Nation* (New York: Knopf, 1949), p. 4.

2. *Ibid.*

3. *Ibid.,* p. 674.

4. The term "one-party system" here includes the disfranchisement of blacks, the dual primary system, and the informal veto over civil rights legislation which southern congressmen maintained as well as the region's attachment to the Democratic party.

5. James G. Maddox et al., *The Advancing South: Manpower Prospects and Problems* (New York: Twentieth Century Fund, 1967), p. 19.

6. In Mississippi the absence of net change favorable to militants simply reflects the original pervasiveness of the strong segregationists. Since more than four fifths of the major candidates ran as militant segregationists, there was little room for improvement in the militants' domination of Mississippi elections. The large net disadvantage (- 16) for South Carolina's strong segregationists, while requiring more explanation, is largely an artifact of atypical Democratic primaries in 1966 and 1970. In South Carolina militant segregationists dominated gubernatorial elections as campaigners and as winners in 1954 and 1958, but in subsequent campaigns most Democratic candidates and winners were not strong segregationists. Because the 1966 and 1970 Democratic primaries were not contested, however, the proportion of militant segregationists among major candidates is exaggerated and the share of moderate segregationists and nonsegregationists among major candidates is lower than it probably would have been had normally competitive conditions prevailed in 1966 and 1970.

7. Hugh Douglas Price, "Southern Politics in the Sixties: Notes on Economic Development and Political Modernization" (paper presented at the annual meeting of the American Political Science Association, Chicago, September, 1964), p. 10.

8. In contrast to his previous campaigns, Texas Governor Price Daniel in 1960 did not discuss racial segregation.

9. Although the scope and substantive focus of the two studies are dissimilar, this finding is roughly analogous to Salamon's research concerning the impact of the electoral process on the types of black candidates who succeeded in Mississippi. A comparison of the socioeconomic backgrounds and public policy orientations of victorious versus defeated black campaigners demonstrated that "the electoral process did indeed act as a kind of screening mechanism in Mississippi, systematically filtering out the less established [that is, less traditional] black candidates." Lester M. Salamon, "Leadership and Modernization: The Emerging Black Political Elite in the American South," *Journal of Politics,* 35 (August 1973), 644. See also the discussion on pp. 633-642, 644-645.

10. See Daniel Patrick Moynihan, "Employment, Income, and the Ordeal of the Negro Family," in Talcott Parsons and Kenneth B. Clark, eds., *The Negro American* (Boston: Houghton Mifflin, 1966), pp. 134-135.

11. Leslie W. Dunbar, "The Changing Mind of the South: The Exposed Nerve," *Journal of Politics,* 25 (February 1964), 18.

11   Explaining Racial Change in Southern Electoral Politics

1. For numerous examples, see Numan V. Bartley, *The Rise of Massive Resistance: Race and Politics in the South during the 1950's* (Baton Rouge: Louisiana State University Press, 1969); C. Vann Woodward, *The Strange Career of Jim Crow,* 3d ed. rev. (New York: Oxford University Press, 1974), pp. 149-168; and Benjamin Muse, *Ten Years of Prelude: The Story of Integration since the Supreme Court's 1954 Decision* (New York: Viking, 1964).

2. Although the proportion of segregationist governors (or major candidates) could have been determined simply by totaling the percentage of militant segregationists and moderate segregationists, the disadvantage of not weighting the segregationist categories would be to treat as equivalently segregationist states (for example, Georgia and North Carolina) that differed markedly in the relative strength of strong segregationists as compared with moderate segregationists. For purposes of a summary index, it was considered less a distortion to control for the intensity of support for segregation, even at the risk of underestimating the strength of moderate segregationists. If moderate segregationists had been counted at full strength, the indexes of racial change plotted in Figure 26 would have been 1.00 or higher for Texas, Tennessee, and Virginia (for major candidates). They would have fallen below 1.00 for Arkansas and the Peripheral South (major candidates only).

3. V. O. Key, Jr., *Southern Politics in State and Nation* (New York: Knopf, 1949), p. 5.

4. Specifically, the numerator of the index of demographic traditionalism consists of the following weighted sum of the vote in Democratic first primaries supplied by the "less traditional" categories: the mean percentage of the total state vote (1950-73 primaries) contributed by the large metropolitan areas (thought to be less preoccupied with the segregation issue per se than any other demographic classification) plus one half of the average medium urban vote (the smaller cities are assumed to be more tradition-bound than the region's major cities but less traditional than the low black rural areas) plus

one third of the low black rural vote (little positive support for racial change is hypothesized for the low black rural areas, merely less intense opposition to racial change than would be expected of the high black rural counties). The index's denominator is the mean proportion of the state vote cast by the high black rural counties. While the specific weights assigned to the demographic categories are clearly arbitrary and reflect the researcher's judgment (following Key, that is) concerning the substantive importance of the various classifications in shaping electoral politics, the weights are consistent with the notion of a demographic continuum running from the big cities to the rural counties with heavy black populations. For a concise discussion of the problem of assigning numbers to ordered categories, see Edward R. Tufte, "Improving Data Analysis in Political Science," *World Politics,* 21 (July 1969), 644-646.

5. Key, *Southern Politics,* p. 9.

6. See Hugh Douglas Price, "The Rise and Decline of One-Party Systems in Anglo-American Experience," in Samuel P. Huntington and Clement H. Moore, eds., *Authoritarian Politics in Modern Society* (New York: Basic Books, 1970), p. 95.

7. *Ibid.* Emphasis in original.

8. *Southern Politics,* pp. 299-301.

9. *Ibid.,* pp. 306-307.

10. Donald R. Matthews and James W. Prothro, *Negroes and the New Southern Politics* (New York: Harcourt, Brace & World, 1966), pp. 158-162.

11. Differences between Key and Matthews and Prothro concerning the behavior of states with cohesive majority factions are due in part to changes in the subregional affiliations of the states so classified. All of Key's "majority faction" states (North Carolina, Tennessee, and Virginia) were located in the Peripheral South. In Matthews and Prothro's study, states with "one dominant faction" were evenly divided between the subregions (Virginia and South Carolina).

12. William C. Havard, "From Past to Future: An Overview of Southern Politics," in William C. Havard, ed., *The Changing Politics of the South* (Baton Rouge: Louisiana State University Press, 1972), p. 690. For a review of factional and party divisions from state to state, see pp. 688-701.

13. *Ibid.,* pp. 691-692.

14. Primaries in which the leading candidate for governor received 60.0 percent or better of the state vote have been treated as unifactional. Bifactional primaries are defined as cases in which the leader received less than three fifths of the vote but in which the two highest candidates obtained at least 75.0 percent. The remaining primaries are classified as multifactional. Following past practice, Texas and Arkansas primaries were omitted in which an incumbent governor was nominated for a second two-year term.

15. See the discussion in Price, "One-Party Systems," p. 89. The topic of factionalism in recent southern politics deserves a detailed monograph which examines (at the minimum) factions in the electorate in addition to factions as organizations.

16. If it is unlikely that differences in factional competitiveness are related generally to elite stances on segregation, in a few states the specific

nature of factional struggles has probably either moderated or intensified racial conflict. Campaign rhetoric in favor of the caste system declined first in Peripheral South states where the conservative wing of the Democratic party apparently concluded that its future could be strengthened by appeals—usually circumspect and tangential—to black voters. John Connally, who emerged in 1962 as the new leader of the conservative Democrats in Texas, had no reputation as a militant segregationist, and this circumstance enabled him to win the support of some black Texans who would not have voted for Allan Shivers or Price Daniel. Once a proponent of school closings, Mills Godwin largely avoided racial topics as the Byrd Organization's candidate in the 1965 Virginia general election. (As has been shown, however, his performance as a Republican candidate in 1973 was another story.) In Tennessee the Clement-Ellington faction ceased to champion segregation, and in 1966 Ellington became the first southerner to be elected governor after publicly repudiating the caste system. Electoral considerations in these states—a fear of liberal Democrats and of conservative Republicans in Texas, a belief that the Byrd Organization could perpetuate itself against a (then) moderately progressive Republican party by loosening its ties to Virginia reactionaries and gaining support from liberals, organized labor, and blacks, and the desire of the Clement-Ellington faction to attract blacks away from more liberal Tennessee Democrats—seem important in understanding the demise of traditional campaign racism. By the same token, it is conceivable that Florida's heritage of multifactionalism (only Florida and Mississippi were invariably classified as multifactional for the post-*Brown* gubernatorial primaries) contributed to the success which segregationists enjoyed through 1964 in Democratic primaries. In the early 1960s Florida factions were much less cohesive and identifiable than the leading factions in Texas and Tennessee. There was no relatively well organized liberal wing of the Democratic party as there was in Texas and Tennessee; and attacks on the opposition as the NAACP candidate still attracted more favorable attention in Florida than they lost votes.

17. Feagin and Hahn argue that one of the conditions necessary in order for minority groups to "maximize their political effectiveness" is a "divided vote among majority electors." See Joe R. Feagin and Harlan Hahn, "The Second Reconstruction: Black Political Strength in the South," *Social Science Quarterly,* 51 (June 1970), 42. For a brief comparative analysis of the mobilization of white voters in the 1960s by Republican parties in the Deep South, see Earl Black and Merle Black, "The Changing Setting of Minority Politics in the American Deep South," in Tinsley E. Yarbrough et al., *Politics 73: Minorities in Politics* (Greenville, N.C.: East Carolina University Publications, 1973), pp. 42-45.

18. The interparty competition index, a modification of Ranney's index of competitiveness, was defined in Chapter 9, above. See note 3 of that chapter for a classification of the states according to the index. In order to present the states in Figure 28 in terms of increasing competitiveness, the index numbers have been subtracted from 1.00.

19. Cosman argued in his 1966 study that a reduction in racial conflict would force "the developing Republican parties . . . to face up to dilemmas of

strategy which, while possibly inevitable, have been delayed by the high perception of the race issue by Deep South voters." Bernard Cosman, *Five States for Goldwater: Continuity and Change in Southern Presidential Voting Patterns* (University, Ala.: University of Alabama Press, 1966), pp. 129-130.

20. J. W. Peltason, *Fifty-Eight Lonely Men: Southern Federal Judges and School Desegregation* (New York: Harcourt, Brace & World, 1961), p. 54. For chronicles of federal intervention through 1954, see Anthony Lewis et al., *Portrait of a Decade: The Second American Revolution* (New York: Random House, 1964), pp. 104-124; and Harold C. Fleming, "The Federal Executive and Civil Rights: 1961-1965," in Talcott Parsons and Kenneth B. Clark, eds., *The Negro American* (Boston: Houghton Mifflin, 1966), pp. 371-399.

21. Lewis, *Portrait,* p. 112. For sharp criticism of Eisenhower's reluctance to enforce the *Brown* decision, see Peltason, *Fifty-Eight Lonely Men,* pp. 46-55.

22. For details, see Lewis, *Portrait,* pp. 117-125. The description of Wallace's behavior is taken from Alexander M. Bickel, "Civil Rights Act of 1963," *New Republic,* July 6, 1963, p. 9.

23. Southern Education Reporting Service, *A Statistical Summary, State by State, of School Segregation-Desegregation in the Southern and Border Area from 1954 to the Present* (Nashville: Southern Education Reporting Service, 1967), pp. 2, 43-44. For additional data, see Harrell R. Rodgers, Jr., and Charles S. Bullock, III, *Law and Social Change: Civil Rights Laws and Their Consequences* (New York: McGraw-Hill, 1972), pp. 81-97.

24. Gary Orfield, *The Reconstruction of Southern Education: The Schools and the 1964 Civil Rights Act* (New York: Wiley, 1969), p. 1.

25. *Ibid.,* p. 3. Another wave of school desegregation occurred in 1969 and the early 1970s after the Supreme Court, tiring of dilatory tactics by various school districts, ordered the immediate abolition of "dual school systems." See Rodgers and Bullock, *Law and Social Change,* pp. 90-94.

26. Thomas R. Dye, *The Politics of Equality* (Indianapolis: Bobbs-Merrill, 1971), pp. 54-56; and Rodgers and Bullock, *Law and Social Change,* pp. 28-29.

27. Schattschneider has argued that "the scope of a conflict determines its outcome" and that civil rights is an issue that benefits from broad attention. E. E. Schattschneider, *The Semi-Sovereign People: A Realist's View of Democracy in America* (New York: Holt, Rinehart and Winston, 1960), pp. 7-8 and throughout. More recently, Grant McConnell has stressed the importance of constituency size as a factor in resolving racial (and other) issues. As long as decisions affecting them were confined to the local level, blacks could expect little sympathy for their grievances. *Private Power and American Democracy* (New York: Knopf, 1966), pp. 91-118, 176-178.

28. Orfield, *Reconstruction of Southern Education,* p. viii. See also pp. 308-309.

29. James Q. Wilson, "The Negro in Politics," in Parsons and Clark, eds., *Negro American,* p. 425.

30. Compare the regional estimates of voter registration by race in the early 1960s presented in Pat Watters and Reese Cleghorn, *Climbing Jacob's*

Ladder: The Arrival of Negroes in Southern Politics (New York: Harcourt, Brace & World, 1967), Appendix 2, with 1970 estimates published in William C. Havard, "The South: A Shifting Perspective," in Havard, ed., *Changing Politics of the South,* p. 21.

31. See, for example, Havard, "The South: A Shifting Perspective," pp. 22-23; Feagin and Hahn, "Second Reconstruction," p. 46; Numan V. Bartley, *From Thurmond to Wallace: Political Tendencies in Georgia, 1948-1968* (Baltimore: Johns Hopkins Press, 1970), pp. 9-11; Chandler Davidson, *Biracial Politics: Conflict and Coalition in the Metropolitan South* (Baton Rouge: Louisiana State University Press, 1972), p. 7; and Black and Black, "Changing Setting of Minority Politics," pp. 35-40.

32. Black and Black, "Changing Setting of Minority Politics," pp. 38-40; and Earl Black and Merle Black, "The Demographic Basis of Wallace Support in Alabama," *American Politics Quarterly,* 1 (July 1973), 290-292.

33. The denominator for all registration rates is the 1960 voting age population. Because Florida's population increased by more than one third between 1960 and 1970, much of the increase in white registration is probably due to migration rather than to white mobilization per se.

34. Feagin and Hahn, "Second Reconstruction," p. 48.

35. There is no comprehensive analysis of the relation of black voter organizations to statewide politics. For a study of black organizations in several large southern cities, see Harry Holloway, *The Politics of the Southern Negro: From Exclusion to Big City Organization* (New York: Random House, 1969), chs. 7-10.

36. These estimates were computed from voter registration data found in Watters and Cleghorn, *Climbing Jacob's Ladder,* Appendix 2; and Havard, "The South: A Shifting Perspective," p. 21.

37. Estimates of the percentage of white voters required to give the Democratic party a regional majority in presidential elections, for varying rates of black participation, are given in Matthews and Prothro, *New Southern Politics,* p. 403.

38. Segregationist senators and representatives, by comparison, with no barriers to their reelection, are better situated to win large white majorities.

39. On this point see, for example, Wilson, "Negro in Politics," pp. 429-430; and Matthews and Prothro, *New Southern Politics,* pp. 478-479. For correctives to any assumption that "the vote will automatically give southern Negroes influence over public policy commensurate with their numbers," see Matthews and Prothro, *New Southern Politics,* pp. 477-481; Allan P. Sindler, "Protest Against the Political Status of the Negro," *Annals of the American Academy of Political and Social Science,* 357 (January 1965), 48-54; and William R. Keech, *The Impact of Negro Voting: The Role of the Vote in the Quest for Equality* (Chicago: Rand McNally, 1968), esp. pp. 93-109.

40. Matthews and Prothro, *New Southern Politics,* p. 481.

41. On the relation between public opinion and the behavior of politicians, see generally V. O. Key, Jr., *Public Opinion and American Democracy* (New York: Knopf, 1961).

42. The most useful sources of data on the racial attitudes of white

southerners are Mildred A. Schwartz, *Trends in White Attitudes toward Negroes* (Chicago: National Opinion Research Center, 1967); Paul B. Sheatsley, "White Attitudes Toward the Negro," in Parsons and Clark, eds., *Negro American,* pp. 303-324; Andrew M. Greeley and Paul B. Sheatsley, "Attitudes toward Racial Integration," *Scientific American,* December 1971, pp. 13-19; Matthews and Prothro, *New Southern Politics,* esp. ch. 12; William Brock and Louis Harris, *The Negro Revolution in America* (New York: Simon and Schuster, 1964); and Brink and Harris, *Black and White* (New York: Simon and Schuster, 1967). Many of the polls on race edited by Hazel Erskine for the *Public Opinion Quarterly* contain information on southerners' racial opinions. See particularly the following compilations: "The Polls: Race Relations," 26 (Spring 1962), 137-148; "The Polls: Negro Housing," 31 (Fall 1967), 482-498; "The Polls: Demonstrations and Race Riots," 31 (Winter 1967-1968), 655-677; "The Polls: Negro Employment," 32 (Spring 1968), pp. 132-153; "The Polls: Speed of Racial Integration," 32 (Fall 1968), 513-524; "The Polls: Recent Opinion on Racial Problems," 32 (Winter 1968-1969), 696-703; and "The Polls: Interracial Socializing," 37 (Summer 1973), 283-294. For brief examinations of white attitudes on race in Texas, see Alan Scott, "Twenty-five Years of Opinion on Integration in Texas," *Southwestern Social Science Quarterly,* 48 (September 1967), 155-163; and Dan Nimmo and William E. Oden, *The Texas Political System* (Englewood Cliffs: Prentice-Hall, 1971), pp. 90-92.

43. In a survey taken in 1961, for example, Matthews and Prothro found that 64 percent of the region's whites preferred "strict segregation" to "integration or something in between." Fewer than one in twenty whites opted for integration (*New Southern Politics,* pp. 332-333). Similarly, southern whites were strongly opposed to the civil rights movement. In late 1963, 78 percent objected generally to "actions Negroes have taken to obtain civil rights" (Sheatsley, "White Attitudes," p. 317), and 81 percent of the white South were convinced in 1966 that blacks were moving "too fast" (Brink and Harris, *Black and White,* p. 221). Yet polls which measure only abstract white preferences probably exaggerate the willingness of whites to resist desegregation. As Pettigrew has argued, in concrete situations "many segregationist Southerners value law and order, public education, and a prosperous economy above their racial views . . . Thus a rounded situational analysis requires the measurement of racial attitudes in the full context of countervalues." Thomas F. Pettigrew, "Social Psychology and Desegregation Research," *American Psychologist,* 16 (March 1961), 107. For a perceptive analysis of the ways in which other values have frequently intervened between segregationist attitudes and actual behavior and a critique of surveys which neglect situational variables, see Howard Zinn, *The Southern Mystique* (New York: Knopf, 1964), pp. 21-42, 53-86. Perhaps the point has been made most succinctly by a Matthews and Prothro respondent: " 'You asked me what I favor,' a white Arkansas housewife who believed in segregation said, 'not what I will accept graciously; not what I thought was right.' " *New Southern Politics,* p. 363.

44. The 1956 and 1965 figures are computed from data in Schwartz, *Trends,* p. 131; the 1970 estimate is from Greeley and Sheatsley, "Attitudes

toward Racial Integration,'' p. 14. Since the polls from which these data are derived include five border states as part of the South, actual attitudinal change in the eleven states of the Confederacy would be less pronounced. It should be emphasized that opposition to school desegregation has remained high when desegregation would place white students in the minority. See Melvin J. Knapp and Jon P. Alston, ''White Parental Acceptance of Varying Degrees of School Desegregation: 1965 and 1970,'' *Public Opinion Quarterly,* 36 (Winter 1972-1973), 585-591.

45. Schwartz, *Trends,* p. 84; Greeley and Sheatsley, ''Attitudes toward Racial Integration,'' pp. 14-15.

46. Schwartz, *Trends,* p. 134; Greeley and Sheatsley, ''Attitudes toward Racial Integration,'' pp. 13-14.

47. Greeley and Sheatsley, ''Attitudes toward Racial Integration,'' pp. 14-16.

48. Schwartz, *Trends,* p. 109.

49. See Hugh Douglas Price, ''Southern Politics in the Sixties: Notes on Economic Development and Political Modernization'' (paper presented at the annual meeting of the American Political Science Association, Chicago, September, 1964), pp. 2-4; and Fred Powledge, *Black Power—White Resistance* (Cleveland: World, 1967), ch. 6. In the absence of pressure for racial change, most businessmen preferred segregation and economic development. See Bartley, *Rise of Massive Resistance,* pp. 312-315; and M. Richard Cramer, ''School Desegregation and New Industry: The Southern Community Leaders' Viewpoint,'' *Social Forces,* 41 (May 1963), 385-386. For examples of economic studies which have argued that the South's racial traditions have been at odds with its urge to industrialize, see William H. Nicholls, *Southern Tradition and Regional Progress* (Chapel Hill: University of North Carolina Press, 1960); and James G. Maddox et al., *The Advancing South: Manpower Prospects and Problems* (New York: Twentieth Century Fund, 1967).

50. Woodward, *Strange Career of Jim Crow,* pp. 182-183; and Dye, *Politics of Equality,* p. 59. The role of the business community in recent southern state politics needs much more research than it has received.

51. The history of the desegregation issue corresponds in several respects to the model of an issue's rise and decline presented in Bernard R. Berelson, Paul F. Lazarsfeld, and William N. McPhee, *Voting: A Study of Opinion Formation in a Presidential Campaign* (Chicago: University of Chicago Press, 1954), p. 208. Desegregation moved from the category of an uncontested issue (no factions or parties advocating it) through a period of maximum controversy (with far more opponents than supporters) to a stage in some states where only unreconstructed segregationists perceive it as a major issue. The desegregation issue, however, does not completely resemble the model elaborated in *Voting.* Institutions outside the South had far more to do with the surfacing of the issue than did the activities of any vanguard of racially liberal southerners. Moreover, desegregation was an issue which, though highly salient, did not arouse true polarization. There were few elections in which nonsegregationists and militant segregationists differed openly on the principle of desegregation.

52. For extended analyses of the relation between national law and

southern racial change, see Frederick M. Wirt, *Politics of Southern Equality: Law and Social Change in a Mississippi County* (Chicago: Aldine, 1970); Rodgers and Bullock, *Law and Social Change:* and Orfield, *Reconstruction of Southern Education.* Two studies which focus not on the impact of national intervention (a variable difficult to operationalize at the county level) but on the relative importance of demographic versus political variables in explaining levels of school desegregation are less impressed with the significance of "stateways." See Donald R. Matthews and James W. Prothro, "Stateways Versus Folkways: Critical Factors in Southern Reactions to *Brown v. Board of Education,"* in Gottfried Dietze, ed., *Essays on the American Constitution* (Englewood Cliffs: Prentice-Hall, 1964), pp. 139-156; and James W. Prothro, "Stateways Versus Folkways Revisited: An Error in Prediction," *Journal of Politics,* 34 (May 1972), 352-364.

53. Clifford Geertz, "The Integrative Revolution: Primordial Sentiments and Civil Politics in the New States," in Clifford Geertz, ed., *Old Societies and New States: The Quest for Modernity in Asia and Africa* (New York: The Free Press, 1963), p. 109.

Index

Abernathy, Ralph, 68
Achievement of economic development.
   See Economic development
ADA, 43, 173-174, 214, 236-237, 382
Adaptive, 19. *See also* Economic develop-
   ment
AFL-CIO, 116, 170, 192. *See also* CIO-
   PAC
Alabama, 1950 first primary campaign in,
   42; political demography of, 49-51, 57-
   58; overview of electoral politics in, 52-
   58; segregationist counties in, 57-58;
   campaign stances of major candidates
   in, 153-154; 1966 first primary campaign in, 184-188; 1962 primary campaigns in, 219-225; campaign stances of
   governors in, 292-293, 296. *See also*
   Deep South
Almond, J. Lindsay, 14, 115, 266, 273
Arkansas, 1950 first primary campaign
   in, 37-39; political demography of, 88-
   91, 99; overview of electorial politics in,
   98-106; segregationist counties in, 99;
   campaign stances of major candidates
   in, 155-157; 1958 first primary campaign in, 174-177; 1966 general election
   campaign in, 269-271; campaign
   stances of governors in, 294-296. *See
   also* Peripheral South
Arkansas Gazette, 176
Arnall, Ellis, 69, 230-233, 269
Ashmore, Harry, 176
Askew, Reubin, as progressive, 21; career
   described, 97-98; as nonsegregationist,
   238, 273, 279; as nonsegregationist-
   redistributive, 288, 296

Barnes, Ben, 131
Barnett, Ross, as strong segregationist,
   14, 141, 212; 1951 first primary campaign of, 39; career described, 59, 63-
   65; compared to Russell, 83; 1959 first
   primary campaign of, 167, 170-171,

376; 1967 first primary campaign of,
   181-183; discussed in 1963 campaigns,
   208, 210, 264; 1959 second primary
   campaign of, 376-377; discussed in
   1967 second primary campaign, 379
Bates, Daisy, 103, 176
Bates, Lester, 80
Battle, John S., 45
Battle, William, 116-117
Beth, Loren, 157
Bifactionalism. *See* Intraparty factional-
   ism
Bilbo, Theodore, 181
Black belt counties, 24. *See also* Political
   demography
Black belt hypothesis, 23, 132-140
Black participation patterns, 326-334
Bodenhamer, William T., 66, 366
Boggs, Hale, 44
Bowles, Hargrove, 111
Brewer, Albert, 56-57
Briscoe, Dolph, 131, 273
Broughton, J. Melville, 110-111, 188
Browning, Gordon, 31-32
Brown v. Board of Education, 4, 12-13,
   173, 339, 341
Bryant, Farris, 93, 96
Bumpers, Dale, 105, 242, 385
Burnham, Walter Dean, 387
Burns, Haydon, career described, 96-97;
   1964 primary campaigns of, 226-228,
   384; 1966 primary campaigns of, 228-
   230, 384; as unsuccessful strong segre-
   gationist, 240, 242
Busing issue, 238, 273-274, 343
Byrd, Harry F., Sr., 113, 118, 140, 375
Byrd organization, 45, 113, 115-118, 318-
   319, 375
Byrnes, James F., 33

Cain, Mary, 34
Callaway, Howard, 69, 267-269, 388-389
Campaign stances, 11-12, 21-22. *See also*

Economic development; Racial segregation
Campbell, Ernest Q., 177
Carlton, Doyle, 93, 96
Carmichael, Stokely, 231, 270
Carter, Jimmy, 70-71, 288, 296
Cashin, John, 249
Caste system, 13. *See also* Jim Crow system
Cherry, Francis, 32, 100
CIO-PAC, 43, 173, 213-215, 382. *See also* AFL-CIO
Citizens' Council, 167, 170, 189
Civil Rights Act of 1964, 8, 324
Civil Rights Bill of 1964, 191-193, 226-227
Clement, Frank, 31-32, 119-120, 122, 173, 249
Coalition formation, 330-334
Coleman, J. P., career discussed, 60, 63; discussed in 1959 first primary campaign, 170; 1963 primary campaigns of, 208, 210-211, 381-382
Collins, LeRoy, 15, 93, 96, 173
Connally, John, as nonsegregationist, 16, 273, 338, 395; as adaptive, 19; career described, 129-132; 1962 primary campaigns of, 235-237, 385
Connor, Eugene, 34, 55
Conservative party of Virginia, 275-277
CORE, 380
Cosman, Bernard, 11, 361-362, 395-396
County unit system, 35
Cox, Jack, 129
Crank, Marion, 242
Cross pressures, 278-279

Dalton, Theodore, 14, 45, 115, 273
Daniel, Price, career described, 128-129; as nonsegregationist, 191, 193, 198, 242, 392; 1962 first primary campaign of, 235-236; 1956 second primary campaign of, 382-383
Dauer, Manning, 230
Davis, Jimmie, as marginalist, 18; career described, 76, 78; 1959-60 first primary campaign of, 189-191, 379-380; 1959-60 second primary campaign of, 215-217
Deep South, definition of, 11; political demography of, 49-51; campaign stances of major candidates in, 152-154; campaign stances of governors in, 292-294, 296; black participation and racial change in, 329-331, 333. *See also* Subregional comparisons
DeGraffenried, Ryan, 55, 219-225
Demographic setting of electoral politics. *See* Political demography
Demographic traditionalism index. *See* Index of demographic traditionalism
Dissimilarity index. *See* Index of dissimilarity
Dixiecrat revolt, 29
Dodd, William, 189, 379
Dual primary system, 7, 162, 199-200. *See also* First primary campaigns; Second primary campaigns
Dunbar, Leslie, 16, 305
Dunn, Winfield, 123

Economic development, classification of campaign stances on, 16-22, 359-360; campaign stances prior to 1954 on, 30-31; campaign stances of major candidates on, 146-152, 160-161; campaign stances of general election contestants on, 252-257; campaign stances of governors on, 283-292, 297-298. *See also* entries for states and subregions
Edwards, Edwin, 78, 238
Eisenhower, Dwight D., 323, 373
Elementary and Secondary Education Act of 1965, 324
Ellington, Buford, as nonsegregationist, 16, 338, 395; career described, 120, 122; 1966 first primary campaign of, 194-196, 381; faction led by, 249
Evers, Charles, 66, 249
Ewing, Cortez, 199

Faircloth, Earl, 97-98
Farenthold, Francis, 131, 238
Faubus, Orval, as redistributive, 20; mentioned in Mississippi campaigns, 60, 171; career described, 99-100, 103-106; compared to other politicians, 106, 122; as moderate segregationist, 173, 191, 272; 1958 first primary campaign of, 174-177; geography of vote for, 176-177; as unsuccessful moderate segregationist, 193, 242, 331, 385; as Rockefeller opponent, 270; as neo-Populist, 296; as strong segregationist, 299; decline of faction led by, 318
Feagin, Joe R., 395
Federal intervention, concept of, 150; and segregationist stances of major candidates, 150-152, 158-159; and first primary results, 166, 172, 183-184, 193-194, 196-197; and second primary results, 202, 204-207, 212, 225, 234-235, 237-241; and general election results, 275, 277-278; and segregationist stances of governors, 288-291, 299-304, 322-326; and racial change, 317-320, 340-342; and black participation, 326-330; and change within white political

elite, 337-338; and campaign rhetoric, 342-344

Federalism. *See* Federal intervention

FEPC, 12, 29, 35-39

Finkbeiner, Chris, 175-176

First primary campaigns, militant segregationists versus militant segregationists, 167-172; militant segregationists versus moderate segregationists, 172-184; militant segregationists versus nonsegregationists, 184-188; moderate segregationists versus moderate segregationists, 188-191; moderate segregationists versus nonsegregationists, 191-193; nonsegregationists versus nonsegregationists, 193-197. *See also* Dual primary system

First primary contestants, 163-169, 197-198

Florida, political demography of, 88-92; overview of electoral politics in, 90, 92-98; segregationist counties in, 92; campaign stances of major candidates in, 155-157; 1964 primary campaigns in, 226-228; 1966 primary campaigns in, 228-230; campaign stances of governors in, 294-296. *See also* Peripheral South

Flowers, Richmond, 56, 184-186, 188, 288

Folsom, James, as redistributive, 20, 297; role in 1950 first primary of, 42; career described, 52; as winner of first primary majority, 186; as moderate segregationist-redistributive, 189; 1962 first primary campaign of, 219-222, 383; as neo-Populist, 296; on campaign rhetoric of Clement, 362

Gardner, James, 111

Gartin, Carroll, 167, 170-171, 376-377

General election campaigns, criteria for "competitive" elections, 251-252; militant segregationists versus militant segregationists, 261-266; militant segregationists versus moderate segregationists, 266-269; militant segregationists versus nonsegregationists, 269-271; moderate segregationists versus moderate segregationists, 272; moderate segregationists versus nonsegregationists, 272-275; nonsegregationists versus nonsegregationists, 275-277

General election contestants, 251-257

General election interest, 246-248, 387

General election winners, 257-262, 277-280

Georgia, 1950 first primary campaign in, 35-37; political demography of, 49-51, 71-72; overview of electoral politics in,

66-72; segregationist counties in, 71-72; campaign stances of major candidates in, 152-154; 1962 first primary campaign in, 177-181; 1966 second primary campaign in, 230-234; 1966 general election campaign in, 267-269, 388-389; campaign stances of governors in, 292-293, 296. *See also* Deep South

Godwin, Mills, career described, 116-118; 1973 general election campaign of, 273-275, 390; 1965 general election campaign of, 275-277, 372, 391; opposition to desegregation of, 390-391; as nonsegregationist, 395

Goldwater, Barry, 182, 255, 263, 316, 391

Governors, 283-292, 296-305

Greeley, Andrew, 335

Griffin, Marvin, 66, 68, 177-180, 233, 377-378

Grover, Henry, 131

Hahn, Harlan, 395

Hamm, Philip, 33, 42

Harris, Roy, 68

Harrison, Albertis S., 18-19, 115-116

Havard, William C., 157, 246, 318

Hawkins, Reginald, 111

Hays, Brooks, 171

Henderson, Bruce, 34

HEW school desegregation guidelines, 182-183, 231

High black rural counties, 24. *See also* Political demography

High, Robert King, 96-97, 226-230, 242, 272-273, 288

Hodges, Luther, 106, 109, 173, 219

Hoffa, James, 216

Hollings, Ernest, 80, 82-83

Holshouser, James, 111-112, 255, 322

Holton, Linwood, as nonsegregationist, 16, 277, 338; career described, 116-118; as nonsegregationist-adaptive Republican, 255; as nonsegregationist Republican, 258, 275, 322; 1965 general election campaign of, 275-277, 391

Hooker, John Jay, Jr., 122-123, 194-197, 277

Howell, Henry, career described, 117-118; as unsuccessful candidate, 238, 279, 288; 1973 general election campaign of, 273-275, 390; as independent candidate, 386

Humphrey, Hubert, 181

Incumbency factor, 162

Index of demographic traditionalism, 313-316, 393-394

Index of dissimilarity, 255-257, 291-292

Index of interparty competition, 244-245, 320-321, 395

Index of racial change, definition of, 310, 393; results of, 310-312, 340-341; and demographic traditionalism, 314-316; and interparty competition, 320-321; and federal intervention, 322-323

Interparty comparisons, 252-262, 277-280

Interparty competition, 244-251

Interparty competition index. *See* Index of interparty competition

Intraparty factionalism, 316-320, 394-395

Jim Crow system, 6, 343

John Birch Society, 231

Johns, Charley, 93

Johnson, Frank, 221

Johnson, James D., career described, 100, 104; 1966 campaigns of, 270-271, 370-371, 375-376, 389-390

Johnson, Lyndon B., in Georgia politics, 69, 231, 268; in Texas politics, 130, 235; in Mississippi politics, 181-182; in Virginia politics, 275; as civil rights advocate, 324

Johnson, Paul B., Jr., 1951 primary campaigns of, 39-41; career described, 59-60, 63-64; 1963 primary campaigns of, 208, 210-211, 381-382; as strong segregationist, 212; 1963 general election campaign of, 261-266; on school desegregation, 387-388

Johnson, Virginia, 193, 385

Johnston, J. Bennett, 78, 238

Johnston, Olin, 83

Jones, Sam, 44

Kefauver, Estes, 44

Kelly, Scott, 97, 228, 384

Kennedy, John F., in Mississippi politics, 63, 208, 210-211, 263-265, 381-382; in Louisiana politics, 76; in Texas politics, 129-130, 235-236; as civil rights advocate, 323-324

Kennedy, Robert, in Mississippi politics, 63, 181, 183, 263-264; in Tennessee politics, 194, 196; in Florida politics, 229

Kennon, Robert, 32, 44

Key, V. O., on regional distinctiveness, 3; on elite analysis, 4-5; on socioeconomic change, 4; on southern political demography, 22-26, 49; black belt hypothesis of, 23, 140, 360; on Texas politics, 42-43, 173; on racial issue in electoral politics, 46; on black belt voting in national elections, 132; on cities and racial conflict, 137; on function of second primary, 199; on southern general elections, 246; on general election interest, 246-248; on regional problems, 281; on failure of southern leadership, 281-282; on determinants of political change, 282; on racial attitudes of black belt whites, 313; on factionalism and racial politics, 317-319; on classification of Democratic factions, 394

King, Martin Luther, Jr., in Georgia politics, 68-69, 178-179, 231, 268; in Alabama politics, 185; in Florida politics, 229; in Arkansas politics, 270

Kirk, Claude, 97-98, 273, 369-370

Ku Klux Klan, 179-180, 193, 231-232, 267, 388

Lake, I. Beverly, 109-110, 191-193, 217-219

Lane, Mills B., 179

Laney, Ben, 37-39

Large metropolitan counties, 24. *See also* Political demography

La Raza Unida, 131

Lipset, Seymour Martin, 278

Little Rock crisis, 174-176, 299, 302-304

Little Rock generation, 336-338

Long, Earl, as moderate segregationist, 15; as redistributive, 20, 297; role in 1951-52 primary campaigns, 44; compared to Folsom, 52; career described, 73, 76; as moderate segregationist-redistributive, 189; role in 1959-60 primary campaigns, 190, 216, 379-380; as neo-Populist, 296; decline of faction led by, 318

Long, Gillis, 78

Louisiana, 1951-52 primary campaigns in, 44; political demography of, 49-51, 72-73; segregationist counties in, 72-73; overview of electoral politics in, 72-78; campaign stances of major candidates in, 152-154; 1959-60 first primary campaign in, 189-191, 379-380; 1959-60 second primary campaign in, 215-217; campaign stances of governors in, 292-294, 296. *See also* Deep South

Low black rural counties, 24. *See also* Political demography

Lowry, Sumter, 15, 93

Lumpkin, Sam, 39-40

McCarty, Dan, 32, 93

McCleskey, Clifton, 381

McConnell, Grant, 396

McGill, Ralph, 179

McGovern, George, 131
McKeithen, John, career described, 76-78; 1967 first primary campaign of, 184; as nonsegregationist, 198, 242, 338; as moderate segregationist, 272
McLemore, James, 44
McMath, Sidney, 20, 32-33, 37-39, 176
McNair, Robert, 83-84, 267
Maddox, Lester, as progressive, 21; career described, 69-71; segregationist views of compared, 194, 270; 1966 second primary compaign of, 230-234; geography of vote for, 233; 1966 general election campaign of, 267-269, 388-389; as unsuccessful militant segregationist, 331, 333
Major candidates, 29-31, 146-152, 157-161
Marginalist, 18-19. See also Economic development
Massive resistance, 113, 115
Matthews, Donald R., on subregions, 11; on white opposition to black participation, 24; on subregional differences in segregationist attitudes, 279; on factionalism and racial change, 317-320; on classification of Democratic factions, 394; on white racial attitudes, 398
Medium black rural counties, 24. See also Political demography
Medium urban counties, 24. See also Political demography
Meredith, James, 63, 208, 210-211, 264
Militant segregationist, 13-14. See also Racial segregation
Militant segregationist vote. See Segregationist counties
Mississippi, political demography of, 25, 49-51, 58-59; 1951 primary campaigns in, 39-41, 363; segregationist counties in, 58-59; overview of electoral politics in, 58-66; campaign stances of major candidates in, 152-154; 1959 first primary campaign in, 167, 170-171; 1967 first primary campaign in, 181-183; 1963 second primary campaign in, 208, 210-211; 1963 general election campaign in, 261-266; campaign stances of governors in, 292-293, 296; 1959 second primary campaign in, 376-377; 1967 second primary campaign in, 378-379. See also Deep South
Moderate segregationist, 14-15. See also Racial segregation
Moore, Dan, 110, 191-193, 272, 380-381
Morrison, deLesseps S., 76-77, 189-191, 215-217, 379

Multifactionalism. See Intraparty factionalism

NAACP, in Alabama politics, 52, 223; in Arkansas politics, 103-104, 175-176; in Florida politics, 97-98, 227-228; in Georgia politics, 66, 68, 179; in Louisiana politics, 76-77, 189-190, 215-216; in Mississippi politics, 60, 63, 170-171, 211; in North Carolina politics, 109, 111, 192, 218-219, 380; in South Carolina politics, 80; in Texas politics, 43-44, 128-129, 173-174, 214-215, 236-237, 382-383; in Virginia politics, 116
National Opinion Research Center, 335
Neo-Populism, 17-21
New South generation, 337-338
Nixon, Richard M., 56
Noe, James, 189, 379-380
Nonsegregationist, 15-16. See also Racial segregation
North Carolina, political demography of, 88-91, 112-113; overview of electoral politics in, 106-113; segregationist counties in, 112-113; campaign stances of major candidates in, 155-157; 1964 first primary campaign in, 191-193; 1960 primary campaigns in, 217-219; campaign stances of governors in, 294-296; 1964 second primary campaign in, 380-381. See also Peripheral South

O'Daniel, W. Lee, 128, 374
One-party system, 244-245, 263-266, 392
Orfield, Gary, 324-326

Parr, George, 173
Party identification, 278-280, 391
Party image, 278-279, 391-392
Patterson, John, 52, 55, 57, 212
Peripheral South, definition of, 11; political demography of, 87-91; campaign stances of major candidates in, 154-157; campaign stances of governors in, 294-296; black participation and racial change in, 328-329, 331, 333. See also Subregional comparisons
Persons, Gordon, 31, 42
Pettigrew, Thomas F., 177, 398
Phillips, Rubel, 261-266, 388
Political demography, classification of southern counties according to, 24-26; of the Deep South, 49-51; of Alabama, 57-58; of Arkansas, 99; of Florida, 88-92; of Georgia, 71-72; of Louisiana, 72-73; of Mississippi, 58-59; of North Carolina, 112-113; of South Carolina,

78-79; of Tennessee, 118-120; of Texas, 123-124; of Virginia, 118-119; of the Peripheral South, 87-91; and segregationist voting, 132-140; and racial change, 313-316
"Port Arthur Story," 213-215
Powell, Adam Clayton, 383
Pre-*Brown* campaigns, 35-45
Preyer, Richardson, 110, 191-193, 380-381
Price, H. Douglas, 138, 297, 316
Progressive, 20-21. *See also* Economic development
Prothro, James W., on subregions, 11; on white opposition to black participation, 24; on subregional differences in segregationist attitudes, 279; on factionalism and racial change, 317-320; on classification of Democratic factions, 394; on white racial attitudes, 398

Racial change index. *See* Index of racial change
Racial segregation, study limited to campaign attitudes toward, 6; classification of campaign stances on, 12-16; campaign stances in pre-*Brown* campaigns, 29-31; as issue in pre-*Brown* campaigns, 45-47; campaign stances of major candidates on, 146-152, 157-159; campaign stances in first primaries on, 163-166, 168-169, 197-198; campaign stances in second primaries on, 200-207, 209, 239-243; campaign stances of general election contestants on, 252-257; campaign stances of general election winners on, 257-262, 277-280; campaign stances of governors on, 283-292, 299-304; and change within white political elite, 336-338, 342-344. *See also* entries for states and subregions
Rainach, William, 76, 189-190, 217, 379-380
Ranney, Austin, 244-245, 386, 395
Ransone, Coleman, 245-246
Rarick, John, 77
Redistributive, 19-20. *See also* Economic development
Republican competition, 244-251
Reuther, Walter, 382
Robinson, Jackie, 180
Rockefeller, Winthrop, as nonsegregationist, 16, 269, 277, 338; career described, 104-105; as organizer of Republican party, 250; as nonsegregationist Republican, 258, 275, 322; 1966 general election campaign of, 269-271,

389; weakness of 1964 candidacy of, 272; as organizer of black electorate, 316, 328
Rogers, Joseph, Jr., 83, 267
Roosevelt, Franklin D., 29
Russell, Donald, 80, 82-83
Russell, Richard, 66

Salamon, Lester M., 393
Sanders, Carl, as moderate segregationist, 15, 233, 241; as adaptive, 19; career described, 68-71; 1962 first primary campaign of, 177-181, 377-378; as nonsegregationist, 238
Sanford, Terry, as moderate segregationist, 15, 241; as adaptive, 19; career described, 109-110; role in 1964 primary campaigns of, 192, 381; 1960 primary campaigns of, 217-219
Schattschneider, E. E., 396
Scott, Robert, 110-111, 188, 269, 272
Second primary campaigns, militant segregationists versus militant segregationists, 207-212; militant segregationists versus moderate segregationists, 212-225; militant segregationists versus nonsegregationists, 225-234; nonsegregationists versus nonsegregationists, 234-239; moderate segregationists versus moderate segregationists, 384-385; moderate segregationists versus nonsegregationists, 384-385. *See also* Dual primary system
Second primary contestants, 200-207, 209, 239-243
Second Reconstruction, 4, 26, 304-305, 310, 338-342
Segregation. *See* Racial segregation
Segregationist counties, demography of, 25-26, 132-140, 374; in Alabama, 57-58; in Arkansas, 99; in Florida, 92; in Georgia, 71-72; in Louisiana, 72-73; in Mississippi, 58-59; in North Carolina, 112-113; in South Carolina, 79; in Tennessee, 119-120; in Texas, 123-125; in Virginia, 118-119; definition of, 353-354
Sheatsley, Paul B., 335
Shivers, Allan, as marginalist, 18; 1950 first primary campaign of, 31; 1952 first primary campaign of, 43-44; career described, 125, 128; 1954 first primary campaign of, 173-174, 377; 1954 second primary campaign of, 213-215; compared to Connally, 236; opposition to school desegregation of, 373-374
Silver, James W., 152

Smith, Preston, 131-132, 338
SNCC, 231-232
Snodgrass, Stanly, 122-123
South Carolina, political demography of, 49-51, 78-79; overview of electoral politics in, 78-85; segregationist counties in, 79; campaign stances of major candidates in, 152-154; 1966 general election campaign in, 267; campaign stances of governors in, 292-294, 296; general election interest in, 387. See also Deep South
Southern electoral process. See Dual primary system; First primary campaigns; Second primary campaigns; General election campaigns; Pre-Brown campaigns
Southern politics, race as primordial cleavage in, 3-4, 343; socioeconomic change underlying, 4; perspective of white elite, 6; demographic structure of, 7, 22-26; electoral process used in, 7, 162, 199-200, 243-246; comparative approach to, 8; failure of leadership in, 281-282; racial composition of electoral coalitions in, 330-334. See also Federal intervention; Racial segregation; Subregional comparisons; and entries for states and subregions
Spaht, Carlos, 33, 44
Stanley, Thomas, 45, 113, 115
Strong segregationist. See Militant segregationist
Subregional comparisons, of demography of segregationist counties, 132-140; of campaign stances of major candidates, 146-152, 157-161; of racial stances in first primary campaigns, 164-165, 168-169; of racial stances in second primary campaigns, 202-203, 209; of general election interest, 246-248, 387; of size of Republican vote, 248-251; of economic development stances of general election contestants, 252-257; of racial stances of general election contestants, 252-257; of racial stances of general election winners, 258-262; of campaign stances of governors, 284-292, 296-304; of index of racial change, 312; of index of demographic traditionalism, 313-314; of interparty competition and racial change, 320-321; of impact of federal intervention, 322-323; of black voter registration, 326-330; of segregationist campaigning in the Second Reconstruction, 340-341. See also Deep South; Peripheral South

Subregional political cultures, 317-320, 322
Sullivan, Charles, career discussed, 65-66; 1959 first primary campaign of, 167, 170; 1963 first primary campaign of, 208, 211, 381-382
Supreme Court, 4, 339, 341
Swan, Jimmy, 59, 65-66, 181-183, 379
Systemic bias, definition of, 282-283; findings concerning, 286, 291-292, 294, 302-304, 392

Talmadge, Eugene, 35, 177, 318
Talmadge, Herman, 35-37, 66, 318
Taylor, Andrew, 122
Taylor, Pat, 111
Taylor, Robert, 123
Tennessee, political demography of, 25, 88-91, 118-120; overview of electoral politics in, 118-123; segregationist counties in, 119-120, 372; campaign stances of major candidates in, 154-157; 1966 first primary campaign in, 194-196; campaign stances of governors in, 294-296. See also Peripheral South
Texas, political demography of, 25, 88-91, 123-124; 1952 first primary campaign in, 43-44; overview of electoral politics in, 123-132; segregationist counties in, 123-125; campaign stances of major candidates in, 154-157; 1954 first primary campaign in, 173-174; 1954 second primary campaign in, 213-215; 1962 primary campaigns in, 235-237; campaign stances of governors in, 294-296; school desegregation in, 373. See also Peripheral South
Thompson, M. E., 35-37
Thurmond, Strom, 79, 84
Timmerman, George Bell, Jr., 80
Truman, Harry S, 29, 32, 39-41

Umstead, William, 31
Unifactionalism. See Intraparty factionalism

Vandiver, Ernest, 66, 68, 366
Virginia, political demography of, 88-91, 118-119; overview of electoral politics in, 113-119; segregationist counties in, 118-119, 375; campaign stances of major candidates in, 154-157; 1973 general election campaign in, 273-275; 1965 general election campaign in, 275-277; campaign stances of governors in, 294-296. See also Peripheral South
Voting Rights Act of 1965, 8, 324

Wallace, George, as militant segregationist, 14, 141; as progressive, 21; career
described, 52, 55-57; compared to other
politicians, 83, 194, 270-271, 385; as
victorious militant segregationist after
federal intervention, 86, 234, 240, 301,
331, 337; mentioned in non-Alabama
campaigns, 178, 379; 1966 first primary
campaign of, 184-188; geography of
first primary votes for, 186-188; 1962
primary campaigns of, 219-225; geography of second primary votes for, 224-
225; impact on Republican party of,
248-249; as militant segregationist-
redistributive, 292; as neo-Populist,
296; as organizer of counter-mobiliza-
tion, 316, 326-327; opposition to school
desegregation of, 323; ability to recruit
industry questioned, 383
Wallace, Henry, 36
Wallace, Lurleen, 56, 184-188, 229, 292,
338
Wallace movement, 299
Waller, William, 65-66, 249, 288, 296
Ward, Lee, 175-176
Watson, Albert, 84

Weltner, Charles, 268
West, John, 84-85, 269, 272
White, Hugh, 39-41, 60
White primary, 12, 199
White southerners, 334-336
Wilkins, Roy, 229
Williams, John Bell, 65, 181-183, 213,
378-379
Winter, William, 64-65, 181-183, 379
Woodward, C. Vann, 199

Yarborough, Don, career described, 130-
131; as unsuccessful candidate, 197,
238, 288, 296; 1962 primary campaigns
of, 235-237
Yarborough, Ralph, as moderate segregationist-redistributive, 33; 1952 first primary campaign of, 43-44; career described, 124, 128; 1954 first primary
campaign of, 173-174; 1954 second
primary campaign of, 213-215; rhetoric
used against, 236; as unsuccessful candidate, 296; 1956 first primary campaign of, 377; 1956 second primary
campaign of, 382-383